PETRUS SACHARIAE NAKSKOW

Articles of Faith

Contents

Forward from the Editor

When I first entered into the Lutheran tradition as a poor college student, I searched the internet far and wide for theological resources that I could access for free. Among the many texts I discovered was this volume from Petrus Nakskow titled *THE ARTICLES OF FAITH, OF The Holy Evangelical Church, ACCORDING TO The WORD of GOD, AND The AUSBURG CONFESSION SET FORTH IN FORTY SERMONS.* Though the PDF was difficult to read, both due its archaic English, and the quality of the manuscript, I knew that I had stumbled upon something truly special. When I first began this publishing house, this was one of the books that I was convinced needed a new edition—one that was modernized in both language and format. Now, ten years later, I am able to present this new edition of this classic work to the world.

Background of this Work

This text is a compilation of sermons from the Danish Lutheran theologian Petrus Sachariae Nakskow (alternatively spelled as Peder Naskov and Peder Zachariæsøn Nackskov) written in the first half of the seventeenth century, generally regarded as the high point of Lutheran orthodoxy. While it is most often Germany that is associated with Lutheran orthodoxy during this period, Denmark had adopted the Lutheran reforms in the church as early as the 1530s.

This led to a number of publications explaining and defending the doctrines outlines in the Lutheran confessional documents in the following centuries.

While Germany retained its significance as the center of academic theological debate among Lutherans—as well as polemics against the Roman and Reformed churches, Danish publications often focused on the communication of complex theological concepts to the laity. It is this spirit which stands behind Nakskow's work. In these sermons, one finds a clear exposition of Lutheran orthodoxy, as the author does not diverge from the dogmatic developments of Lutheran scholastics in Germany during this era on any significant point. Yet, as a pastor, Nakskow explains these ideas in a way that is accessible and practical in the life of the average congregant. Each of these sermons begins with Scripture, and using the Scriptural text, Nakskow explains the distinctive characteristics of Lutheran doctrine. Nakskow's writing makes it apparent than one need not divide doctrine from practice, as he combines robust orthodox theology with pastoral care.

This book first entered into the English language in 1754 through a translation produced by Rev. Joachim Melchior Magens (1715-1783). A century prior to the growth of American Lutheranism with the Saxon immigration, Magens migrated to the United States from the West Indies, and eventually settled on Long Island in New York. At this time, apart from some selected writings of Martin Luther, there were no major Lutheran theological publications available in the English language. Even the Book of Concord did not receive a complete English translation until the Henkel edition in 1851. Seeing this lack of available resources, Magens translated these forty sermons, and thus presented the first major Lutheran theological work published in the United States. For interested readers who did not speak German, this text became their sole source for Lutheran doctrine in the post-Reformation era.

About this Edition

The present text is based upon the Magens translation, and thus is not itself a new translation of the work. Instead, it is a revised text with the simple goal of making the book readable for a lay audience who would not prefer to delve into the text in its archaic eighteenth-century English. This revision has taken several hours of work, as I attempted to keep this as close to the original text as possible, while also accounting for maximum readability. Some of the changes made to the text are as follows:

The original work is full of archaic spellings which often were not even self-consistent within the work. These have all been changed to reflect modern spelling conventions in the United States. The work also had a large amount of seemingly random capitalization throughout. I could not discover any discernable pattern as to why some words were capitalized and others were not. This has been fixed. Several words, such as: thou, hast, saith, etc. have been replaced with their modern equivalents throughout the text. There have also been some minimal changes to sentence structure to increase the text's readability for a modern audience. Finally, this has all been placed into a modern typeface to create an enjoyable reading experience.

It is my hope that you will enjoy this work as much as I have through my original reading of the text and the many re-readings through the process of editing and revising this book. Though written nearly four hundred years ago, the truths contained within it remain as relevant today as its original date of publication. May you be strengthened in your knowledge and trust in your Savior throughout these pages.

Jordan Cooper
  Ithaca, NY
  March, 2021

Publishing Info from the 1754 Edition

THE ARTICLES OF FAITH, OF The Holy Evangelical Church,

ACCORDING TO *The* WORD *of* GOD,

AND The AUSBURG CONFESSION

SET FORTH IN FORTY SERMONS

By Magist. *Petrus Sachariæ Nakskow*,

Præpositus, and Minister of the Gospel in *Jutland,* in *Denmark*

Translated from the Original into English,

By Jochum Melchior Magens

NEW-YORK:

J. PARKER and W. WEYMAN, at the New Printing-Office in

Beaver-Street; Also to be GODFRIED MULLER, Reader in the

Lutheran Church, in *New-York*, and Mr. SCHLEYDORN in

Philadelphia, MDCCLIV.

To the HONORABLE *VESTRY*, OF THE EVANGELICAL CHURCH, IN
The City of *NEW-YORK*

Reverend Fathers, and Brothers in Christ,

    IT is now going on five years since I arrived here from the *West-Indies*, in order, if I should like the place, to settle here, or else remove to *Copenhagen*, where I have had my education, in the Royal University; though born in the island of St. *Thomas*, under subjection of his most sovereign majesty the king of *Denmark:* But I cannot express how I was grieved in my mind, when, upon inquiry after the state of our Holy *Evangelical Church* and brethren, I mostly met with a general contempt and disrecommendation, partly occasioned by the bad and immoral lives of so well preachers as some of their hearers; partly by the great prejudice that prevailed among the other congregations, concerning our holy doctrine: And therefore I resolved to translate the *Forty Sermons,* of the worthy magister *Petrus Zachariæ Nakskow,* upon the articles of our faith, in order to have them printed; *First,* For the better conviction of all who are unacquainted with the purity of our holy doctrine; and, *Secondly,* for the edification of them that are desirous to be instructed in the true way to salvation. And since the honorable *vestry* have chosen me to be an elder of our church, in the city of *New York,* I thought it proper to dedicate this, my well-meaning labor, to them.

I shall always endeavor to help the promoting of this our found doctrine, and remain with due regard.

Reverend Fathers and Brethren,

Flushing, Jan. 31, 1754.

Your most Obedient,

J.M. MAGENS.

Nakskow's Preface

THERE is a common Proverb: Everyone is saved by his faith. *This saying is both truth and untruth.*

It is truth that when we understand by the word "faith," *as a sincere relying on the mercies and grace of GOD, revealed in his Son* Jesus Christ; *such a faith must everyone have that will be saved. For, as none can see with another's eye, neither live by another's breath, so can none be saved by another's faith, but by his own alone.*

It is not truth when we take the word "faith" *for profession; for then the* heathens *would be saved by their* idolatry; *the* Jews *by* Judaism; *and the* Turks *by* Islam; *which is impossible: For, as there is but one true GOD, so there is likewise but one true faith, by which man can be saved, and that is the* faith *in* Jesus Christ, *which GOD has revealed to us in his Holy Word, wrote by the* prophets, evangelists, *and* apostles.

They that pass by the word of GOD, and follow traditions of men, have not the true faith; *for they believe in men, and not in GOD. What is tradition to the word of GOD?*

Neither have they, who will not believe anything, but what they can apprehend with their own reason, a true faith. For, if they would but follow the dictates of their reason, they would give unto GOD full honor in all things, and take their reason captive under the obedience of faith.

He therefore that will know which is the true faith, *let him read these* SERMONS *comprehended in this book, and prove the same by the word of GOD; and he shall find, that all the articles of this* Evangelical Faith, *are grounded on the word of GOD alone, and not on the tradition nor reason of men.*

GOD Almighty, by his Holy Spirit, graciously turn the hearts of everyone, that they may put a right value on this his revealed word, and seem it as their greatest treasure, and ground their faith alone on it, so that they may at last, receive the end of their faith, which is the salvation of their souls, for the sake of our blessed Savior, *Jesus Christ*; AMEN.

1

Scripture

The text stands in the Gospel of St. JOHN, Chap. 5 verse 39. *Search the Scriptures; for in them you think you have eternal life; and they are that which testify of me.*

INTRODUCTION

TROUBLE without profit is tiresome, and also is labor without gain: We seldom undertake any trouble, without having in view some reward for it. The merchant undergoes many dangerous voyages for money's sake. The farmer toils and cultivates his land, in expectation of a good harvest. The soldier goes into the war, and exposes his life there, for to get salary and spoil. This may oftentimes fail in temporal cases, but in spiritual it never fails: Those who serve God with a true spirit and upright heart shall again receive grace and salvation; for God is not unjust, that he should forget anyone's actions, provided they are done to the glory of his name. If we pray, he promises to hear, and to help us, saying: *Whatsoever you shall ask the Father in my name, he will give it to you.* If we give alms, he promises reward, saying: *Whosoever shall give to drink unto one of these little ones, a cup of cold water, only in the name of a disciple; verily I say unto you, be shall in no wise lose his reward.* If we suffer, he gives us strength in sufferings, and crowns us afterwards with glory everlasting; for so we read in the holy records: *If so be, that we suffer with* Christ, *that we also may be glorified together.* If we spend any time in reading, hearing and preserving the word of God, the Lord will certainly reward us for it. *Blessed is be that reads, and they that bear the words of his prophecy, and keep those things which are written therein*; says the Spirit of God, Rev. 1:3. Consider herein;

FIRST, *An encouragement to read, bear, and keep the word of* GOD.

SECOND, *An assurance of great gain, to be blessed thereby.*

First, concerning the encouragement: The Spirit of God requires three of our members to be employed and used, when we have to do with the word of God namely, the eyes in reading, the ears in hearing, and the heart in keeping.

1. Open your eyes when you read the word of God: There is not one single tittle in the Holy Scriptures, that is not full of wisdom; the Lord himself regards the least tittle in his word, and says, therefore, *It is easier for heaven and earth to pass, than one tittle of the law to fail.* The Holy Scripture is a letter from God to man, wherein he revealed, how he will be honored and served: Should now God, in such a high cause, wherein his own glory, and the salvation of mankind, are concerned, write otherwise than truth? We account ourselves happy when we receive a letter from a friend; we read the same over and over again, and consider every word, the better to know the meaning of our friend. More blessed then are they who read the Scriptures, for thereof to learn the will of God, in order to live accordingly thereafter; So says our Blessed Savior, *You are my friends, if you do whatsoever I command you.* If we will then know the commands of God, we must learn it of reading and hearing his word; and if we will do his commands, then must we keep his word in a pure heart: And why

should we not be willing and diligent in the reading and hearing of God's word; since the Bible is the best book in the whole world; for it is holy, true, and instructing.

The Bible is holy, because it contains holy things; the Lord Jesus Christ is the center in this book; and therefore, he that reads the Bible must read it as if every line was marked with the blood of Christ.

The Bible is true, because it contains nothing but truth; if we should find any text therein, that the Lord had spoken or promised, and it was not truth, then was our hope in vain: Well do we find many things related in the Bible in a historical way, that are spoken against the truth by the wicked and ungodly, though all that the Lord himself has said is truth.

The Bible is instructing; we can be instructed thereof in whatever condition we live: Will a preacher make good and instructing sermons, so that his words can be as the words of the wise, *which are as goads, and as nails fastened by the masters of assemblies:* Then must he diligently pursue the word of God: The Bible must be his first book in the morning, and the last at night. The tree of the Scripture is so fruitful, that the more it is shaken, the more fruit grows on it. St. *Paul* had read many books, but found in none such wisdom and content, as in this; and therefore persuaded *Timothy*, saying, *But continue you in the things which you have learned, and have been assured of, knowing of whom you had learned them; and that from a child, you have known the Holy Scriptures, which are able to make you wise unto salvation, through faith, which is in Christ Jesus.* Will a magistrate know what book he shall use? The holy *Psalmist*, king *David*, shows it him; saying, *Your testimonies are my delight, and my counselors:* Yea, the Lord commands all rulers, diligently to read the word of God; saying, *This book of the law shall not depart out of your mouth; but you shall meditate therein day and night, that you may observe, to do according to all that is written therein; for then you shall make your ways prosperous,*

3

and then you shall have good success. Would a merchant cast so often up in the Bible as in his account book, there should not be found in his house balances and measures of deceit, which is an abomination to the Lord. Would any laborer prosper in his undertakings, then must he learn of this book, to fear God, walk in his ways, and maintain his family in honesty: Would a warrior have success, and bring his life as a booty out of the battle, then must he know the word of God; for it is the book of the wars of the Lord; besides, everyone can learn of this book, how to arm himself against the devil, the world, and his own flesh, which war against the soul.

2. Open your ears, when you hear the word of God; it is not so easy to hear the word of God, as men think in common: We can soon go to church, and set there in order to hear, but the heart must first be prepared with and by prayers and devotion, by removing all fleshly thoughts, by captivating our own reason, and by denying all worldly affections; which is the meaning of our Savior, when he says, *He that is of God, hears God's word:* The Lord will, we shall not alone read his word, but also hear it: Therefore has he ordained ministers to preach, and what are they, but a*mbassadors for Christ, as though God did beseech by them.* Although we can read the word of God at home, yet must we not neglect the public assemblies: Therefore, says the Psalmist, *For I had gone with the multitude; I went with them to the house of God.*

3. Open your heart, when you read or hear the word of God; blessed are they that hear the word of God, and keep it: We never let gold and precious stones lay before everyone's eyes, but we keep them in the safest places. Is not the word of God better than gold and jewels? Every text therefore, is as a precious golden ornament, wherewith we can adorn our hearts; and thereby, *Lay up in store for ourselves a good foundation against the time to come, that we may lay hold on eternal life.* By reading and hearing the word of God, we may grow

wise in our brains; but by keeping it, we will grow wise in our hearts. If an angel from heaven did preach to us; yea, if the Lord Jesus Christ did himself preach to us, it would be of no service nor use, if we kept not the words in our hearts: We must do as *Mary, who kept all these things, and pondered them in her heart:* And then, when we read, hear, and keep the words of God, it follows thereupon,

Second, an assurance of great gain; we will be blessed thereby. This salvation and blessing can we better discern, when we consider the profit and gain we have of reading, hearing, and keeping the word of God. For,

1. We receive faith; *Faith comes by hearing, and hearing by the word of God.* Faith purifies the heart from sin: The Lord Jesus says, *Now you are clean through the word which I have spoken unto you:* And St. Paul says, *By grace are you saved through faith.*

2. We become thereby able to withstand sin: When *Joseph* was persuaded to adultery by his master's wife, then was his knowledge in the word of God, the only armor by which he defended himself from temptation: *How*, says he, *can I do this great wickedness, and sin against God?* When sin arises in our thoughts, then can we be hindered therefrom by the word of God: For by holy and godly meditations, can we drive away all worldly thoughts, that may arise in our hearts.

3. We become thereby zealous in our devotion; the Lord complains, that the prophets were light: A light Christian is soon persuaded to sin: We can lightly blow a feather where we will: There are many feather-light Christians, who, when there arises a little storm of temptation, at once are ready to fall off and sink: On the contrary; the word of God makes a Christian strong in his faith.

4. We come thereby apt to prayers; for prayer is a lamp, and God's word is the oil in the lamp; as the lamp, having no oil, goes out, likewise goes the lamp of our prayers out, when it is not nourished

by the word of God; besides, the word of God gives us words, when we will pray, and can't utter our meaning.

5. We become thereby bold and patient in sufferings: See how bold Job was in all his sufferings: *Though the Lord slay me,* says he, *yet will I trust in him.* What made St. *Paul* so bold in his troubles? That he says, *We glory in tribulations, knowing that tribulation works patience, and patience experience, and experience hope, and hope makes not ashamed.* The reason of this boldness was, as he says afterwards, *Because the love of God is shed abroad in our hearts by the Holy Spirit, which is given unto us:* A child of God under affliction, is as the lily under the snow, and *like a tree planted by the rivers of water, that brings forth his fruit in his season, his leaf shall not wither.*

6. We become thereby partakers of the Kingdom of Heaven after this life; for the Lord says in our text; *Search the Scriptures, for in them you think you have eternal life; and they are they which testify of me.* We will then, in the name of the Lord, take the Holy Scripture before us, and see what book it is, since it contains such high and holy things, that we thereof can be instructed, and have eternal life. The Lord give his grace hereto. *Amen.*

EXPLANATION of the TEXT

There was at Jerusalem, by the sheep market, a pool called Bethesda, having five porches; in these laid a great multitude of impotent folks of blind, halt, and withered, waiting for the moving of the water; for an angel went down at a certain season into the pool and troubled the water; whosoever then first after the troubling of the water, stepped in, was made whole of whatsoever disease he had. There was a certain man which had an infirmity thirty and eight years, him did Jesus make whole on the Sabbath Day: *This vexed the Jews, that* Jesus *had wrought miracles on the Sabbath, and began therefore to dispute with him, accusing him of breaking the Sabbath; Christ used many arguments against this accusation, by which be shows that he was the Son of God, and Lord over the Sabbath; and among other arguments, Christ calls upon the Scripture, saying,* "Search the Scriptures; for in them you think you have eternal life; and they are that which testify of me."

Our Savior means by the word "Scriptures," the Bible, that is, the Word of God, written by the prophets, evangelists, and the apostles, whom God used in this cause, as secretaries or clerks; and they were holy men, inspired with the Holy Spirit, in order that we should be instructed by their writings, to know and to do the will of God, and there by obtain eternal life and salvation.

We have to observe here,

First, the certainty of the Holy Scripture. That there is such a book, which is the word of God, dictated by the Holy Spirit, can be proved by these three following arguments.

1. The own testimony of this book; the Holy Scripture shines of its own light, not having occasion to borrow from anywhere else; as the light of the sun convinces us of its brightness; so has the Scripture its own convincing testimonies of its godliness: *It is the Spirit that bears witness, because the Spirit is truth.* Read in the Old or New Testament, and you shall find, that all that is said there, is said of the Lord himself, or his Son Jesus Christ; or spoken by holy men by God's order. We will find here and there the words and actions of the wicked; but they are related for us to abhor them: Who dares then say, that this book is not from God, showing its authority by its own testimony? We have therefore no need of going to the Pope, or anywhere else, for to get a confirmation hereon. Is the disciple more than his Master? Is the Pope more than *John* the Baptist? The Jews did send to him, and he bore witness of Christ, but Christ refuses his testimony, saying, *I receive not testimony from man.* When a minister is in the pulpit, he must take his authority from his

doctrine; so takes the Scripture testimony from his own authority; for that is the true light, where from all doctrine must take their light. Also we find in the Holy Scripture, great power to instruct, to reveal all secret and hidden thoughts, to withstand all false doctrine, to drive away idolatry, and to comfort in all tribulations, and oppose all temptations; all which can be effected by the Word of God alone: Thereby were the *Thessalonians* persuaded to believe, and to embrace the doctrine preached by St. *Paul*; thereby did the hearers of St. *Peter*, become so pricked in their hearts, that they did not know what to do, before St. *Peter* advised them, *To repent, and be baptized in the name of Jesus Christ, for the remission of sins:* Thereby was one of the malefactors converted before ever he knew where to find the apostolic church.

2. The testimony of the church; for, since the Holy Scripture is so full of godly words, wonderful miracles, and deep mysteries, from the beginning to the end, is all so harmonious, and is all truth; therefore has the whole Christendom always acknowledged this book to be the word from God's own mouth; and none has ever dared to contradict or thwart it, with any sound reason; so that this book, which has been consented to, and has been received by so many millions who lived at the time, or just after it was wrote, and has been since acknowledged in so many hundred years, can in no manner be now contradicted by anyone. They might as well dispute the sun her light; wherefore, so long as the church acknowledges this book to be the word of God, lives conformable to its commands, and alters not the least tittle thereof; so long is such a church, a true catholic church; therefore did St. *Paul* call the Christian church, *The pillar and ground of the truth:* For as sovereigns have their orders on public pillars, that everyone can read them, so we find the word of God in the church, that everyone can learn of them the Lord's will and commands.

8

3. The testimony of the Holy Spirit in the conscience. If any doubts of this book, let him read in it; consider and ponder on what he reads; live conformable to it, and pray to the Lord for the assistance of his Holy Spirit, and he shall find such pricking in his heart, and, by the testimony in his own conscience, be convinced, to confess, that this book is the word of God. It will go with him, as with the *Samaritans*, who, after the woman had told them that Christ was there, and they had spoken to him; *said unto the woman, Now we believe not because of your saying; for we have heard him, and know that this is indeed the Christ, the Savior of the world:* Likewise can the Christian church testify the Holy Scripture to be the word of God: But by reading, hearing and meditating thereon, the Holy Spirit will testify it in our hearts. We have now to consider,

First, the great necessity of the Holy Scripture. Our Savior commands to search the Scriptures; and what is there that we can do with greater profit? There are two reasons that should bring us to the searching of the Scriptures.

1. God's command. "Search" is a word of command: Christ did not say what the Jews did, but what they ought to do: He had in the foregoing 38th verse, upbraided them of their unbelief and neglect of the Scriptures: Thereupon he commands them in our text's words, what they should do with greater attention. It has pleased the good and gracious God, always to preserve the Bible, that it is not altered in the least; although the Jewish church erred greatly against it, as we may observe of our Savior's complaints. As God would not suffer the book of nature altered by the heathens, although they corrupted it with sin against nature; so did the Bible always remain unaltered, although the Jews erred greatly against the true doctrine thereof; yea, not in the greatest wars, when whole countries were destroyed, has this holy book suffered any damage. When *Jerusalem* was destroyed the first time, by the king of *Babylon*, and the tribes

brought into captivity, and even the temple burnt, then were the Scriptures preserved, as we can conclude from the words of the Prophet *Daniel*, who was one of the captives, and understood of the Scripture; the time when Israel was to be relieved; which Scriptures were *Moses's*, and the other prophets.

Afterwards when they came home to their own country again, in order to rebuild the city and temple, they had the Bible with them: In the last destroying of *Jerusalem* by the *Romans*, the Bible was preserved; as we can see, since we have it yet.

2. Our own need and want. If we did not have the Bible, then we would be heathens, of whom St. *Paul* says, *That they are strangers from the covenant of promise, having no hope, and without God in the world.* It would go with us, as with them that were on board with St. *Paul*, who, *When neither sun nor stars appeared, and no small tempest arose, had no hope to be saved.* But, *the word of God is a lamp unto our feet, and a light unto our path.* It is a perfect light, that enlightens us in all that is necessary for us to know to salvation. It is a clear shining light, so that everyone can see thereby, and learn what is required of him: It is a true light, having light of itself like the sun: It is a continuing light, that shall burn so long as the world stands. *We have also a more sure word of prophecy; whereunto you do well that you take heed, as unto a light, that shines in a dark place, until the day-dawn, and the day-star arise in your hearts.* Next have we to consider,

Thirdly, the writers of the Holy Scriptures; our Savior says in our text, Scriptures. Who has then written these Scripture? The Bible is not written from the beginning of the world; for then did the parents learn their children by heart, and was in them days, the doctrine transplanted from generation to generation by word of mouth, until the time of *Moses*, who was the first that began to write by the command of God, after the children of Israel were gone out of *Egypt*, 2454 years after the creation. It is worth observing, that although *Moses* did not live at the time of the creation, yet has he wrote such a true and exact history of the whole transaction, as if he had been present from the first day, and had heard or seen the order and words that the Lord used: The reason therefore is, that the Spirit of God dictated to him, all what he should write; for *Moses* was a high instructed man of God, with whom the Lord spoke face to face, as a man speaks unto his friend. Afterwards the Lord wrote with his own finger the Ten Commandments upon the two tables of stone, and delivered them to *Moses*; since that, have the other holy men wrote, all by the Inspiration of the Holy Spirit; for if they had written without orders from God, they would have committed a high and treacherous crime: These holy inspired men have been,

1. True and just: They did not write after their own thoughts, but alone by the inspiration of the Holy Spirit, and wrote what they had heard and seen; for they did not hide away even their own faults.

2. Harmonious. Although the prophets and apostles wrote at different places, times and languages; yet, for all, they agree, and don't write against one another, contrary to temporal writers, who oftentimes contradict themselves. Herefore are the prophets said to speak with one mouth.

3. Sound in faith and doctrine; For, since they were all inspired by the Holy Spirit, and God himself dictated to them, then could they not err; neither write against the truth.

4. Mean and ignorant before their call. *Moses* was a shepherd; *Elijah* a ploughman; *Amos* a herdsman, and a gatherer of sycamore fruit; *Mathew* a receiver of custom; *Lucas* a physician, and the apostles all fishermen; but after their call to this office, they received knowledge and intelligence, of what they should write and speak; for when the Holy Spirit instructs, can man be soon instructed to perfection.

The reasons why it has pleased the Lord, to give and reveal his

Word, are as follows:

1. Since the memory of men was not to be depended upon, especially in supernatural causes. We can hardly apprehend the earthly, much less the heavenly things; and it is a great blessing that writing is invented, since it is the greatest help to memory.

2. Because men did increase and multiply. For since one country after another, did receive the word of God, and the Christian church became enlarged; therefore did the apostles and evangelists write to them, whom they could not personally instruct with preaching.

3. For the greater certainty. The doctrine we receive by word of mouth, is not so durable, neither to be so much depended upon, as what is wrote down, especially, if it concerns spiritual things; for if the true doctrine had not been written down, there would have been many more erroneous opinions in Christianity, than there is already. We have to consider,

Fourthly, the division of the Holy Scripture. *Search the Scriptures*, by which we must not alone understand the Old Testament, as it was of old, in the time of Christ's incarnation, but also of the New, so as it is now in our days.

The Old Testament is that part of the Bible, containing the books that were wrote before the birth of Christ, called the time of Promise, or the time under the law; of which books *Genesis* is the first, and the prophet *Malachi* the last.

The New Testament is the other part of the Bible, containing the books wrote after the birth of Christ, called the time of revelation, or the time under the gospel; whereof the Gospel of St. *Matthew* is the first, and the Revelation of St. *John* is the last.

The Scriptures in the Old and New Testament, are called canonical or fundamental, since they contain the grounds of the Christian Faith, wherefore Christ and the apostles did always use them, to confirm their preaching and doctrine with.

We find besides in the Old Testament, some books called apocrypha, which are good and exemplary to read, but can in no ways serve to the confirmation of any article of faith; for they are not wrote by the inspiration of the Holy Spirit, as having many faults and contradictions in them; and therefore not counted among the canonical: We have to observe,

Fifthly, the holiness of the Scriptures. Our text says: *For in them you think, you have eternal life.* What is the end and aim of all our troubles, sufferings, and desires? Is it not the eternal life? This we can find in the Holy Scriptures; not as physic in a box, but as the only means that can help us to the eternal life; therefore are the Scriptures like warning lights, by which we can see to arrive through this wicked world, into the heavenly glory.

Our Savior says in our text: you *think*. We must not accuse the Scriptures with any falsehood, as if it should promise us what we can't find in it: No! but Christ accuses here the Jews of their uncautiousness, and own conceit, and likewise their explanation of the Scriptures; wherefore St. *Paul* writes of them; *Even unto this day, when* Moses *is read, the veil is upon their hearts:* Like many among the Christians, who are of the opinion, that because they read and hear the Scriptures, go to church, receive the Sacrament, give alms, sing and pray, they therefore shall enter into the Kingdom of Heaven, and receive eternal life, although they have no living faith: No! but they who read the Holy Scriptures, hear the Word of God, go to church, receive the sacrament, or performing any pious or charitable actions, thereby seeking Jesus Christ, by a true faith, have the eternal life: *He that has the Son, has life, and be that has not the Son of God, has no life.* Let us also consider,

Sixthly, the glory of the Holy Scripture. Our Savior says in our text; *They testify of me:* The Holy Scriptures testify of the person, offices, and benefits of Christ.

1. Of his person. That he is the second person in the Blessed Trinity, true God and true man in one person; true God, born of the Father from eternity; and true man, born in the time of the Virgin *Mary*.

2. Of his offices. That he is our King, Priest, and Prophet: Our King, for he reigns over us with his Spirit and word. Our High Priest; *Who through the eternal Spirit, offered himself without spot to God; and shall therefore his blood purges our conscience from dead works, to serve the living God.* Our Prophet: For he has revealed to us the will and pleasure of his Father; has reconciled us with God, and intercedes for us.

3. Of his benefits towards us. He is the *Alpha* and the *Omega*, the beginning and end of our faith. He is our bridegroom, who has betrothed us unto himself in righteousness, and in judgment, and in loving kindness, and in mercies, and in faithfulness, that we should know the Lord. He is our Christ; for God anointed him with the Holy Spirit and power. He is our judge; for he is to judge everyone, according to that he has done, whether it is good or bad. He is our *Ebenezer*; for hitherto has the Lord helped us by him. He is the Prince of Peace; for he has obtained the everlasting peace with God for us. He is the Good Shepherd; who has given his life for his sheep, for to free them from the power of Satan. He is our redeemer; for he has redeemed us not with corruptible things, as silver and gold, but with his own precious blood. He is our physician; and has healed our spiritual sicknesses. He is our Savior; for he has saved us when we were lost. He is the promised Seed of the Woman; who has bruised the head of the Serpent. He is our guide; for he is the Way, and the Truth, and the Life; the way we should walk in, the truth we should walk after, and the life we should walk unto. He is the way in his example, the truth in his doctrine, and the life in his sufferings and meritorious death; and there are a great many more benefits which are innumerable.

Who would not then search the Scriptures, since they bear such a glorious testimony of Christ: And is the Bible a heavenly apothecary, wherein we can find a true remedy for all our spiritual diseases? It is a prayer book, and we can learn therefrom to pray rightly. It is a book of virtue and vice; for we find therein the virtues we must practice, and the vices we must abhor. It is a book of examples; for therefrom we can learn how to behave ourselves in temptation. It is a receipt-book; for therein we can find the receipts for our sins, by the blood of Christ. It is a book of testimony; for all the prophets witness, that, through his name, whosoever believes in him, shall receive remission of sins. Yea, the Bible is an armor, whereon there hangs a thousand bucklers, all shields of mighty men. Search therefore the Scriptures, all men, high and low, young and old, big and small, since you are entreated and commanded thereunto; and you shall thereby receive such great reward. You might ask, how shall we search the Scriptures?

1. Buy you a Bible, that is the best furniture we can have in our houses; we oftentimes lay out money on small matters, whereof we have little or no profit; why won't we then lay it out for a Bible, whereof we can reap so many benefits. *Solomon* says: *Get wisdom, get understanding.* But how shall we get wisdom? Buy a Bible, and you have wisdom in your hands; read diligently therein, and you will get wisdom in your head; and keep the word, and live according to its commands, and you will get wisdom in your hearts.

2. After you have bought a Bible, read diligently in it; we can bestow whole days, weeks, months, yea, even years, in reading temporal and worldly books; but for to read the Bible, we cannot, and oftentimes will not, find any spare time. Worldly men are like quicksilver, which has no rest; their thoughts are always here and there, to and fro, like a bird from one limb to another.

3. In reading of the Bible, search the Scriptures with reverence and

devotion. He that will read, or hear the word of God, to any profit or purpose, must first put away all fleshly and worldly thoughts, and beseech the Lord for the assistance of his Holy Spirit, for to enlighten his reason, and incline his heart to preserve what he hears or reads. What will it signify, if we read or hear the word of God, and are not truly resolved to live according to it. That seed is evil sowed that yields no harvest; so is reading of no profit, if not accompanied with outward actions, and likewise with a sincere resolution. To search the Scriptures is the work of the soul, not in flying thoughts, like the dog who sobs of the water, and runs away from it: But in the perusing of the Scriptures, take this advice; do not read much at one time, but break off, and ponder, and consider, with sincere meditations, on what you have been reading.

If you are not able to buy a Bible, get a Catechism, and search in that; for that is an extract of the Bible, and contains all what is necessary for you to know and believe to salvation: If you can't read, get another to read for you; go often to church, and listen with due attention and reverence to the preaching of the Scriptures, by which you will be instructed.

The Lord give everyone of us his Spirit and grace, that we may always put a true value on his holy word, for the sake of our Savior, Jesus Christ. AMEN.

2

God

T he text stands in the Gospel of St. JOHN, Chap. 4 verse 24. *God is a spirit; and they that worship him, must worship him in Spirit and truth.*

INTRODUCTION

IT is a mournful complaint, that the Lord made of the ignorance of his people, in the cause of their own salvation; saying, by the prophet *Isaiah*, the first chapter, third and fourth verse. *The ox knows his owner, and the ass his master's crib; but Israel does not know, my people do not consider: Ah sinful nation.* The prophet sets forth three things in these words.

First, the natural sense of the beasts. *The ox knows his owner, and the ass his master's crib.* The Lord is pleased here, not to take example or similitude of the subtlest sort of beasts; as a serpent, stork or dog; but of the dullest sort, as an ox and ass, who, although they are dull by nature, yet know their owners and benefactors. *Balaam's* ass knew her owner; for when *Balaam* smote her with a staff, then did the Lord open her mouth, and she said unto *Balaam: What have*

I done unto you, that you have smitten me these three times? Am not I your ass, upon which you have ridden, ever since I was yours, unto this day? Likewise do we find several other creatures praised in the Scriptures; as the ant of carefulness, the spider of laboriousness, the stork, turtle, crane, and swallow, of observing the times.

But here the Lord complains of,

Secondly, the scandalous ignorance of his people. *Israel does not know, my people do not consider.* Men should be careful, since the Lord has been pleased to give unto them reason and sense, by which they are separated, and above the beasts; but they are oftentimes worse than even the dullest of beasts; in wickedness, they are subtle enough; but in the knowledge of God, they are dull and ignorant: Israel won't know, that the Lord gave them *corn, wine, oil, wool and flax.* When a man is in honor, and don't consider it, then is he worse than a beast. *Adam* was in great honor in *Paradise*, but since he did not remain in it, he became like the beasts; for the Lord made him coats of skins of the beasts, that he should learn of them, to be obedient to his Creator: So scandalous can men become by disobedience. The beasts never leave off their beastly nature; but many men lose their human nature, by disobedience, and become dogs, hogs, lions, bears, scorpions, vipers, and even devils themselves, as our Savior says of *Judas* the traitor. Men are apt enough to understand the world, and all worldly things; but to know, and serve God, as their Lord and Maker, are they dull and unwilling. The heathens had more regard for their gods, than Israel for the true God, who had brought them out of bondage, by so many miracles; whereof the Lord complains, saying: "*Has a nation changed their gods, which are yet no gods? But my people have changed their glory, for that which does not profit. Be astonished, O you heavens, at this, and be horribly afraid, be desolate,*" says the Lord.

Thirdly, the Lord puts therefore by the punishment. *Ah! sinful nation.* Ah, is a little word, but contains all temporal punishment, and eternal damnation; the Lord calls them, sinful nation! for they that don't know God, are sinful; since they want by which they can abstain from sin; and that is the knowledge of the living God. He that says, I know him, and keeps not his commandment, is a liar, and the truth is not in him. They knew God, but would not obey him: They thought if they did but offer their sacrifices, and observe the outward ceremonies, that was enough, and were not further concerned how they lived; as we can see of the following in said chapter. The punishment of such senseless people, will be greater and harder, since they knew the will of God, and lived not according to it; *For that servant that knew his Lord's will, and prepared not himself, neither did according to his Master's will, shall be beaten with many stripes.* For, besides that, they shall not prosper in their undertakings; as the Lord threatens, saying; *Because there is no knowledge of God in the land;* therefore shall everyone that dwells therein languish; so shall this *Ah!* befall them after death, *In flaming fire, for vengeance on them that know not God, and that obey not the gospel of our Lord Jesus Christ.* And it will be the harder in the Day of Judgment, when it will go better with *Tyre* and *Sidon,* than with *Corazin* and *Bethsaida,* where Christ had often preached, and wrought many miracles.

Therefore, that we shall not be like horses and mules, who have no sense, but must be ruled with the bridle, will not we be in our own light; but, according to our duty, strive to learn to know God rightly; whereof our text will serve. Whereof we will take to consideration, these three heads.

FIRST, *That there is a GOD.*

SECOND, *What this God is in his essence.*

THIRD, *What honor and service we owe to this God.*

EXPLANATION of the TEXT

First, we have to enquire that there is a God.

Our Savior coming on his journey to a city of *Samaria*, called *Sichar*, near the Mount *Gerizim*, where the *Samaritans* had built a temple, where there was a well called *Jacob*'s well, sat him down by this well, being weary of his journey; there comes a woman of *Samaria* to draw water, Jesus said unto her: "Give me to drink. Then said the woman to him: "How is it that you being a Jew, ask me for a drink, when I am a woman of *Samaria*? For the Jews have no dealings with Samaritans." Jesus answered and said unto her: "If you knew the gift of God, and who it is that says to you, Give me to drink; you would have asked of him, and he would have given you living water."

The woman thinking that Jesus spoke of the water in the well; said unto him, "Sir, you have nothing to draw with, and the well is deep; from where then have you that living water?" Thereupon explains Jesus this living water, saying, "Whosoever drinks of this water, shall never thirst, but this water shall be in him a well of water, springing up into everlasting life." And when the woman again understood that Jesus spoke of natural water; then did he break off the discourse, and said unto her, "Go call your husband, and come here." The woman answered, "I have no husband." Jesus said unto her, "You have well said, I have no husband; For you have had five husbands, and him whom you now have, is not your husband." The woman finding that Jesus knew her secrets, took him to be a prophet, and began to talk of religion, saying, "Sir, I perceive that you are a prophet. Our fathers worshiped in this mountain, and the Jews say, that in Jerusalem is the place where men ought to worship." She wanted to know, which of the two parties were in the right. Jesus thereupon instructs her concerning the true worship, saying, "Woman, believe me, the hour comes, (when the Messiah is come, and has satisfied with his own blood, by which all Levitical offerings will be ended, and the gospel is preached over the whole world,) when you shall neither in this mountain, neither at Jerusalem worship the Father: But in every place shall a pure offering of devotion, be offered unto the name of the Lord." Thereupon explains Jesus to her, in our text's words, how the true worshipers shall pray and worship God, and that in Spirit and Truth; because God is a Spirit, saying; *God is a Spirit, and they that worship him must worship him in Spirit and Truth.* Of this we have to consider, that there is a God.

The Samaritans knew very well that there was a God; Therefore said the woman, "Our fathers worshiped on this mountain." We know better, the Lord's holy name be praised for it, that there is a God; although the fool say in his heart, "there is no God." They acknowledge an almighty power with their mouths, but deny it with their actions; Such fools can be convinced that there is a God.

1. Of nature. The heathens who don't know God, know for all that there is a God; which they can conclude, of the creation of the world; as St. *Paul* writes of them which knowledge is a natural knowledge, wherewith everyone is born. So that there is not one nation in the universe, that does not acknowledge the being of a God; yea, many nations have chosen rather sticks, stones, and other images for their gods, than to be without a God. This inbred natural knowledge of the being of a God, increases by the sight of the world, and of all that is therein. So says the Psalmist; *The heavens declare the glory of God, and the firmament shows his handy work.* So many stars in the skies; so many birds in the air; so many drops of water in the sea; so many grains of sand on the earth; so many flowers in the fields; so many days in the year; so many hours in the day; so many moments in an hour, are all so many evidences of the being of an almighty God. The firmament, with sun, moon and stars, have stood so many thousand years without support or pillar. The earth gives its seed,

and produces in due season: Winter and Summer, day and night, follow one another so regular, and man is so wonderfully formed in his mother's womb: All this is the work of an almighty artful Master, who has created, preserved, and daily brings forth everything in such complete and ample order, so that nothing is lost; and therefore says *Solomon*; *God has ordered everything, by measure, weight and number:* Just as if everything in nature was numbered and weighed; for if there was too much in nature, that would be burdensome; if too little, that would weaken nature.

2. Of the conscience. The woman of *Samaria*, was convinced in her conscience, that Jesus knew all her secret wickedness; also our conscience convinces us, that there is a God, who knows and sees all our doings; for conscience is a letter from God to the soul, and is the vicar of God; and is as the echo of the voice of God, which occasions such a fright and terror in the mind, that a sinner cannot forbear it: Hereof comes it, that the wicked is always chased even of a shaken leaf. We have many examples of murderers, and other malefactors, who could never rest in their own consciences, before they revealed their crimes; and if others would not punish them for their crimes, have even laid violent hands on themselves. What made *Cain* say "*My punishment is greater than I can bear?*" A guilty conscience. What made *Judas* say, "*I have sinned, in that I have betrayed innocent blood?*" A guilty conscience. He was very ready and willing to receive the thirty pieces of silver; but now he was so pricked and troubled in his conscience, that he went and hanged himself.

3. Of the Holy Scripture. There is not one single leaf in the Bible, that do not confirm that there is a God. Who created heaven and earth, the sea, and all that in them is? God. Who promised unto men redemption by the seed of the woman? God. Who brought the sin-flood over the world? God. Who destroyed *Sodom* and *Gomorrah*, with brimstone and fire from heaven? God. Who spoke with *Abraham*,

Isaac, and *Jacob*, and promised unto their seed the land of *Canaan*? God. Who brought the children of *Israel* out of *Egypt*? God. Who wrought so many miracles? God. Who spoke with the prophets and others? God. Who would then doubt that there is a God, who sees and knows all things? yet we see many live in the world, as if there was no God, but the Spirit of the Lord calls them *foolish people.*

Secondly, we have to consider what this GOD is in his essence.

Since we are now convinced that there is a God: What is then this God in his essence? No man is able to understand or describe the essence of God; for this is a mystery; therefore says the prophet *Isaiah: "You are a God that hides yourself."* And St. *Paul* says, *"God dwells in a light, which no man can approach unto, whom no man has seen, nor can see."* Of this mystery can we talk but as children, in as much as the Scripture has revealed to us, and we can apprehend or understand.

God is a spirit, eternal, infinite, incomprehensible, omnipresent, all-knowing, almighty, free-making, true, holy, good, just, merciful, honorable, *&c.* These are some attributes by which God is described, and signify his essence in itself; we cannot understand and describe the essence of God better, than of his attributes: And although we find in the Scripture more attributes of God, yet are these the most principal; for the essence of God is nothing else but the nature of God, by which God is of himself, and in himself.

We must then consider, that the attributes of God are essential and personal. The essential attributes of God, are attributed to all the three persons in the Holy Trinity, without difference, and is the essence of God in itself; for the attributes of God, is God himself; which, although they are many towards us, since our weak minds can't comprehend it otherwise, are but one in God.

Personal attributes are attributed to every person in the Trinity in particular, as the personal attribute of the Father, is to generate or beget a Son; the personal attribute of the Son, is to be born of the Father; and the personal attribute of the Holy Spirit, is to proceed from the Father and the Son.

God is a spirit. The angels are spirits, and likewise the souls of men; but *God is the Father of all spirits*; and is so much and high above all other spirits, as eternity is above this present time. And since God is a spirit; then by consequence follows,

1. That he has no body nor members. We often read in the Scripture, of the members of God; but, that is, because the Spirit has written according to our simplicity, that we should and could better apprehend what God is. And we must understand this way of writing in the Scripture, in a higher and godlier style.

2. That he cannot be seen. Therefore said the Lord to *Moses*; *You cannot see my face; for there shall no man see me, and live.* By our own souls, which are likewise spirits, we can partly conclude what the essence of God is. The souls within us are spirits, who can't be seen nor handled; God is in a higher way a spirit, not created, cannot be seen nor apprehended, and is without body and members. The soul is whole in the whole body, and whole in every part of the body, and rules the whole body: God is in the whole world, and in every part of the world, and governs the whole world. The soul cannot be seen, but can see all that is in and without the body; so can nobody see God, but God sees everything. The soul can in a moment travel through the whole nature; so is God over all, and can pass through the whole nature in an instant: For, when it blows, He is said to walk on the wings of the wind; when it rains, He is said to water the earth; when it thunders, He is said to let hear the voice of his strength; and when it snows, He is said to give the snow like wool.

God is eternal. God is always the same, without beginning, change or end; therefore is he said to inhabit eternity, and is called king, *forever and ever.* Who lives forever? *The eternal God, whose arms are everlasting*. This eternity of God, is concealed in that holy name, that the Lord told unto *Moses*, when he asked what his name was; *And God said unto* Moses, *I AM THAT I AM, this is my name forever, and this is my memorial unto all generations.*

In this name is concealed many deep meditations.

I AM THAT I AM; that is, I am eternal; I am that I am, in present time, and know not of time past nor to come; for the essence of eternity is to be always the same; wherefore St. *John* says: *Which is, and which was, and which is to come, the Almighty.*

I AM THAT I AM; that is, I am the beginning and offspring of all what is: An essence, whereof all other essences have their essence; and all what is divided into certain degrees in others, all flows out from me.

I AM THAT I AM; that is, I am unchangeable and constant; for all that can change, is not so much as what remains always constant.

I AM THAT I AM. I am alone, that has essence of himself; all other things are not of themselves, but have their essence and being, from my will and pleasure.

I AM THAT I AM; that is, all what in me is, is my essence; I am not composed of parts, as other things are, but I am of myself.

I AM THAT I AM; that is, I am the ONLY God; *I am the Lord, and there is none else*; *there is no other God besides me.*

God is infinite and incomprehensible. God is in his essence and power so great, that he cannot be measured: He fills heaven and earth, and cannot be comprehended of any place. He is over ALL. He gives life and motion to everything. He is higher than heaven; what can you do? deeper than hell; what can you know? The heavens, and heaven of heavens cannot contain him. "*Can any hide himself in secret places that I shall not see him?*" *says the Lord.* "*Do not I fill heaven and earth?*" says the Lord.

God is omnipresent. The angels can be but in one place at a time, but God is always over all, not as *the house was filled with the odor of the ointment:* Neither as *the cloud filled the House of the Lord.* Neither is he defiled of the unclean things, by which he is present; like the sun, who is not stained of the things whereon it shines. If any should ask, was God over ALL before the creation? He must know, that God was well infinite and incomprehensible before the creation; but we can't say that God was over all, and filled everything before the things were. The old fathers have made this question, "Where was God, when there was nothing but himself?" Whereupon they answer: "He was in himself, for he is himself enough." The omnipresence of God is not idle, without effect and power; no, but is always working in the wicked, with terror and fear; and in the faithful, with grace and comfort; neither is it a bare and simple godly effect, without the presence of his essence. As the sun is in the air, not with its body, but alone with its beams, light and power: For since the Lord fills heaven and earth, and is Lord himself in his essence; so fills this essence, heaven and earth with power. But therein consists the omnipresence of God, that he fills everything essentially.

Yet, for all, the omnipresence of God has its degrees.

The common omnipresence of God, stretches unto all that is in heaven and earth. The heaven is his throne, and the earth his footstool. His gracious presence stretches to the Christian church, and the faithful on earth. It is worth observing, that our Savior commands us to pray; *Our Father who art in heaven;* and not, *Our Father who art over all:* For this is a prayer that belongs alone to the Christian church; and God will, that all Christians should be his in heaven: And the nearer the faithful keep themselves to God, the nearer is God to them. And in regard to this we can say, that God is not even nigh unto everyone in the Christian church. For, as the spirit of *Elias* did rest double on *Elisha:* So the presence of God works more holiness in one than in another. His glorious presence, is by the angels and saints in heaven; who, of the continual seeking of his face, are filled with glory and honor. When we read in the Scripture, that God is departed, is gone away, or is come again, it must be understood of the different ways of his presence. When God is said to depart, then comes punishment and misfortunes: When he is said to come again, then comes blessing, comfort, grace, and all other good things, (understand to the faithful.) *Gen.* 19.

God is all-knowing. He knows all, what has been, is, and shall be, in, and through the whole nature. There are three things that men do not know, namely, what is absent, secret, and to come. But God knows all things; he knows what is absent; for he is the whole eye, and sees all things; he is the whole ear, and hears all things; he is the whole foot, and is over all: He knows all what is hidden and secret; he knows all secret thoughts of the heart; he sees in the bottomless pit; he searches the heart and reins. He knows all what shall happen, good or bad; for it stands all before his eyes; so that we may say, that, in regard to this, the knowledge of God stretches further than his power and will. God knows more than he can do, as sin. God knows more than he will do, as the things that are possible, but happens never. The old *Hebrews* have said of this knowledge of God; there are three things above us that we should never forget; that is, an eye that fees all things, an ear that hears all things, and a book wherein all our thoughts, words and deeds are numbered.

God is almighty. The almighty power of God shines forth: *first,* of his titles and names he is called by in the Holy Scriptures; as, He is *the Almighty God, the King of Glory. The Lord strong and mighty, the Lord mighty in battle.* A man of war; a giant, *who makes wars to cease unto the end of the earth; he breaks the bow, and cuts the spear in sunder; he burns the chariot in the fire. Secondly,* of his words. By his almighty word, he made heaven, earth and sea, and all that in them is, of nothing. *He spoke, and it was done; be commanded, and it stood fast:* And he still preserves by his almighty word everything. *Thirdly,* of his actions. *He is mighty, and can do what he pleases in heaven and upon earth.* His hand is not shortened. *He can do exceeding abundantly, above all that we ask or think.* We must for all consider hereby; 1. That what is against, or impossible in nature, God can't do; and even if he could, he would not; For God is not against himself; neither can God do what is against his holiness and perfection. 2. That when we read in the Holy Scriptures, that God can't do it; we must then understand it in regard to his promises, that he has made and will not break. So said the Lord to *Lot*, when he would destroy *Sodom* and *Gomorrah: Move quickly, escape from here; for I cannot do anything till you depart.* The reason thereof was, because the Lord had promised to save *Lot*.

God is free-making. He is not subject, neither tied to any natural cause; but all that he does, he does freely after his own will and pleasure, and decree, so that none can say, what do you do? The will of God is all that God wills, and all that God wills, has he decreed, which in a Scriptural way is called, *the secret will of God:* And all that God has decreed, and afterwards revealed, is called, *the revealed will of God.* But since the will of God is not always fulfilled by men, through the wicked and bad disposition of men's self, therefore fulfills God his will and decree to the praise of his glory, wisdom and justice, because the wicked should have nothing to cloak their wickedness with. Hereof arises the difference between the antecedent, and consequent will of God, which are in God but one will, but is called so in regard to us men. The antecedent will of God is his mercy towards men, that they shall be saved through the faith in Jesus Christ: The consequent will of God, is his justice to save the faithful, and damn all unbelievers. The antecedent will of God is grounded on this: *I do not desire the death of a sinner, but that he shall repent, believe in Christ, and be saved.* The consequent will of God has regard to the faithful, and unbelievers, the first to be saved and the last to be damned. As our Savior says, *He that believes on the Son has everlasting life, and he that believes not the Son shall not see life, but the wrath of God abides on him.* The antecedent will of God, contains on God's side, the offer of salvation, with the means thereof: The consequent will of God contains on man's side, the reception of salvation, and the right use of the means; and they that shall use these means rightly, shall be saved; but they that neglect and abuse the means, shall be damned. Hereby can we understand these words: *O Jerusalem, Jerusalem, how often would I have gathered your children together, even as a hen gathers her chickens under her wings, and you would not.*

God is true and faithful. He is called in the Scripture, not true alone, but Truth. The Father is Truth, the Son is Truth, and the Holy Spirit is Truth. He has shown himself true in his word, and it is therefore called the Word of Truth; true in his works; for all that he has promised or threatened, he fulfills. *God is not a man, that he should lie, neither the son of man, that he should repent. Has he said, and shall be not do it? Or has he spoken, and shall be not make it good?* And this shall be the comfort of the faithful in afflictions, that God will certainly fulfill what he has promised. He has not two tongues in one mouth, nor two hearts in one breast; the Lord shall cut off all flattering lips. Therefore, says St. *Paul*; *It is impossible for God to lie.* God is holy; he is holy in his essence; *I am holy,* says the Lord. He is holy in his effect. He sanctifies all that come unto him. The Father sanctifies us in truth. The Son sanctifies us by his blood and baptism. The Holy Spirit sanctifies us by the gospel. Therefore shall the children of God endeavor to be holy; as the Lord commands; *Sanctify yourselves; for I am holy.* We shall be holy by faith in Christ; for faith cleanses the heart from sin, and sanctifies us. We shall be holy by works, for we must endeavor to serve God without fear, in holiness and righteousness, all the days of our lives.

God is good. He is good in himself, of himself, and through himself. All goodness that we find in creatures, is but a glance or brightness of the essential goodness in God. God has shown his goodness towards all creatures in the creation, particularly towards men; first, in the creation. God created man in his own image; afterwards in the redemption and sanctification. He redeemed us by the blood of his Son, and brings us, by the Holy Spirit, upon the right way to salvation, and since God is goodness itself, and the fountain of goodness, then consequently follows, that God is not the cause of sin: For, *first*, he had given unto man in the creation, such reason, and sense, and strength, that he could have withstood Satan and all his temptations; For Satan did not force man to eat of the forbidden fruit. Can a child of God after the Fall, withstand the devil, by the power of the Spirit of God; much more could *Adam* and *Eve* before the Fall. *Secondly*, God forbid them to eat of the fruit and since he had forbidden them, he had given unto them in their minds, not to do against his commands; for God hates sin. *Thirdly*, God ordained the punishment that should follow, which God could not have done in justice, if he had been the cause of sin.

God is just and righteous. He rewards the good, and punishes the wicked; he won't let one sin pass unpunished, without repentance. We shall not think that God is unjust, because he punishes the wicked, some with temporal and some with eternal punishment; for although their sins are finite, yet God is, whom they sin against, infinite. And since no man could satisfy for his own, much less for another's, therefore did God accept the person of Christ, and laid his merits in the one scale of the balance of his justice, and in the other scale the sin of all men, and received thereby full satisfaction; the one is justification by the law, that God according to his justice requires of us after the law; the other is justification by the gospel, that God according to his mercy imputes righteousness to the faithful by Christ, who is become a justification for us. And, since the faithful are become hereby pleasing in the sight of God, through faith, therefore is God said to respect some faithful, not for the sake of his own person, but for the merits of Christ. According to the first, God will punish the wicked with temporal and eternal punishment; and according to the last, God will reward the faithful with temporal and eternal blessings. Although we don't perceive this always in this world, (for the wicked prosper oftentimes best, and the faithful worst) yet shall the justice of God not suffer hereby: For in the Day of Judgment, *God will render unto everyone according to his deeds: Then shall it be well with the righteous; for they shall eat the fruit of their doings. But woe unto the wicked, for it shall be ill with him; for the rewards of his hands shall be given him.*

God is merciful, in general unto all men; to whom he has given body and soul, and preserves them daily with his fatherly providence. *What do you have that you did not receive?* Afterwards he has given unto them his Son Jesus Christ, and offers them in his word and gospel, his grace and mercy in Christ, that none shall be lost, but all be saved; in particular, against the faithful, whom he forgives their sins and transgressions, chooses for his children, and makes them eternally happy. For Christ is the Savior of all men, especially of those that believe.

God is glorious. In majesty and essence is God glorious: He has his majesty and glory in himself, and of himself; he will glorify the faithful, in his glorious Son Jesus Christ, and they shall again glorify and praise him here in grace; and afterwards in the glorious Kingdom of Heaven: *You are worthy, O Lord; to receive glory, and honor, and power; for you have created all things, and for your pleasure they are, and were created.*

We must observe these two things of God. 1. That there is but one

God. 2. That there are three persons in this Godhead.

First, we have to observe, that there is but one God: The angels and men are innumerable; but God is only ONE. *Hear, O Israel, the Lord our God is one Lord. I, even I am the Lord, before me there was no God formed, neither shall there be after me.*

Secondly, we have to observe, that there is three persons in this Godhead: Christ speaks here in our text, as the eternal Son of the Father, of his heavenly Father, saying, *God is a Spirit*; and includes herein the Holy Spirit; for the word "Spirit" is used two ways in the Holy Scriptures.

1. Essential. For the three persons in the Godhead, and the Holy Spirit is not excluded; for he is a Spirit as well as the other persons are.

2. Personal. For the third person in the Holy Trinity, that proceeds from the Father and the Son, and these three persons makes out that godly essence; *There are three that bear record in heaven, the Father, the Word, and the Holy Spirit; and these three are one God.*

God the Father is the first person, not that he has been before the other persons; for they are all three even eternal: Neither, that he is more or worthier than the others; for they are all three even, glorious and mighty; but since he is the first fountain and offspring in the godly essence, but not the cause.

God the Son is the second person, born of his Father from eternity, and in the time of his mother, the Virgin *Mary*.

God the Holy Spirit, is the third person, proceeding from the Father and the Son, and was sent visible upon the apostles, and is yet sent in the hearts of the faithful, and fills them with spiritual gifts.

3. We have to consider, what honor and service we owe to this God.

Since we have such a mighty and glorious Lord and God, it is certainly then our duty, to honor and serve him, and we can never employ our time better, than on the knowledge and service of God. It is his godly will and pleasure, that we should learn to know and serve him; and therefore, says our Savior; *He must be worshiped in Spirit and Truth:* Many people worship God as the *Samaritans*, of whom Christ said, you *worship, you know not what.* So do many worship God, who have not received the saving knowledge of God. The *Samaritans* worshiped God on Mount *Gerizim*, without command: So do many worship God without faith. Christ says in our text; *They that worship God, must worship him in Spirit and Truth.* We must know, that,

To worship God in Spirit, is to worship him, *First*, with faith and true devotion, raised by the Holy Spirit. That prayer that is not inspired by the Holy Spirit, is vain and useless. *No man can say that Jesus is the Lord, but by the Holy Spirit. Secondly*, with a broken and contrite heart. *The sacrifices of God, is a broken spirit: A broken and contrite heart, O God! you will not despise. The Lord loves to look to him that is poor, and of a contrite spirit, and trembles at his word. Thirdly,* with gathered thoughts and attention. God can't bear, nor will not suffer scattered thoughts, when we pray to him. Many are more concerned in their prayers for their worldly business and profits, than devotion. Attention in prayers, agrees best with the nature of God.

To worship God in truth, is to worship him without hypocrisy, consisting only in going to church, and all other outward ceremonies and actions, by which we only show the shadow of religion outwardly, but have not the real religion inward in our hearts. God is not pleased with such devotions, as we can see of the offering of *Cain*, in the tears of *Esau*, and of the prayers of the Pharisees. We may compare such hypocrisy with an inn, having an angel as a sign, but a devil in the house; or as the cake of the prophet, *that was not turned*, but was baked on the one side, and raw on the other.

God will not alone be worshiped in spirit and truth, but he will also be praised in spirit and truth: When he has heard and helped us, then are we obliged to praise his holy name for it. He commands us: *Call upon me in the day of trouble, I will deliver you, and you shall glorify me.* It is his gracious will, that we shall praise him: *I will praise the Name of God with a song, and will magnify him with thanksgiving. This also shall please the Lord, better than an ox or bullock, that has horns and hoofs.* The praise of God is a spiritual offering; and since God is a Spirit, therefore is he best pleased with a spiritual offering. God is worthy of our praise, and what can man do better, than to praise his Creator. *It is a good thing to give thanks unto the Lord, and to sing praises unto your name, O most high! to show forth your loving kindness in the morning, and your faithfulness every night.* Besides, in praising of God, we become like the angels, who praise the Lord always. *The Host of Heaven worships him. Bless you the Lord, all you his hosts, you ministers of his that do his pleasure.*

We should praise his goodness and mercy; that, although we are but poor sinners, yet he is so merciful, that he will we should be saved. He has therefore given his only Son, who bore all our sins; and if we sin, he does not punishes us instantly, but has patience with us. We should praise his justice, that he will recompense all our enemies, as they have deserved, if not in this world, then in the world to come. It is a righteous thing with God, to recompense tribulation to them that trouble you. We should praise him for all his blessings, that he gives us peace, rest, health and prosperity in all our undertakings: Even if he sends us crosses and affliction, we should not forget to praise him; for who knows, wherewith he has deserved it. *Shall we receive good at the hand of God? And shall we not receive evil?*

When we are so joined unto the Lord, then do we become one Spirit with him, and partakers of the divine nature; that, as God is an immortal Spirit, so shall we become likewise, blessed, happy, and immortal, through faith in Jesus Christ.

The Lord enlighten our hearts by his holy Spirit, that we may daily

34

increase in the true knowledge of God, and his Son, become strong in faith, and receive at last the crown of everlasting Life. AMEN.

3

The Holy Trinity

T he text stands in the first epistle of St. JOHN, Chap. 5 verse 7.

There are three, that bear record in heaven, the Father, the Word, and the Holy Spirit, and these three are one.

INTRODUCTION

IN the year, that King *Uziah* died, did the prophet *Isaiah* see the Lord sitting upon a throne, high and lifted up, and his train filled the temple. Above it stood the Seraphim, each one had six wings; with two he covered his face, and with two he covered his feet, and with two he flew; and one cried unto the other and said: *Holy, Holy, Holy, is the Lord of Hosts, the whole earth is fall of his glory*; as we can read by the said prophet *Isaiah*, in the sixth chapter, the 1, 2, and 3 verses.

In this sight we have to consider three things,

First, the sight in itself. The Lord appeared here unto the prophet in a sight, and not in a dream, for to confirm him publicly in his prophetical office, whereto he was called. And the Lord showed to the prophet in this sight,

1. His godly majesty; whose pomp and grandeur is described, *First*, of the throne he was seated upon. Worldly kings have their thrones to sit upon. *Solomon* had a great throne of ivory, there was not the like made in any kingdom. But the throne of God is more pompous; heaven is his throne, and the earth his footstool: He has built his stories in the heavens. The throne of *Solomon* had six steps; but the throne of God is above all heaven: Therefore is the Lord called, *The high and lofty One that inhabits eternity. Secondly*, of his garment. His train filled the temple. As the train of God filled the temple, so has Christ in his time filled the temple in *Jerusalem* with glory in his manhood. *The glory of this house shall be greater than of the former*; and so is Christ always present in his church, not alone with his godly, but also human nature, *and fills all things:* And the faithful shall receive *of his fullness, grace for grace.* For he is given, *to be the head over all things to the church, which is his body, the fullness of him that fills all in all. Thirdly*, of his waiters. Above it stood the Seraphims; *the holy angels are the ministers of the Lord to do his pleasure:* That they stood, we can thereby remember the happy state wherein they remained, and did not fall like the bad angels, from their original truth and holiness. *Fourthly*, of the cloud that filled the temple. by which we can remember the mysterious essence of God, which cannot be seen: *clouds and darkness are round about him.*

2. The mystery of the Holy Trinity. The angels did cry one to another three times, *Holy*. Herein is concealed the mystery of the Holy Trinity. The first *holy* belongs to God the Father; see *Revelation* chapter 4. The second *Holy* belongs to God the Son; see the Gospel of St. *John*, chapter 12. The third *Holy* belongs to God the Holy Spirit; see *Acts* chapter 28. Hereof we can see and perceive, that this mystery has been known and acknowledged by the forefathers in the Old Testament, although not so plain as in the New.

3. The praise of the work of God. *The whole earth is full of his glory.*

If we consider the creation; everything is full of the glory of the Lord. If we consider redemption, then is Christ given a Savior, not of few but of all. If we consider the Christian church, we shall find that God protects his church against tyrants, and reigns among his enemies.

Thirdly, we have to consider in this sight, the humbleness of the angels. We have a description here of the angels:

1. Of their order and number. Seraphim signifies glowing and burning; for the holy angels are like fire, and burns of love to God, and of zeal for his glory, to cleanse the good and consume the bad. Therefore is this name given to the angels nowhere in the Scriptures than here, where there is spoken of touching the unclean lips of the prophet, and of the punishment of the unconverted Jews. These Seraphim have been many and innumerable. The prophet *Michael saw the Lord sitting on his throne, and all the hosts of heaven standing by him, on his right and on his left hand.*

2. Of their posture. They stood, whereof we can observe their willingness to serve God; for, to stand, signifies in the Scripture, to serve and to wait upon.

3. Of their nimbleness. Each one had six wings. The creatures with wings are always nimbler than those without; since wings causes nimbleness: *Daniel saw an angel fly swiftly.*

4. Of their humbleness. With two they covered their faces, in order to show their humility toward God, and their bashfulness to see God in his glory; and to acknowledge, that they cannot understand the divine mystery of the Holy Trinity, and the human nature of the Son of God. Whereof St. *Peter* says; *The angels desire to look into.* And with two they covered their feet, for to show their deep reverence. *The heavens are not clean for the sight of the Lord, and he puts no trust in his saints.* What goodness and holiness there is in the angels, they have of and from God. Who has confirmed them in goodness, and preserves them in their original holiness.

Thirdly, we have to consider in this sight, the complaint of the prophet; *Wo is me, for I am undone, because I am a man of unclean lips, and I dwell in the midst of a people of unclean lips; for mine eyes have seen the King, the Lord of Hosts.* The prophet considers here, the holiness and majesty of God on one side, and on the other, his own uncleanness and sinful nature; and is therefore astonished, it would cost him his life and salvation; for, what is a man to be compared to God? Men have often been afraid, when they have seen an angel, much more must they then be to see God, who can spoil soul and body. God is an invisible Spirit, and no man can see him and live, therefore was the prophet so frightened. And since the prophet *Isaiah* said that *he had seen the Lord in his majesty and glory:* Therefore did the Jews accuse him of blasphemy, and afterwards destroyed him, because the Lord had said unto *Moses: "No Man can see me, and live."*

In the New Testament God has shown himself with less pomp, in the incarnation of his beloved Son. The high and lofty throne, is the glory and majesty of Christ, that was seen in his miracles, and heard in his sermons. His garment is his words and the Sacrament. His train is his mercy and grace. The Seraphim are, in part, the holy angels, that protect his holy church, and, in part, the ministers that preach and declare unto men the mystery of the Holy Trinity. Whereof our text says; *There are three that bear record in heaven, the Father, the Word, and the Holy Spirit, and these three are one.* We will, in the name of our Savior Jesus Christ, undertake to speak of this high and holy mysterious Trinity, although we must cover our faces like the seraphim, and acknowledge with *Abraham, that we are but dust and ashes:* And in the deepest reverence, consider these two heads of our text.

FIRST, *That there are three persons in the Godhead.*

SECOND, *The testimony and unity of these three persons.*

EXPLANATION of the TEXT

I. That there are three persons in the Godhead, St. John testifies in our text, when he speaks,

First, of the number of them; *There are three.* This mystery is hid for the nature, but revealed in the church, though clearer and plainer in the New, than in the Old Testament. The forefathers in the Old Testament, have had knowledge of the three persons in the Trinity, or else, how could they have know Christ, believe in him, and be saved through him? In the Old Testament, we can see and be convinced of the Trinity.

1. Of the creation. *Moses*, in describing the work of the creation, speaks of the three persons, saying: *In the beginning God created heaven and earth, and the Spirit of God moved upon the face of the waters; And God said: "Let there be light," and there was light.* Herein are all the three persons named. God the Father, is the first person, who created heaven and earth. The Word he said, is not alone his word of command, but also the essential Word, the second person; by whom all things were made. The Spirit of God, the third person that moved upon the face of the waters. In regard to this, says *David: By the Word of the Lord were the heavens made, and all the hosts of them, by the breath of his mouth.* The Psalmist names and mentions here all the three persons. The Lord is the first person. The Word of the Lord is the second person. And the breath of his mouth is the third person. Likewise, when God would create the first man, he said; *Let us make man in our own image, after our likeness.* God spoke here not to the angels, but to the other persons in the Trinity: For to whom should God speak than to them whose image and likeness man was to bear?

2. Of the way of blessing, wherewith *Aaron* and his sons, were to

bless the people, saying; *The Lord bless you, and keep you:* That is, God the Father, the first person, who blesses us with all blessings in Jesus Christ. *The Lord make his face shine upon you, and be gracious unto you:* That is, the Son, the second person, who enlightens us with the true knowledge of God, and has obtained grace of God for us. *The Lord lift up his countenance upon you, and give you peace:* That is, the Holy Spirit, the third person, who preserves us from sin; that the countenance of God can shine in our hearts by a good conscience, and seals unto us the remission of sins, which is the eternal peace of our conscience. With this blessing does the greeting of St. *Paul* agree, wherewith he concludes his second epistle to the *Corinthians*, saying; *The grace of the Lord Jesus Christ, and the love of God, and the communion of the Holy Spirit, be with you all.*

3. Of the sight *Moses* had in the desert, in the burning bush, *that did burn with fire, and was not consumed.* He that revealed himself to *Moses* in the bush, was God, which is without doubt; for none else could do such works, as to bring the children of *Israel* out of *Egypt*, and to give the law on Mount *Sinai.* He that was seen in the bush, was the Son of God, the uncreated Angel; the Angel of the presence of God. For, as we can know a man by his face, so can we know the Father in the Son. *Moses* calls him afterwards his mercy, that was in the bush. *The same Angel went before them in a pillar of a cloud, to lead them the way:* And in the same Angel was the name of the Lord. The Holy Spirit, the third person, was also in this work; for the children of Israel were said, *to have vexed his Holy Spirit,* in the wilderness. And therefore said the Lord unto *Moses,* in the same sight; *I am the God of* Abraham, *of* Isaac, *and of* Jacob. Had there not been a mystery in it, he would have said, of *Joseph,* or any other patriarch too.

4. Of the words of *David. The Spirit of the Lord spoke by me, and his word was in my tongue. The God of Israel said, the rock of Israel spoke to me, He that rules over men, must be just, ruling in the fear of God.* The

mystery of the Holy Trinity is concealed in these words. *The Father, the God of Israel spoke to* David: *The Son, the Rock of Israel, and the Word of God, spoke with* David: *And the Ghost, the Spirit of God, spoke likewise with* David.

In the New Testament we can find plainer proofs of this mystery.

1. In the words, as here in our text, besides in the command of Christ; *To baptize, in the Name of the Father, the Son, and the Holy Spirit.*

2. In divers sights, as in the baptism of Christ. *The voice of the Father was heard from heaven; the Son stood in the river, and was baptized, and the Spirit of God descended like a dove.* In the transfiguration of Christ; *There was the voice the Father heard out of the cloud:* The Son was transfigured, and the Holy Spirit appeared in a bright cloud.

3. In several effects; it is the promise of Christ: *I will pray the Father, and be shall give you another Comforter, that he may abide with you forever.* In these words, we have a plain testimony of the three persons. It is attributed to the Father, to have begotten a Son in eternity, and in time, to send this Son and the Holy Spirit. It is attributed to the Son to be born of the Father, and to pray the Father, that he will send the Holy Spirit: For he is our only Propitiator, and the High Priest, in the New Testament, by whose satisfaction and merits, the Father sends the Holy Spirit. It is attributed of the Holy Spirit, that he is sent a Comforter from the Father in the name of the Son. Our Savior says in another place: *When the Comforter is come, whom I will send unto you from the Father, even the Spirit of Truth, which proceeds from the Father, he shall testify of me.* Here we have again a plain proof and testimony of the three persons. *I,* said Christ, that is, the second person, *will send unto you from the Father,* that is, the first person, *the Comforter, the Spirit of Truth;* that is, the third person. Further, our Savior says; *The Comforter, which is the Holy Spirit, whom the Father will send in my name.* The Son attributes here

to himself, the sending of the Holy Spirit; which, in another place, is attributed to the Father. Whereof follows, that the Father and the Son, are of one power and essence. The Son sends the Holy Spirit from the Father; therefore has the Father and the Son one Spirit; and they that have one Spirit, cannot be separated in essence. The Son sends the Holy Spirit from the Father; therefore is the Son one person for himself, from the Father. The Holy Spirit proceeds from the Father and the Son, and is one essence with them both; and since the Holy Spirit proceeds from the Father and the Son, therefore is he another person for himself, from the Father and the Son.

St. *John* describes in our text,

Secondly, the name of every person, the Father, the Word, and the Holy Spirit.

The Father is one person, the first person, and a godly person; that is, true God. God the Father is one person, since he has his own essence, and consists of himself; is perfect, living and reasonable, and cannot share with others of his person: For a person is described also, that it has,

1. Its own essence, and consists for itself, as by comparison. The speech, wisdom, and beauty in man, are no persons, for they do not consist of themselves, neither have their own essence, but they belong to the man, and are common.

2. A person has a perfect essence; as, a man consists of body and soul: When these two parts are separated, then is the man no longer a person. The perfections in God are yet greater; he is not composed of any parts, for all that is in God is God.

3. A person is living and reasonable; therefore are trees, stones, and all the beasts, no persons, for the first are without life, and the others without reason.

4. A person doth not share with others of his person. *Esau* and *Jacob* are two persons, the one cannot share with the other of his

person; but everyone of them remains a person for himself: The human nature in them both, cannot be called a person; but *Esau* is one person, and *Jacob* another, for they can't share their persons with one another; *Esau* remains *Esau*, and *Jacob* remains *Jacob*.

Although the Godhead is a perfect essence, yet it is not a person, for it is common to all the three persons. But the Father, the Son, and the Holy Spirit, are everyone for himself, a person, since the one don't share with the other of his person; but everyone for himself, is a person for himself, yet are these three persons but one God, and have one godly essence.

God the Father is the first person, in regard to,

1. The origin, for he is of none, but is as the original fountain of the divine essence.

2. The order, not in regard to any dignity, as if the other two persons should be less than he, but alone, in regard to the nomination, because he is commonly called and reckoned the first in the Scriptures.

3. The appearance. So did he appear in the Baptism of Christ, and Christ has likewise instructed us so in the form of baptism.

The Father is a godly person, that is, a true God. This cannot be doubted, nor in reason, disputed by anybody.

The Son, or the Word, is one person; the second person, and a divine person, that is, a true God.

God the Son is one person, separate from the Father and the Holy Spirit; which can be seen in the description of the person of the Father. The Son is one person for himself, and consists for himself. He is perfect, living, and reasonable, and does not share with the others of his person: Besides, he is called the Word, which name is never given to the Father nor the Holy Spirit. The Son of God is called the Word, in respect to,

1. The Father. As our mind, when we think, forms the words yet

remaining in the mind; so is the divine Word born of the Father in eternity, and remains unseparated by the Father; therefore is the Son of God called; *The Image of the invisible God. The brightness of his glory, and the express image of his person.*

2. As men, with words we reveal our thoughts and pleasure; so has the heavenly Father sent the Word Jesus Christ to us, and by him revealed his fatherly will and affection: Yea; *This Word, the Son of God is a propitiation for our sins, and an advocate for us by the Father.*

The Son of God is the second person, in regard to,

1. The order. He is always placed next the Father in the Scriptures.

2. His office. *He is a Mediator between God and men.* He has always the middle place. He was born at midnight. When he was twelve years old, *He sat in the temple, in the midst of the doctors.* He preached over all in the midst of the coast. He was crucified between two malefactors. After his resurrection, he went in the midst of the two disciples to *Emmaus.* He stood afterwards in the midst of his disciples. He was seen after his ascension; *Like unto the Son of Man in the midst of the seven candlesticks.* Besides, he has promised; *where two or three are gathered together in my Name, there am I in the midst of them.*

God the Son is a divine person, that is, a true God; which can be affirmed,

1. Of his godly names. He is called not alone Lord, but *Jehovah*, which is the essential name of God. He is called *God over all, blessed forever.* True God, *God manifest in the flesh.*

2. Of his godly attributes. He is of the same essence with the Father, and is one with the Father, even eternal, even almighty, and infinite with the Father. In him we are elected before time; by him we are redeemed in time; and he will glorify us after time. All which, is a plain proof of the Godhead of Christ.

3. Of his godly works, as to create, preserve, redeem, justify, and sanctify. It is the faculty of God to do miracles: The many

miracles Christ wrought here on earth, in the time of his incarnation, convinces, us of his Godhead; and therefore, said he to the Jews; *The works that I do in my Father's name, they bear witness of me.* He wrought all these miracles by his own power, that comes from himself, as from a fountain; wherefore he could give unto others the power of doing the same, to the glory of his Name. Truly that one miracle, that he raised himself from the dead, was a plain proof that he was God, and the Son of God.

4. Of the divine worship and adoration. We must worship the Lord God only; therefore, since we are commanded to worship him; *At the Name of Jesus every knee shall bow.* The disciples worshiped him, when he ascended into heaven. *The elders in heaven fell down before him.* It follows by consequence, that he is a true God.

The Holy Spirit is one person, the third person, and a divine person, that is, true God. God the Holy Spirit is one person; he is called Spirit in our text, which cannot be understood here, essential of the three persons, as in them words *God is a Spirit*; but personal of the third person in the Holy Trinity; who, in other places of the Scripture, is called: *the Spirit of God.* The Spirit of the Lord. The Holy Spirit of God. This word holy, shows us the office of the Holy Spirit; that he is not alone holy in his essence, but also in his effects. He sanctifies all them he comes to, and makes them faithful. The Holy Spirit calls us through the Gospel; enlightens us with his gifts; sanctifies and preserves us in the true faith.

The Holy Spirit is the third person; not that he is less than the Father and the Son, for he is of equal divine essence, glory, and majesty with them both; but because he is named in the third Place in the Baptism of Christ, and several other places in the Scripture, and likewise here in our text; though it is no sin, much less blasphemy, to alter the order in naming the Son before the Father, or the Holy Spirit, before the Father and the Son.

The Holy Spirit is a divine person, that is, a true God: Which we can prove,

1. Of his divine Names. He is called *Lord, Lord God: He that Ananias lied to, was God the Holy Spirit.* St. *Paul* says, *There are diversities of the gifts of the Spirit; but the same Lord and God, which works all in all.*

2. Of the divine faculties. The Holy Spirit is of one essence with the Father and the Son, these three are one: He is therefore called; *The eternal Spirit. The breath of the Almighty. The Spirit that searches all things.*

3. Of his divine works. *All the Hosts of Heaven were made by the breath of the mouth of the Lord. The Holy Spirit came upon the Virgin Mary in the incarnation of Christ.* He preserves all things, he sanctifies the faithful, and we are baptized in his Name.

4. Of divine worship. *The angels praise him, and likewise we.*

Thirdly, the difference between these three persons, is some inward and some outward tokens.

The inward tokens have respect to the persons inwardly; as the inward token of the Father is, to beget or generate a Son; that of the Son is, to be born of the Father; and that of the Holy Spirit, to proceed from the Father and the Son. We cannot apprehend, much less understand this high mysterious *knowledge of God, therefore we must bring our thoughts into captivity, to the obedience of Christ.*

The outward token have respect to us men, according to the three articles of our Christian faith; That of the Father is the creation; That of the Son, redemption; that of the Holy Spirit, sanctification.

II. We have to consider the testimony and unity of these three persons; whereof St. John says in our text; There are three Persons that bear record in heaven.

St. *John* will prove, *that Jesus Christ, is true God and man.* Therefore to prove that he is true God, St. *John* produces three evidences, that bear record in heaven. As we are obliged to prove our right and causes with evidences, which cannot be less in number than two or three; so does St. *John* prove here, the true God and manhood of Christ, with three evidences in heaven, for the surer confirmation of our faith.

The first evidence is God the Father. He has testified of his Son, *You are my Son, this day have I begotten you:* That he is a priest, after the order of *Melchizedek: That he is his beloved Son, in whom he is well pleased: That he should bruise the serpent's head.* God the Father testified likewise of Christ, by *John* the Baptist; *There was a man sent from God, whose name was John, the same came for a witness, to bear witness of the Light, that all men through him might believe.* He was not that Light, but was sent to bear witness of that Light. Christ did acknowledge this testimony, saying to the Jews; you *sent unto John, and be bear witness unto the truth. But I have greater witness than that of John; For the works which the Father has given me to finish, the same works that I do, bear witness of me; That the Father has sent me.*

The second evidence is the Word; *The Son of God has testified to us on earth what he had seen in heaven.* He has testified not alone by his word; *That he is the Savior of the world, and the true Messiah, the light of the world, the way, the truth, and the life:* But he has also confirmed this his testimony with his painful death and suffering: He is therefore called, *The faithful witness, who loved us, and washed us from our sins in his own blood.* He testifies of his Godhead, with his descending into hell, resurrection, and ascension.

The third evidence is the Holy Spirit: He has testified of Christ three times.

First, *When Christ was baptized in Jordan by John.* Second, *When Christ was transfigured*; and the third time, on the day of Pentecost, *when he was sent upon the apostles.*

Since we have such glorious heavenly testimony of Christ, and the Christian doctrine; then we must surely believe and acknowledge, that the same testimonies are true, and to be depended upon; *For he that believes not God, has made him a liar, because he believes not the testimony that God gave of his Son.*

Every child of God can therefore rely and depend upon his faith, and say, *I know in whom I have believed, and I am persuaded, that he is able to keep that which I have committed unto him against that day.*

Will the inward testimony, that is, our heart, condemn us; God, who has given record of the merits of Christ, is greater than our hearts.

Although there are three persons in the Trinity, yet there is but one God. St. *John* says, *These three are one:* They are not one alone in consent and will; for what the Father wills, that wills the Son and the Holy Spirit: But also in testimony; for what one testifies, that testifies the other likewise, and in effect; for what one does, the other two do likewise. Therefore says St. John, *"They are one,"* that is, in essence and nature.

This we cannot comprehend with our human reason; and the pit of this holy mystery is so deep, and the cord of our reason so short, that we cannot reach to the bottom; therefore we must take our reason captive, and remain by that knowledge, that the Lord has pleased to reveal to us in his holy word. If we look too long at the shining sun, we shall become blind: In the life to come, we shall see God, as he is, and be satisfied with the sight of his glorious presence.

Unto thee, O holy and blessed Trinity, Father, Son, and Holy Spirit, be all honor, praise, might and majesty, now and forever more.

AMEN.

4

Creation

T he text, GENESIS, Chap. 1 verse 1, 26, inclusive.

INTRODUCTION

IT is worth observing, what the apostle St. *Paul* writes to the
Hebrew's, Chap. 11 verse 3. *Through faith we understand, that the*
worlds were framed by the word of God; so that things which are seen,
were not made of things which do appear.

In these words we have three things to consider,

First, by which we can understand, that the world is framed; St.
Paul says, through faith. There was no man, when God created the
world, therefore can none know how it was transacted, neither can
we comprehend it with our reason; therefore some have wrongfully
concluded, that the world is eternal; others, who have heard something of a creation, but could not rightly understand it, are fallen
on diverse ridiculous opinions, as: that the world is blown together
and composed of sun-grains. Others said that there had been some
substance before, whereof everything is created, as fire, water and

air; for, they said, "Of nothing comes nothing." But they did all err, and when they thought themselves wise, they became fools: St. *Paul* corrects us herein, saying, *through faith we understand it.*

Faith is built upon the word of God, which teaches us, that the world is neither eternal, nor composed of sun-grains, but framed by the word of God; so that faith is the looking-glass, through which we can see the absent things as present. The unbelievers will not consent to this, for they are willingly ignorant of this; but a true Christian beholds the creation with a faithful eye, not as the heathens, who worshiped the creature more than the Creator. Therefore says St. Paul, "*through faith we understand.*" We must have knowledge to apprehend the creation; not a philosophical knowledge, which human wisdom can teach, but a knowledge, that the Holy Spirit has instructed us in by the word of God, whereof comes faith; and when we follow this knowledge, then we do understand through faith, not alone that the world is framed, but also,

Secondly, whereof the world is framed: St. *Paul* says, "*The world is framed by the word of God.*"

In which words the apostle shows us, as with his finger on the Creator, and the tools. On the Creator, who is not an artful and cunning master among men, as *Micemides* a carver, who made a coach, horses and coachman, in such little figures, that a fly could cover it all with her wings. Another formed in a cherry-stone, a ship with all her tacklings. Such cunning masters are nothing but mockers of nature; since they can do nothing but what they have seen before, and that of things already made to their hands: But here has the Almighty God himself, been the work-master, and has built this beautiful work of the whole creation. In particular, the work of the creation is attributed to God the Father, the first person in the Holy Trinity; when we confess in the first articles of our Christian faith, *I believe in God, the Father Almighty, maker of heaven and earth.*

For in the creation is God the Father gone out the first time of his sacred godly light, and has shown himself in his work.

The tools, by which God framed the world, is called here, "the Word of God." This is not a word that anyone can speak, but it is the essential Word, the Son of God, as St. *John* declares; *In the beginning was the Word, and the Word was with God, and the Word was God: The same was in the beginning with God; all things were made by him, and without him was not anything made, that was made.* This Word stands yet, and has its full power and effect, or else the world could not consist. It was likewise the word of God's command. *God said, "Let there be," and there was.* The Apostle says: *"By this Word was the world framed."* Which word *framed*, comprehends a comparison, taken of one broken in his limbs, that again must be put in order, if the body shall have its right shape; by which is laid before us the beautiful creation, composed in an ample order, of divers contrary parts; which, in part, were nothing, and in part something, though nothing in respect to the unformed chaos, wherein everything was mixed. The apostle calls them here,

Thirdly, the things that do not appear. What are the things that do not appear? That is, *in part, nothing.* There is still something that does not appear in our sight, as air; therefore this nothing is explained in other places in the Scripture, by things that are not. *Moses* calls it: *Without form and void; and darkness upon the face of the deep.* So, when the apostle says here, that the things which are seen, are made of things which do not appear, is to say, that the world is created of nothing: For, since the world is not made of things that do appear, then it is certainly made of nothing; therefore, said the wisdom of God; *When there were no depths, I was brought forth.*

In part nothing; that was still something, but wholly unformed, and unable to make anything of, otherwise called the unformed chaos, wherein everything were mixed together, which was as good as nothing: So, as the Scripture calls this unformed matter, heaven and earth, because heaven and earth were created thereof; so are likewise them things that are created thereof, said to be created of nothing, because the same unformed matter is created of nothing. Hereof did God bring forth, by his almighty word, one thing of another: light from darkness, wet from dry; and did put a glorious form thereon. Also is then what was in the beginning nothing, made first to something, and afterwards to something beautiful.

Must we not therefore be astonished? For what master can make something of nothing? When a church, palace, or house is to be built, then must all the materials be provided beforehand, and then build a long time thereon, before it is finished and completed. But God had alone power to create, in a little time, the whole world, and everything, and that of nothing. *For the Lord spoke, and it was done: The Lord commanded, and it stood fast.* Of this creation does our text make mention, and give a full description. We shall, in the name of our Lord Jesus Christ, take a walk into the world, and consider of our text, these two heads;

FIRST, *The creation in itself.*

SECOND, *The Creator.*

EXPLANATION of the TEXT

1. We have to consider the creation in itself.

We shall consider the work of the creation, as if it was done yesterday; for with God, ten thousand years are as one day; therefore, here are all new things before us in our text; whereas *Moses* gives us such a description: *"In the beginning, God created the heaven and the earth."* Consider here,

1. *The time*, when the world was created: in the beginning. We can't call this time, for before the beginning there was no time, but all

eternity. But time begun in the beginning. Likewise, when the world is at an end, there will be no longer time, but eternity. Hereof we can see, that the world is not eternal, but was created in the beginning; neither could the world be from eternity, for then it would be even with God, and by consequence be God. Since nothing is eternal, and without beginning but God, who is alone from everlasting to everlasting; *Before the mountains were brought forth, and the earth was made.* The world is created with time, and time with the world, in the beginning, when it did please God, to draw the thread of time out of the ball of eternity. Will anyone know, what God did before the creation? *Moses* makes no mention thereof, neither is it of any consequence for us to know, as not belonging to our salvation. Though we can answer such inquisitives, what St. *Paul* says; *God chose us in Christ, before the foundation of the world*: And we can conclude of the words of our Savior, that God made, in the beginning, the Kingdom of Heaven for the faithful, and hell-fire for the devil and unbelievers.

2. *The manner or mode* how the world is framed, is comprehended in this word, *create*; which word signifies here, to make a stately and glorious work, either of nothing or of something, whereon human reason and sense must doubt, that anything could be made of, much less, so complete and well; so that all they who are no gods, are here defied to make such a work, which did cost God but one word, and it was there. *Moses* shows us in this word *create*, three things: *First, that* there was nothing to create of, or else he could not say, create; neither does he mention any matter. *Secondly, that* God did create of nothing this unformed chaos, wherein all the elements were mixed, and whereof heaven and earth were afterwards created. *Thirdly, that* God did divide this unformed chaos from one another, and did put everything in their proper places in the three first days: For the first day he divided the light from darkness; the second day,

he divided the waters under the firmament, from the waters above the firmament; The third day, he divided the dry land from the seas; and in the other three days, God did adorn and fill the same. On the fourth day, he adorned the firmament with light and stars: On the fifth day, he adorned and filled the waters with fish, and the air with birds. And on the sixth day, he adorned and filled the earth with all sorts of creatures; and at last with man, who was to rule over all. God had nothing to create and adorn this of, but he created and made all of nothing; and as God did then create all things, so does he yet preserve them daily, that nothing shall be lost or go to decay.

3. *To what end* has God created the world? When a thing is made, it is commonly made for profit's sake. A house is always built for the profit of the builder; likewise has the creation its intent; as the *glory of God.* So says the Psalmist; *The heavens declare the glory of God, and the firmament shows his handiwork: Day unto day utters speech, and night unto night shows knowledge.* We can see in the creation, the glory of God's almighty power. It is a great and plain proof of the infinite power of God, that he, by one word, could create all visible and invisible things; some of nothing, and some of a coarse unformed chaos. When he said, *Let there be light,* and there was light. When he said, *Let there be a firmament,* it was so. When he said, *Let the waters be gathered together in one place,* it was so. When he said, *Let the earth bring forth grass, herbs and trees,* it was so. When he said, *Let there be lights in the firmament,* there was sun, moon and stars. Here we must fall in astonishment, and cry out, *Ah, Lord God, you have made the heaven and earth by your great power and stretched out arm, and there is nothing too hard for you.* We can see further in the creation, *the glory of God's wisdom.* The work praises its Master. All that God has made, is divided in certain order: Some have no life, as heaven, earth, stones and metals; some have life, as the trees and the beasts; and some have reason, as man; and for all, they do

all consist. Is not this a great wisdom? We can likewise see in the creation, the glory *of God's goodness and mercy.* God, who is perfect, and needs nothing, is pleased here, to communicate His goodness to creatures, and give them life and spirit; which goodness and mercy of God, the prophet *David* praises with these words; *O give thanks unto the Lord, for he is good, for his mercy endures forever: O give thanks unto the God of gods, for his mercy endures forever: O give thanks unto the Lord of Lords, for his mercy endures forever: To him, who alone does great wonders, for his mercy endures forever: To him that by wisdom, made the heavens, for his mercy endures forever: To him that stretched out the earth above the waters, for his mercy endures forever: To him that made great lights, for his mercy endures forever: The sun to rule by day, for his mercy endures forever: The moon and stars to rule by night, for his mercy endures forever.*

The use and profit of man. God created man for his own sake, that he should honor, serve, and obey him, as his Lord and Maker: But the world, and all what therein is, God created for the use and profit of man, either in clothing, feeding, or diversion: We can be better convinced hereof, when we consider the work of every day by itself.

On the first day, God created the light. Is not the light a precious thing? For, what would we do, if we had no light to see by? If there was no light, then the world would be nothing else but a land of darkness; yea, as darkness itself, and of the shadow of death, without any order, and where the light is as darkness. The old fathers are of opinion, that the angels are created the same day, as the light; for they are called angels of light, glowing fire. So says St. *Paul* of them, *Are they not all ministering spirits, sent forth to minister for them, who shall be heirs of salvation.*

On the second day, God created the firmament; by which is understood, *First, in common,* that place, from the earth and sea, to the highest regions, and comprehends the element of fire and air, likewise *the circuit*, where the sun, moon and stars have their turn, otherwise called the heavens. *Secondly, in particular*, the uppermost part of heaven, which we call the blue sky, or starry heaven. The Psalmist calls it, *the firmament of God's power.* This firmament was before nothing but a thick moist air, as a thick sky, wherein the earth laid concealed. Here happened now, according to the command of God, a division: For there rose up a firmament, which was stretched out as a curtain, and spreads out as a tent, and remains hanging in his own circle some thousand miles broad: This firmament was to divide the waters above the firmament, from the waters under the firmament. The waters above the firmament are unknown to us, although the Scripture makes mention thereof in other places. The waters under the firmament, are the sea and sky, which are drawn together of the vapors that rise out of the earth, and pressed together by the coldness of the air, and falls down again in rains, snow, hail, and dew; this is all for the profit of man.

On the third day God created heaven and earth; that is: He divided the dry land from the waters; so that we can walk, live, sow, and plough on the land; and he adorned the earth with grass, herbs, and trees, everyone after its kind, and filled its inside with metals, minerals and stones. The waters of the sea were gathered together as a heap, and were shut up with doors, and is kept in subjection, that it should not list up its waves too high. We can daily see how subservient or profitable the waters are; for when it rains, how quick do the waters run to the sea, which is their right gathering place? Who can number up all the use and profit men have of the earth and waters? We live, are fed, and clothed of the earth, and find at last a place of rest in her when we die. The waters furnish us plentifully with fish, we drink it, we fail on it, and wash our stains off with it.

On the fourth day, God created sun, moon and stars, that they should give *light upon the earth, and divide the day from the night,*

58

and to be for signs and for seasons, and for days and for years. For signs
natural, as heat, cold, rain, and good weather; as supernatural, as
when the sun stood still, or went back: *For seasons,* that we thereby
could know the four seasons of the year, when we should plough,
sow and reap: *For days and for nights,* that we should know when to
work and to rest. We should be careful that we do not attribute unto
the sun, moon and stars, more power and effect than we find here
summed up.

On the fifth Day, God created all the birds in the air, and the fish
of the sea, whereof the whale is alone named; which, in the ground
text signifies, a great and monstrous sea creature; for the greatest
creatures are to be found in the sea. We have the fish and the birds
for our food, and the feathers of the birds to lay on; yea, we have
many innumerable profits of them.

On the sixth day God created all living creatures and worms,
everyone after his kind. What use and profit have men not of the
creatures? Some of them we ride on, they work for us; of others,
while they live, we have butter, milk and cheese; and afterwards
their flesh for food, and their hides for shoes. Of poisonous worms
we prepare antidotes against poison. Besides, we have other profit of
the creatures; for we can learn of them, as of the ant, diligence; of the
ox and the ass, thankfulness; of the stork, turtle, crane, and swallow,
carefulness; of the dove, simplicity; and of the serpent, subtlety. On
the same day God created man after his own likeness, and concluded
therewith the work of the creation. This was a masterpiece, and an
epitome of all what God had created on the other days; since it was
above all the other creatures in magnificence and glory, by reason of
the speech and rational sense; which is the power of the immortal
soul, that God had laid in particular in man. And after man was
created, God rested on the seventh day, to show, that he would have
his rest in man, and man should again rest in him; that they could at

last come to the eternal rest in heaven.

II. We have to consider, the Creator.

Let us now lift up our thoughts higher, and consider this glorious and great Creator. *Moses* called him with one word, *GOD*; that is, the holy and blessed Trinity, *which is, and which was, and which is to come, the Almighty.* In the ground text there stand gods; not as if there had been many gods, but thereby is alone showed the three persons; who are all named here by *Moses*, in the description of the creation. The first person is called *God.* The second person is called *Word*; for this Word was not alone a simple word of command, but also the essential Word, the Son of God; wherefore *Solomon* explains this Word by the Wisdom of God. St. *Paul*, speaking of Christ, said; *He is the image of the invisible God; the Firstborn of every creature: By him were all things created.* The third person is called, *the Spirit of God that moved upon the face of the waters.* This was not a wind, for the winds were then not created, but the Holy Spirit; who by his divine power kept up the unformed lump of the earth, and made it fruitful as a hen that sits upon her eggs, and hatches out her chickens. We have now named here the Almighty Creator of all things; that is, the holy and blessed Trinity, the Father, the Son and the Holy Spirit: As St. *Paul* declares, saying: *Of him,* (that is, God the Father) *and through him* (that is, God the Son) *and to him;* (that is, God the Holy-Ghost) *are all things: To whom,* (that is, the Holy-Trinity) *be glory forever.* AMEN.

This Creator is unsearchable, wondrous, unalterable, bountiful and generous, worthy of praise, and glorious.

Unsearchable. He dwells in the light, which no man can approach unto; whom no man has seen, nor can see; yet is he gone out of this light, and has showed himself in the creation, where we can see his back parts.

Wondrous: There is nothing imperfect in the creation; but such a harmony, that although one thing is against another, yet is there no disagreement: the night releases the day; the moon the sun; one season the other; One thing is against another; as fire and water, air and earth, hard and soft, four and sweet, wet and dry, thick and thin, black and white, heavy and light; notwithstanding all which, nature is not corrupted.

Unalterable. All what is in the world is subject to alterations; but the Creator is always the same. So says the Psalmist; *The heavens shall wax old like a garment, as a vesture shall it be changed; but you are the same, and your years shall have no end.* We see everything alters, even man himself, who is created after the image of God, is subject to alterations, from his birth to his grave: For from children we become youth, from youth boys, from boys young men, from young men to man's old age, and at last we alter to dust in our graves.

Bountiful and generous. He has showed his bounty so plentifully in the creation; where He has given unto men, all what is needful for them.

Worthy of praise, and glorious. This is the final cause wherefore God created us, that we should praise and glorify him; therefore has he given us a rational soul, that we should know, love, and eternally possess him, as the only and highest good. He that does not love and acknowledge this highest good, forsakes the final cause for which he was created. Our soul is created after the image of God, therefore ought the same to love that God and Creator, of whom it has all things and everything. If a shadow had life, it would certainly love that body whose shadow it is. If a picture had life, it would love the master that drew it. Should not then our souls in a higher degree love that Lord and God, who made it after his own likeness? This grace we can alone receive by prayers; therefore will I conclude with this short one,

O Holy Lord God, Heavenly Father, draw our hearts unto you with the cords of your love, that we may forget all earthly things, and cleave unto thee, and alone seek the heavenly things, whereto we in the beginning, were created, and which you have preserved for them that love Thee, that when we quit these earthly tabernacles, we may be received into the everlasting ones. Hear us, O Lord, for Jesus Christ Sake, AMEN.

5

The Good Angels

he text, PSALM 91:11th and 12th verses.

He shall give his angels charge over you, to keep you in all your ways: They shall bear you upon their hands, lest you dash your foot against a stone.

INTRODUCTION

FRIENDS have all things in common. God has this way, that they who are his friends, have everything in common with him. He has heaven in common with the angels, and the angels in common with the faithful: so says the apostle St. *Paul*, in his Epistle to the *Hebrews*, 1st chapter, 14th verse: *The angels are all ministering spirits, sent forth to minister for them who shall be heirs of salvation.* Of these words we have to consider two things,

First, the ministry of the angels. The angels are here described by their essence, their glory, and their willingness.

Of their *essence.* They are spirits, by which they are separated from all visible creatures. They have often appeared in the form of men;

But of the angel, whereof we read in the history of *Tobias*, we can see, that they only kept such form so long as they were sent out.

Of their *glory*. They are angels; angel is a name of ministry, and signifies errand, for they are errands from God, and we can see thereby their glory: For, as there are two things which make a man great, *to wit*, his own qualities, that he can merit a high charge; and his office that he gets according to his qualities, so are there two things that make the angels glorious; their nature and their office; on account of the first are they called *holy*, and on account of the last are they *glorious*.

Of their *willingness*. They are sent forth to minister: God did not keep the angels for himself in heaven, but he sent them forth to minister for men; therefore are they called ministering spirits. This is not to the disgrace of the angels; for, as an ambassador accounts it a great honor to be employed in the king's service; so is it likewise a great honor for the angels to be sent forth in the service of God to men.

Secondly, for whom the angels are ministering. They are sent in particular for them that shall be heirs of salvation. God sends his angels to save the faithful in dangers, as *Lot* in *Sodom*; *Daniel* in the lion's den; the three men in the fiery furnace; *Paul* in the danger of the sea; *Peter* in prison. God sends his angels to destroy and withstand the enemies of the faithful. An angel smote the Sodomites with blindness. An angel destroyed the first-born in *Egypt*. An angel withstood *Balaam* on the road. An angel smote the camp of the *Assyrians*. And an angel smote *Herod*, so that the worms did eat him. Yea, the holy angels minister for the faithful, from their cradles to their graves, and carry them then into the bosom of *Abraham*.

We shall speak here of these holy ambassadors, and heavenly ministers, and of our text consider these two things.

FIRST, *The sending of the angels, from what Lord they are sent.*

SECOND, *Their ministry, in this their sending to men.*

EXPLANATION of the TEXT

I. We have to consider, the sending of the angels, from what Lord they are sent.

As the holy angels ministered unto Christ in the time of his incarnation, from his birth until his ascension; so do they minister unto them, that through faith are made members of Christ. Therefore, after the Psalmist had described, how the man shall be, who shall have the protection of the angels; namely: *He shall dwell in the secret place of the Most High, and abide under the shadow of the Almighty:* He shall say of the Lord; *He is my refuge, and my fortress, my God, in him will I trust;* Then follows the gracious promises, that God had made to such a man, as we can see in the words of our text: And we have to consider here, the Lord and the ministers.

1. The Lord that sends them. He is no earthly king, as the king of *Babylon* sent letters and presents unto *Hezekiah* in *Jerusalem*; but he is Lord above all lords, and King above all kings: He is almighty, commanding and protecting.

Almighty. Heaven and earth, and all what therein is, are created by the word of his mouth. The Scripture makes no mention of, on what day the angels were created; though we can conclude, that they were not before the creation; for what is, or has been, before the beginning of time, is, according to the way of speaking in the Scripture, eternal; neither were they created after the six days, for then did God rest from all his work; therefore they must be included in the creation of the six days. The old fathers are of opinion, that the angels were created on the first day, when the light was created, because light agrees best with the nature of angels; therefore, since

God has created the angels, he has the best right and title to use them, when and where he pleases.

Commanding. He has power and authority to command, and to send the angels, therefore is he called, *The Lord of Hosts. For he spoke, and it was done; he commanded, and it stood fast.* Can an officer having soldiers under him, say to this man; *"Go," and he goes: And to another, "come," and he comes: And to his servant, "Do this," and he does it.* Should not God then have more command over his angels, whom he has created.

Protecting. He has care over us men, that no evil shall befall us; therefore He sends these noble ministers, that the whole world shall see how precious the faithful are in the sight of God: The Psalmist therefore says; *How excellent is your loving kindness, O God! Therefore the children of men put their trust under the shadow of your wings.*

2. The ministers, who are sent, are his angels. God has many angels that minister unto him. *Daniel* saw God, as an Ancient of Days, upon his throne, and thousands upon thousands ministered unto him; and ten thousand times ten thousand stood before him: Although there are so many angels, yet they were created all at one time.

The Scripture ascribed unto the angels several titles, particular qualities, order, appearances, and offices.

Several titles and names. Here in our text, they are called angels of God and ministering spirits. In other places in Scripture, they are called, *children of God, elect angels, God's morning-stars, holy watchers, wind, flames of wire.* Otherwise we have six names of angels in the Scripture; as *Michael*, who is as God; *Gabriel*, the Strength of God; *Raphael*, the physician of God; *Uriel*, the light of God; *Jeremiel*, the mercy of God; *Sealthiel* the desired of God. The two first names we find in the canonical books, and the four last in the apocrypha.

Particular qualities; as, goodness, holiness, immortality, power, nimbleness, wisdom and will.

Goodness. God created all the angels good, but some fell off, and some remained constant in their goodness; and these were so strengthened by the grace of God, that they can never depart from their goodness, and are therefore called good angels.

Holiness. Our Savior calls them himself holy angels, for there was no sin at all found in them that remained steadfast, as they were created.

Immortality. The angels can never die; their immortality is natural to them; belonging to the perfection of spirits: This immortality is a grace and blessing to the good angels, but misery and punishment to the bad.

Power. We can see their power partly of their titles, partly of their actions. They are called, *the mighty angels of Christ*, who have done mighty things. An angel smote in one night, all the first-born in *Egypt.* An angel smote in three days in *Israel*, in the time of *David, seventy thousand.* An angel smote in one night, in the camp of the *Assyrians, one hundred and eighty five thousand.*

Nimbleness. They are seen with wings, and to fly; as the creatures with wings are always nimbler than those without.

Wisdom. The angels are endowed with great wisdom, yet they do not know all things; they do not know the Day of Judgment, neither the thoughts of men, nor the mysteries of God, without God reveals it to them; though they know many deep and secret things of God; For they always behold the face of God in heaven, of themselves: The Spirit in us, knows everything in us: Why should not the angels likewise know what is in themselves? The angels speak with one another, and reveal their thoughts unto one another, in a manner wholly unknown to us. God speaks likewise with the angels when he enlightens them, we suppose, as he used to speak to the prophets, of the condition of the world. Since God uses the angels to defend the faithful, and punish the wicked, and to guard over the world, then do they certainly know how it goes in the world. The devil goes round in the world, and contrives mischief; much more are the holy angels striving to defend the faithful from the power of Satan. If the bad angels know the condition of the world; much more can the good angels know it. And if the good angels know the prayers of the saints upon earth; much more can they know the condition of the world; of some things to come, though not all; for to know all what is to come, is alone becoming unto God: *Who, as I*, says the Lord, *shall call the things that are coming? and they all come.* The angels know most the things to come, partly of their own knowledge and wisdom, that they, of foregoing accidents, can conclude what shall happen, partly of revelations from God: So did God reveal unto the angel *Gabriel*, the mystery of the seventy weeks, which *Gabriel* again revealed unto the prophet *Daniel*. Likewise did God reveal unto the same angel, the conception of Christ, which he was to annunciate to the Virgin *Mary*.

Will. The will of the angels is so confirmed in good, that they can never fall from it in eternity: Shall the children of God become after the resurrection, equal unto the angels; then shall they become unchangeable, holy like the angels. And since our souls shall be perfect spirits after this life, how much more perfect spirits are the holy angels? The angels have not this confirmation in goodness of themselves, or through their own natures, but of the grace of God: For who can deserve anything from God through his own means? Though there are some reasons, why they were confirmed in their goodness; as, partly, that they did use the gifts well, wherewith they were created; partly, that they did endeavor to improve the gracious gifts they had received, and partly, that they saw how horribly the fallen angels were punished.

Their order. There is a certain order among the angels, one is above another. The Scripture speaks of cherubim, seraphim, thrones, dominions, principalities, powers, arch-angels and angels; but what orders they are we cannot understand. We can well think, that God, who is a God of order and decency, and has placed everything in order in the world, has likewise put order among the angels; but which of them is the highest or lowest, is nowhere in the Scripture revealed; therefore we must rest contented so, until we come into the glorious Kingdom of God, and become equal unto the angels.

Their appearances. The angels are by nature invisible; for they are spirits, and have no flesh nor blood, though they have appeared in several forms. For *Abraham*, they did appear as men; in the grave of Christ as young men; in the resurrection of Christ, as fire and lightning: For the prophet *Ezekiel*, as four creatures, everyone with four faces: For the prophet *Elijah*, as chariot and horses of fire. For the prophet *Zachariah*, as men riding upon horses.

The uncreated Angel, the Son of God, has often appeared in human form, in the Old Testament, before his incarnation; wherefore the Spirit of the Lord said; *I rejoiced in the habitable parts of the earth, and my delights were with the Son of Man.* We will number up some examples.

The Angel that appeared before *Hagar in the wilderness*, was the Son of God; for he is called afterwards *Jehovah*, which is the proper name of God; besides, the same Angel promises afterwards, that he would multiply her seed, which no created angel could do.

One of the three men that *appeared unto* Abraham, *in the plains of Mamre, when he sat in the door of his tent*, was the Son of God; which we can conclude thereof; *First*, because there stands in the beginning of the Chapter, *And the Lord appeared unto* Abraham; thereupon follows the manner how he appeared. *Secondly*, says the Lord, *I will certainly return unto you according to the time of life*; *and lo*, Sarah *your wife shall have a son*. These words are afterwards ascribed to God himself. *Thirdly*, the same Angel is called in the same chapter,

Jehovah. Fourthly, the two angels went from *Abraham* towards *Sodom*, but the third being the Son of God, did remain, and spoke with *Abraham*, and *Abraham* prayed unto him for *Sodom*.

The Angel that *spoke unto* Jacob *in a dream*, when he had laid the piled rods in the gutters before the flocks, was the Son of God, which we can conclude from the following, where the same Angel says; *I am the God of Beth-el, where you anointed the pillar, and where you vowed a vow unto me.*

The man that wrestled with *Jacob* in the night, was the Son of God, in human form, and we can thereby prove it. *First*, that the Angel said; *As a prince you have power with God and men, and have prevailed. Secondly*, The same man blessed *Jacob. Thirdly*, Jacob himself did confess, that he had seen God face to face, and therefore called the place *Peniel*.

TheAngel that *appeared unto* Moses *in the bush, burning with fire, and was not consumed*, was the Son of God. For, *first*, God the Father is never called an angel, because he is not sent. *Secondly*, says the same Angel unto *Moses; I am the God of your father, the God of* Abraham, *the God of* Isaac, *and the God of* Jacob. *Thirdly*, He afterwards revealed his name unto *Moses*, saying; *I AM, THAT I AM*, which name Christ did apply to himself, when he was in dispute with the Jews, who did deny his Godhead, saying: "*Before* Abraham *was, I am.*" *Fourthly, Moses* himself declared this sight of Christ, and called it; *The goodwill of him that dwelt in the bush.*

The Angel that went before the Camp of *Israel, by day in a pillar of a cloud, and by night in a pillar of fire*, was the Son of God; for the same angel is called *Jehovah*; and God himself said of this Angel, "*My name is in him.*"

The offices of the holy angels, is described in the Scripture, to be the following.

To praise God in eternity. The prophet *Isaiah*, did hear the angels cry

70

aloud; *Holy, Holy, Holy is the Lord God of hosts.* The shepherds abiding by night in the field at *Bethlehem*, did hear the angels sing to the glory of the newborn Christ; *Glory to God in the highest, and on earth peace, good will toward men. St. John the divine* saw in a sight, *that all the angels stood round about his throne, and about the elders; and the four beasts, and fell before the throne on their faces, and worshiped God, saying, Amen: Blessing, and glory, and wisdom, and thanksgiving, and honor, and power, and might, be unto our God forever and ever.* They are willing and ready to obey and execute God's command; therefore are they said to stand before God; for to stand, signifies in the Scripture, to serve; so *stood* Joseph *before* Pharoah; David *stood before* Saul. The children of the Hebrews were nourished in the palace of the king of *Babylon that they might stand before the king.*

Are the holy angels, who are strong giants, the most noble creatures, and clear-shining spirits, so willing to serve God and obey his commands? Should not then we poor earth-worms, who are but dust and ashes, strive to be more willing to serve God and obey his commands? Our Savior makes us sensible thereof, when he teaches us to pray "*Your will be done on earth, as it is in heaven.* We must not pray thus alone with our lips, but we should do all our endeavors, to do the will of God here on earth, as it is done in heaven of the holy angels.

They minister unto Christ. They worship him. All the angels worshiped him in the state of his humiliation and exaltation; They ministered unto him when he was born, when he was in danger of *Herod*; when he was tempted in the wilderness; when he sweats drops of blood; when he laid in the grave; when he rose up, and when he ascended into heaven: And they shall minister unto him, when he shall come again to judge the living and the dead, at the great Day of Judgment.

II. We have to consider the ministry of the angels in their sending to man.

This ministry consists herein, to keep men in all their ways, to bear them up in their hands, and to defend them from all evil.

They keep men in all their ways; as,

On the way of our birth, we are kept by the angels. If the devil had his will, there would never be a child born without defect; yea, our mother's womb, would often become our grave.

On the way of our life, we are kept by the holy angels, in all conditions.

In spiritual. They help to promote the word of God and the gospel; when St. *Paul* was in *Troade*, he saw a vision in the night; there stood a man of *Macedonia*, and prayed him saying; *Come over and help us*; whereof St. *Paul* concludes, that the Lord had called him to preach the Gospel. They defend likewise the servants of God in their lawful callings, as we can see of the examples of *Elias, Elisha, Daniel*, and all the prophets and apostles.

In temporal. They defend all pious magistrates against their enemies, as we can see of kings *Hezekiah, David*, and others.

In household conditions. They defend pious married people, promote their matrimony, protect them, have care over their children; tends them in sickness, and after death carries their souls into the Bosom of *Abraham*. If it happens that a child of God comes to any misfortune, in his lawful calling and way, then we must not think that the holy angels have neglected their ministry, or are gone away from such persons; no, but we should consider, *That a sparrow cannot fall on the ground, without the will of God:* And the very hairs are numbered on our heads; then can no misfortune befall us without the will of God.

Who is he that says, and it comes to pass, when the Lord commanded it not? There happens many things in the world, whereof we can find no cause. We can see the finger on the dial of God, but not the wheels that turn the finger; and we must therefore say; *I was dumb, I opened not my mouth, because you did it.* Has God his eyes by the casting of the lot, much more by his children? Misfortune rests at everyone's door, and takes up lodging as soon by a pious *Job*, as a wicked *Herod*; though with this difference, that it is a trial by the faithful but a punishment by the wicked. *Jacob* had the Son of God in his arms, and went away from him lame. *Lazarus* was a child of God, and had the angels about him, yet he laid in misery with sores and boils: God will thereby try the faith, patience, and constancy of his children; as St. *Peter* says; you *are in heaviness through manifold temptations. That the trial of your faith being much more precious than of gold that perishes though it be tried with fire, might be found unto praise, and honor, and glory, at the appearing of Jesus Christ.* As the Spirit of God is not departed from a faithful one, because he is sick, miserable or unhappy; so are neither the angels gone away, because misfortune happens.

On the way of our calling, do the holy angels keep us. They who walk in their lawful calling, and are careful in the fear of God, in that calling where it has pleased the Lord to place them, praying and beseeching the Lord's help and grace, trusting in God, and depending on the gracious promises of God; have this privilege and assurance from God; *He shall give his angels charge over you, to keep you in all your ways.* It is the same promises that the Lord gave by the prophet *Zachariah*, saying: *"If you will walk in my ways, and if you will keep my charge, then I will give you places to walk among those that stand by."* On the way of crosses and afflictions, are the holy angels by the faithful. The Psalmist says: *"The angels of the Lord encamps round about them that fear him, and delivers them."*

On the way of death are the holy angels present by the faithful, in order to carry their souls *into the Bosom of Abraham.*

They shall bear them up in their hands, like parents that are very careful and tender of their infants, and bears them up in their hands or arms, that they should not be hurt; so is God watchful over his children, and is said; *To bear them as a man bears his son. To carry them in his bosom, as a nursing father bears a suckling child. To take them by their arms.* Which service God shows to the faithful by his holy angels, whereof we can see his great bounty and mercy toward us poor Sinners. We were not able to withstand Satan, *who casts out of his mouth water as a flood,* to carry us away, if the holy angels did not guard and protect us. God could well protect us from the devil, and defend us from misery, without the help of the holy angels, as well as he made us men, and created our first parents without them, or their help. He could likewise govern and rule the world, without kings and princes; and he can likewise give us seed of the ground, without sowing and plowing: But it has pleased the gracious God, to do things by means, and likewise to protect us in our lawful ways by his holy angels.

They shall defend them from all evil, *Lest you dash your foot against a stone.* There are many stones in our way through the course of our lives. Satan rolls big stones of temptation, with wicked thoughts and objects, before us. He hinders us in doing good; he represents to us the grace of God too small for the greatness of our sins, in order to bring us to despair; yea, he contrives all manner of mischief for the destruction of our souls and bodies. Our own sinful flesh and blood throws in our way, stones of pride, ambition, revenge, covetousness, lasciviousness, and such like more: The wicked world throws in our way, stones of blasphemy, slander and offence. The holy angels are here ready, in order to defend us, and remove out of our ways the following Stones; as,

Stones of sin; by taking away the cause and occasions of sin, or by hindering us from sin; as we can see of *Balaam*, who was hindered by the angel of the Lord, from cursing the children of *Israel*.

Stones of misery. When there is danger, then do the holy angels protect the faithful, as we can see of *Noah*, in the sin-flood; *Lot*, in *Sodom*; *Daniel* in the lion's den; the three men in the fiery furnace; *Elisha* in the dearth, and many other examples.

Stones of death. When death, as a heavy stone, will bruise the image of our body, and separate the soul from the body, then shall the holy angels carry our souls into the bosom of *Abraham*, and guard our bodies in the grave, and keep our bones there, that not one shall be lost. And at the Day of Judgment, shall the holy angels gather out of the Kingdom of Christ all things that offend, and cast them into a furnace of fire. And the righteous shall be then, *as the angels of God in heaven.* Since God has been so gracious to us, and has ordained his holy angels to be our watches and protectors, in and through this wicked world, where the devil goes round, and strives either himself, or by his adherents, to devour and destroy us; then we ought seriously and heartily, to thank God for this his great mercy, and so frame the way of our living, that the holy angels may desire and be willing to stay by us. Uniformity in manners increases friendship. The angels are ready and willing to obey God, and so must we be, if we will keep them by us. The angels are clean, chaste, humble, and ministering spirits, and love one another; likewise we must endeavor to practice the same virtues, if we will gain their friendship and protection. The angels are loving children of God; we must likewise be in the number of God's children, according to the will of God, if we will keep the holy angels by us. The angels are clear-shining lights; therefore, if we will keep them by us, *We must walk as the children of light, and cast off the work of darkness, and put on the armor of light.* The angels have great desire and delight in the Word of God, and are always there where the Word of God is learned.

Likewise, we must always have a true desire for the Word of God, and frequent the Assemblies where we may be instructed therein. *The angels fight against the devil*; likewise we must wrestle against Satan, and all temptations, with spiritual weapons and prayers, if we will keep the holy angels by us for our assistance.

If everyone did believe, that the holy angels sees all their actions, which they commit in darkness, there would many a private sinful action be omitted: Therefore have the old fathers said: *Wherever you are, honor your angel*; though we must not worship them, for such honor belongs to God alone; as the angel told St. *John* the divine, *We know that the angels are rejoiced in heaven over the conversion of one sinner*, much more will they be rejoiced of, when a man is strong in the fear of God, and remains in the state of grace.

The Lord send his holy angels, that can keep and protect us in all our ways; to the glory of his holy name and our own salvation, for the sake of our blessed Savior, Jesus Christ. AMEN.

6

The Bad Angels

The text stands in the epistle of JUDE, 6th verse.

The angels which did not keep their first estate, but left their own habitation, he has reserved in everlasting chains under darkness, unto the judgment of the Great Day.

INTRODUCTION

BAD root, bad fruit, bad seed, bad breed. *From thorns men do not gather figs, nor of a bramble bush do men gather grapes. A good man, out of the good treasure of his heart, brings forth that which is good; and an evil man, out of the evil treasure of his heart, brings forth that which is evil.* When Christ was in argument with the Jews, who did boast, that they were children of *Abraham*; then said Christ unto them, (as we can read in the Gospel of St. *John*, Chap. 8 verse 44. *"No, you are not children of Abraham, because you seek to kill me; but you are of your father the devil."* "For," says he, *"the devil was a murderer from the beginning, and did not abide in the truth."*

Christ describes the devil in these words, by three things.

First, of his blessed state. When Christ named here the devil, saying; *The devil was a murderer:* He does not mean one devil, but all the devils, who are one in wickedness and punishment, and gives us to consider their blessed state, wherein they were created in the beginning; namely, in truth; for, since Christ said, *They did not abide in truth*, it is certain, that they were created in truth. This truth has regard to the devils and God.

To the devils. They were created in the beginning, in truth, holiness and goodness, as well as the good angels; for *Moses* declares, *that God saw everything he had made, and behold, it was very good*, though, was this truth and holiness not their essence, or else had they lost of their essence when they fell, neither was their will so unalterable, but that they could fall from the state wherein they were created; for it becomes God alone to be essential and unalterable: Therefore, since the angels had their free-will, which in itself was changeable, then it was in their power to use or abuse their will, and to obey or disobey; but, because they abused their free will, and departed from truth, so has their fall regard to God, from whom they departed. For God is truth, and loves truth; therefore, when the angels departed from truth, they departed likewise from God, and from the faith, obedience, and service they were obligated to, unto God their Lord and Maker, and were cast out of heaven. God is not bound to keep any from falling, especially, when he has given power and will, by which they might stand and withstand, and will not use their power and will rightly. As soon as man was created, then did these fallen angels, who were cast out of heaven, go into paradise, where man was, in order to deceive him, and told a great lie for him; namely, that his case would not be so dangerous as God had told them, and that they should not die, although they did eat of the forbidden fruit; and that is,

Secondly, the fall of the devil. *They did not abide in the truth*; they left off their own free-will, their inbred truth, and rose up against God their Creator, and lies for men; and there is now no more truth in them, but all deceit, lies, murder, and all other wickedness and abominations. The fall of the devil was,

Obstinate. They were not forced nor tempted to it, but did it of their own free-will, wherein they were created good with the other angels, who remained steadfast. It was in their free-will to remain with the good angels with God, and afterwards to be confirmed in goodness; but they would not wait for this, but fell from God. And their fall therefore is, untimely. Our Savior says. *The devil is a murderer from the beginning*; not from the beginning of the world, but from the beginning of their fall: When they left truth, fell from the highest good, and turned to lie and murder; therefore is their fall,

Frightful. They were cast out from eternal joy and glory, to eternal darkness and misery; from honor to dishonor; from holiness to sin; from good to bad; from life to death; and they do now love lies and deceit instead of truth; hatred, malice, envy and dispute, instead of the grace and love of God; and death and murder, instead of life. wherefore our Savior Christ says, *They are murderers and liars*; and this shows us,

Thirdly, their wickedness. They are murderers and liars; what can be more abominable? The devil showed in the beginning his murdering mind against our first parents, for he did not alone murder them, but also in them, the whole human generation, and brought death into the world. How he has afterwards been the cause of murder and mischief, we can find many examples of, as well in the holy records, as of daily experience. The devil is a liar, and the father of lies, for he brought the first lie in the world, and casts daily these poisonous arrows out, as well in young as old; for, what vice and crime is now more common than lies?

The apostle St. *Jude*, explains in our text, what punishment the devils have received, and what they have to expect; whereof we will consider the fallen angels:

FIRST, *In the State of their Perfection.*

SECOND, *In the State of their Fall.*

THIRD, *In the State of their Damnation.*

EXPLANATION of the TEXT

I. We have to consider the fallen angels, in the state of their perfection.

No person is so glorious, nor place so holy, that it can free any from punishment after sin. The devils were in the beginning, in a glorious state, and had places in heaven, though they were not pardoned when they fell; for, so says the apostle in our text; *The angels which kept not their first estate, but left their own habitation.* The apostle here lays before us, the perfect state of these angels before their fall; which can be seen;

First, of their names. They are called angels: God had created them for to minister in holy cases, as well as the good angels, therefore had he given unto them the same titles as the good angels, yea, as Christ himself, who is often called an angel; they were created after the image of God as well as the good angels; and that the angels were created after the image of God, we can see of our Savior's words, when he says: "*In the resurrection are the faithful as the angels in heaven,*" and in heaven shall the image of God be perfected in us. St. Paul says, That, "*the new man is created after God, in righteousness and true holiness.*" The angels were created in righteousness and true holiness; then consequently follows, that they were created after the image of God.

Second, of the grace and favor wherein they were created by God.

Since they were created in righteousness and holiness, then were they in the grace of God, as his dearest friends, and beheld the face of God; and God turned his face to them, which is a sign of grace: For as it is a token of grace to see and speak with the king, so was it a sign of grace that the angels did see and converse with God, and fulfill his commands: But after they fell, they were cast out from the sight of God in disgrace, and they will never again see the gracious sight of God. When the bad angels appear before God, they appear for him, as their severe judge, full of malice, hatred, and envy against God, the holy angels, and men; and they are never better contented than when they can contrive mischief, breed quarrels among men, and tease them to murder, though all with God's leave, for to punish the wicked and try the Good, and for to make the wickedness of the devil public, and his fury ashamed, when he is withstood by the faithful.

Third, of their order. The apostle ascribes unto them in our text, a principality, saying, *"They did not keep their first estate."* We can conclude hereby, that the devils had a principality before, and were princes in the kingdom of light; but now after their fall, they are become princes of darkness, and rulers in darkness. No man can know what order there is among the devils; though, as well as there is order among the good angels, so is there among the bad likewise. The Scripture calls the chief of the devils *Beelzebub*, that is, King of Flies; which name the inhabitants of *Ekron* gave to their idol, either because he was made as a great fly, or because his temple was full of flies that gathered there by the blood of the sacrifices; or because they desired help and relief of this idol, from the many flies, wherewith their country was plagued. The devil may well be called *Belzebub*, King of Flies, for the following reasons: The fly flies high in the air; the devil is a proud spirit, and comes never so high, but strives to come higher. There are many flies, and where we come in the world, we do find abundance of flies; likewise there is innumerable many devils, and the air is full of them: If we could see spirits with our bodily eyes, we should be astonished to see such a quantity of devils flying in the air. We can conclude of that one example, namely, the man of *Gaderene*, in whom was a legion of devils, that there must be a great number of them. The fly is shameless and bold, and lights as well on the pulpit or Communion-table in a church, as on a drinking, or gaming table in a tavern; and is over all, in king's palaces, and in all houses, and chambers; likewise is the devil bold, and has regard to no person, neither spares he any, high or low, wise or unwise, rich or poor. He is in the church, to take away the words from the hearers; he is in kings' palaces, to entice them to war, bloodshed, and tyranny; he is in all the houses, for to smite the four corners of the houses, that they fall; he is over all in companies, for to breed disturbance and quarrel; he is in the bed, for to breed disorder between man and wife. The fly is an unclean thing, and daubs everything it lights on; and the whiter a thing is, the sooner will the fly light upon it. The devil is an unclean spirit, and where he comes he makes everyone unclean, with thoughts, words and deeds; therefore did he ask leave of our Savior, *to go into the herd of swine.* The fly is not long in one place, but always flying about; likewise has the devil no rest, *but walks about as a roaring lion, seeking whom he may devour.* The fly is shy, and is soon driven away. The devil is never so furious, but we can drive him away from us with the word of God, and one word of God can tie him.

The Scripture makes mention of other names, as *Asmodæus*, the devil of matrimony; *Abadon* and *Apolion*, the devils of spoil; *Belial*, the devil of disobedience; *Mamon* the devil of avarice, *Python*, the devil of prophecy; *Satan*, the devil of strife. Our Savior himself says that, *"the devil has a kingdom, and is not divided, or else his kingdom could not stand."* Therefore, although there is such abundance of devils, yet they keep always together, and agree in wickedness. The chief of them has so ordered his kingdom, that some are church devils, some court devils, and again, others are household devils.

Church devils contrive misdeeds as well by the teachers as hearers. They deceive the teachers in many ways; first with false doctrine, *and sow tares among the wheat*; then, *with lying wonders and signs*; then, *with binding pious ministers in their lawful calling*; then, *with persecution*; then, *with immoral lives*: For a minister who teaches well, and lives bad, serves God with his lips, but the devil with his life. He builds upon heaven with his doctrine, but upon hell with his works. The devil deceives likewise the hearers in many ways. *They take away the word of their hearts, that they should not believe and be saved. They blind the minds of them that do not believe, that the light of the glorious gospel of Christ should not shine unto them.* They harden the hearts of the wicked, that they do all what they will. Which St. *Paul* calls to *"be taken captive by the Devil."*

Court devils contrive mischief at court; they oppose and hinder the peaceable and good propositions of pious kings and princes, and on the contrary, inspire them to war. Who did provoke King *David* to number *Israel*, wherefore God did send three days plague? Satan. *Daniel* was preferred in the court of the king of *Babylon*, above the presidents and princes, because an excellent and pious spirit was in him, which provoked the presidents and princes so against him, that *Daniel* was cast into the lion's den, through their accusation. Who was the promoter of this? Satan, who instigated them to malice and hatred against *Daniel.*

House-devils contrive all disturbances among families. First, between man and wife; then between parents and children; then between sisters and brothers; then between master and servant; then between fellow-servants; then between neighbor and neighbors. And as the devil is a declared enemy to Christians, so does he mostly oppress the Christians, first, with deafness, then with dumbness or other defects, throws them in fire and water, and then damnifying their goods and estate, as *Job*; then their good name and character, as *David*. The devil endeavors to spoil the soul, for to gain which, he does not spare any trouble, night or day. He preaches for the thought, that he can thereby persuade the hearts and minds; and all his preaching consist in these three words: *sin, continue, despair.* He does not pardon the holy; He deceived *David* with lasciviousness, *Peter* with denying; *Judas* with covetousness, and the other apostles with ambition.

For to promote wickedness, the devil is bold, subtle, furious and mighty.

Bold. There is no crime so great, but the devils dare put it in practice: If it goes on, they are glad, but if it fails, they are not ashamed, for they are shameless.

Subtle. He is therefore called artful and cunning: They have many deep things hidden in their hearts; they watch every opportunity; sets out their nets, and throws out tempting baits for to draw souls into their snares.

Furious. The devil is compared to a *roaring lion, a great red dragon, having seven heads and ten horns.* The *seven heads* shows his many contrivances, *and the ten horns* his might and strength.

Mighty. What the devil will, he can do, as far as God permits him; therefore did the devil, who tempted Christ, confess and acknowledge, "*that God had power and might over all the kingdoms of the earth*;" for, he says, "*that is delivered unto me.*"

II. We have to consider the fallen Angels in the State of their Fall.

What was the crime of the angels, since they were punished so severely? The Spirit of the Lord mentions not in the Scripture, what their crime was in particular; but the apostle *Jude* says in our text; *They kept not their first estate, but left their own habitation:* That is, they were not so obedient to God as they ought, but as rebellious subjects, did rise up against God their Lord and Maker. Hereby we can conclude, that the crime of them was disobedience towards God, pride towards themselves, and lies towards men.

Likewise we can, according to the opinion of some, explain this their habitation also: That, as God would, by his special grace and presence, have his habitation in the angels, so should the angels again by their faithful obedience and constancy, have their habitation in God; but they left this their habitation, and fell from God; and yet do they lie in this their fall, wherefrom they shall never rise up again. Here happened a great alteration to the angels, by this their fall, for they lost something, and kept something.

They lost their goodness, holiness, truth, cleanness and free-will.

Their goodness; wherein they were created they lost, and became bad, and are therefore called bad angels, for they are bad, will bad, have bad, and shall receive worse.

Their truth. They are now liars; when the devil speaks a lie, he speaks of his own; if he speaks truth, that is, either through the command of God, or he does it for his own advantage, for to deceive men, and to confirm his own kingdom.

Holiness and cleanness. They are called unclean spirits, masters of mischief, using all weapons of subtlety and unrighteousness.

Free-will. Before the fall, they had a free-will to choose good or bad, but after their fall, their will was entirely bent to evil and all mischief.

On the contrary, they kept following faculties, though greatly weakened: As, their *knowledge and power.* The devils believe God and Christ, but tremble. They know themselves, as the soul in man knows all what is in man, so know the devils all what is in themselves. They know the condition of the world: *The devil walks round about in the world*; should they then not know how it goes therein? They know some things to come which have natural causes, but the things that have no natural causes the devils do not know, for that belongs to God alone; therefore it comes, that the devil always gives doubtful and equivocal answers. So did he deceive *Adam* and *Eve* with false words that seemed to be true; and said, you *shall not surely die.* He meant in the same moment; you *eat thereof; for God does know, that in the day you eat thereof; then your eyes shall be opened, and you shall be as gods, knowing good and evil.* This became likewise true; they became as gods, to know in their Thoughts, their eyes were opened, that they saw their own nakedness. *Eve* thought to become like God, as the serpent said, but the devil who spoke through the serpent, thought to get her like himself in damnation. They knew good and evil; Good, as long as they obeyed the command of God; Evil, after they had sinned, for then they learned to consider the good they had lost, and the evil they had received. Also the devil is a liar and deceiver, in all that he says. Likewise did this lying spirit deceive king *Ahab* to war, with this false answer: *"Go up and prosper, for the Lord shall deliver the city into the king's Hands,"* but he did not mention what king.

We must observe this of the devils, that, however wise the devils are, yet is their knowledge but in darkness; likewise, as we cannot plainly discern anything in dirty and troubled waters; for since the devils are always troubled and disturbed in their minds, so they do not know everything plainly; wherefore they often contrive not alone foolish things, but even push on things that are against themselves and their Kingdom. What was more to the destruction of the devil's kingdom than the death of Christ? Yet, for all, the devil did all his endeavors to forward the same. The devils can much less know the thoughts of Men, except as far as he can conclude of the outward tokens he sees.

We can best know the power of the devil by his *titles* and *works*.

The title shows the man, so likewise does the title of the devil show what mighty man he is. He is called, *the Prince of this World*, for his tyrannical power he uses in the world. If we will consider and behold the world, and all men therein after the Fall, so far they are without Christ; then we shall find, that they are all, for the sake of sin, under the tyrannical power of Satan, which the many idols among the heathens, and even death itself, convinces us of. He is called, *the God of this world*; partly, because he is the sole author of all mischief in this world; partly, because the men of this world, that is the wicked, live after his will; and partly, because the greatest Part of the Inhabitants in the World are entered into his Service. He is called a prince that has power in the air, because he can, with the leave of God, raise thunder, lightning, and storms in the air.

The work of the devils, shows what they can do. They can throw down fire from heaven; they can plague men in their bodies with deafness, dumbness, and other defects. They can break iron bolts as straw; they can instigate wicked thoughts in men's hearts; they can blind the minds of the unbelievers, so that the glorious light of the gospel shall not shine for them; they can hinder the conversion of men, and can take on the form of an angel of light; they can possess man spiritually, as *Judas Iscariot* was, whom the devil brought first to covetousness, then to theft, and then to treachery, and brought him so from one sin to another, 'till he became a servant captivated under the snares of Satan, and ghostly possessed. The devil can possess men bodily, when he goes in their bodies and plagues them; whereof we have many examples in the New Testament. This bodily possession can, with the permission of God, befall even the faithful; and it is to be imputed to the impudence of the devil, that he dares to possess the body of men; for the good angels, although they have some time committed or revealed anything in the minds of men, by dreams or apparitions, have never dared to possess the habitation of their Lord and Master.

The devil can often frighten men by apparitions, so that it is taken to be a forewarning, or the soul of some departed; but it is nothing else but the contrivance of Satan himself; for they that are dead do not come again. The apparition which the woman in *Endor* brought forth out of the earth, in the shape of *Samuel*, by the desire of king *Saul*, was not the true *Samuel*, but the devil, in the shape of *Samuel*; which we can prove by the following; for, *First*, Who will believe that a woman, who had given herself up entirely to the service of the devil, should have power over *Samuel*, whose soul was with God? *Second*, should the devil be able to raise up any from death? No, surely, for this becomes God alone. Could any of the dead have sent an errand to the living, certainly *Dives* would have procured this, when he entreated *Abraham* to send one of the dead to his five brethren; but we see it was not granted. *Third*, we read in the foregoing of the same chapter, that the Lord did not answer *Saul*, neither by dreams, neither by *urim*, neither by prophets: Who would then believe, that this was the true *Samuel* sent from God? *Fourth*, as soon as the apparition appeared, he said, *"Why have you disquieted me, to bring me up?"* Can any disquiet befall the blessed and elect in heaven? Then was their state and condition is not perfect. *Fifth*, the apparition said to *Saul*, *"Tomorrow shall you and your sons be with me;"* which we must understand not alone of the condition of the dead, but also of the place and condition after death, that is, in hell; for we read, that *Saul* died in his transgression. But notwithstanding the might of the devil, and the wonderful things he can do; yet, he can do no miracles or supernatural things, but all his work and actions are either according to nature, or has natural causes; which seems wonderful to us, because we do not understand them, or he blinds our eyes. We read, *that everyone of the sorcerers in* Egypt, *cast down his rod, and they became serpents.* Who will not think that these rods became serpents by conjuration? But the most part are of opinion that, when the sorcerers threw down their rods, the devil snatched them away, and threw living serpents in their stead. We can conclude the same of the other wonders.

What will now they, who are of opinion that there is neither devil or hell, say to this? There have been seen divers apparitions and devils, in several shapes and forms; and likewise many bodily possessed. Should we then not believe that there are devils? There were many bodily possessed in the time of Christ's incarnation, yet did the Sadducees, who were a sect among the Jews, deny that there was a devil or spirits. Should we but take a view of the world, and consider the course thereof, then we should perceive, that the devil is loose in all states and conditions. In spiritual, with false doctrine; in temporal, with wars, destruction, and ruination of whole countries and nations; in household, with abominable crimes and vices. Well, what can we conclude of this, but that there is a certain cunning contriver and promoter of all such? and who should it be but the devil, who is a liar and murderer from the beginning.

We will now consider, how the state of the devils are after their fall. The same is become horrible, scandalous, remarkable, furious, and unpardonable.

He is become *horrible.* We find in the Holy Scriptures several horrible examples of the wrath and vengeance of God against sin, as the sin-flood, the fire and brimstone from Heaven over *Sodom,* the drowning of *Pharoah* and his men in the Red Sea, the driving out of the *Canaanites*; the destruction of *Jerusalem*, and many others. But this example of the angels is yet more horrible, for they were cast out of heaven, and are reserved in everlasting chains, under darkness. *Since God did not spare the angels that sinned, but cast them down to hell, and delivered them into chains of darkness*, neither spared the first world, but punished them with the sin-flood; what an abomination must then be sin, while it deserves and receives such horrible punishment? It is become,

Scandalous. When a servant rises up, and becomes rebellious against his kind and affectionate master, is not that scandalous? God had made the angels mighty, heavenly princes; he had given unto them states, and in the same states, habitations; but they rose up and became rebellious, against their God, Master and Maker.

Is not that very scandalous? *David* was fore grieved in his heart, when his own son rebelled against him; much more had God cause to be offended at the angels.

It is become *remarkable.* It was not one angel that fell, but a multitude; the number thereof is unknown to us, but we can conclude, that the higher place they had in heaven before their fall, the deeper place they received in hell after their fall.

It is become *furious.* The devil will never leave off sinning, nor be satisfied of contriving wickedness and mischief. His only and greatest delight, is to blaspheme God, to spoil men's souls, and bodies, and goods, as often as he can; so that it may well be said: "*Woe to the inhabitants of the earth.*"

It is become *unpardonable.* The fallen angels can never be pardoned, and receive the grace of God; therefore is the fire that is prepared for them, called, *an everlasting fire.* We have herein a great preference before the angels, since we have a Savior, and they not. Our Lord Jesus Christ, took not the part of the angels, but the seed of

Abraham, and he has not redeemed them whose part he did not take. The bad angels may accuse themselves for their fall; for they abused the free-will wherewith they were created, and therefore, were cast out into everlasting disgrace, but men were received through Christ, into everlasting grace, because they were betrayed to sin through Satan. This brings us to consider,

III. The fallen Angels in the State of their Damnation.

The apostle *Jude* says in our text, *God has reserved them in everlasting chains, under darkness, unto the judgment of the Great Day*. This their state of damnation, consists in, that they are cast out forever from the sight of God, that they are *reserved unto the judgment of the Great Day*, and that they are tied *with everlasting chains under darkness*.

They are cast out forever from the Sight of God. God had cast them out from his glorious sight in his wrath, and this wrath of God will remain over them forever and ever. This is their greatest punishment in hell.

They are reserved unto the judgment of the Great Day. The devils received their sentence and punishment the same moment they sinned, but on the Great Day shall they appear before the tribunal of Christ, and their judgment shall then be made public. In regard to this, says St. Paul, *"Do you not know that we shall judge angels?"*

They are tied with everlasting chains under darkness. By these chains we must understand,

First, the power of God over the devils; that they can do nothing without permission. As wild and ravenous creatures are always chained, that they shall not do what they will; and as a mad dog, who can only howl and bark, but not bite, except we come too near to him; so is the devil chained of Christ. The devil can persuade us to sin, but not force us, and he loses a great deal of his hope and expectation, when he is resisted.

Secondly, the shame of the devils. They have lost their former liberty, and are now become slaves. When one is tied or chained, he has lost his freedom and honor, and is a shame for everyone, as we can see of King *Zachariah*, and King *Manasseb*. The devils are said to be chained, because they have lost their freedom, honor and glory, and cannot move without God's permission. St. *John* the Divine, saw a sight hereof, when he *saw an angel coming down from heaven, having the key of the bottomless pit, and a great chain in his hand. And he laid hold on the Dragon that old Serpent, which is the devil and Satan, and bound him.*

These chains are called in our text, *everlasting chains under darkness.* First, of the place where the devil is chained, that is Hell, which has its name of darkness, because it glistens of darkness. He was before his fall an angel of light, and had his state and habitation in light; but after his fall he received his habitation in darkness, where he is chained with everlasting chains. God Almighty permits them to go round in the world and make prey; but they bear always their hell with them, wherever they are, unto the judgment of the Great Day, when they shall be sent into Hell as an everlasting prison, and be punished there, in the highest degree forever. Secondly, of the pain they shall suffer: They shall be bereaved of all hope of salvation, and suffer pain from the sight of God, in everlasting shame and misery; for, as nothing can be more pleasing and blessed, than everlasting light in the presence of God, so can nothing be more miserable and cursed, than everlasting darkness. The devils themselves are hereof afraid, and dread the time to come, and therefore cried unto our Savior: *"What have we to do with you, Jesus you Son of God? Have you come here to torment us before the time?"* The bad angels know very well that they shall be eternally tormented; wherefore they are afraid, and are also never without torment; though there is a time when their torment shall be without measure and end; and for this time they do dread most. As long as the devil flies about in the air, and is among men on earth, their torment seems to be moderated; but on the Great Day, when they shall be cast out into everlasting fire, then shall their torment first begin; and they shall then be tormented in *the lake of fire and brimstone, day and night, forever and ever.*

Let us then thank God with all our hearts, that he hath pleased to reckon us, poor mankind, so worthy, that he would help us up again from our fall, and give us grace and mercy, in his Son Jesus Christ. He passed by the angels that fell, and suffered them to remain in their damnation; but us, poor earthworms, he took again into his fatherly grace. Let us therefore now be cautions, that we do not come too near Satan, with our thoughts, words or deeds; and if he should be so bold as to come too nigh us, let us withstand him, and remain steadfast in faith, having on the full armor of God; for the devil goes round like a roaring lion, and they that come too nigh to him, with unbelief or sin, will certainly be devoured as a prey to him.

The Lord be gracious unto us, and preserve us from Satan, and all his works, and all his tools, and make all their projects and contrivances to naught; for the sake of our blessed Lord and Savior, Jesus Christ.
AMEN.

7

Our First Parents

The text stands in GENESIS, chap. 2:7, 8, 18, 21, 22, V.

And the Lord God formed man of the dust of the ground, and breathed into his nostrils the breath of life; and man became a living soul. And the Lord God planted a garden eastward in Eden; *and there he put the man whom he had formed. And the Lord God said, It is not good that the man should be alone: I will make a helpmeet for him. And the Lord caused a deep sleep to fall upon* Adam, *and he slept: And be took one of his ribs, and closed up the flesh instead thereof. And the rib, which the Lord God had taken from man, made be a woman, and brought her unto the man.*

INTRODUCTION

WHEN the faithful Jews would prevail upon God for to have compassion over them, in their miserable condition, they represented unto God, that he was their Father and Creator; saying, with the prophet *Isaiah*, chap. 6:8. *You, O Lord, are our Father, we are the clay, and you our Potter and we all are the work of your hands.* When anything befalls a child, it runs to his father, and takes him by the hand and heart, with that loving name *father*, and makes his complaints. Likewise do the Jews here in our words; they take or move, 1*st.* the heart of God, calling him *Father*; and 2n*d.* by the hand, calling him *Potter*, and themselves *the clay*, and *the work of his hands.*

First, they take God by the heart, calling him *Father.* Nothing can prevail more with God, than when we appear before him, using the loving name, *Father*: For he is an *Almighty Father*, whose hands are not shortened. Parents would often help their children, especially in sickness, but they cannot, as we can see of the officer and the woman of *Capernaum*, and of daily experience: But the hand of our Almighty Father, is able to do all things.

He is a *merciful Father.* Our Savior makes a comparison between the affection of parents towards their children, and the affection of God towards the faithful, saying: *"What man is there of you, whom if his son ask for bread, will he give him a stone? Or if he asks for a fish, will he give him a serpent? If you then being evil, know how to give good gifts unto your children, how much more shall your Father in heaven, give good things to those that ask him?*

He is a wise Father. He knows best what is needful for us; if not justly when we desire, yet when he pleases. We should therefore wait patiently, and say; Lord, you are our Father, although it pleases you sometimes to visit us with crosses, and it seems as if you did hide your fatherly sight from us, yet, you are our *Father:* We have often neglected to show our obedience as children; yet you hast never refused to be our Father; for, you are faithful, and cannot deny yourself.

Secondly, they take God by the hand, saying, *"We are the clay, and you our Potter, and we the work of your hand."* They lay before God in these words, three things: 1. That God is their Creator. 2. That they are his creatures, and, 3. For what end and purpose God created them. In the first they acknowledge, the power of God; in the second, their own weakness; and in the third, the glory of God.

The Creator is here compared to a potter; *You are our Potter.* A potter is always careful over his pots, and works them carefully: Likewise has God created men carefully, and his carefulness is daily over them. A potter makes what pots he pleases, and gives to every pot its shape, and adorns them with glazing and painting. Likewise has God created all things in the world; and has made two creatures more noble than the other, *to wit*, man and woman, and has adorned them so gloriously, that no Creature is to be compared to them; yea, what a potter could not give to his pots, has God given to these two noble creatures, namely, mind, sense, speech, life, and even an immortal soul.

The creature is compared here to the clay; *We are the clay.* What is sooner broken than clay? Although the image of *Nebuchadnezzar* was excellent, yet it was easily broken, since it stood upon legs partly of clay. What is man in the world but earth, dust and clay? As the clay is in the potter's hands, so are we in the hands of God. The clay cannot say to him that makes it, "Why did you make me so?" None can argue with God and say, "Why have you made me of such brickly stuff?" God created the sun, moon and stars of fire; the weather and wind of the air, and the birds and fish of the water; but man of the earth, which is the coarsest element; yet did God give to the frail, brickly body of man, a precious and immortal soul, and this is,

The glory of the Creator. We are all the work of your hand. The other creatures can likewise be called the work of his hand, for they are also created of God; but man is the most noble work of his hands.

Our text makes mention thereof, and shows us how God created the first man of the dust of the ground, and gave him, to the remembrance of his creation, the name *Adam*, which signifies man, created of red clay; and of a rib of this man, while he was asleep, God made a woman. Of these two are all humankind generated, so that we are all of earth and clay; and when it shall please this Almighty Potter to break these our vessels of clay, then shall we return again unto dust, from which we were taken: Let us therefore learn by our text,

FIRST, *The Creation of* Adam, *of Dust.*

SECOND, *The Creation of* Eve, *of one of* Adam's *Ribs.*

EXPLANATION of the TEXT

I. We have to consider the creation of Adam of dust.

The Lord God had built his stories in heaven, for himself and the angels. He had likewise founded the earth, and had adorned the same with grass, herbs, trees and creatures; had filled the air with birds, and the sea with fish: But the precious and noble creature man was yet wanting, and he was to be created last, for to be Lord over all what God had made, and likewise for to praise and glorify the great Creator for his power, wisdom and goodness, from where we can judge, that God built first the house, then the inhabitants. *Moses* gives us such a description of the creation of man, as we can see in our text: "*And the Lord God formed man of the dust of the earth,*" &c. Herein we have five things to ponder upon. *First*, is to be observed,

The foregoing conclusion of God, concerning the creation of men. God went as in a consultation with himself, before he created man, and said; *Let us make man in our image, after our likeness.* In these words are concealed two mysteries, 1. The three persons in the Holy Trinity. The Father spoke to the Son the Word, by which everything is created, and to the Holy Spirit, who moved upon the face of the waters; therefore says God, "*Let us make man in our image, after our likeness.*" If there had been but one person in the divinity, God would not have said, *our image*, but, *my image*; whereof we can understand, that there are more than one person, and that he said, *our image*, and, not *our images*, convinces us, that there is but one essence in these three persons. The *second* mystery, is the nobleness of man. God used but one word in the creation of the other creatures; but when he did create man, he goes, first, deliberately about it; and says, "All the other visible things which I have created, have no sense to know me their Creator; therefore will I make one creature more in our image, who shall have sense and reason to judge of all what I have made, and who shall honor and praise me, and whom I will keep for my own service and glory." This should persuade men to live to the praise and glory of God, not alone, because he has created us in his own image, and given us reason and sense, for to judge of all the works of his hands, but also, because he hath given us dominion over all the other creatures. *Secondly*, we have to consider,

The time when man was created. On the sixth day, *that is*, according to our account, on Friday, or the same day that the other creatures on earth were created. We can give three reasons why man was created last: The first reason is natural; God has divided the creatures in certain order and degree, one above the other: Some live as trees, plants, herbs and grass: Some live and can feel, as the beasts. Some can understand, as the angels; all this we can find in men. They live, feel, and understand. Some are invisible, as the angels. Some are visible, as all the other creatures; but man is both. His body is visible, and his soul is invisible. The second reason is temporal. Man should have dominion over all what God had created, and was therefore created last. The kingdom must first be prepared, before the king can be brought into it. The third reason is spiritual. That man is created last of all; therein is a mystery, which St. *Paul* declares with these words: "*The first man* Adam, *was made a living soul: The last* Adam *was made a quickening spirit.*" The meaning hereof, is, that as the first man *Adam*, of whom we are all generated, was created on the sixth day, being the last of the creation; so is the last *Adam*, Christ, born, and come into the world, when the seventy weeks were expired, and the time was fulfilled, that he should restore what was lost by the first *Adam*. The first man *Adam*, was made a living soul, but he brought a curse and damnation on himself and his offspring, by whose disobedience we are all dead in sin, and he could not quicken them again. But the last *Adam*, was made a quickening spirit, and we are again quickened in him. wherefore, the time after Christ coming to the world, is called the end of the world, the last time; and this last *Adam* is expected again to judgment, and shall then quicken the dead, and judge the quick and the dead. Thirdly, we have to consider,

The stuff, whereof man is created. *Moses* says in our text,

Of the body. *The Lord God formed man of the dust of the ground.* *Moses* compares God here to a potter who takes a lump of clay in his hand, and forms thereof a beautiful vessel, wherein we may admire the might, and wisdom of God, who of such mean stuff as dust, has formed man's body, which is apt and able to do so many works, and would have stayed incorruptible, if man had not sinned. God does yet, daily, this masterpiece, in forming our bodies in our mother's womb; which the Psalmist explains, with a comparison taken of embroidery, saying; "*My substance was not hidden from you, when I was curiously wrought.*" The comparison is in this word: *wrought*. That, as an artful embroiderer can curiously embroider close with silk of different colors, and with thread of gold and silver, shades the colors so nicely, and places not one stitch without great care, that one flower can be formed like the other: so has God likewise shown his masterpiece in the creation, and with forming us in our mother's womb. There is not one sinew or vein in us, which is needless, and every limb is proportioned one to another; there is neither any part or limb in us, but is useful and necessary. Therefore, *Job* calls the body of man, "*The work of God's hands.*" When we consider the wonderful forming of our bodies in our mother's womb, then calls our bodies to us, as with a three-fold voice.

First, with a voice of instruction: We are instructed by our creation of three blessings God has shown us: The 1st is past. The 2nd is present. And the 3rd is to come.

The blessing past, is, that God, of his great love and grace, has created our bodies, and has placed all of our members in such complete form and shape, so that everyone of them is for a proper use, and none is needless, or can be wanted. If we will consider human nature in itself, then is man but little to be valued; but if we consider the glory and honor God has given unto man, we must then admire this masterpiece, that the great Creator has formed such a beautiful image, not of gold or silver, but of the dust of the ground.

The present blessing, shows us the love of God, that he has made us so wonderfully in our mother's womb. It is as wonderful, that God lets a child be conceived, and grow to full perfection in its mother's womb, as that he created *Adam* of a lump of clay. Therefore *Solomon* proposes this question, for the wise and learned of this world to resolve: "*Who knows how the bones do grow in her that is with child?*" It seems as if *Job* would answer hereto, when he said: "*Have you not poured me out as milk, and curdled me like cheese? You have clothed me with skin and flesh, and have fenced me with bones and sinews.*" This cannot be taken for a fundamental answer; but for an explanation, to make the question plainer. The blessing to come makes us remember the transformation of our bodies of earth again at the Last Day. The same Almighty God, who has created our bodies of earth, is yet so mighty, that he can transform them again of earth, and raise them out of the dust again at the Last Day, by his almighty and powerful word.

Secondly, it calls to us with, *a voice of compassion*, which brings three evils in our memory. *First*, the uncleanness of our bodies. *Second*, the sufferings of our bodies. And, *third*, the mortality of our bodies.

The uncleanness of our bodies. Dust and ground is unclean, likewise is our bodies become after the Fall. *Shall mortal man be more just than God? Shall a man be more pure than his Maker? Behold, be puts no trust in his servants, and his angels be charged with folly; how much less in them that dwell in houses of clay, whose foundation is in the dust?* Therefore calls St. *Paul* our bodies *earthly*; then, *vessels, and earthly; houses of this tabernacle.*

The sufferings of our bodies. An earthen vessel is not to be compared to a gold or silver vessel. The best children of God suffer most crosses and afflictions; when, on the contrary, the wicked spend their days in wealth.

The mortality of our bodies. An earthen vessel is never so beautiful, but it is broken at last; likewise, our bodies are never so well formed, but they must die, and turn again to dust. Thirdly, it calls us with,

Thirdly, it calls us with, *a voice of admiration.* Our bodies advise us to three things. *First*, to love, obedience and thankfulness towards God. *Second*, to charity towards our neighbors. And, *third*, to humility.

To love, obedience and thankfulness towards God. Since God has given unto us such a complete body, let us then thank him for it, and use these bodies to the honor and glory of the Creator. It is believed, that we have so many joints in our bodies, as there are days in the year. If we would now thank God every day through the year for one joint, then we have always cause to thank God through the whole year, and by consequence all our lifetime.

To charity towards our neighbors. All men are made of one stuff by God, and none is made of finer stuff than another; we have all one entrance into the world, and all one exit again; therefore we ought to love our neighbors as ourselves, and not reckon ourselves better.

To humility. Since man is created of such unclean stuff as earth, and shall again return to earth: wherefore will then this poor earth and stuff extract itself, and reckon itself better than another? If one is in a higher station, or honor, or wealth than another, yet he must consider, that we all have but one origin. Never flies a bird so high in the air, but he must come down to the earth for his food. None is so high and mighty, but he is taken of dust, and shall return to dust again. The earth bears us, the earth feeds us, and the earth shall consume us again. Why should we then exalt ourselves and be proud above others?

Of the soul, says *Moses*; *And God breathed into his nostrils the breath of life, and man became a living soul.* This was no bodily breathing done with the mouth, for God has no body. It may be possible, that this breathing was done with a small still voice, as a testimony of the quickening power of the presence of God; for it has been the way of God, to let a still small wind or voice come, when it has pleased him to do any miracles, or to show his presence, as we can see of the example of *Elias*, unto whom the Lord appeared in *a still small voice:* And likewise, when God would raise up the dead bones in the time of *Ezekiel*; he did let come a breath from the four winds: By this breathing did the reasonable soul come in man, who became thereby able to stand, walk, breathe, speak, and understand. This soul is not of the essence of God, for the godly essence cannot be separated, but the Lord created the Soul in time of nothing, and breathed it into his nostrils, which are the place or tools of breath, as *Job* says: "*All the while my breath is in me, and the Spirit of God is in my nostrils.*" So long as we breathe does the reasonable soul have its effect and operation in the body.

This proves the immortality of the soul, because it is breathed in man by God. The souls of the other creatures were created with their bodies, and are therefore mortal, and goes to naught, when their respective bodies die: But the soul of man is breathed in of God, and is therefore immortal. We can make this conclusion hereof: Is the soul breathed in of God? Then it is created after the image of God; and if it is created after the image of God, then it is immortal like God, though the soul is not immortal of its own nature, but through the will of God, who has given such immortality to the soul; wherefore our Savior says that *none can kill the soul.*

God created the soul in the first man, but afterwards are the Souls planted in children, by the conception, which we can prove. *First*, of,

The Scripture. Adam begat a son in his own likeness, after his image. This son did receive both soul and body, in the conception from his father, and was of the same nature with his father: Body and nature, that he was his son; soul, that he had his likeness; for the image consists mostly in the soul. We read, *that all the souls that went down into* Egypt *with* Jacob, *came out of his loins.* We must understand these words of the man's whole body and soul. We read of *Levi: That he gave tithes to* Melchizedek, *in the loins of* Abraham. The Psalmist complains of his sinful conception, saying; *I was formed in iniquity, and in sin did my mother conceive me.* These words do not have regard to the body alone, but also to the soul, for it is the principal place of the original sin: Hereof we can conclude, that, since the original sin is planted in children by the natural conception; likewise is the soul planted in them by the same conception; for the body cannot be defiled with sin before the soul, since the soul received sin first, and the body is but the tool of the soul. *Secondly* of,

The blessing God has given to man, to conceive souls, as well before as after the sin-flood. If this blessing did belong alone to the conception of the bodies, then were the beasts more happy and perfect than men, since it is the nature and quality of every beast, to get young ones in their own kind and likeness. *Thirdly*, of,

The examples of Eve and Mary. When the Lord God created *Eve* of

Adam's rib, he did not breathe new breath in her, for we do not read thereof. But she received body and soul from *Adam*. If that Holy One that was born of the Virgin *Mary*, had not received soul from her, then she could not have been the mother of Christ. *Fourthly*, we have to consider,

The place wherein God did put Adam *after he was created. Moses* describes the same with these words; *And the Lord God planted a garden eastward in* Eden, *and there be put the man whom he had formed.* This garden has been *paradise*, a beautiful and pleasant place, planted by God on the third day of the creation. It seems by the words in the ground-text, to have been fenced in by nature, and separated from the other part of the earth. It was planted by God, and was therefore so complete and pleasant, *Eden*, wherein this garden was planted, was a country so called for its delightfulness; for when *Moses* says that *the Garden was planted in* Eden, *and a river went out of* Eden, *to water the garden*, then we must conclude, that *Eden* is the name of a certain country, and that the garden was planted eastward of this same country.

Paradise has been a place upon earth, and has lain, according to the opinion of the learned, in *Mesopotamia*, between the two rivers *Tigris* and *Euphrates*, called by *Moses, Hiddekel* and *Phrat*; and was likewise contained therein *Babylonia* and *Chaldea*. This *paradise* was destroyed by the sin-flood, when the waters went fifteen cubits above the highest mountains. We know now nothing more of that *paradise* than the bare name, neither is there any token or remnant left thereof in *Babylonia, Mesopotamia, Chaldea. Fifthly*, we have to consider,

The famous name of paradise, of these two particular trees, the Tree of Life and the Tree of the Knowledge of Good and Evil. The Tree of Life was an apothecary, and the Tree of Knowledge as a school: The Tree of Life was called so, because the fruit thereof should keep man in perpetual health and immortality, so that they should have gone alive into eternity, without suffering death, if they had not sinned. The Tree of Knowledge was so called, according to the opinion of a great many, that man by this tree, as by a temple or altar, should learn how good it was to obey his Creator, and also remain steadfast in righteousness; but on the contrary, how miserable it would be, if he departed from God by disobedience: And therefore, when they eat of the fruit of this tree, their eyes were opened, and found how miserable their condition had become through disobedience, and what good they would have received, if they had obeyed.

II. We have to consider the Creation of Eve, of one of Adam's Ribs.

After *Adam* was created, and put in *paradise*, then did God bring unto him all the creatures, for to see what *Adam* would call them; but when *Adam* saw that the creatures had their fellow, and found no helpmeet for himself; then God went into counsel with himself, and said; *It is not good that the man should be alone: I will make him a helpmeet for him.* Herein we have to consider,

First, the consideration of God: *It is not good, that man should be alone.* When God would create *Adam* after his image, then he went in counsel, saying: "*Let us make man in our image.*" Likewise does God consult with himself, now he is to make a *helpmeet for man.* Hereby we can see, 1*st*, the worth and honor of matrimony. God could well have created all human creatures at once, as the angels; but it pleased the infinite and godly wisdom to create man, both male and female, that all men could be generated of them, by and through matrimony; and are also all men upon earth *of one blood.* We can see hereby,

2n*dly*, the necessity of matrimony. It would not have been good had *Adam* remained alone, for then would the unreasonable creatures have been more happy than he, since they could multiply their kind, and he would have stayed alone; therefore did God conclude, *I will make him a helper*. The woman shall then be a help to the man, not alone in multiplying their seed, to rule the house, to keep all things in order, to help and assist him in family care; but also in prayers and in worshiping of God. She shall faithfully stand by him in need, want, sickness, and other calamities. She shall suffer good and bad with him, and encourage him in crosses and afflictions: therefore says *Solomon*, *"Two are better than one, because they have a good reward for their labor: For if they fall, the one will lift up his fellow: But woe to him that is alone when he falls, for he has not another to help him up. Again, if two lie together, then they have heat, but how can one be warm alone: and if one prevail against him, two shall withstand him.* "We can see,

3*dly*, the loving conversation in matrimony: *A helpmeet for him*. The words which are used in the text, shows the uniformity of the woman with the man, in nature and essence, and the readiness of the woman towards man. She shall always be before him, not as a servant, but as a help, that is, a second I.

Second, the fulfilling of God's conclusion. This comprehends,

1. The sleep of *Adam*. *And the Lord God caused a deep sleep to fall upon* Adam. This was no natural, but a supernatural sleep; as that of *Abraham, Sisera*, and the soldiers of king *Saul*; for the same word is used here as there. Hereof we can see the secret council of God: He would give *Adam* a help, but would not let him know where she should come from; so does God often do with his children, that he gives them his blessing as in sleep, that they shall be more rejoiced and thankful. It comprehends,

2. The taking of the rib. *And be took one of his ribs, and closed up the flesh instead thereof*. This was not a naked rib, but it had certainly some flesh on, as we can conclude by the words of *Adam*, when he

106

said: *"This is now bone of my bone, and flesh of my flesh."* God created the woman of the man's rib, not without particular consideration; not of his head, that she should not be above him; neither of his foot, that she should not be used as a servant; but of his rib, which is not far from his heart, because man should love her, and reckon her as himself.

3. The creation of the woman. *And the rib, which the Lord God had taken from man, he made a woman.* The word *made*, is in the original text, *build*, for *Eve* was to build the house of *Adam*,

1. By the begetting of children. For children are as pillars whereupon the house is built; the building was begun in *Adam*, but perfected in *Eve*.

2. She was to build it with good education of the children, which was very needful after the Fall; for if children are not well brought up, then is the house sooner broken than built, as *Solomon* says: *"Every wise woman builds her House, but the foolish plucks it down with her hands."*

3. She was to build it with diligent care in the house, which is likewise needful, that the gain and profit can be sure; for, *What the man gathers must the woman not spread, but be sparing, and be as a fence round about the house, and keep off all damage, and promote the good and interest of the family.*

Fourth, the institution of matrimony; *And brought her unto the man.* God would not, that man and woman should run together, as beasts, who, after their creation, did run together through natural lust; but as he had valued them more than the other creatures, and had created *Adam* with his own hands, of the dust of the ground, and *Eve* of one of *Adam*'s ribs, so would he now make their matrimony holy and worthy of honor, separated from the natural pairing of the beasts; and brought her therefore unto the man; which was a great honor; like a father, who can give his daughter in marriage; and like a minister, that can marry a couple together; so that the Lord God did not alone give the bride away, but acted likewise the part of a priest, and married them together, and tied, besides, their hearts with a cord of love, which made *Adam* say: *"This is now bone of my bones, and flesh of my flesh, therefore shall she be called woman, because she was taken out of man."*

Fifth, thereupon follows the words of the copulation, which the Lord uses, saying; *Therefore shall the man leave his father and his mother, and shall cleave to his wife, and they shall be one flesh.* That the Lord spoke these words, we can see by the words of Christ, when he, being in dispute with the *Pharisees*, concerning matrimony, said: *"Have you not read, that he, which made man at the beginning, made them male and female? And said, for this cause shall a man leave father and mother, and shall cleave to his wife, and they twain shall be one flesh."*

This copulation concerns not *Adam* and *Eve* alone, but also all married, for God said *the man;* besides, *Adam* had neither father nor mother. The Lord instructs with these words all married people, how they shall live in matrimony.

1. They shall have an inward love to one another: *The man shall leave his father and mother.* We must not understand here, as if the man should conclude matrimony without the advice of his parents, and not converse with them after matrimony, nor help and assist them in their wants; no, for all this is forbidden in the fourth commandment; but the meaning is, that the love between man and wife should be greater, and exceed the love between parents and children.

2. They shall never be separated, before death separates them: *And shall cleave to his wife.* St. *Paul* explains this conjunction with a comparison taken of a thing glued together, which keeps so fast and close, that it cannot be separated; likewise is the knot of matrimony

so strong, that none can loose or untie it. There is sometimes divorce for certain reasons, but this is not done by men, but by the command of God, whose servants the magistrates are, for to declare his sentences.

3. They shall have everything in common: *They shall be one flesh.* Single persons have all that they have for themselves alone; they eat alone, they drink alone, and sleep alone; but married people have all and everything in common; they have one house, one table, one bed, one family, one relation, and one interest in common.

O Lord God, who has created man in the beginning, male and female, and has instituted the holy matrimony as a sacred order, for the multiplying of mankind; be always within doors of all Christian married people, that they may live to your glory, and their own comfort and joy here in this life; and that they, at last, may receive the everlasting joy hereafter; for the sake of our Savior, Jesus Christ. AMEN.

8

The Image of God

The Text, GENESIS, 1:27th Verse.

God created man in his image; in the image of God created he him: male and female created he them.

INTRODUCTION

THE old fathers have said, *We must consider these three words*; BEFORE, NOW, *and to* COME. What we have been before, what we are now, and what we shall be hereafter. For to consider these words rightly, we will use the words of the Apostle St. *Paul*, in 1 *Cor.* 15:49. where he says; *As we have borne the image of the earthly, we shall also bear the image of the heavenly.* We have here to consider,

First, what we have been before. *We have born an image: Moses* declares whose image man bore before the Fall, saying; *God created man in his image*; as the Lord is, so is likewise his image: God is holy, righteous, and immortal; so did our first parents bear the same image; and their whole generation would have born the same, if they had not sinned. As a king, when he makes one to be a lord, gives and grants this honor not alone to such a person, but also to his

110

offspring and generation; whom therefore we can say of, that they are made lords in their fathers. So did God likewise, when he created *Adam* in his image, and gave unto him the dominion over all the creatures; created all mankind in *Adam*, after his own image, and gave dominion unto them. *Adam* bore the image of God, as a son his father's; as a servant his master's; as a subject his king's; and as a householder his lord's; that we thereby should be encouraged to love and fear God, as a son his father, as a servant his master, as a subject his king, and as a householder his lord. But,

Second, what image do we now bear? The image of the earthly: When *Adam* lost, by his disobedience, the image of God, then *be begat children in his own image*, even sinful and mortal, as he was himself. *Who can bring forth a clean thing out of an unclean thing?* We bear now the image of *Adam*, both in our bodies and souls. Where is our holiness? Where is our righteousness? Where is our immortality? Where is our wisdom? Our silver is become dross; the image of God is darkened in us; yea, entirely lost, both in soul and body. If we find yet in us, some remaining sparks of the image of God, as that the soul is immortal, being a spirit that we can rule and govern, and can discern God by the created things; that is to be imputed to the goodness and grace of God; and it is no more, in comparison, to the first image wherein man was created, than darkness is to light; neither is it regarded in the sight of God, unless it is renewed through the regeneration in Christ by the Holy Spirit. For, *except a man be born again, he cannot see the Kingdom of God.* The image of God must be renewed in us, partly by regeneration, and partly by renewing of the Holy Spirit. By *regeneration*, we become from children of wrath, children of God: We are freed from sin, and are made partakers of the righteousness of Christ, which is appropriated to us by living faith. By *renewing:* We let the Holy Spirit govern in us; we crucify the flesh and all its lusts; and walk according to God's command;

so that it is engraved upon the heart of the faithful, as it was on the breastplate of *Aaron*; *Holiness to the Lord*; and this is that heavenly image, the apostle says here, that we shall bear, although it doth not yet appear what we shall be, but we know, that when he shall appear, we shall be like him.

Third, hereafter, when death shall be no more, but we shall begin another life, how shall then the image be? The wicked, who would never bear the heavenly image, but have always extinguished the same by sin and a wicked life, shall bear the image of the devil, forever and ever. On the contrary, the pious, who have believed in Christ, and did remain steadfast in their faith to the end, God shall know by this image, and place them in the heavenly *Jerusalem*, where the words of the apostle shall be fulfilled in them; *That as we have borne the image of the earthly, also shall we bear the image of the heavenly.*

Of this first image of God, wherein man was created in the beginning, we shall discourse of here, and of our text consider,

FIRST, *The author of this image.*

SECOND, *The description of this image in its honor, dishonor, and restoration.*

EXPLANATION of the TEXT

I. We have to consider the author of this image.

When we see a beautiful image, we always ask: Who is the creator of this? Admiring his great skill: *Bezaleel*, and *Aholiab*, were two cunning masters, and were filled with the Spirit of God, in wisdom and in understanding, and in knowledge, and in all manner of workmanship, to devise cunning works, to work in gold, and in silver, and in brass, and in cutting of stones, and in carving of wood, to work in all manner of workmanship: But here this Master, who made man after his own image, is the greatest Master; the holy, blessed Trinity, Father, Son, and Holy Spirit: for so did God the Father, the first person, speak to the other two persons, the Son and the Holy Spirit: "*Let us make man in our image, after our likeness;*" then follows the words of our text; *God created man in his own image; in the image of God created he him; male and female created he them.* Also is then the whole blessed Trinity, who is one in essence, but three in persons, the Master of this image: This Master is the most glorious, wisest, kindest, and most beautiful Master.

He is the *most glorious Master.* He has already show his masterpiece in the creation of heaven and earth, and what is therein, of nothing, by his Word; yet for all, he would make one masterpiece more glorious than the rest, and that after his own likeness. The holy angels do admire the beauty of this image; the devils are offended at it, and do envy the same; and all the creatures acknowledge the same for their Lord and Master.

He is the *wisest Master.* We cannot say, that God created the other creatures without a foregoing decree; though it is worth observing, that when *Moses* did speak of the creation of man, he mentions, first, that God went in deliberation with himself before; neither can we say, that God did not know how to create man; no, but we have thereby to remember the excellency of man above the other creatures; for man is a copy of the whole creation, in the world, and is therefore called the little world, and a miracle above all miracles; he grows like the trees; he feels like the beasts, and understands like the angels. The head, where reason has its place, we can compare by the highest heaven, where God and the angels are. The heart is as the sun, who gives life and motion to everything. The eyes are the light in the world; the natural health is the fire; the breath is the air; the water and blood is the sea; The body is the earth; the hair the grass; the bones are the stones and minerals: Besides, is not that a great miracle, that among so many millions, we cannot find two faces alike? Hereof we can form this question: What is the greatest wonder in the least?

He is the *kindest Master*. When great men offer their image to anyone, it is always accepted as a gracious token; should not we then account it a great grace, that the Almighty God, Lord of Lords, and King of Kings, has pleased to create us after his own likeness, and has placed his godly image not alone inward in our souls, but also, outward in our bodies. As an earthly king, when he has built a city, has always his image made of some stuff or other, placed in the city, for to show his power and authority: So has the Lord God, after he had created heaven and earth, placed man, created after his own image, in the world, that every creature should see of this image, how powerful their Creator is.

He is the most *beautiful Master*. The work praises its Master. Is the world so beautiful, and man, the ruler thereof, so excellent? Then must certainly the Master and Creator of all this, be more beautiful and excellent. All what we can call pretty here on earth, has its beauty from him, and is but as a little spark of his glory and beauty. Might we do as *Job* says: "*Ask the beasts, and they shall teach you, and the fowls of the air, and they shall tell you; or speak to the earth, and it shall teach that; and the fish of the sea shall declare unto you.*" We should find, that all of them would answer as with one voice: "*We are all beautiful, but our Creator exceeds us all; and although we are so beautiful, yet are we subject to alterations: But he is unchangeable and infinite.*"

When we consider this, then we must be rejoiced, thank our Creator, and glorify him.

We must be *rejoiced*, that God has thought us so worthy, as to create us after his own image. Where-with have we deserved this? or what have we contributed hereto? Not more than clay in the hand of a potter can help that a vessel is made thereof to honor. And we must say with the Psalmist: *What is man, that you are mindful of him? And the son of man, that you visit him?*

We must *thank our Creator. Solomon* admonishes us: *"Remember your Creator in the days of your youth."* The Psalmist explains this word *Remember*, with thanks, saying: *"I will praise you; for I am fearfully and wonderfully made."* Hereof complains the Lord, saying, *"Israel has forgotten his Maker."*

We must *glorify our Creator.* We honor a man in his image: If the king was to give his image to a subject, then he ought to keep it in great honor and value; but if the subject was to despise and disregard this image of the king, and throw it away, then certainly the king would be very much offended at it, and punish this subject for so doing. Since God has created us in his own image, then it is just and reasonable, that we honor him in his image, and not abuse our souls and bodies, wherein his image is placed; for he will not let it pass unpunished; *Therefore glorify God in your hearts and spirits, which are God's.*

II. We have to consider the description of this image.

Let us now go farther, and consider the Image in its honor, that is, before the Fall; we may often see an image that is beautiful and pleasing on the outside, but the inside is worm-eaten, and full of cobwebs; but this Image of God in man, was before the Fall, as well in, as outward, beautiful and complete.

The image of God did shine inward in the soul, 1st, In the sense. 2nd, In the will. And, 3rd, in the heart, and all the effects and faculties of the soul.

First, the sense was full of wisdom; which appeared thereof, that

Adam knew God above him, the angels about him, himself in himself, and the creatures under him. The man had perfect knowledge, of God above him; for, as God knows himself, and none knows the Father without the Son, nor the Son without the Father, nor the Father and the Son without the Holy Spirit; so man knows God, perfect in essence and will, though not without God: As none can see the sun without the sun's own light, so can none see God, without the light of God, which shines in the soul of man. *Adam* had knowledge of the angels about him; for they were his fellow servants: *Adam* had knowledge of himself; for as man loves himself by nature, before any other, so knows man himself before any other. *Adam* had likewise knowledge of the creatures under him; which we can conclude by the following;

That *Adam* gave names to all the creatures; not a simple name, according to the sound of the letters, but also a name that shows the nature of every creature, as if he had seen in the nature of them, and given them names accordingly. Could *Solomon*, by the wisdom he had after the Fall, know the nature of the creatures; much more could *Adam* know it before the Fall, when he was yet in the state of innocence.

That *Adam* did know *Eve*, and knew where she came from, and therefore called her woman. See what a deep wisdom is concealed in this name: It shows, *first*, the stuff whereof *Eve* was created; *This is bone of my bones, and flesh of my flesh*: *Secondly*, It shows the sex, that *Eve* was a woman; and, *Thirdly*, it shows the decree of God, that she was to be his wife, more bound to him than to her father and mother, if she had had any. Will anyone say, where comes it, that *Eve* was deceived, since she was so wise? For it seems to be contrary to such high wisdom, wherewith she and *Adam* were created: Hereto we can answer, that *Eve* was not deceived, before she departed from God and his command; but when she departed through unbelief, then had Satan power over her: She knew, and could easily conclude, that it was a spirit which spoke to her out of the serpent; but she knew not whether it was a good or evil spirit; which we may suppose, when she laid the fault upon the serpent.

Second, the will was naturally inclined to all Good, and was free and willing, and in perfect uniformity with the will of God; so that, what God would, man would and did willingly; and thereby, shines forth in the will of man, holiness and righteousness: Holiness, according to the first table; righteousness, according to the second table, holiness towards God, and righteousness towards others. Also was the Law, which was given after the Fall, fulfilled by *Adam* and *Eve* before the Fall.

That they were created in holiness and righteousness, we can prove of the Scripture; by the admonition of the Spirit of the Lord; and by the example of Jesus Christ, and of their freedom from sin and punishment.

Of the Scripture. There stands; *And the Lord God saw everything that he had made, and behold, it was very good.* If everything that God had made was good, then was certainly man, for whom everything was made, likewise good. So says *Solomon:* "*God has made man upright.*" There was no difficulty in the sense, nor disagreeableness in the flesh by them. He that is lame, cannot be said to be right; neither can he that is inclined to wickedness, be said to be upright. Although man was created with a free-will, yet was this freedom not so wholly inclined to Good of itself, but it could fall to wickedness; for what happened afterwards, was caused through the abusing of their freedom. God made man from the beginning, and lest him in the hands of his council. If you will keep the commandments, and perform acceptable faithfulness, it is, set fire and water before you, stretch-forth your hand unto whether you will. The Lord has commanded no man to do wickedly, neither has he given anyone license to sin.

Of the admonition of the Spirit of God. That we should be renewed in the spirit of our mind; and that we put on the new man. A thing that must be renewed, has certainly been new, but is waxed old. And shall we put on the new man, which, after God, is created in righteousness and true holiness? then there has been a man before, who was created in righteousness and true holiness; and this man is *Adam*, who was created after the image of God, and who was in the state of his innocence, an example of righteousness and holiness.

Of the example of Jesus Christ; who is always set up in the Word of God, as an example for us to follow, in righteousness and holiness. He was perfect, holy without sin; perfect, upright, without crimes; and perfectly righteous, without any ill desire. What was not in Christ, that is the second *Adam*, was neither in the first *Adam:* Christ did not know of sin, neither knew *Adam*, in the state of innocence, of sin.

Of their freedom of sin, and the punishment thereof. Adam and *Eve* did not seal before the Fall, any effect of sin, as afterwards, namely, a fearful and accusing conscience; terror for the presence of God, and the thoughts of death and damnation.

Thirdly, in the heart was a great harmony between all the faculties: The sense did agree with the light of the reason, and the desire of the will; yea, with the holy law of God, which was written in their hearts; so that, what the law did prescribe outward, was wrote inward in their hearts; namely, a perfect love to God, and all men; and thereby shines forth the image of God, in holy cleanness and chastity; so that they needed not to strive and war against the desire and lusts of the flesh; as the Apostle St. *Paul* afterwards complained of: In all the other faculties of the soul there was a great harmony; likewise between the reason, will, heart, and all the members of the body, so that man did walk as a visible God on earth, and was the living temple of the Holy Spirit, and a holy tabernacle of the Trinity.

In this glorious estate of honor, were both *Adam* and *Eve* naked, and were not ashamed; for they had no ill desire, neither had they committed anything whereof they should be ashamed; their nakedness was a testimony of their wisdom; that, as the angels did rejoice of their innate heavenly light, so did *Adam* rejoice of his inbred nakedness. It was also a testimony of their holiness, where there was no inward ill desire; there was nothing outward to covet; *Adam* and *Eve* felt no ill desires, and had therefore no occasion to cover themselves; likewise their nakedness was a great honor to them, like a pretty lady, never hides away her beautiful face, wherein the honor and glory of the Creator appears.

The image of God shines outward in the body of man, in immortality; in the government over the creatures.

Immortality was natural to *Adam* and *Eve* from the Creation; for,

1st, Since the image of God was created with them of nature and immortality is part of the image of God; then follows, that immortality was created with them, and therefore natural to them.

2ndly, If *Adam* and *Eve* had been created mortal of nature, then God could not have said; *In the day that you eat of the forbidden fruit, you shall surely die:* For how could death be a punishment for sin, if it was natural to man to die? It would be ridiculous, to forewarn a blind born, not to behold the daylight, nor the vanities of the world; therefore, since *Adam* and *Eve* were created holy and righteous, then were they certainly immortal, and they would never had died, if they had not sinned.

3rdly, There was no cause of death found by them; for their bodies were of so good a complexion of nature, that they could not be sick, neither had they reason to be afraid of any outward hurt or damage from anything, since they were rulers and lords over all things; besides, they had the Tree of Life, by which they could strengthen themselves.

The government over all the creatures, is likewise a part of the image of God, though the least; for men do not please God more, by having government; since not all the mighty are valued before God: Although this government over the creatures is greatly lessened since the Fall, yet we can find great remnant thereof by man.

That man has yet power over the fish in the sea, the birds in the air, and the creatures upon earth, we can see by the fear and dread of them; for when any fort of creature in any of the elements, feet or hears a man, then they are afraid, and run, away hiding themselves like servants on their masters coming unaware of them; which is the power of the words God spoke to *Noah* after the flood: *"And the fear of you, and the dread of you, shall be upon every beast of the earth, and upon every fowl of the air; upon all that move upon the earth, and upon all the fish of the sea."* Further, we can see man's power over the creatures, by the catching of them; for man can with art, catch the great beasts, the birds, and the fish, and employ them to use, either for service, provision, or diversion and remedies, as daily experience convinces us of.

The proof of man's government alone over the creatures, we can see thereof, that man alone is created with a straight and upright body, where again the greatest part of the creatures, walk with their heads bent down to the ground. God has given this upright form to man, partly for difference, and partly for testimony.

For difference: That man should differ from the other creatures. As it has pleased God to bless man with more precious gifts than the other creatures, namely, the immortal soul, the reason and the speech; so has he likewise given unto man a more perfect and beautiful form, that they always walk straight up; wherefore *Augustine* says: *"That we go up straight; thereby we are admonished of God, who has created us, that we, in our best part, that is, the soul, should not be like the beast, from whom we differ in the form of our bodies."*

For testimony: The straight posture of man testifies,

First, of their power over the creatures; for, as man walks with an upright head, and the creatures with theirs bent down, that shows that they, as subjects, will submit to their lord and king, according to the command God has pleased to plant in nature.

Secondly, of their uprightness. A man, considering his straight and upright body, must remember the words of *Solomon*, when he says: *"Man was made upright."* He must therefore be upright in all his doings, without fraud or frowardness, as the Psalmist says: *"Let integrity and uprightness preserve me."*

Thirdly, of their origin. God, who lives on high, has made man here below, with a straight body, because they are created for higher purposes than the other creatures; namely, that they should set their affections on things that are above, and not on things that are below on earth; that they should love and honor God; that they should seek after a heavenly treasure; and, that they should practice Christian virtues.

Fourthly, of the providence of God. Man is created with a straight body; for to consider, that God who has created them, will certainly provide for them; and therefore has our Savior taught us to pray: *"Give us this day our daily bread."* And when we consider our redemption, then ought we to lift up our hands towards heaven, and praise God, who did send his Son from heaven, in the time, born of a woman, and granted us through him, the adoption of children, and will, for his sake, receive us into heaven, where from the Fall of *Adam* had excluded us.

Fifthly, of help in crosses and affliction. When we suffer and are afflicted, then we must list up our eyes towards heaven, to him who lives in the highest, and who can, and will help, when none else can, according to the example of *David*, who said; *Unto you do I lift up mine eyes, O you that dwell in heaven.* This is now the description of the image of God in its honor; by which we may reckon, besides their felicity, that they had the Garden of *Paradise*, which was the pleasantest place of the whole earth, adorned with all trees and rivers for their abode and habitation; and that the Lord himself did converse with them as a father with his children; and the holy angels had delight in seeing man love God, and being again beloved of God.

But what became afterwards of this image of God? The devil envying that man should be adorned with this image, did all his endeavors, and at last, with fraud and lies, did so stain this image, that it lost all its former honor, and became on the contrary full of dishonor, as well inward as outward.

Inward. The sense became darkened: They who knew God before, and did converse with him as with a Father, and were convinced, that he was almighty and all-knowing, did now flee from him, as from a severe judge; and wanted to hide away from him, as if he could nor should see or find them: Their will became stubborn, and against God. God would, that they should come forth, and confess their faults and crimes; but they would do the same, and therefore blamed one the other. Their hearts became full of wicked thoughts, which their guilty and accusing consciences convinces us of: And all the faculties of the soul became against one another, by which arose disorder and strife in their bodies; and therefore sewed fig-leaves together, and made themselves aprons for to cover their outward nakedness.

Outward. Their bodies became subject to all sorrowful accidents, slavery, hunger, thirst, poverty, sickness, and even death; so that if we will now consider *Adam* and *Eve* after the Fall, we shall see, that they are become of God's friends, his enemies; of the delight of the angels, a spectacle for the devil; of free-born lords, sinful servants. We may now rightly compare *Adam* with *the man who went down from Jerusalem to Jericho, and fell among the thieves, who stripped him of his raiment, and wounded him, and departed, leaving him half dead.* As the image of God became spoiled in *Adam* and *Eve*, likewise it is spoiled in us, their offspring: This we can prove,

First, of the words of St. *Paul*, when he says, "*All have sinned, and come short of the glory of God.*"

Secondly, of the *original sin*. Where the original sin is, there is certainly the image of God lost. We find the original sin in us, therefore have we all lost the image of God; and are therefore said in the Scripture; *To be conceived and born in sin; and to be by nature the children of wrath. The imagination of man's heart is evil from his youth:* We are transgressors from our mother's womb: *Who can bring forth a clean thing out of something unclean?*

Thirdly, of the *admonition* of God's Spirit, who says: "*Be renewed in the spirit of your mind; and that you put on the new man, which after God is created in righteousness and true holiness.*

Fourthly, of *several* sins, sicknesses, and adversities, and death itself, whereto men are subject on account of sin.

We find several Scripture texts, whereof we might conclude, as if the image of God was yet in man; though we must not understand them, as of the principal parts of the image of God, which consists in holiness, righteousness, cleanness, and innocence: No, but alone, as of some small sparks of this light, that did remain after the Fall in the hearts of men: As for instance, that we have an immortal soul; that we, by the check of our conscience, can beware of sins; that we, of the creation, can make some conclusion of the Creator; that we have government over the other creatures, and such like, &c.

When the Lord God saw his image so shamefully spoiled in man, then would he not let Satan go off so victorious, and rejoiced of, that man should now bear his hellish image: But the Lord had great compassion over the miserable condition of fallen mankind, and promised unto them another image from heaven, who should be the image of the invisible God, the brightness of his glory, and the express image of his person; who should come down upon earth and be born like another man, and should take away the image of the devil, and tread it underfoot, and again, renew the image of God in man. This image was the Lord Jesus Christ, whom mankind should embrace in faith, till such time that he came in person, and they could be assured of him, as they had him already in the promises and sacrifices. The promise of God hereof is; *The seed of the woman shall bruise the Serpent's head, and the Serpent shall bruise his heels:* This was the first Gospel preached in the world, of the Lord Jesus Christ, who was to be born in the world, for to renew the damage of man. Herein are comprehended three things: The *person* of Christ, the *office* of Christ, and the *sufferings* of Christ.

The *person* of Christ. *That he is true God and true man in one person*; this is contained in these words: *the seed of the woman.* His human nature is concealed in the word *seed*; for seed signifies in the Scripture children; besides, what is born of a woman, is certainly a true and natural man. His divine nature is concealed in this word; of the *woman*; for, since he was to be the seed of the woman, and not of the man, then follows, that his mother should not conceive by the man, as other woman, but it should be in a supernatural way, that the should conceive and beget a Son, by the power of the Holy Spirit, who was to come over her.

The *office* of Christ. *He shall bruise the Serpent's head.* The Devil having brought men under his power, knew full well, that no simple man was able to take away his booty: *Shall the prey be taken from the mighty?* None therefore but God could do this: But how did it go? The Lord did cause the seed of the woman to throw the Devil underfoot, who thought to devour him, and took away his honor and life; so that at last, nothing was left unto Christ, but shame, dishonor, and death; though what happened here; this seed of the woman was God, and could therefore not lie under, nor be conquered. The Devil had here to do with another; then he thought, and did not expect that he had to do with God, who is Master over all, and even over himself; therefore the Devil was obliged to give it up; and the seed of the woman, the Lord Jesus Christ, did remain an eternal king, having got victory over sin, death, the Devil, and hell. All this did the Devil strive to oppose; for, in

The *suffering* of Christ, did the Devil bite after our Savior with his lion's teeth, stung after him with his prickle, like an old serpent; but he could not reach further than his heel, that is, his human nature. This did the Devil bruise, and brought it at last to the cursed cross. By these words of life, were *Adam* and *Eve* again revived, after they had lost the image of God: This was the first gospel wherein *Adam* and *Eve* could see, as in a glass, the image of Christ, and became like it through faith, and at last, receive thereby the grace of God, and eternal salvation. *Adam* and *Eve* were proud, and would be like God; *Jesus Christ, when he was in the form of God, thought it not robbery, to be equal with God, but made himself of no reputation, and took upon him the form of a servant, and was made in the likeness of men. Adam* and *Eve* did reject the command of God, and acted contrary to it. Jesus Christ did fulfill the law and commands of God. *Adam* and *Eve* did leave the conversation of the good angels, and conversed with the Devil. Jesus Christ did leave heaven, and was tempted for our sake; *Adam* and *Eve* did not withstand the temptation of the serpent; Jesus Christ did conquer Satan's temptations; *Adam* and *Eve* were to die the eternal death, Jesus Christ has by his death, made death to naught, and did overpower him that had the power of death, namely, Satan the old serpent.

Now, as *Adam* and *Eve* did believe this promise of Christ, who was to come into the world, to raise them and their offspring up again from the Fall, and did thereby receive the image of God renewed again; so does the image of God become renewed in us in baptism, by the preaching of the gospel, by faith, and in the Lord's Supper.

In *baptism*. Where God washes off the sinful stains of Satan, takes us on as children; declares us free from sin, and clothes us with the holiness and righteousness of Jesus Christ, so that we are made partakers of the eternal blessings alone by faith. But since the old *Adam* often will return in us, when we grow up in years, so God teaches us,

By the *preaching* of the gospel: wherein the image of our Lord Jesus Christ is presented to us, whom God has ordained to be a Savior and propitiator for all. He was a man full of love, obedience, humility, patience, meekness, chastity, justice, and all other virtues. He was in his whole life, a clear shining example of all goodness; and all his doings was to do the will of God, to promote the salvation of men, and restore the image of God: We must always have this image of Christ before us, and strive to follow the same.

By *faith*. By and through faith, we do always look on, and behold Christ, as if he was evidently set-forth before our eyes, thereby we make him wholly our own. He, that beholds his natural face in a glass, stands not always for the glass, and beholds himself; but after he had beheld his face, he goes straight away, and forgets what manner of man he was. But we shall never take away our faithful eyes from the image of Christ, whether asleep or awake; and we shall cleave to him, till we come to see him hereafter in eternity: We should, in our conversation with others, have before us his learned discourses and humility; when we are alone by ourselves in devotion and prayers to God. In our discourses we shall follow his temperance, truth and justice; in our thoughts his holiness; in our actions his love; in our devotion his submission and sincerity; in temptation his meekness, and strength to withstand; in sufferings his patience; and in death his firmness. When we also behold the Lord Jesus Christ with our faithful eyes, and follow his example, then do we become the same image from glory to glory, as of the Spirit of the Lord, and then becomes our reason enlightened from its inbred darkness and ignorance: Our will becomes subject to the will of God, and contrary to its own natural stubbornness. Our desires become subdued: our affections become meek, and all our members alone to the service of God; and then will the image of God be again more fully renewed in us. But since our faith is not always even strong, and clear-sighted, to behold the Lord Jesus Christ; neither have we always alike, desires to follow his example; and, besides, the Devil, the world, and our own flesh, makes us careless thereof; so shall we when we perceive such, strengthen our faith.

By the *Lord's Supper*. This is the right salve, wherewith we shall appoint our eyes that we may see; that as the eyes of *Jonathan* were enlightened, when he tasted a little of the honey in his faintness, so do the eyes of our soul, that is, our faith, become enlightened, and we receive new strength, to behold the Lord Jesus Christ, and to follow his example.

O Lord God, strengthen our faith, and revive in us a hearty desire to follow the example of your beloved Son, that thereby, your image may be again renewed in us; for the sake of our blessed Savior, Jesus Christ. AMEN.

9

Free Will

T he Text, JOHN 8:34, 35, 36 Ver.

Whosoever commits sin, is the servant of sin; and the servant abides not in the house forever, but the Son abides forever. If the Son therefore shall make you free, you shall be free indeed.

INTRODUCTION

IT is an old proverb, *a man's will is a man's heaven or hell.* The meaning is, if a man can obtain his will, then it is as pleasing to him as heaven; but if this will be evil, then it opens hell for him. After God had created man, then he placed him between heaven and hell, and granted unto him free-will to choose which he would, saying: *Genesis* 2:16, 17. *Of every tree of the Garden you may freely eat, but of the tree of knowledge of good and evil, you shall not eat of it; for in the day that you eat thereof, you shall surely die.* In these words is spoken; *First,* Of a free-will; *Second,* of a free-will's measure; And, *third,* of a free-will's want.

First, of a *free-will,* there stands; *Of every tree of the Garden you may*

128

freely eat. Man had here in *paradise* a good store to choose and use of. God had caused to grow out of the ground, every tree that was pleasant for the sight, and good for food. Man had here not alone delight for his eyes, but also for all his senses. He could eat of them without scruple, and use them as he would; if he did not like the taste of one sort, he might take of another,; wherein we can see.

1. The *goodness of God.* Since he, as a liberal Master, gave man full leave to eat of all the trees in the Garden. We can see,

2. The *felicity* of *Adam*, not alone of the place wherein he was placed, which was the Garden of *Paradise*, the most delightful place in the whole universe, where there was all sorts of (all for man's delight) serviceable necessaries; but also of the freedom, God had granted him, *That he might eat of every tree:* Yet was there by this freedom,

Second, A free-will's measure. But of the tree of the knowledge of good and evil, you shall not eat of it. It was just, that there should be something wherein *Adam* should and could acknowledge God to be his Lord and Master, or he might have thought, that there was no Lord over him; therefore God did forbid him to eat thereof, and that under a severe threatening; *That in the day he did eat thereof, he should surely die: Adam* could easily have fulfilled this command; but, no, he abused his freedom, and broke the command of God, and without cause or necessity, took and eat of the forbidden tree's fruit: The anger of God was therefore greater, since there was abuse of the free-will.

1. *Unjust. Adam* is called *the Son of God*, because he was created of God. Is it not just and right, that a son should obey and honor his father?

2. *Shameful.* God had blessed *Adam* with a clean soul, and with a perfect body, and full power; so that he could easily have obeyed God's command; but *Adam* acted here quite contrary; it was as if he would accuse God of lies, that he should not fulfill his threatening;

For he that does not believe God, has made him a liar.

3. It was *hurtful.* It caused himself and his offspring temporal misery, and eternal death and damnation, and therefore lost the image of God, and therewith their free-will.

Thirdly, a *free-will's want. Adam's* will before the Fall, was free, and could be bent to good or evil: He could eat of the forbidden tree's fruit, or let it alone if he would; but after the Fall, was his will alone inclined to evil; so that we are now, *not sufficient of ourselves to think anything as of ourselves, but our sufficiency is of God.* Our Savior lays this before us in our text, how we have lost our freedom, and are become servants, though Christ has again procured our freedom; wherefore, the Lord be praised; we will of our text, discourse on these three heads.

FIRST, *What a noble freedom God had given to man in Paradise.*

SECOND, *How man lost this freedom by sin.*

THIRD, *How the Son of God has made us free again.*

EXPLANATION of the TEXT. PART I

I. What a noble freedom God had given to man in Paradise.

When a king favors one of his subjects so much as to make him a lord or knight, then he grants him certain privileges for himself and his posterity. God had made *Adam* a lord and ruler over all his handy work; he was as a monarch on earth, and was blessed with glorious privileges, as,

1. *With freedom from sin.* Our Savior says; *Whosoever commits sin, is the servant of sin. Adam* had not committed sin, therefore was he neither a servant of sin: For, since he was created after the image of God, in holiness and righteousness, so was he likewise without sin,

because the image of God cannot consist with sin. After *Moses* had given us a full description of the creation, then he concludes with these words: *And God saw everything that he had made, and behold it was very good.*

2. *With freedom in his will.* The sense, understanding, and will of man, was, before the Fall, so perfect, that he knew God according to his essence: He understood all divine and human things, and all what he understood, he could either accept or reject. They had a free-will in corporal cases: They might eat of every tree in the Garden, yea, even of the tree of knowledge of good and evil, was in their own free-will, though God had commanded not to eat thereof, which command they ought to have obeyed. Now should anyone think that *Adam* was not free, since God had given him a command? *For he that stands under a law, cannot be free in his will to do as he pleases:* He must know that this freedom did not go beyond the command of God, which we are obliged always to obey. But his freedom is placed against a tyrannical power, and absolute necessity. Now there was none, who could force them to eat of the forbidden fruit; nay, even the Devil could not do it, for he was himself obliged to persuade them for to eat thereof. Neither had they any occasion to eat thereof, since they had abundance of other fruit that was pleasant to the eye, and good for food; therefore it cannot be doubted, that they had a free-will; for, since they did abuse their free-will, it is a certain sign that they had one; for we cannot abuse a thing which we have not. Though this their free-will was not so confirmed in goodness, but that they could choose evil, as their issue has convinced us of. They had free-will in spiritual cases; besides, that they knew God, his command and will, and could easily have obeyed the same; So did they likewise know that they were created to an eternal life; which they could conclude thereof, that God did threaten them with eternal death; and since they knew God, and to know God is perfect righteousness; and to

know his power, is a root to immortality; so should immortality have been their portion, if they had not abused their free-will.

3. With freedom from the punishment for sin. In Paradise, there was no sorrow nor grief, adversity nor misery, need nor death, but a free and glorious life. Men should have been as children in their Father's house, and would never have been drove out, as happened afterwards; but they should have lived some time here on Earth, in the greatest felicity, and afterwards been taken up into Heaven.

PART II

We have now to consider,

II. How man lost this freedom by sin.

We may now ask: How is the free will of man become after the Fall? Our Savior answers hereto in our text, saying: "*Whosoever commits sin is the servant of sin.*" A servant has no freedom to do as he will, but he is subject and bound and can be punished. So happened it with us, that since we would not be servants of God, but did abuse the freedom wherewith we were blessed; So we have shamefully lost our freedom, and from servants of God are become servants of Satan, and have now no free will of ourselves, to do anything that is good or pleasing in the sight of God; and we have thereby thrown ourselves, and are entered,

First, in the service of sin: *Whosoever commits sin, is the servant of sin.* When *Adam* and *Eve* departed from God's command, they departed likewise from his service, and with fulfilling the desire of Satan, they entered into his service, and Satan became their lord; and human generation is now become since the Fall, wholly subject to this devilish dominion, wherein they can do nothing but sin: *For of whom a man is overcome, of the same is he brought in bondage.* All men have lost by the Fall their honor, and are become abominable and despicable before God. Satan made cords of their evil will, and bound them with; and he made rods of their wicked actions, and whipped them with; Like children born in servitude are servants, so are we all servants to sin; being the offspring of *Adam* and *Eve*, who for a short pleasure sold their freedom shamefully. A servant must labor a great deal, has little or no rest, day or night. Likewise they that are entered in the service of sin, *They devise iniquity, and work evil upon their beds, and when the morning is light, they practice it.* The eyes of the thief and adulterer, waits for darkness, and when others sleep, they contrive mischief. A servant must be contented with mean food, and often with nothing: Satan shows riches enough, and promises great things, but at last gives nothing: For, what have the servants of sin and the world for all their works of iniquity at last, but unrest and trouble in their consciences and mind here, and hell-fire and eternal damnation hereafter.

2. In the service of a disobedient will. The will of man is after the Fall, no longer free but slavish. Man has lost free will, with losing the image of God: He has yet in some cases a free will, but the best thereof is gone; it is with him as with the blind, who, although he has the balls of his eyes in his head, yet has lost the glance and luster to see with. We have as yet our free will.

In *natural* cases; as, when we can eat, drink, stand or walk, set or lie, skip or dance when we will; we can speak, sing, laugh or bawl when we will. These and such other natural cases do stand in our own free will, though greatly diminished; *For the preparations of man's heart, is in the man, but the answer of the tongue is from the Lord. A man's heart devises his way; but the Lord directs his speech.* We have yet a free will,

In *moral cases.* A man can, of his own will and choice, strive after all manner of virtues, and abhor crimes and vices, as we can see of the old heathen philosophers, who did, in their morality, exceed a great many Christians. We have free will,

In *temporal cases.* A king can rule and govern a nation and country; a merchant can buy, sell, and trade; a laborer can work, and a householder can order his family; and everyone of them may do their respective work wisely enough; yet in this their free will is greatly diminished; and they can do nothing without the assistance of God. *Bezaleel* and *Aholiab*, were two cunning workmen to work, yet *God filled them with his Spirit, in wisdom and in understanding. Gideon* was to war against the *Midianites, But the Spirit of the Lord was to come upon him first.*

There comes several hindrances in the course of our lives against our free will, so that the same cannot have its progress; as,

The Devil, who is mighty in the children of unbelief, oftentimes hinders, that men cannot obtain their will. He can raise our affections to evil; he can blind the eyes, so that man's sight is blind, and goes astray from the right way. King *Saul* was troubled by an evil spirit, Satan entered into the heart of *Judas Iscariot:* The *Pharisees* thought they did well, in giving the tenth of *cumin, mint* and *dill*; and, who will not believe, that it was the Devil, who made the *Gentiles change the glory of the incorruptible God, into an image made like to corruptible man, and to birds, and four-footed beasts, and creeping things.*

Our own frailties often hinders our free will; for our reason is often blind, and judges that to be good, which is evil: So that it goes with us as with the night-owls, who, by a small light, are dim-sighted; by a greater light are quite pur-blind, and by a great blaze are stone-blind. Our will inclines us to evil, and our affections are so passionate, that we often do a thing which we afterwards repent of. There is none so wise but he may fail.

Outward causes hinders likewise oftentimes our will, and deceives us; for, if they seem pleasing, they delude us; if they seem evil, they put us against; as the example of our first parents convinces us thereof.

God himself often hinders our free will in outward cases. The preparation of man's heart is in his own power; but it is directed and governed by God: *Man proposes, but God disposes.* The way of man is not in himself; it is not in man that walks, to direct his steps; *Sennacharib* king of *Assyria*, had an evil intention against *Hezekiah* and *Jerusalem*, but the Lord did *put a hook in his nose, and a bridle in his lips, so that he could not come into the city, nor shoot an arrow therein, neither cast a bank against it.* In regard to this, says St. *James; Go to now you that say, today or tomorrow we will go into such a city, and continue there a year, and buy and sell, and get gain: Whereas you know not, what shall be on the morrow: For, that you ought to say, If the Lord will, we shall live, and do this, or that.* Therefore must we say of the actions of men, as *Job* says, *They meet with darkness in the daytime, and grope in the noon-day as in the night.*

In spiritual cases, concerning our salvation, a man has a free-will, in the outward, but not in the inward actions.

The spiritual outward actions are, to go to church, to hear, read, and meditate upon the word of God, to use the sacraments, to sing Psalms, to pray, to give alms, and many more actions of piety and charity; wherein a man that is not reformed nor regenerated, may have his own free will: *The Queen of* Sheba, *hearing of the fame of* Solomon *concerning the name of the Lord, came to* Jerusalem. *The wise-men from the East, were desirous to know the place where Christ was born:* Herod *did gladly bear* John, *and did many things: The deputy of* Paphos *called* Sergius Paulus, *did desire to hear the Word of God, that* Barnabas *and* Saul *did preach, although he favored* Elymas *the sorcerer;* Felix *the governor in* Judea *a heathen-man sent for* Paul, *and heard him concerning the faith in Christ.* How many are found in the world, who are very diligent in hearing and reading the word of God, and are for all ungodly? Therefore can such outward actions, not procure faith nor conversion in us, except with the inward working of the Holy Spirit; for if one would practice all his lifetime, all outward pious and charitable actions, and had not the living faith enlightened by the Holy Spirit in his heart, yet could he not be converted and saved: *Neither is he that plants anything, neither he that waters; but God who gives the increase:* Could the apostles not convert any by their preaching without the grace of God, and the working of the Holy Spirit; then can a man, neither by hearing and reading the word of God be converted, and believe without the assistance of the Holy Spirit. We read therefore of the apostles, that, *when they preached, the Lord was working with them:* Though we shall not condemn the outward actions; *for faith comes by hearing, and hearing by the Word of God: And it has pleased God by the foolishness of preaching to save them that believe.*

The spiritual inward actions are a true faith and love towards God, and likewise a sincere attention. Herein a man has no free-will, but is as a slave born in sin. A man cannot of himself, nor of his own strength believe in God, receive the Word of God, convert himself, believe in Christ, depend and rely on the death and sufferings of Christ, hate sin, better his life, worship God in Spirit and truth, be patient in crosses and afflictions, expecting help from the Lord, and wait with a hearty longing for a life eternal: In these and many other such like inward spiritual actions a man has no free will; which we can see of the following.

First, a man's reason is blind in godly and spiritual cases: *The natural man receives not the things of the Spirit of God: For they are foolishness unto him; neither can he know them, because they are spiritually discerned.*

Secondly, the will and affections in man, who is regenerated, are in themselves evil and obstinate against God; so that we have no natural inclination to what God will, but on the contrary incline always to what God abhors: Can an *Ethiopian* wash himself white? If we withstand one sin, another breaks forth; and our free will in this case, is as a colander, if we stop one hole, the water runs out of another; if we guard against one sin, than breaks forth another; *therefore is man's heart said to be deceitful, and desperately wicked; to be rebellious and revolting*, stony, blind, and working against the Holy Spirit; *the neck* is said to be, *an iron sinew, and the brow brass.*

Thirdly, all strength and power in spiritual cases are entirely lost; therefore is man said to be dead in trespass and sins: As a dead body cannot commit anything, much less raise itself up again; so can neither a man, who is dead in sin, do any spiritual action of his own power, nor raise in himself the eternal life.

Fourthly, our conversion is in the Scripture attributed to the Holy Spirit, and the grace of God. So says the Spirit of God: *I will take the stony heart out of their flesh, and will give them a heart of flesh.* When God commands us in his word: *To turn unto him; to circumcise the foreskin of our hearts: To make us a new heart and a new spirit,* then can we do no more than a lump of clay can form itself into a vessel; nay, than the dead who were raised by Christ in the time of his Incarnation could have raised themselves. But the meaning of the Lord is, that when he offers us his grace, we should not obstinately resist the working of the Holy Spirit; but implore the mercy of God, to give us strength and power to do, what we are not able of ourselves to perform: Also then is the will of the unregenerate, slavish, dead and powerless persons in spiritual cases; and cannot of themselves do anything to the promotion of their own conversion and salvation: For, as after we have taken poison, are sure of death, so is the inclination of men towards heavenly things dead, through the unhappy eating of the forbidden tree's fruit by our first parents.

3. In the service of punishment; Our Savior says in our text, *The Servant abides not in the house forever, but the Son abides forever:* When our first parents became servants of sin, then were they not allowed to stay longer in Paradise; but God drove them out as a token, that, as the earthly Paradise was shut up from them, so should the heavenly likewise be shut up against them, and all servants of sin. A servant can well abide in a house for some time, and be one of the family, obtain liberty, and be employed about family work; but when it comes to heirship, then do we see the difference between the son and a servant: The son abides in the house as heir forever, but the servant is turned out, so will it go with all servants of sin; such a one can well remain in the house of God, namely the church, and be looked upon as a member of the family, yea, even be entrusted with some care, and prosper. For the wicked hides themselves always among the godly; but on the great Day of Judgment, when we shall appear before the tribunal of God, then shall the Son abide in the house forever, but the servants shall be put away; then shall the faithful, being adopted unto children, go into eternal glory; but the unbelievers unto eternal shame and misery. This was the comfort of the Psalmist King *David*, when he said, *I will dwell in the House of the Lord forever.*

PART III. Let us also enquire,

III. How the Son of God has made us free again.

Here one should think: should all they, who are servants of sin, be excluded from the heavenly house of God; who can then get a portion in this house, since all men are sinners and servants of sin? Our Savior answers hereto in our text: *If the Son therefore shall make you free, you shall be free indeed.* The Son of God Jesus Christ, who alone is Son and heir in his heavenly Father's house, has alone power to make us free. As the first *Adam* brought us into a triple service, namely the service of sin, disobedient will, and punishment for sin; so has the second *Adam* again procured us a triple freedom; namely,

1. Freedom from sin. The Son of God has freed us from sin, for God laid our sins upon him: *He has made him to be sin for us, who knew of no sin; that we might be made the righteousness of God in him:* He has freed us from *the wrath of God, by having made peace through the blood of his cross;* He has *freed us from the curse of the law, being made a curse for us:* He has *freed us from accusing conscience:* He has *purged our consciences with his blood from dead works, to serve the living God:* He has *freed us from Satan's anger, and has bruised the head of the old Serpent:* He has *freed us from eternal death; for he is become a plague to death, and destruction to hell.*

2. Freedom from a disobedient will. A servant cannot do anything for himself, except he has a master who favors him: So is it with us before our conversion, we cannot do of ourselves anything concerning the cause of our own salvation; but we are as slavish servants, unable, yea, dead in all that is good. Shall we be regenerated and converted to the glorious freedom of God's elect, then must God take on our cause, and help us, which he will certainly do, and will promote our conversion, and will incline our disobedient will to obedience. *It is God who works in us both to will and to do of his good pleasure.* Our Savior says, you *cannot do good, except you abide in me; no man can say that Jesus is the Lord, but by the Holy Spirit.* We confess this likewise in the third article of our belief, when we say on the explanation thereof: *I believe, that I, by the strength of my own reason cannot believe, nor come unto my Lord Jesus Christ, unless the Holy Spirit has called me through the gospel, enlightened me with his gifts, sanctified and preserved me in the true faith.* God uses here two

means,

First, the Word of God, as well that which is preached and heard, as that which is seen. The word which is preached and heard is the law and the gospel: The law increases in us dread and sorrow for our sins: The gospel comforts us again with the satisfaction of Jesus Christ for our sins: When also true faith in Jesus Christ is joined with a dread and sorrow for our sins, then can we be sure; *That a godly sorrow works repentance to salvation not to be repented of:* The Word of God which is seen, are the Holy Sacraments; for, since they assure us of the grace of God promised to us in his word, so are they called the word of God, which we see in regard to the outward signs that we see with our eyes; *to wit,* The water in Baptism, and the bread and wine in the Lords Supper: Both of these Sacraments help and free us from sin: Baptism is a means of the forgiveness of sin, of the deliverance from death and hell, and of obtaining life-everlasting; for everyone that believes the word and promise of God, according to the Words of our Savior, *He that believes and is baptized shall be saved*; shall certainly reap the benefit of this promise. The Lord's Supper assures us of the forgiveness by Jesus Christ.

Second means is, the ministers of God, who assist likewise towards the conversion of men. John *the Baptist did turn many of the children of* Israel *to the Lord God.* St. *Paul* says of himself and apostles, *Who then is* Paul, *and who is* Apollos, *but ministers by whom you believed, even as the Lord gave to every man.* The Lord uses the following order in our conversion; he causes his word to be preached by his servants, and offers his grace and mercy therein. God will that we shall receive this word so preached, and obey the same, and he promises his grace and assistance to them that receive and obey his words, that they shall thereby be converted and enlightened: He promises likewise his Holy Spirit, who shall renew their corrupted nature, and give them holy thoughts and affections, create in them a new heart, take the stony heart from them, and give them a heart of flesh, and guard them; that they shall not fall again into willful sins; but go forth daily in a pious and godly life, *and serve God in holiness and righteousness*; And then is a man free indeed; *For where the Spirit of God is, there is real freedom.* Then has a child of God freedom to do good, and to shun evil. *The heart that by nature was a wild olive-branch, is then by faith grafted into the good olive-tree, Jesus Christ*, and is become thereby strengthened to do spiritual and God-pleasing actions; then has man freedom to obey the commands of God, to strive after good works, to remain in goodness, and not to be tired thereof, but to increase daily more and more, which man cannot do himself, by his natural power and strength, but alone by the working grace of God, and the assistance of the Holy Spirit. *He that has begun a good work in you, will perform it until the Day of Jesus Christ:* But, although God has, for the sake of Jesus Christ, renewed a free-will in the regenerated, for to serve him in holiness and righteousness, yet there is often an infirmity in them; so that a child of God must complain, *to be sold under sin:* For the remnants of sin is in us as long as we are in this world, and draws us back in many ways from godliness: Therefore is man so far regenerated, free in spiritual things; but so far the remnants of sin is in them, they are servants unable of themselves. As there is always a natural aversion between water and fire, so is there likewise between spirit and flesh; which aversion will continue until we lay off our earthly house of this tabernacle, and shall appear at the resurrection with glorified bodies, according to the glorified body of Jesus Christ. Then shall the image of God be perfectly renewed in us, and our will shall be *free indeed*, and inclined to good, and we shall be confirmed in goodness, holiness, righteousness, and truth, and shall never fall again from the grace of God: *For they shall be equal unto the angels.*

3. Freedom from the punishment for sin. Although we must be in this world subject to adversity, sorrow, crosses, misery, and

even death itself, yet do we know and believe, that all this comes from a gracious Father, who will glorify us afterwards in his Son. Christ has freed us from eternal punishment and damnation, and has procured for us a sure hope of salvation, and everlasting life, where our freedom shall rightly begin, and we shall not know of sin nor the punishment of sin. Our reason shall be enlightened, to know God and the godly things. Our will shall be alone inclined to do the will of God. Our hearts shall be chaste, full of holy and godly thought, and all our affections shall be joined together, desiring nothing but holiness and goodness: *Then shall this corruptible put on incorruption, and this mortal shall put on immortality.* And it shall be perfected what the apostle St. *Paul* says: "*O death, where is your sting? O hell, where is your victory?*" What this freedom is, for we shall be perfectly convinced of hereafter in the eternal Glory.

O Lord God Heavenly Father, govern our will with your Holy Spirit, that it may always be inclined to godliness, so that we may daily he strengthened in the true faith, and at last receive the end of our faith, even the salvation of our souls alone; for the sake of our blessed Savior Jesus Christ. AMEN.

10

On the First Sin

The text, GENESIS 3:1, 2, 3, 4, 5, 6, 7, verses.

Now the Serpent was more subtle than any beast of the field which the Lord God had made: And he said unto the woman, yea, has God said, you shall not eat of every tree of the Garden? And the woman said unto the Serpent, We may eat of the fruit of the trees of the Garden: But of the fruit of the tree which is in the midst of the Garden, God has said, you shall not eat of it, neither shall you touch it, lest you die. And the Serpent said unto the woman, you shall not surely die. For God does know, that in the day you eat thereof, then your eyes shall be opened: And you shall be as gods, knowing good and evil. And when the woman saw that the tree was good for food, and that it was pleasant to the eyes, and a tree to be desired to make one wife; she took of the fruit thereof, and did eat, and gave also unto her husband with her; and he did eat. And the eyes of them both were opened, and they knew that they were naked.

INTRODUCTION

WHAT God makes good, strives the Devil always to make bad, and is therefore called a destroyer; God created man to be immortal, and made him to be an image of his own eternity; nevertheless, through envy of the Devil came death into the world. In these words is laid before us three Images. 1st. Of *God*. 2nd. Of the *Devil*, and 3rd. Of *Death*.

First, the *image* of God. Which is the noblest and most beautiful image: For as God is the highest good, so had he favored man with the same image, for all what is good, he will willingly part to others of his goodness. Here we can see how holy, wise, true, righteous and good God is in his essence. According to this image did God create man. As God is immortal, and governs all things, so had he likewise created man to life everlasting, and to be a ruler over all his handy works; and as a father can see his own image in his child, and be rejoiced thereover, so could God see his own image in man, and be rejoiced thereover, as over his best and noblest creature.

Second, the *image* of the Devil. The Devil being envious over the happy state of man, did begrudge them the precious image, where-with they were honored in the creation, and strove to bereave them thereof, and to give unto them his own devilish image; wherefore, under the shape of a natural serpent, did deceive them by lies, to eat of the forbidden tree's fruit, by which they lost the precious image of God, and received, instead thereof, the image of the Devil; which consists in darkness in their senses, unbelief in their reason, bad desires in their affections, great disorder in their members, and horrible terrors in their consciences.

Third, the *image* of death. Death was no ways to be found before the Fall. But after the Fall, *sin entered into the world, and is now over all*. The transgression of our first parents was a port, through which death entered into the world, so that we must all die now for their sake. This image of death entered into the world, with three horrible faces; wherefore we must be afraid, and call him, *the king of terrors.* The first face terrifies the body, the second the soul, and the third both soul and body. The first is the temporal death, the second the spiritual, and the third the eternal. The first is when soul and body part, the second is when God departs from us with his grace, and the third is the pain of the damned in hell. This triple death is comprehended in these words; *You shall surely die.*

In such misery are we brought through the sin of our first parents, as we can see of our text's words; whereof we will remark these three parts,

FIRST, *How Satan in the shape of a natural serpent did deceive our first parents.*

SECOND, *How they were persuaded and did consent.*

THIRD, *What punishment followed thereon.*

EXPLANATION of the TEXT. PART I

I. How Satan in the shape of a natural serpent did deceive our first parents.

When Satan was plunged out of heaven, he did not tarry long; but after men were created and placed in Paradise, then went this turbulent and wicked spirit in there and tempted them to fall off from their obedience; he was now become so raving, that, if it had been in his power, he would have destroyed the whole creation, and therefore began first with man; who was the noblest creature on earth, made in the likeness of God, after his own image, and for better execution of his hellish proposal, chose the serpent on account of its subtlety. We see herein following,

1. The description of the Serpent, whereof our text says: *Now the Serpent was more subtle than any beast of the field which the Lord God had made:* birds of one feather, flock together. The Devil is subtle, and having a subtle intention, thought therefore that the Serpent, being likewise subtle, was best able for the executing of his wicked design. There is great subtlety ascribed unto the Serpent; so well in defending itself, as in hurting of others. In defending itself, when he wants to change his hide, then creeps he between two stones, when his eyes are dim, because he is all the winter in dark holes; then rubs he them in the Spring with fennel, by which they become clear again; when anyone will beat them with a stick or stone, then is he most careful of his head, wrinkling his body round it, knowing that he cannot live after his head is hurt; he keeps always his poison in his throat, that he can have it ready when it is wanted; when he goes to drink he lays down first his poison, which he takes up again after he has drunk; he stops his ear with his tail, that he shall not hearken to the voice of charmers, charming ever so wisely; he does not stay in his holes, neither in unfrequented places, but always by the paths by the way; such subtlety can we find by the Serpent after the Fall; much subtler has he then been before the Fall. In this natural serpent had the Devil hid himself, and is therefore called, *The old Serpent, which deceives the whole world*; and spoke with *Eve* out of this natural serpent. We see,

2. The address of the *Serpent* to the woman. *Eve* was made of God mistress over all the creatures; and was therefore not afraid of the Serpent, whom she knew to be one of the creatures, but she was not aware of, that it was the Devil who spoke to her out of the Serpent; she was astonished, thinking there was some mystery in it; wherefore St. *Paul* says; Adam *was not deceived, but the woman being deceived was in the transgression.* The meaning is, that *Adam* was not deceived of the Serpent, but persuaded of the woman. We see,

3. The speech of the *Serpent* to the woman. The Devil uses not here his own words to *Eve*, entreating and persuading her to eat the forbidden tree's fruit: No, but he uses God's words; saying, *Yea, has God said:* He speaks to her, *First*, by way of questioning, as if he would say, should that be the true intent of God's words, that you should not eat of that one single tree, since he has given you free leave to eat of all the other trees in the Garden? Certainly *Eve* you hast not understood God's words rightly; he never intended to bereave you the use of the best tree, and, if he had even said so, it is not his earnest, and even if it was his earnest, what great crime would that be to eat of one tree's fruit, more than of another? Should that be so dangerous that God should forbid it under threatening of such severe punishment; that cannot be, it is a bad construction of your own. *Secondly*, by denying the words of God, saying to the woman; you *shall not surely die:* Ah, you liar, hereof can we see and perceive, that the Devil is a liar, blasphemer, deceiver, and a proud spirit.

He is a *liar*; for he says, you *shall not surely die.* Whereof we all are convinced to the contrary; therefore did our Savior call him, *a liar, and father of lies*; for he was the first inventor of lies.

He is a *blasphemer.* His words are always against God; God had said, you *shall surely die*; he says the reverse, you *shall not surely die.* Is not this the greatest blasphemy?

He is a *deceiver.* He speaks one thing and thinks another; he gives good words of a false heart, and covers his hellish intention with honey-words. He must therefore be the king of the *locusts*, who had *faces as the faces of men; and hair as the hair of women, and teeth as the teeth of lions, and tails like unto the scorpions, with stings therein.*

He is a proud *spirit.* He places his own words before God's, and will be believed before God; as here in our text. *Thirdly*, speaks the Devil to *Eve* by turning the word of God, saying, *God knows that in the day you eat thereof, then your eyes shall be opened: And you shall be as gods, knowing good and evil*; God had never said this; but barely forbidden the eating of the fruit, under punishment of a sure death. Also did the Devil deceive *Eve*, and brought her to doubt on God's words; and she consented at last. Everyone must therefore be cautious for the first instigation and temptations of the Devil, and let his saying be ever so flattering and pleasing, yet must we be on our guard. He appears as a fox, but turns at last to a lion. Hence follows two questions, namely, what cause there was for man's fall? And, what method the Devil uses commonly in his temptations.

The first question is: what cause was there for man's fall? Not God: For he had absolutely forbidden the eating of the tree's fruit. And what God forbids, he will not have done. Besides, God had threatened the eating thereof with certain death. Therefore shall no man say; It is through the Lord, that I fell away: For, you ought not to do the things that he hates; and he hath no need of the sinful man. But there is three causes of the Fall of our first parents; as, 1*st*, the Devil. 2nd*ly*, themselves. And, 3rd*ly*, the natural serpent.

The first cause of the Fall of *Adam* and *Eve* was the Devil, who did deceive them; he did use two moving arguments to deceive them with, the first, was that in shewing them the great advantage they would have thereby; *that they should be as gods.* The second, the losing or missing of the punishment, wherefore they were afraid that they should not die. The Devil knew full well, that if he could but remove their dread of the wrath of God, he then might easily prevail upon them, and so obtain his desire and intention.

The second cause was *Adam* and *Eve* themselves, who, of their own free-will, without any necessity, did consent, and transgress the command of God; which they easily could have obeyed, for God had given them power enough to withstand, and a free-will to do as they would; therefore are they the cause of their own fall, since they did abuse their free-will. Will anyone say, God consented hereto, since he could easily have prevented it if he was willing? We answer hereto, that the cause cannot be ascribed to God, who had consented thereto; for he had given them strength and power enough to withstand all temptations, since they were created in his own likeness. I will illustrate this with a similitude: When a king builds a fort or castle, and provides therein necessary means for the defense thereof against an enemy who is approaching, and orders, in the meanwhile, the governor, not, on pain of death, to deliver the city to the enemy; could the king be blamed if the governor was to surrender? No; is not the fault in the governor who acted against orders? And the king, who had furnished the place so well, is blameless; but the governor is worthy to be punished: Likewise is it with the Fall of our first parents; God had created them in his own image, where-through they were adorned with such precious gifts, that they could have withstood temptations. They knew God's command; God was not obliged to defend or guard them, for that would have been, as if the image of God was not in full perfection in them; therefore their fall can be ascribed to none else but their own abusing of their free-will; neither would God have prevented their fall, because he wanted to prove their obedience: The command was not so difficult but that they could easily have obeyed the same. The command that God gave after the Fall to *Abraham*, concerning the sacrificing of his son *Isaac*, was more difficult and hard; yet he was willing and ready to obey, and would have fulfilled the same, if God had not hindered him in the fact. *Jonadab*, the father of the *Rechabites*, commanded his sons, and their posterity, that they should drink no wine; this command they did obey, and even when the prophet *Jeremiah*, according to the command of the Lord, did ask them to drink wine, answered; *We will drink no wine:* Much easier could *Adam* and *Eve*, being in the state of innocence, have obeyed the command of God, concerning the eating of the forbidden fruit.

The third cause is the natural serpent, in whom the old serpent the Devil was hid. *Moses* mentions the serpent; and that it was a natural serpent, we can see by the curse God pronounced against him; *Upon your belly shall you go, and dust shall you eat:* And, that the Devil was in this serpent, we can prove, partly, that the serpent spoke; partly of the subtle speech; partly of the saying of our Savior; *That the Devil is a murderer and liar from the beginning:* And partly of the words of St. *Paul*; *The Serpent beguiled* Eve *through his subtlety*; and therefore is the Devil called, *an old serpent.*

The second question is: What method does the Devil use commonly in his temptations? This we ought to observe well, the better to guard ourselves, since it helps greatly towards the obtaining a victory, rightly to know the strength of our enemy; and we shall find that,

1st, the Devil attacks men always on the weakest side, for his better advantage: He entered first into a parley with *Eve*, and not with *Adam*; he thought her the weakest of them both, and therefore the easiest to persuade. He acts always in his temptations the part of an experienced general; therefore we should always be watchful and careful, *And take on the whole armor of God:* For the Devil can, of little cause, take opportunity to tempt us.

2ndly, the Devil begins mostly with small, but ends with great temptations. He made *Eve* believe first, that the eating of the tree's fruit was not such a great crime as she imagined. When he tempted our Savior in the wilderness, he began with stones, but ended with the kingdoms and glory of the world. *Judas* began with a kiss, but ended with a halter. We should therefore withstand temptations in the very first beginning, and not let the Devil spend the least thread in our thoughts; for he will at last make cords thereof to bind us with. Had *Eve* stopped her ears from the Serpent, then she would not, nor her offspring after her, have heard of so many misfortunes, that happened daily in the world.

3rdly, the Devil brings forth, and makes use of the word of God; but he either alters it, takes from it, or adds to it, as he sees most advantageous. He began in his tempting of our Savior with God's word, but left out what he found against himself. When pirates intend mischief, then do they hang out false Colors; so does the Devil, when he uses God's word; and he will always gain thereby, if we are not on our guard: And how horrible the Fall of our first parents was, we can better discern, when we consider the following circumstances, of the second part of my discourse; which is,

PART II.

II. How Adam and Eve were persuaded, and did consent.

Here we have to consider the following; *First*, who did sin; and, *Secondly*, The crime or sin itself.

1. Who did sin. *Adam, Eve*, and all their posterity.

Eve made the first step towards the Fall; first, by entering into parley with the Serpent. We may suppose that *Eve* was walking in the Garden, admiring the beautiful creation that was given under the dominion of men; at last she came to the forbidden tree, where she stood, beholding the tree, and wondering at the fruit thereof; and likewise meditating on God's command concerning the eating thereof: Thereon appeared the Serpent, and entered into discourse with her, and at last deceived her. We can see hereof, that it is not good to enter into familiarity or discourse with the Devil, for he is too subtle for us. Secondly, by departing from the word of God. He is certain that *Eve* had no thoughts of departing from God's words, neither of transgressing the command; for we can see that she began in her own defense with the words of God; had she continued so, she would have withstood the temptation; but, when she afterwards began to sickle, first with adding to the word of God, namely, *neither shall you touch it*; and then with a sort of a doubtful may-be; *Lest you die*. Then found the Devil it easy to deceive her; When we begin to doubt on the word of God, then begins our faith to diminish, and when that diminishes, then comes the Devil nearer and nearer; as we can perceive of *Eve*; as soon as she began to doubt on the words of God, then began bad desire for the forbidden fruit to rise in her thoughts; for so stands it in our text: *She saw that the tree was good for food, and pleasant to the eyes, and a tree, to be desired to make one wise.* We should therefore remain firm by the words of God, and not add to it, nor take from it, for we show the greatest obedience to God thereby.

Adam's Fall is described with few words. *And she gave also unto her husband with her, and he did eat.* Although *Adam* was not deceived of the Serpent by the woman, yet was their crime alike, as the issue has convinced us of. None of them could be excused, for they transgressed both; *Adam* acted here foolish, thoughtless, and despising.

Foolish. For he obeyed his wife more than God, and showed thereby, that he loved her more than God. He is more to blame, than *Solomon* was, whose *heart was turned away from God by his wives.*

Thoughtless, he took the fruit from *Eve* in his hands, not considering from what tree it was taken.

Despising, he saw that *Eve* did not die on the spot, according to the threatening of God, and therefore doubted on the truth thereof. Hereof we can now be convinced, that departing from the word of God is a beginning to all sin. It went worse here, than our Savior says: *When the blind leads the blind, they both fall into the ditch: Adam* and *Eve* did not alone fall into the ditch of God's judgment through their transgression, but also,

Their whole offspring were brought thereunder: *For as a little leaven leavens the whole lump of dough*; So has the transgression of *Adam* and *Eve* corrupted all mankind; and it goes as the prophet says: "*The fathers have eaten sour grapes, and the children's teeth are set on edge.*" For we have all sinned in *Adam*, and are disobedient, desiring what is forbidden, yea, *the imagination of man's heart is evil from his youth.*

2. The crime of sin itself, consisting in these three parts; First, the departing from God; Secondly, the eating of the forbidden fruit, and, thirdly, in the transgressing of all the commandments.

In departing from God. When *Eve* believed the Serpent, she departed from God, in doubting his word, and God departed again from her; whereupon followed darkness and unbelief, and *Eve* became *as an unclean thing, and her righteousness as filthy rags, and faded as a leaf.*

In the eating the forbidden fruit. It went with *Eve*, as St. *James* says, "*Everyone is tempted, when he is drawn away of his own lust, and enticed. Then when lust has conceived, it brings forth sin, and sin, when it is finished, brings forth death.*" *Eve* did hearken to the words of the Serpent, and was taken in with his subtlety; thereupon beheld she the tree, *and saw that it was good and pleasant.* Also did the sin enter from her sight into her thoughts, and from her thoughts into her heart, with bad desire to eat and taste thereof, which she at last fulfilled. We can see hereby, how gradually sin comes; it arises first in the thoughts, then in the heart with bad desire to fulfill the same; then, after our inclinations are gratified, follows death; therefore should we always withstand wicked thoughts, that may arise in us, that they may make no progress. It seems a small crime to eat of a tree's fruit; but in the commands of God, we should look mostly on the person, who commands, and not on the command itself.

In the transgressing of all the commandments. When *Adam* and *Eve* broke the command of God, and eat of the forbidden tree's fruit, then broke they likewise all the commandments; for in this first law was concealed the second law, comprehending the ten commandments, and made themselves liable by their transgression to the judgment pronounced; which brings me to the third part of my discourse; which is,

PART III.

III. What punishment followed thereon.

We read in our text, *And the eyes of them both were opened, and they knew that they were naked.* Their conscience awakened, and they saw how much good they had lost, and how much evil they had brought on themselves and their offspring, with their disobedience. We see here, that,

First, their eyes were opened, namely, the eyes of their conscience, and of their body. The eyes of their conscience were opened. They remembered two things, 1st. the command of God, after which they were to live; and 2ndly, their sin, wherewith they had transgressed; and did conclude thereby, that the punishment wherewith they were threatened, would certainly follow. For, what is conscience but a conclusion in our thought, that, considering on one side the commandment, and on the other side the transgression of such commandment, there follows thereon, the conclusion of a punishment? Hereby arose terror in their conscience, so that they did hide themselves among the trees in the Garden: *For the wicked flee when no man pursues; and everyone that does evil, hates the light.* Their hearts did shake like the trees, and they trembled even like a shaken leaf, and could complain as king *Saul: We are sore distressed, for God is departed from us.* The conscience regulates itself by our actions, like our pulse after our health, and the disposition of the body. If we do right, it excuses as; but if we do wrong, it accuses us, and condemns us. *Adam* and *Eve* had no accusers, yet they were afraid and hid themselves by which came their fright on them? By their consciences, making this conclusion; He that transgresses the command of God, is liable to punishment. We have transgressed the command of God with eating of the forbidden fruit; therefore are we liable to the punishment pronounced by God, which is, you *shall surely die.* Such a power has the conscience, and everyone must bend under it; for none can run away from himself. It goes with a troubled conscience as with a sick person, who changes his bed often, and is carried out of one room into another, and cannot get rid of his sickness: The conscience is as a sleeping lion, who, when he awakes roars, and tears his booty. When does conscience awake? Sometimes, when the crime is committed, as here in *Adam* and *Eve,* who, after they had eat, *saw that they were naked.* When king *Manasseh* was led captive to *Babylon,* then awakened his conscience, and he prayed unto the Lord his God; sometimes long after. The conscience of *Joseph's* brethren, did not awake before twenty-three years after they had sold him. Sometimes when our proposal mishappens; as *Ahithophel.* The thief, who was taken in a murder, said, when his conscience awakened; *We receive the due reward of our deeds.* Sometimes does the Lord himself awaken our consciences, either by an outward token, or an inward thought. By an outward token, as here in *Adam* and *Eve,* who, when *they heard the voice of the Lord God walking in the Garden, hid themselves among the trees.* When king *Belshazar* saw the *part of the hand, that wrote upon the plaster of the wall, then became his conscience so terrified, that his countenance did change, and the joints of his loins were loosed, and his knees smote one against another.* *Baalam's* conscience was awakened by the opening

155

of his *ass's mouth*; and St. *Peter's* by a *cock's crow.* By an inward thought, either of the action, which we find is not right, as *Judas*; or of the Place where the Crime is committed, as the Prophet says; *The Stone shall cry out of the wall, and the beam out of the timber shall answer it.* But the conscience shall never continue sleeping always. We can well subdue our conscience for some time, but we can never destroy it; although we may make him fall asleep, like a drunken man; but when he awakens, he will be worse: As one who has got a thorn in his foot, the longer it has stayed in, the more pain it causes; and is therefore more dangerous.

The eyes of the body were opened. *They knew that they were naked.* They were naked before the Fall, but this nakedness was an honor to them; but after the Fall it became a shame, therefore did *they sew fig-leaves together, and made themselves aprons.* Here began the strength of God's judgment to have effect on their bodies: They did not die on the spot, yet the messenger of death began to work in their bodies, and made them remember that they should die. Their souls were naked, they lost the garment of holiness and righteousness, wherewith they were adorned in their creation; and became like the man fallen among the murderers. As one staring up in the air after what he cannot reach, falls in a pit; so did *Adam* and *Eve*, striving after what they could not obtain, fall into the pit, that the Devil had dug for them; namely, in the wrath of God.

2. They were afraid of God. They did converse with God before the Fall, as children with their father: But now after the Fall they flee away from him, like criminals from a severe Judge; and hid themselves, as if God could not see nor find them. Hereof we can perceive, the darkness in their understanding, which they received instead of their former wisdom. *Adam* was now become so wicked, that when the Lord called him, instead of giving God full honor, and confessing his crime, he thought to hide the same; and when he

found that would not do, then wanted he to excuse himself, and to lay all the blame on the woman, and consequently on God, of whom she was given, saying: "*The woman, whom you gave to be with me, she gave me of the tree, and I did eat.*"

3. They were afraid of the severity of the judgment, you *shall surely die. Adam* did not die at once, but lived nine hundred and thirty years after, yet found he the effect of death, as well in his body as soul. In his body, with sickness, misfortunes, and hard labor. In his soul, with despairing to overcome that which the Lord was so gracious to promise, *The Seed of the woman shall bruise the Serpent's head.* This promise was the only comfort to *Adam* and *Eve*, and everyone shall, by a true faith in the same, be saved to life-everlasting.

The Lord help us graciously in all our need and wants, both temporal and spiritual, and free us from the eternal death and damnation, for the sake of our blessed Savior Jesus Christ. AMEN.

11

Original Sin

T he text, PSALM, 51:5th verse
Behold, I was formed in iniquity; And in sin did my mother conceive me.

INTRODUCTION

AS the tree is, so is its fruit. A good tree does not bring forth bad fruit, neither a bad tree good fruit. Our first father *Adam* was in the beginning a good tree; he was created after the likeness of God in righteousness and holiness, but he became through his own folly, a bad tree, full of sin and bad desires, and we his offspring are become like him; as the apostle St. *Paul* says to the *Romans*, Chap. 5:12. *As by one man sin entered into the world, and death by sin, and so death passed upon all men, for that all have sinned.* The apostle lays before us three things, in these words;

First, the root and origin of all sin. All evil in the world, either sin itself, or punishment for sin, namely, sickness, plague, war, hunger, and at last death, are entered into the world by *Adam* and *Eve*; for

158

they were both but one: wherefore *Adam* said; *This is flesh of my flesh, and bone of my bone. Syrach* says: *By the woman came the beginning of sin, and through her we all die. Syrach* has regard, in these words, to the order in the sin-fall of *Adam* and *Eve: For Eve was deceived first, and afterwards* Adam; yet bears *Adam* the fault thereof, since sin was transplanted by him in men, and they have the original sin from him. And the transgression of *Adam* in *Paradise* is become ours by heirship. *Adam* sinned when he took the forbidden tree's fruit, and eat thereof, by which he lost the image of God, and for fear of judgment, *hid himself among the trees in the Garden.* We have sinned in communion with *Adam,* for we were in him, and are his offspring, and are become guilty in the same punishment of sin like him; likewise, we have part with him in the promise concerning the seed of the woman.

Second, how this evil has spread itself over the whole world, and passed upon all men: Not one of *Adam's* children is free from sin: *Who can give a clean thing from an unclean thing? Not one.* When *Adam* did promote his generation by procreation, then did he in the moment of conception, communicate the original sin to them. *And* Adam *begot children in his own likeness.* Now if the likeness of *Adam* after the Fall was sinful, therefore could his children not be otherwise. Also is then evil brought down from generation to generation, and is passed upon all men. Whereupon follows,

Third, punishment: Death entered into the world, and passed upon all men. As a great warrior, who after a victory enters into the camp of the conquered, and cuts down and destroys everyone without exception of persons. The holy children of God, have always complained heavily over *original sin,* and in particular, the Psalmist king *David,* in our text, whereof we will speak under these two heads,

FIRST, *That there is original sin.*

SECOND, *Wherein original sin consists, and how it deforms men.*

EXPLANATION of the TEXT. PART I

I. That there is original sin.

The children ought not to lay up for the parents, but the parents for the children. Abraham gave unto his Son *Isaac*, all that he had. King *Jeboshaphat*, gave unto his children many gifts of gold, silver, and jewels. But our first parents *Adam* and *Eve*, have left unto us their offspring, a miserable heirship, namely, the original sin; whereof the Psalmist complains in our text, saying, *Behold, I am formed in iniquity: And in sin did my mother conceive me.* The Spirit of the Lord will, with the word *behold*, show us as with a finger, *Adam* and *Eve*, who transgressed first, and thereby, lost the image of God, and afterwards begot children in their own likeness in sin; which is extended to us all. The Psalmist will say, thereby: *Behold my miserable condition. Is that a wonder that I have sinned, since I am formed in iniquity, and conceived in sin? My whole nature is polluted with sin; not alone my body, and all its members, but even my soul, and all its faculties, so that there is not one drop of blood in me but what is sinful; yea, the malice is bred in me, even from the moment of my conception.* Is not this a charming heirship? What can be said plainer? The Psalmist says not, *I have killed* Urias, *I have committed adultery?* No, but he comprehends his whole nature, as in one bundle, saying, *I am formed in iniquity, and conceived in sin: The seed whereof I am conceived is, and was polluted: The clay whereof this my vessel was made, was unclean and cursed:* We can prove of these words of *David*,

   1: That there is a sin derived from *Adam* and *Eve*, and extended to all men, called, the original sin. Which sin we of our first parents, and bring with us into the world, when we are born; yea, even the seed of our first parents is so transplanted, *That the seed of our parents whereof we are conceived, is polluted and cursed.* This we can prove,

1st, Of many other texts in the Scripture, as well in the Old as New Testament. We read of *Adam*; that *he begot a son, not after the image of God in holiness and righteousness; but in his own likeness, after his image.* Since the image of *Adam* was after the Fall, become sinful, therefore did he beget such-like children. The Lord himself complains over the corruption of man's heart, saying: *The imagination of man's heart is evil from his youth.* The word in the ground text signifies not alone *youth*, but even *infancy*; and in another place it is continually explained. *Every imagination of the thoughts of his heart is only evil continually.* Is it a continual evil? Then certainly it begins on the day of our birth, and ends on the day of our death. *Job* says, *Who can bring a clean thing from an unclean thing? Not one.* In a hospital there is none but sick and infirm: Of leprous parents are leprous children born: Of an unclean fountain flows forth unclean water: Of a bad tree comes bad fruit. And these are the words of our Savior, *That which is born of the flesh is flesh.* The meaning is: they that are born of sinful parents, are likewise sinful; excluded from the Kingdom of God, wanting the regeneration, although they may be born and conceived of pious and regenerated parents: For, as a learned father begets an unlearned son; so do regenerated parents beget unregenerated children. We can prove it,

2ndly, of other certain proofs grounded on the word of God. Why did God ordain the circumcision in the Old Testament? For no other reason, than that men should be thereby received again into the covenant with God; and without receiving this covenant, they were to be cut off from the people of God. Why was the purification of woman after child-bearing, ordained by God? Not because they became unclean by child-bearing, but for the natural inbred sin, wherein children are conceived and born. Yea, why are children baptized now a-days? *That they may be sanctified, and cleansed from the original sin, with the washing of water by the word in baptism:* Therefore is baptism called, *the washing of regeneration, and renewing of the Holy Spirit.* We can prove it,

3rdly, of experience. Conscience convinces everyone, that there is in him a bad root, and a poisonous fountain, wherefrom arises all evil actions, words and thoughts; and this foundation is man's heart, which is the office of all wickedness. We can perceive it of children, that they are naturally more inclined to evil than good; and that they are more apt to learn vice than virtue; and if they had their full freedom, they would grow up in all wickedness and immorality; yea, even against their own parents. How unwilling is not a child to go to school? What labor and trouble has not a school master, with instructions and other ways, to bring the child to what is good? And yet for all this, some children are so corrupted, that nothing will prevail upon them: All this arises from the inbred wicked nature, polluted with sin.

1. We can prove of our text, that this sin is called the original; net that it has been from the beginning of the creation; for God did not create any evil, much less sin and death; neither, that man's nature was created evil, for man was created upright: But it is called original, in regard to the three following reasons.

First, in regard to the root, which is, *Adam* the first father, who sinned first, and from him is the original sin transplanted upon all men; for as *Adam* did transgress against the divine majesty, so are we, his offspring, partakers not alone of his crime, but also of the punishment.

Secondly, In regard to all men, who never receive life from their parents, except in and by this original sin, which sprouts up with us even from the moment of our conception like a bad tree, sprouting up from a bad seed.

Thirdly, in regard to the actual sin, which is the fruit of the original sin: Foul water of an unclean fountain. Therefore is original sin called by several names in the Scripture; as, *the secret faults*; because it is so deep rooted in nature, that none can rightly understand the power and effect thereof, except God will place it in *the light of his countenance.* Human nature may seem as clean as possible, yet is the sinful corruption so deep rooted in it, that we can never get quite rid thereof, before we depart this life; St. *Paul* calls it, *a sin that dwells in us.* We cannot turn him away like a stranger; it takes lodging in and by us, when we are conceived, and will not quit his lodging, before the earthly house of our bodies shall be dissolved, and our souls shall be *clothed with a house, which is from heaven.* The Psalmist prays, that *God will not remember the sins of his youth.* It is called sin of youth, because sin appears always first in youth; as long as a child lies in the cradle, or is carried on the arm, we cannot well perceive the original sin; but when the child grows up to three, four or five years of age, then does the original sin appear, which must be corrected; for, *foolishness is bound up in the heart of youth or child, but the rod of correction shall drive it far from him.*

The old church fathers have called this original sin; *The enmity of the Serpent; the old sickness; the first sin; the inbred sin; Nature's fault and infirmity, and the natural evil*; not that it is nature itself, but because it begins with nature. We come now to the second head,

II. Wherein original sin consists, and how it deforms mankind.

We can conclude of my text's words, wherein the original sin consists, *Behold I am formed in iniquity, and in sin my mother did conceive me:* Which, according to the ground text, is; *My mother is become warm with me*; thereby confessing and acknowledging, that his whole nature, both in soul and body, is polluted with sin; yet is this original sin not nature or essence of men, but it is natural; for we must make a difference between nature and the faults of nature. Nature was good from God, but the fault of nature is evil from the Devil. Christ took on human nature, but not the fault of human nature; for, *he was without sin:* Also is then the original sin, a natural, a corporal, a universal, and a pernicious wound.

It is a *natural* wound. It is not cut in our clothes, but born in our flesh: And this natural evil shall remain in us, as long as we live in this world.

It is a *corporal* wound. Not that it is alone in our flesh, or in them parts; which we have in common with the beasts, but because it begins in us at the conception of our bodies, and remains in us until the dissolving again of our bodies.

It is a *universal* wound, and extends to all men. The greatest king must complain hereof, as well as the meanest beggar; yea, even the Virgin *Mary*, the mother of our Savior, was not free from the original sin. This honor alone is attributed to Jesus Christ, *Who is holy, harmless and undefiled, and separate from sinners.*

The children of pious and regenerated parents, are likewise born and conceived in the original sin; for the begetting of children is a work of nature, and not of grace. Well, says St. *Paul, if the root be holy, so are the branches.* We must not understand here, an inward cleanness or purity of heart, wherewith children should be born; no, but we must understand it, partly of the freedom which the children of the faithful have before the children of unbelievers; namely, to be made partakers of the covenants and means, by which the spiritual regeneration and holiness is given, partly, of the good and holy life of the children themselves, that if they should walk in the steps of their pious parents, they will be holy branches of a holy root; but if not, then they will not be holy branches, although the root might have been holy, as we can see of the words of our Savior to the *Jews; if you were* Abraham's *children, you would do the works of* Abraham.

164

It is a *pernicious* wound, and has corrupted the whole man, and is, soul and body, both inward and outward, defiled with the original sin. Doesn't *Job* say of the whole man? *Who can bring forth a clean thing of an unclean thing?* And in another place; *What is man, that be should he clean? And be, which is born of a woman, that he should be righteous?* Likewise complains the Psalmist in our text; *That he is formed in iniquity, and conceived in sin.*

The soul is so deformed, that the reason is become darkened in godly cases: *The natural man receives not the things of the Spirit of God:* The will is turned from God, and all what is good to all evil; we are by nature, as little inclined to good, as a stone thrown in the air can stay there of itself. We always omit what God commands, and commit what he forbids. *The heart is full of all evil imagination and thoughts, and is desperately wicked, and contains the depths of Satan.* The affections are unruly, as a young horse that prances, not because he is pricked with the spur, but because the bridle is taken off from him: Also are the affections, that, if we but see or hear of anything that is pleasing, whether good or bad, we at once, without further consideration, strive to obtain the same; and therefore, we often do what we repent of afterwards, and act against our better knowledge. The body is so deformed, that it cannot be longer called the Temple of God, but, *the body of sin*, and, *the body of death.* The members should be armors of righteousness, but are now become armors of iniquity. *The tongue is a fire, a world of iniquity; it defiles the whole body, and sets on fire the course of nature, and is set on fire of hell. The hands are full of blood; The eyes are full of adultery, and the feet are swift running to mischief.* Therefore, if the Lord should look on us in his justice, we would be an abomination in his sight, and be destroyed in his vengeance. *When the anger of the Lord smote* Miriam, (*Moses*'s sister) *the cloud departed from the tabernacle:* When king *Saul* had sinned, and been disobedient; *The Lord would not answer him:* The holy angels are become our enemies; for, as they are rejoiced of the repentance of a sinner, so are they likewise grieved of transgressions. We ourselves must complain of our *stinking wounds*, and be ashamed thereof. The Lord himself compares man's heart to a fountain casting up its water, saying; *As a fountain casts up her waters, so casts she out her wickedness.* And this wickedness will become, if full freedom is granted, worse than that of the unreasonable creatures. Anger will turn men to dogs, lies to sows; subtlety to foxes; unrighteousness and extortion to lions and bears; gluttony and drunkenness to swines; envy and hatred to night-owls, and pride to peacocks, and *so forth.* Herein we are all alike, and one is not better than another. King *David*, who is called in the Scripture, *a man after the heart of God*, shows us with his example, *that the most pious is as well polluted and corrupted by nature, as the wickedest and ungodliest:* Nature has made us all alike; for, *what is born of the flesh, is flesh.*

One might think we see, by daily experience, that there are many; yea, even among the heathens, who do not live according to the bad desires of their corrupted nature; but on the contrary practice virtues and morality in all their actions, live decent, and are very charitable. They have certainty no corrupt nature; and must we not then therefore make difference between man, and man's nature? We answer thereto, that we are all without exception, children of wrath by nature: And that we find some, who do not commit any outward great crime; but seem to live a good and moral life: Whereof we give the following reasons,

First, their own reason, or the law of nature, which shows us what is good or evil, lawful or unlawful; for although the reason is of human nature, yet do they not live according to it, as they ought; but the greatest part live according to nature itself, which is inclined alone to evil. But they who have higher thoughts and desires to correct the faults of nature, by virtue and morality; strive to conquer nature by a

166

moral life, in order thereby to obtain a good name, and the praise of men; such were many heathens, who because they found that nature was so corrupted, and subject to so many faults, did endeavor to subdue their natural faults, with and by a moral life; yet for all was their virtues, nothing but shining vices, because they had no faith. *For whatsoever is not of faith, is sin.* There are likewise many among the Christians, who will not commit any bad action, alone for the sake of a good name; yet, if such could, under the cloak of justice, deceive anyone, so that it should never be found out, they would not omit it. This proceeds from the original sin; therefore seek they to hide away their wickedness under the cloak of vain glory; but they are in the sight of God, yea, even in their own consciences, nothing else *but eye servants*, as our Savior said of the *Pharisees*.

The *second* reason is the dread of punishment. Men would often do their neighbor injury, or commit some gross crime or other, if they were not afraid of the punishment, which the law of the country indicts them to, if they were found out.

The *third* reason is the word of God. They who are convinced by the word of God, and in regard thereto, do not put their bad desires in execution, but abstain from all wickedness through love and obedience towards God, are the best Christians. *Joseph* would not consent to the desire and wicked delusion of his mistress, *because he would not sin against God.* A true Christian obeys the word of God, and bridles thereby his passions and affections, and subdues his corrupted nature, and is therefore regenerated. *For as many as are led by the Spirit of God, they are the sons of God.*

We should strive after, and endeavor to understand the articles of original sin rightly. *Luther* said, *None should think that he is a good divine, or understands the Scripture rightly, if he don't understand; or if he even diminishes original sin.* Whereof arises so many errors and misapprehensions about man's free-will in his conversion, and the cause of his salvation, and of the merits of our good works? Thereof alone, in that we do not rightly consider the greatness of original sin: We can never give due honor and reverence unto God, as long as we do not know our sins: We can never sincerely confess, that God is true, just, and merciful, if we do not acknowledge ourselves to be sinners, and of a corrupted nature, and offspring of *Adam* and *Eve:* Neither can we rightly understand the love of God, the merits of Jesus Christ, and the comfort of the Holy Spirit, except we know the original sin rightly: Who can rightly understand the words of Christ? *God so loved the world*; or the words of St. *John, Behold the Lamb of God, which takes away the sins of the world*; or the words of St. *Paul, Christ bath redeemed us from the curse of the law:* Who can understand what a divine mystery it is, that little children should, by the washing of water by the word, become regenerated? Likewise, that the children of *Adam*, should by the word and the Holy Spirit, be renewed, sanctified and enlightened, except they understand rightly the doctrine of the original sin. When we know our sins, and acknowledge that we are thereby in the sight of God, sinners and transgressors, by whom no good is to be found; then begins the grace of God, the love of Jesus Christ, and the comfort of the Holy Spirit, to be well-tasting.

Since then nature is so corrupted and defiled in us, let us then praise God for his goodness, that he has ordained us means thereby against the washing of regeneration, and renewing of the Holy Spirit, in baptism. Let us keep God and his words always before our eyes, abstain from sin, govern our actions by the command of God, comfort ourselves by the holy and undefiled conception and birth of Jesus Christ; put our whole trust and confidence in him, and show our Christian faith in a godly life; that we at last may receive the end of our faith, even the salvation of our souls. The Lord give us his grace hereto, for Christ's sake. AMEN.

12

Actual Sin

T he Text MATTHEW 12:31, 32, 33, 34, 35, 36, 37, Verses.

*All manner of sin and blasphemy shall be forgiven unto men:
But the blasphemy against the Holy Spirit shall not be forgiven
unto men. And whosoever speaks a word against the Son of Man, it
shall be forgiven him: But whosoever speaks against the Holy Spirit, it
shall not be forgiven him, neither in this world, neither in the world to
come. Either make the tree good, and his fruit good; or else make the
tree corrupt, and his fruit corrupt: For the tree is known by its fruit. O
generation of vipers, how can ye, being evil, speak good things? For out
of the abundance of the heart the mouth speaks. A good man out of the
good treasure of the heart, brings forth good things: And an evil man out
of the evil treasure, brings forth evil things. But I say unto you, that every
idle word, that men shall speak, they shall give account thereof in the
Day of Judgment. For by the words you shall be justified, and by your
words you shall be condemned.*

INTRODUCTION

IT goes with sin, as with the conception of a child, whereto is required, 1. The seed. 2. The conception of the seed. 3. The nourishment thereof; and, 4. The birth of the child. These four parts are included in the words of St. *James*, when giving a description of the conception of sin; he says in his epistle, Chap. 1:14, 15. *Every man is tempted when he is drawn away of his own lust, and enticed. Then when lust has conceived, it brings forth sin, and sin, when it is finished, brings forth death.* Consider here,

First, the seed, whereof sin is conceived, is the thoughts, and instigations, and desires in the heart: This proceeds either from outward or inward. From outward it arises, when we see, or hear of anything that is pleasing: *Eve* saw the forbidden fruit: *Esau* saw the red pottage: *Achan* saw the *Babylonish* garment, and *Judas* saw the thirty-pieces of silver, these outward things are not bad in themselves, but the Devil uses them as a bait, to catch us by; and if we are captivated by them, then do they become bad. When the Devil tempted Christ, on the *high mountain, and shewed him all the kingdoms of the world, and the glory of them, as in a moment*; then Christ beheld them without deceit and desire. Without deceit; for, as he who considers the paper to be white, that by another is blackened, does not err; so did Christ behold *the kingdoms and glory of the world*, brought here before him as a cheat. Without desire; for there was no bad inclinations nor desires in him. If we would also behold and consider the outward things that Satan brings before us, in order to deceive us with, then should we not be drawn so soon into his snares.

From inward, comes bad desires of a wicked heart, naturally inclined to all evil; and from thence arises all bad thoughts and imaginations. This is the seed whereof sin is conceived. Thereupon follows,

Second, the conception of this seed, which is consent. When we fully consent to our wicked thoughts and imaginations, and do not resist them; As *Solomon* says of the house: *By much slothfulness the building decays, and through the Idleness of the hands the house drops down*; so can we likewise say of wicked thoughts; Are we slothful and negligent in the fear of God, and the spiritual war; then can we soon be deceived of our own thoughts. For, when lust has conceived by consent, then follows thereon,

Third, the nourishment of the seed, that is the lust. We do not alone consent in our wicked thoughts; but we have lust and pleasure therein, and contrive all manner and ways, to put them in execution: And this is the bait that the the Devil throws out for us; deceiving us with the prospect of some gain or pleasure we shall have thereof. After this seed has conceived, and is nourished by our wicked lust and appetites, then comes forth;

Fourth, this *viper breed*, which is sin. It is a breed from the Devil; for he sinned first, and afterwards poisoned all men. *When sin is finished it brings forth death.* A woman after her child is born is overjoyed; but a sinner, after sin is committed, becomes troubled in his conscience, it telling him, that he must surely die. We can show this plainer in examples. When *Eve* saw the forbidden tree, and listened to the voice of the Serpent, then was she enticed by her own lust. *Eve saw that the tree was good for food, and pleasant to the eye, and to be desired, to make one wise.* After the lust was conceived in her heart, and her will consented, then was the sin finished: *She took and eat of the fruit, and gave also unto her husband with her.* But at last, after she had sinned, then became her conscience awakened. When king *David* saw the naked *Bathsheba*, he was inflamed with bad desire for her, and when he withstood not this desire, but strove to obtain it, then became the sin finished, *and be lay with her:* But as soon as the sin was completed, death followed. Of such *actual sins* we will discourse of here in our text, under these three heads;

FIRST, *What sin is.*

SECOND, *How many sorts of sin there are.*

THIRD, *What punishment follows on sin.*

EXPLANATION of the TEXT. PART I

I. What sin is.

Christ shows in our text, that the *Jews* and *Pharisees*, who would not acknowledge themselves to be sinners, were great sinners, which could be concluded by their words and actions; and he compares them therefore to *corrupt trees bearing corrupt fruit*; he calls them *a generation of vipers, of whose hearts proceeded nothing but wickedness and blasphemy against the Son of Man.* Christ compares them likewise to *evil men, bringing forth evil of their evil treasure*; and wills, that they should behold themselves in the law as in a glass. Well could they of the law of nature planted in their hearts, know what sin was, but of the law of God they could be better instructed. For the law of God is a glass that shows us our corrupt and sinful nature; since the law of God is a rule of righteousness in the will of God, after which we should regulate all our actions, if we will become well pleasing in the sight of God; so is all that is against the law transgression, and transgression is sin: So says the apostle St. *John: Sin is the transgression of the law:* Will we understand what actual sin is, then must we know, that it is a departing from the law of God, or a transgression of the law of God, either in thoughts, words or deeds. This word *actual* comprehends following,

First, the first motion in the mind, by which the heart is persuaded to sin; either it is done willfully or not, either big or small, if it is but against the command of God, and such first motions, are the sinful sparks kindled in our hearts from the original sin.

Secondly, all unlawful actions, either that we omit what is commanded, or commit what is forbidden, either knowing, or unknowing: For we can sin unknowingly, as St. *Paul* confesses of himself; that he *persecuted the church of Christ ignorantly.* Such, and other actual sins are called in the Scripture by several names, as: *The works of the flesh; the unfruitful works of darkness; the works of the old man; dead works; unlawful deeds.* They proceed from the Devil, and may therefore well be called like the *Pharisees* in our text: *Generation of vipers.*

We are instigated and persuaded to sin by the following.

1. The Devil who is the first author of sin: He deceived *Adam* and *Eve,* and deceives men many ways: He *deceives the whole world,* says St. *John* the divine: He provoked *David to number* Israel: He put it into the heart of *Judas,* to betray his Master: He *filled the heart of* Ananias *and* Sapphira, *to lie to the Holy Spirit.* Therefore are all they who commit willful sins against their own conscience, called in the Scripture, *children and servants of the Devil.*

2. The world betrays and deceives us likewise to sin; it is a teaching thing given to men, as *Michael* was given unto *David,* to be a snare. One man lays snares for another, first with bad examples, then with wicked persuasions, then with words and deeds. *Adam* was deceived by *Eve, Solomon* by his many wives, *Samson* by *Delilah.* The world is full of snares, as covetousness, ambition, pride, lasciviousness, and many other crimes.

3. Man himself commits sin, and is therefore called actual sin. As man consists of two parts, body and soul, so are both parts guilty in the actual sin. The soul is the chief worker of sin, and the body is the tool or instrument wherewith sin is committed; like an artificer, when he proposes to complete a piece of work, forms always a scheme first thereof in his thoughts, also is sin first conceived in

the thoughts, and afterwards executed; wherefore both parts in man are alike guilty in sin, therefore are our members called, armors or *instruments of unrighteousness.*

The Scripture makes a difference between to sin and to commit sin. We sin all, yea even the godliest, for the remnants of sin continues in us as long as we live; but we are said to commit sin, when we let the same rule over us, following our bad lust and inclinations, commit evil willfully, and are rejoiced in the gratifications of our passions. This difference is showed to us,

First, In the Scripture: so says our Savior: *Whoever commits sin, is the servant of sin.* The apostle St. *John* says: *He that commits sin, is the servant of the Devil: Whosoever is born of God, does not commit sin, for his seed remains in him.* It is demonstrated,

Secondly, by examples; St. *Paul* complains, that he was *sold under sin.* His condition was as one sold under slavery, who must work and slave daily with his body, even against his own will, also was *Paul sold under sin; so that he did what he would not do.* Contrary was it with king *Ahab, who sold himself to do wickedness as a slave:* By such, sin shows its tyranny over their souls; they are stubborn against God, they sin with stretched out hands, and say with *Pharaoh: Who is the Lord, that I should obey his voice?* They drive away the Spirit of God, they slay the firstborn of the Spirit, and entangle their poor souls in innumerable vices, and their bodies must always consent and execute the evil that arises in their thoughts; also are they that commit sin the servants of sin, and slaves to Satan, *who takes them captive by his snares, and keeps them at his will: For of whom a man is overcome, of the same is he brought into bondage.*

I come to the second head of my discourse; which is,

II. How many sorts of sin there is

Although original sin is alike by all, yet arises from the same many different sorts of actual sins; like a tree who having but one root, grows up in many branches: It would be too tedious and most impossible to sum up all the sorts of actual sins. Therefore we will discourse of the most principal. There is,

1. Deadly or pardonable sins, which we commit either through ignorance, that we know not better, or of infirmity through the perverseness of our corrupt nature, or through carelessness, that we do not consider better. They are called pardonable sins, because God is so gracious, and forgives them when we confess them; and even if we cannot, or do not understand them, God is so merciful as to pardon them. Therefore must we always say, with the Psalmist, *Lord, who can understand his errors? Cleanse you me from secret faults.* Therefore had God ordered in the Old Testament; that everyone that sins either through ignorance or malice, should bring his certain sacrifice, and his sins should be forgiven.

2. Deadly sins are they which men commit willfully against their own knowledge and conscience, and continue in the same without repentance, and Christian proposal of a better life. They are called deadly sins, because they wound the conscience, they extinguish the faith, they grieve the Holy Spirit, and cause eternal death and damnation, except the sinner repents, and receives forgiveness.

3. Small and great sins. Christ compares the small sins by *motes,* and the great ones by *beams.* We can perceive therefore, that all sins are not alike; Sins against God are greater than against men; likewise against many than against one; against a friend, than against a stranger; against a widow or orphan, than against any other. He that has authority, or is in any post, and subdues another through spite or malice, commits a greater sin, than a particular man having no

authority, revenges his own spite on his neighbor. A sin committed willfully is greater than one committed ignorantly; a sin in the church is greater than in another place; and a sin of a believer being enlightened is greater than of an unbeliever.

4. Our own and strange sins. Our own sins are they which we commit ourselves; strange sins are committed by others, but may in some regard be attributed to ourselves, as full as if they were committed by ourselves: The accidents by which we may make ourselves partakers in strange sins are following.

First, when we command another to do a wicked action. King *Saul* ordered his *footmen to slay the priests of the Lord:* King David *wrote in a letter to* Joab, *that he should set* Uriah *in the forefront of the hottest battle:* King *Jeroboam* did put up *two calves of gold*, and brought *Israel* to idolatry: *Jezebel* wrote false letters in king *Ahab*'s name, and deprived thereby *Naboth* of his life and vineyard.

Secondly, when we give bad council and advice. *When* Herod *kept his birthday, and the daughter of* Herodias *danced before him, it pleased* Herod *so well, that he promised with an oath, to give her whatsoever she should ask. But she being before instructed of her mother, said, give me here* John *Baptist's head in a charger*. The mother was here guilty in the death of *John*, through her wicked advice.

Thirdly, When we consent or join with others in their Sin; the Receiver is as bad as the Thief; not alone they who commit the Sin, but also they who consent therein, are guilty. *Saul*, who consented in the death of *Stephen*, was as guilty as they who stoned him, although he took only care of their clothes.

Fourthly, When we delude another to sin, and say, *Come with us, let us day wait for blood, let us lurk privily, we shall find all precious substance; we shall fill our houses with spoil: Cast in your lot among us, and let us all have one purse.* The Jews were willing to destroy Christ, but they wanted *Judas* to betray him.

Fifthly, when they who should punish malefactors, pardons them, and lets them escape; which can and may happen in all conditions in spiritual: So says the Lord: *When the minister, who is placed as a watchman, does not speak to warn the wicked from his way, the wicked shall die in his iniquity, but the blood will I require of the minister's hand.* When *Pilate* released *Barrabas*, then he became guilty in his wickedness. *Eli* the High Priest was judged and punished, because he, knowing the iniquity of his sons, he restrained them not.

5. Crying and dumb sins. Crying sins are they that cry to heaven for vengeance from God; there are four sorts according to the Scripture, *First*, bloodshed or manslaughter: *Secondly*, the sin of *Sodom*: *Thirdly*, the oppression of the poor; and *Fourthly*, the keeping back the hire of the laborer. Dumb sins are they that are committed either with beasts, as the men of *Sodom*; or with our own sex, as the heathens; or with ourselves as *Onan*; which the Apostle St. *Paul*, calls *effeminacy*. These, although they may be called crying sins, are dumb sins, in regard that they are so heinous, that we cannot with modesty speak of them.

6. Corporal and spiritual sins. Corporal sins are the actions, whereto we are brought through the remnants of sin which is in us, and in our flesh. St. *Paul* calls them, *the filthiness of the flesh*; and these are *adultery, fornication, uncleanness, lasciviousness*, and so forth. Spiritual sins are they which arises in us, to hinder and draw us off from the work of regeneration, and the progress of our spiritual condition; as negligence in using the means God has given of his grace, for the promoting of our regeneration, and renewing of the Holy Spirit; as the unfaithful servant who hid away his talent in the earth; or ambition, and the exalting ourselves above others, through the abundance of revelation.

7. Sins without the body, or against the body. Sin without the body, is when the thing, wherein we sin, or the instruments wherewith

we sin, is without the body; as, when one drinks until drunk, then is the liquor wherewith the sin is committed without his body; when a thief steals, then is the goods without his body. Sin against the body is, when the body is both the thing where against we sin, and the instrument wherewith we sin, as in fornication.

8. Sin against the Holy Spirit: Whereof Christ says in our text, *All manner of sin and blasphemy shall be forgiven unto men; but the blasphemy against the Holy Spirit shall not be forgiven unto men. And whosoever speaks a word against the Son of Man, it shall be forgiven him; but whosoever speaks against the Holy Spirit, it shall not be forgiven him, neither in this world, nor in the world to come.* Christ speaks in these words of two sorts of sin.

First, of sin against the Son of Man, which shall be forgiven. This sin consists in denying of Christ, and his word, and in the blaspheming of him, though not willfully and provokingly; but either through ignorance that we know no better, or through fear or force. St. *Peter*, St. *Paul*, and the crucifiers of Christ were guilty of this sin. St. *Peter* did deny and forswear Christ with his will, but not willfully, through fear that he should be taken, and condemned with his Master: St. *Paul* did persecute Christ and his followers, but did it ignorantly. The crucifiers of Christ did it ignorantly: *For had they known it, they would not have crucified the Lord of Glory.*

Secondly, of sin against the Holy Spirit, which shall not be forgiven, neither in this world, neither in the world to come. That we may rightly understand the nature *of the sin against the Holy Spirit*; then must we consider the following, namely, why it is called *sin against the Holy Spirit*; wherein it consists, and why *it shall not be forgiven.* Why it is called, *Sin against the Holy Spirit.* Not in regard to the person of the Holy Spirit, as if this sin was and is committed against him exclusive of the Father and the Son; for he that sins against the one person, sins against them all three; for they are three persons in one godly essence. But it is called so, in regard to the ministerial office of the Holy Spirit, wherein he instructs, enlightens, and admonishes men, and thereby seals and confirms them to be children of God: He that condemns this work of the Holy Spirit, and will not be corrected by the Word of God, neither, will be guided by the Spirit of God, but continues willfully in his wickedness, even against his knowledge and conscience, until his death; he commits *sin against the Holy Spirit*; and this is called here *blasphemy against the Holy Spirit.*

Wherein consists *the sin against the Holy Spirit.* There are four parts belonging to this sin, and they must all four be together, if it shall be *the sin against the Holy Spirit.* Namely,

1. That we know and understand the word of God, and acknowledge the same, so that we have been enlightened: St. *Paul* calls them that commit *sin against the Holy Spirit; who were once enlightened, and have tasted of the heavenly gifts, and were made partakers of the Holy Spirit, and have tasted the good word of God, and the powers of the world to come, and have received the knowledge of the truth.* We can see hereof, that they who have been enlightened, can alone be guilty of this sin.

2. That we, although we are enlightened, deny, forswear, and blaspheme God, and his word, and oppose the same willfully, through malice, against our own conscience and knowledge.

3. That we thereupon persecute the followers and true believers of Christ, and his word.

4. That we continue therein till the end of our life, and at last die in the same; and therefore is it called *a sin unto death*; not that other sins are no sins unto death, but because, that he who *sins against the Holy Spirit*, continues therein until his temporal death, whereupon follows certainly eternal death.

Of these four parts shall we know *the sin against the Holy Spirit*, and they must all four be together, and continue so, in order to make out *the sin against the Holy Spirit*; which sin cannot be forgiven. We will now see the reasons.

Why the sin against the Holy Spirit, shall not be forgiven. It is not because the grace of God is not great enough to forgive all sins, neither that he will not forgive: No, for the grace of God is greater than the sins of the whole world. *And the Lord has no pleasure in the death of a sinner, but that the wicked turn away from his wickedness and live*; neither is it because the merits of Christ is not sufficient atonement for sins; but it proceeds from man himself, whose ungodliness is so great, that he rejects and condemns all the gracious means from God, by which his conversion and salvation should be worked out. Can anyone that condemns the means of salvation, obtain salvation? God uses no other means for the promoting of man's salvation than his Word, wherein is declared his grace, the merits of Christ, and the confirmation and testimony of the Holy Spirit. How therefore can he, that has abused the grace of God, *has trodden underfoot the Son of God, and has counted the blood of the covenant, wherewith he was sanctified, an unholy thing, and has done despite unto the Spirit of God*; and dies at last in this his wickedness, and abomination, expect forgiveness and salvation? That is impossible as our Savior says in our text.

I come to the last part of my discourse, which is,

III. What Punishment follows on Sin.

Every sin deserves punishment both temporal here, and eternal hereafter, if there is no sincere repentance and conversion; it goes with sin and the punishment thereof, as with *Esau* and *Jacob*, whose *hand took hold on the others heel*; and as *Goliath*, who had his sword, wherewith his head was to be cut off, hanging by his side. That sin shall be punished either in this world, or in the world to come, we can prove by the following.

1. Of the justice of God; since God is just in his essence, then is it his immutable will, that man, who is a reasonable creature, should live according to the rule of righteousness prescribed in his law; and if man does not live according to that, he will certainly be punished therefor.

2. Of the serious threatenings of God, which we meet with through the whole Scripture: For, as God will not be served of us for nothing, but rewards us in all our good actions, with temporal and spiritual blessings; so will he neither let our bad actions pass unpunished, but he will certainly visit us for them, here or hereafter.

3. Of several examples: The angels who sinned were plunged into hell; the first world perished by the sin-flood; *Sodom* and *Gomorrah* were consumed with fire and brimstone from heaven; the *Egyptians* were destroyed in the Red Sea; the children of *Israel* were troubled in the wilderness; the *Canaanites* were drove out of their country: What are such and the like examples, than plain proofs of God's vengeance. The punishment that follows on sin are following.

The *first* punishment, is remorse of conscience, which arises oftentimes as soon as the sin is committed. We can see therefore the justice of God, that, as the thoughts are the first place where sin is conceived, so are they likewise the first place, where sin is punished: We may escape from man, but never from our conscience: Why is conscience so terrified, after sin is committed? Because it is afraid of God, who is a just avenger of all evil; and this terror is nothing else then a post errant from the justice of God, who has pronounced this sentence in his Law. *Cursed is he, that confirms not, all the words of this law, to do them.* Thereupon follows.

The *second* punishment, is the anger of God, and the curse of the law, God has revealed his will in the law, and threatened the transgressors of his law with a curse; and since God is vexed with

Sin, then follows thereon,

The *third* punishment; which is, the departing of the Holy Spirit. For into a malicious heart or soul wisdom will not enter, or dwell in a body that is subject unto sin; and the Holy Spirit of discipline will free deceit, and remove from thoughts that are without understanding: When the Spirit of God is departed, then follows thereon.

The *fourth* punishment; which is, that God punishes sin with sin. Not that God should cause anyone to sin, or put Satan on to do it; no, but that God in vengeance of our sins, and the contempt of his word and grace, draws his help and assistance from us, and then goes it with the sinner, as the Lord said of the *Jews* by the prophet *Isaiah. Hear you indeed, but understand not; and see you indeed, but perceive not, make the heart of this people fat, and their ears heavy, and shut their eyes; lest they see with their eyes, and hear with their ears, and understand with their hearts, and convert, and be healed.* When that comes, then follows;

The *fifth* punishment, which is hardness of heart, consisting in hardness of mind, and blindness in the spirit: This befalls obstinate sinners for their former crimes, and wherewith God punishes them, either, that there happens to them such things, by which they could be converted, but through the malice of their own heart, they became hardened as *Pharaoh's* was; or that God do not grant unto them his grace and Spirit, which they have so long and so often resisted, that they could be converted thereby, as the *Jews*; or, that God permits Satan to take them with his snares, as *Judas*. They who are of opinion, that God hardens the heart of men, because the apostle St. *Paul* says, *God has mercy on whom he will have mercy, and whom he will he hardens.* They do injustice, for God hardens none; but man being of his own obstinate will, disobedient to the word of admonition from the Lord; he is himself the cause of his own hardness of heart, though this hardness of heart is ascribed to God; since he of a just vengeance over sin, takes away his Holy Spirit and grace, from such abominable condemners of his word and gracious means; whereupon the Devil takes full possession of their hearts, as a king of his palace; and they become like a ship without a rudder driving before wind and weather. We cannot accuse God for injustice herein, since they had so shamefully refused his grace; also it is, that God is said to harden man's heart, although they themselves are the cause thereof, in resisting the gracious means offered unto them: In this sense must we understand the Scripture, when it says, *That the Lord hardened* Pharaoh's *heart*; for what is here ascribed unto the Lord, is in other places ascribed to *Pharaoh* himself, who *hardened his heart*; also, since the Lord showed *Pharaoh* his grace, and did send *Moses* and *Aaron* to him, for to procure the liberty of the children of *Israel* from their bondage, whom *Pharaoh* would not obey, neither when he saw the many miracles wrought before him, would be convinced; is the Lord said to have hardened *Pharaoh's* heart; because he in his wrath gave him over as a just judge a criminal, to his obstinacy, as a punishment for his wickedness and disobedience. At last follows.

The *sixth* punishment, which is eternal death and damnation. *The wages of sin is death*, not alone the temporal, but also the eternal hereafter. Therefore must we always be careful, and cautious of sin, and flee from sin, as from the face of a serpent; for, if we come too nigh to it, it will bite us; *the teeth thereof are as the teeth of a lion*, slaying the souls of men.

The Lord give us his grace, and enlighten our hearts with his Holy Spirit, and keep us from all evil and mischief, that we may be found unpunishable on the Day of our Lord Jesus Christ. AMEN.

13

God's Providence

T he Text Acts 17:24, 25, 26, 27, 28, Verses

GOD that made the world, and all things therein; seeing that he is Lord of heaven and earth, dwells not in temples made with hands: Neither is worshiped with man's hands, as though he needed anything; seeing he gives to all life and breath, and all things: And has made of one blood, all nations of men, for to dwell on all the face of the earth, and hath determined the times before appointed, and the bounds of their habitation. That they should seek the Lord, if happily they might feel after him, and find him, though he be not far from everyone of us: For in him we live and move, and have our being.

INTRODUCTION

WHEN *Simon* the High Priest had finished the service before the congregation of all *Israel*, in the temple in *Jerusalem*, then he went down, and listed up his hands over the whole congregation, and gave the blessing of the Lord, and after the blessing was ended, he bowed himself down to worship, and to receive a blessing from the Most

High, and said, *Now bless you the God of all, who only does wondrous things everywhere, which exalts our days from the womb, and deals with us according to his mercy: He grants us joyfulness of heart, and that peace may be in our days in* Israel *forever: That he would confirm his mercy with us, and deliver us at his time*; as we may read in *Ecclesiasticus Sirach*, 22, 23, 24.

Simon the High Priest encourages here, with these words, the congregation of *Israel*, to thanksgiving to God for all the blessings they had received. We must likewise be encouraged as true spiritual *Israelites*, to praise and thank the Lord for all his blessings bestowed upon us; whereof some are past, some are present, and some are to come.

The past blessings are *again some* before we were born, and *some* after: Some concerns the goods of nature, some the goods of grace, and some the goods of fortune. Before we were born, God exalted our days in our mother's womb; our days cannot well be said, to begin perfectly before we were born, for as long as a child lies in his mother's womb, it cannot be said to have days, as well as after the birth, when it begins to breathe the common air: Though God has exalted our days from our mother's womb; for he knew us, when we were yet unborn, as the Psalmist says: *Thine eyes did see my substance yet being imperfect:* And he has wonderfully formed our bodies in our mother's womb, as *Job* says, *Have you not poured me out as milk, and curdled me like cheese? You have clothed me with skin and flesh, and hast fenced me with bones and sinews, and has brought us forth alive in the time of our birth*: And after we were born, he exalts our days in our cradles, that we grew up with sound and heal your bodies; has carried us as upon his hands, and guarded us by his angels in our infancy; has guided us by his hands in our youth, has advised us in our manhood, and he deals yet daily with us according to his mercy. O! how often have we vexed him in our lifetime, yet he has not cut off the thread of our life, but exalts daily our days, and grants to us one joyful day after another. And this is,

The present blessings; they are,

First, he deals with us according to his mercy. The mercy of God is a fountain, whereof flows all other heavenly gracious gifts; like the river in Paradise, that was parted in four heads; so is the mercy of God parted in four heads to water men. The *first* is the creation. The *second* the preservation. The *third* the redemption; and the *fourth* the sanctification. All these have their origin from the bottomless pit of God's mercy; *Of mercy* he forgives us our sins; *Of mercy* he has compassion over his people; *Of mercy* he comforts us; *Of mercy* he grants to us all what is needful for this and the eternal life; *Of mercy* he keeps us from evil; *Of mercy* he has created us; *Of mercy* he rises us up, when we fall; *Of mercy* he holds us up when we stand; *Of mercy* he guides us, when we walk; *Of mercy* he comforts us, when we are afflicted; *Of mercy* he rejoices us, when we are troubled; and *Of mercy* he strengthens us, when we are weak. We cannot praise the mercy of God enough, for it is as great as he is himself, and it is infinite and immeasurable.

Secondly, he grants us joyfulness of heart. There are two forts of joyfulness, namely, corporal and spiritual.

The corporal joyfulness is either lawful or unlawful: *Lawful* joyfulness is what a man has, *to whom God has given wealth and power, to eat and drink thereof, and to take his portion, and to rejoice in his labor*; *this is the gift of God:* Likewise when we are rejoiced over the blessings of God, thank him for them, and employ them to the glory of his holy Name, and to the help of our wanting neighbor. *Unlawful* joyfulness is, when we are but rejoiced over riches and wealth, and will not do any good therewith, as *Nabal*, or over honor and power as *Haman*, or over luxury and plenty, as *dives*. The foolish children of this world can tickle themselves with such, but it is no true joyfulness of heart, for there is no root nor ground of true joy herein; therefore do they deceive themselves, who think that the joy of this world is true joy. *They may well for some time spread themselves like a green bay-tree, but they will not be found more at last.*

Spiritual joyfulness is a true undeceivable joyfulness of heart, proceeding from the grace of God, and the comfort of the Holy Spirit, which flows out always with living nourishment in the Lord in the midst of the greatest grief; for it assures a child of God, that he has peace with God through Jesus Christ, *and has a conscience void of offence towards God and men*; and therefore always rejoiced although in the greatest calamity, for he knows that his cross comes from God, with a good intention. *Since God does not afflict willingly, nor grieve the children of men.* He never permits any evil to happen, without having in view, to make some good of it: He gives strength in sufferings; and when the Lord has given unto his children so much of the red wine, as is poured out in the cup of salvation, and that he knows they can bear, and they are thereby become unable to sin, and strong to pray; then crowns he them at last with salvation, and he is likewise rejoiced in death; for he does not look on death with natural eyes as the heathens; but with faithful eyes as being a door and entrance to life everlasting, and an unbinding of this worldly.

Thirdly, he gives us peace in our days: There is three sorts of peace, *outward, inward*, and *eternal.*

Outward peace is again either common or particular; *common* peace is, when kings and princes on earth live peaceably and in alliance: This is a great blessing, and comes from God; and when we have this peace, we must thank God therefore, and pray that it may continue so in our days; and when it is gone, we must again in humility seek it from the Lord. *Who makes wars to cease unto the end of the earth, he breaks the bow, and cuts the spear asunder, the burns the chariot in the fire.* Particular peace is between neighbor and neighbor, friend and friend, relation and relation. *This is one of the fruits of the spirit; when a man's ways please the Lord, he makes even his enemies to be at peace with him.*

Inward peace is the peace of conscience, and is called the peace of God, because it comes from God; is procured by Christ, is sealed and confirmed by the Holy Spirit; is offered in the gospel, is preached by the ministers of God, and is received by faith. This peace consists herein; *That we are assured of the forgiveness of sin, have peace with God, through Jesus Christ; makes the word of God shine in our hearts, and subdues our will from wickedness, alone through love and obedience to God, that we shall not disturb again the peace of our conscience.* We often feel the sparks of the inbred sin, but through the grace of God we quench the same, and are willing to receive all that comes, being assured that, *although the mountains should depart, and the hills be removed, yet shall not the covenant of the peace of the Lord be removed:* Let the whole world, and even death, storm against a heart, it is not affected, as long as the conscience rests in the Lord, and has peace with God: In regard to this, says the Psalmist: *Rest in the Lord, and wait patiently for him.*

The *eternal* peace we shall receive in heaven, when we have conquered all the enemies, that troubled and tempted us in this world; then shall the people of God *dwell in a peaceable habitation, and in sure dwellings, and in quiet resting places.*

The blessings to come are,

First, that he confirms his mercy with us: The greatest mercy and grace God shown to the *Jews,* was that he entrusted them with his word, and dealt not so with any other nation. St. *Paul* says of them therefore; *Who are* Israelites, *to whom pertains the adoption, and the glory,* (in the many miracles) *and the covenants,* (God made his covenant with *Abraham* by the circumcision, and promised unto his seed a new covenant) *and the giving of the law,* (on Mount *Sinai*) *and the service of God* (the *Levitical* offerings and ceremonies) *and the promises*, (not alone temporal of the land of *Canaan*, but also spiritual of the *Messiah*); but, because they condemned the word of God, and rejected his grace, God did depart from them, took his holiness from them, and chose another people, who will put a higher value on his mercy; God has now entrusted us with his word, and with his mercy, therefore let us walk circumspectly therewith, left God take it from us again; God has not entrusted us with his word and mercy on other conditions, than that we shall be accountable thereof; as we can see of the parable of the king, who called his servants to account.

Secondly, that he delivers us at this time, not alone from all evil wherewith we are surrounded in the time of our life, but also in the time of our sickness; but especially in the time of our death. We must pray to God for this, and thank him for the manifold blessings he has bestowed upon us, and say, *Now bless you the God of all:* We cannot pay God cheaper for all his blessings, than with thanksgiving; which can best be done, when we acknowledge them with our hearts, speak of them with our mouths, and show it in our actions. The Apostle St. *Paul* praises this bountiful God and his almighty providence in our text. Whereof we will consider,

FIRST, *That God has not alone created all things, but preserves all things yet daily.*

SECOND, *Wherein providence consists in particular.*

EXPLANATION of the TEXT. PART I

I. That God has not alone created all things, but preserves all things yet daily.

When we see a neat and beautiful piece of work, then falls always on our thoughts, who is the Master who has projected, completed and finished the same: Do we behold the world, and all that is therein, then our thoughts draw us to the Master, who has created all: We see in all the created things in nature such a complete order, that one thing is above another, the reasonable above the unreasonable, the heavenly above the earthly; that one creature must serve the other, and that the whole nature is in amity together, and nothing is against another, or else it would cause confusion; We behold ourselves, then points our creation to us the Master thereof; although nature learns us, that one is born of another, and that everyone has his father and mother, of whom he is generated; yet our reason tells us, that the first man, from whom we all are descended, could as little have created himself, as men can now do; therefore has there certainly been a Master who created him, and gave him life, and who preserves yet daily the race of mankind, and gives them life and breath. This is it, that the apostle will have the *Athenians* to understand, and preaches therefore to them in our text, of God and his providence; for when he, as the apostle of the gentiles, came in his travels to the city of *Athens*, where there was a high school, and beheld their devotions, then found he an altar with this inscription, *To the unknown God*; the meaning whereof should be, that if there was any other God, besides their gods, then should this altar be erected to this unknown God. St. *Paul* took hereby Occasion and Cause to instruct the *Athenians* of the true God, and carried them to the creation and preservation of the world; that they thereof should acknowledge the Creator; of whom St. *Paul* says, that he is

1. *The only Lord*: The *Athenians* had many altars, and the city was

wholly given to idolatry, but the apostle will convince them, *that there is but one God*, and speaks therefore of God as of one, saying, *God that made the world:* We shall not take the name God, as a title of honor, so as when the angels and magistrates are called gods; but for the only true God, in opposition to the false Gods, whom the *Athenians* worshiped; for when God is called in the Scripture with this name, then is shewed therein his godly essence, by which he is separated from all others, who are no gods. He is the,

2. *Almighty, that made the world;* The heathen philosophers were of opinion, that the world was eternal, and had no beginning, neither would have an end, but St. *Paul* will convince them here of their error, and says therefore, *God that made the world.* Who of their invented gods could do such a work? This is a plain and visible proof of the infinite majesty, power and wisdom of God, by which the Lord distinguishes himself from all false gods. *He has made the earth by his power, he has established the world by his wisdom, and has stretched out the heavens by his power:* And as he has created all things, so does he preserve them daily, that nothing shall be lost and destroyed. Directly otherwise does an artificer, who, after the building is finished, goes away, and is not further concerned about it. *Who knows not*, says *Job, in all these, that the hand of the Lord has wrought this? In whose hands are the soul of every living thing, and the breath of all mankind.* His providence governs and upholds all things; the Son of God upholds all things by the power of his word; *he is before all things, and by him all things consist:* He answered therefore the *Jews* who accused him with the breaking of the Sabbath, because he had healed the impotent man on a Sabbath day; *My Father works hitherto and I work.* The meaning hereof is; you accuse me with breaking the Sabbath, but you shall know that I am not so bound to the law of the Sabbath, as you think; for, as my Father, although he rested on the seventh day from creating, does not rest from preserving, but he

preserves all things as well on the Sabbath, as working days; in the same manner do I work as a true God with the Father; especially as this is a work that cannot be fixed on a certain time or day, but must be done continually. He is

3. *Commanding*; He is Lord of heaven and earth: *When he speaks it is done, and when he commands, it stands fast*: If he will have a thing done, none can withstand it, neither can anyone say, *What do you do?* Therefore is he called *Lord Sabaoth*; that is, the Lord of Hosts. That as a general has to command over his army, so commands God the whole nature, and has a mighty, a well ordered, and obedient army.

A mighty army has the Lord. If we look up to heaven, *he has there millions and his millions of angels, that do obey commands: He has the stars, and brings out their hosts by number, he calls them by names. The stars in their courses fought against Sisera. He has the thunder and lightning, and therewith is the voice of his excellency heard. He has the stormy winds, to fulfill his words; he commands the clouds to go over the whole world, he has fire and hail for vengeance over the ungodly:* The sun stood still in the time of *Joshua*, and went back on the shadow, in the time of *Hezekiah*, and was darkened in the time of Christ's sufferings. The elements are likewise belonging to the army of God; *the earth swallowed up* Corah, Dathan *and* Abiram, *and their company*: The waters drowned the first world, and swallowed up *Pharaoh*, and all his might; fire and brimstone consumed *Sodom* and *Gomorah*, and on the contrary did not hurt the three men, that were cast in the fiery oven. The beasts and unreasonable creatures are likewise reckoned in the army of God: A lion, tore the disobedient prophet; two bears tore forty-two children of *Bethel*, and the Lord threatens, that he will send wild beasts among the disobedient, who shall bereave them of their children, and destroy their cattle: The insects and vermin, are also under the army of God; palmer worm, locusts, canker worm, and caterpillars, destroys the harvest of the field. The devils and evil spirits are also under this mighty army of God, and the Lord uses them as executioners over the disobedient and ungodly.

A well-ordered army has the Lord. Can a general put all his whole army in good order, before a battle begins; much more can God, being a God of order and decency, bring forth his army.

An obedient army has the Lord. When he calls for famine, it comes; when he calls for corn and fruit it comes, and there is plenty; yea, all that he calls for, sword, drought, they come all at his command. He is,

4. *Holy.* He will be honored, served, and worshiped, not in such ways as human reason can invent; for our reason is blind in the godly things; neither as we think it right in our own eyes; neither dwells God in temples made with hands, as if he was enclosed or confined there, as the heathens thought, for he needed no temple: King *Solomon* builds a stately temple in *Jerusalem*, there was no such other in the world; and yet said *Solomon, should God surely dwell on earth?* The heathens had temples for their idols, but they were only synagogues of the Devil, with whom God will not have any fellowship; neither will God be worshiped alone with outward ceremonies: Therefore said he to the prophet; *I hate, I despise your feast days, and I will not smell in your solemn assemblies:* And as God dwells not in temples made with hands, so will he neither be worshiped with man's hands, as though he needed anything: *For the earth is the Lords, and the faithfulness thereof, the world, and they that dwell therein: Yea if we would offer to the Lord,* Lebanon *is not sufficient to burn, nor the beasts thereof sufficient for a burnt-offering.* He is,

5. *Mild,* He gives to all life and breath, and all things. He created the two first men, *Adam* and *Eve, Adam* of the earth, and *Eve* of one of *Adam*'s ribs. From them again are all men descended by the natural conception and birth, wherein God acts the chief part, *for he gives all life and breath,* as *Job* and *David* acknowledge; yea all that is needful

for the preservation of the whole nature, God gives daily: Hereby can we be convinced of the providence of God. He is,

6. *Wise*, which we can best perceive of the following three articles.

First, he has made of one blood, all nations of men, for to dwell on all the face of the earth, from the origin. One man is not higher nor more worthy than another, for all are made of one blood; we are all descended from *Adam* and *Eve*, and afterwards from *Noah*.

Secondly, he has determined the times before appointed; we can see, that the times and seasons have their regular order, one after another; *He appoints the moon for seasons, the sun knows his going down*; the stars shine in their watch and order.

Thirdly, and the bounds of their habitation; God had in the beginning divided the whole earth among men, and given the earth to the children of men. After the flood God settled all the bounds, and gave to every nation their limits and inheritance, as *Moses* said to the children of *Israel: When the Most High divided to the nations their inheritance, when he separated the son of* Adam, *he set the bounds of the people, according to the number of* Israel. He is,

7. *Omnipresent.* He is not far from us, for in him we live, and move, and have our being; a worldly king or lord cannot be over all his dominions, therefore has he stewards or viceroys, to govern in his stead. But God is over all; *Can any hide himself in secret places, that I shall not see him says the Lord*; *do not I fill heaven and earth says the Lord:* None can fly away from the presence of God, he hears all what we say, he sees all what we do, he counts our steps, and knows our thoughts.

We have here to consider, PART II

II. How it consists with the providence of God

We must know that the providence of God, is the all-knowing knowledge and foresight of God over the whole creation, and all the creatures, which he governs and preserves wisely, justly and freely, to the glory of his holy Name, and the welfare of men: The providence of God is called likewise in the Scripture; *The eye of God:* One having clear eyes, can plainly see all that comes before him, much plainer sees and knows God everything that is committed, either in public or privacy. His eyes are clearer than the sun: *The darkness and the light are alike to him*; and shall we not think that this is a simple sight without effect and power? No, for it is called in other places of the Scripture; *The ordinances of God, by which heaven and earth consist*; *the upholding of all things, and the care of God.*

We cannot call the providence of God with a more proper name, than the economy of God, since the earth, sea, heaven, and all what is in them are his; and he, as a householder and Father, upholds and preserves them all, daily and continually: If a father of a house governs his house rightly and wisely, then he must observe these three things. *First*, he must be well acquainted, and have a foreknowledge of his house. *Secondly*, he must form to himself a purpose and conclusion, concerning the governing, preserving and upholding of his house. *Thirdly*, he must have thoughts, and be concerned for the work of his house in itself; likewise do these three parts belong to the providence of God.

1. A foreknowledge of everything. This foreknowledge is but ascribed to God by us in a human way, in order to help our weak understanding. God has knowledge of everything, not after the alteration and change of times and seasons, as if he needed to gather this knowledge by experience; no, but the knowledge of God is in a moment, that he sees and knows all and all in an instant: God

knows all his work from eternity. This foreknowledge of God, is either common, particular or personal.

The *common* foreknowledge of God extends to all things. That God sees all things before, and knows the hour and moment when everything shall happen, and sees it all in one sight; *The Lord looks from heaven, he beholds all the sons of men, from the place of his habitation*; *he looks upon all the inhabitants of the earth*; *yea, he understands our thoughts afar off.*

The *particular* foreknowledge of God extends to the faithful: He knows before, and has seen from eternity, who should believe in Jesus Christ, and remain steadfast in their faith to their lives end. And, they are the elect; he knows all their actions and inclinations, and is pleased therewith; *The Lord knows the way of the righteous:* The foundation of God stands sure, having this seal; *The Lord knows them that are his:* In regard to this says St. *Paul* of the Jews: *Has God cast away his people? God forbid. God has not cast away his people whom he foreknew*; namely, that should believe in Christ, and remain steadfast to their lives end.

The *personal* foreknowledge of God extends to Christ, whose incarnation, suffering, death, resurrection and ascension, God had foreseen from eternity; yea, even them who should betray, condemn, and crucify him; so that nothing happened to Christ but what God had foreseen, and knew from eternity, that should befall him, and had therefore foretold the same by the prophets. We should not be of that opinion, that all this befell Christ, because God had foreseen and foretold it: No, for thereof would follow, that God had instigated the enemies of Christ, to complete their wickedness, because he should not be deceived in his foreknowledge: A thing happens not because God knew it should happen, but because it shall happen; therefore God knows and sees it, for he knows and sees everything. Therefore said St. *Peter* to the Jews; *Jesus of Nazareth being delivered*

by the determinate counsel and foreknowledge of God you have taken,
and by wicked hands have crucified and slain: St. Peter says in another
place: *He was foreordained before the foundation of the world:* It was
the council and will of God, that Christ should die for us, though God
did not drive the enemies on, to take and crucify him: The action
displeases God, but the suffering pleases him.

2. A purpose and conclusion concerning the welfare of the house:
This extends,

First, to all creatures in general; when God decrees from eternity
to create all things; for all what God makes in time, he has ordained
from eternity.

Secondly, to men alone, when God had decreed from eternity,
to create men in holiness and righteousness after his own image,
and saw that men would fall; then decreed he likewise, to take the
fallen men again in his grace, and not plunge them into hell, as the
fallen angels, and therefore to send his beloved Son Jesus Christ;
who should raise up again the fallen men, and reconcile them to
God, through his death and sufferings, and thereupon ordained the
gracious means of salvation. In regard to this, says St. *Paul; God*
made known unto us (in the Gospel) *the mystery of his will,* (to save us
through Christ) *according to his good pleasure, which he hath purposed*
in himself: That in the dispensation of the fullness of time, be might
gather together in one, all things in Christ, both which are in heaven and
which are on earth. This purpose of God concerning the salvation of
men, belongs to the antecedent will of God; after which he will, that
all men should be saved, and come to the knowledge and confession
of truth.

Thirdly, to the faithful in particular, *who are predestined according*
to the purpose of him who works all things after the counsel of his
own will: For, it pleased God by the foolishness of preaching, to save*
them that believe. Thereby likewise to the condemners of God's

197

word, to hide from them the mystery of the gospel concerning the obtaining of salvation, through faith in Jesus Christ: For, since so many are careless and neglectful of their own salvation, that they do not thank God for such high grace, but condemn and despise the same, although so plainly revealed in the gospel of Christ, in whom salvation is offered to all; so has God decreed in his justice, to hide from them this mystery, and to condemn them for the sake of their ingratitude and contempt; therefore did Christ thank his heavenly Father, saying; *I thank you, O Father, Lord of heaven and earth, because you have hid these things from the wise and prudent, and have revealed them unto babes; even so Father, for it seems good in your sight:* This belongs to the consequent will of God, after which he will, *that all the unbelievers shall be damned.*

3. The work of God's providence, and the upholding of all things in itself, comprehends these two parts.

First, the preserving of all things. This is so, that God has not alone endued everything in the first creation with its own natural power and virtue, by which the same shall be preserved; but that he likewise daily preserves them, so that nothing can move without the help of his almighty hand. The sun was created by God in the beginning, that he should rise every morning, and by his continual course, show us four seasons; yet says our Savior; *That God makes his sun to rise daily.*

Secondly, the governing of all things: that is, that God is the supreme ruler and governor of all things, so that nothing in the whole nature can escape his all-seeing and watchful eyes: But everything must come to the end and purpose of God's will, and serve to the glory of his holy name, and the salvation of the faithful.

God does this either by a natural or supernatural course.

By the *natural* course, God governs all things as well in the big as little world: In the big world, when he lets the sun go up daily; when he sends rain, thunder and lightning; when he lets everything grow out of the earth, and governs everything, and all the creatures. In the little world, namely, man, man himself, and all his actions, good or bad, stand all under the governing eye of God, both in the natural and gracious Kingdom.

In the *natural* kingdom, man stands under the providence of God, in the entrance, progress, and exit of his life. Let the atheist think and say what he will, concerning the conception and birth of men; that the same is mere accident of natural causes.

Can their lies and inventions make the truth of God's providence to naught? No truly, for the hands of the Lord formed us in our mother's womb; brought us forth in birth, and preserves us through the course of our lives; and, when we die, will carry our souls, by his holy angels, into *Abraham*'s bosom. Though I cannot think what these profaners will bring in, concerning the birth of cripple and defected persons. Here, say they, has God been either blind and mistaken, like a potter who may mistake in the forming of a vessel. We can give unto them no better answer hereupon, than out of the Lord's own mouth, who said, *Who made the dumb or deaf, or the seeing, or the blind? have not I the Lord? God is the potter and man is the clay. As the Potter has power over the clay of the same lump to make one vessel unto honor and another unto dishonor:* So has God much more power over men, to create one well-shaped, and another deformed. God does not do this out of any secret hatred; no, he loves all the things that are, and abhors nothing which he has made. Deformed and defected men, who live in the fear of God, are more pleasing in the sight of the Lord, than strong and wholesome who run in sin and disobedience. If such deformed had been an abhorrence to God, our Savior would not have healed so many in the time of his incarnation; besides, we read, that he called the woman, who was bowed down through infirmity, *a daughter of* Abraham: the reason hereof is alone known to God; there hangs a vail before the judgment and counsel of God, where through human reason cannot see: Though parents are often in the fault, and guilty of the deformity of their children, especially women, when they are careless in their travels. And therefore, God did order such *severe punishment for them who hurt a woman with child.* Malicious and thoughtless men have a common proverb, when they see a crippled or deformed person; 'Be cautious,' say they, of him 'whom God and nature had marked.' But we can and may answer such wicked men; *Who are you that replies against God? shall the thing formed say to him that formed it: Why have you made me thus?* God cannot forbear such wicked expressions and judgments over his creatures; *For be that mocks the poor, reproaches his Maker.* Sirach says; *Laugh no man to scorn in the bitterness of his soul, for there is one who humbles and exalts:* We often see, that God blesses such deformed persons with such abundance of sense or other qualities, that they become wonders in nature; yea, some are deformed in their bodies. God who is almighty, can again give unto them a fuller portion of his Spirit in their souls, until he at last, shall give unto them transfigured bodies, with the saints and elect, in the resurrection of the flesh.

In the gracious Kingdom, that is, the Christian church, has God care over all, but in particular over the faithful. The Lord said unto the Jews, whom he had chosen for his own people; you *have seen how I bore you on eagles wings, and brought you unto myself:* He protects his church by his holy angels; he sends faithful ministers, and brings the faithful through fire and water, and guards them among lions and dragons.

Man's actions both good and bad, are likewise under the providence and care of God.

The good actions stand two ways there under, *first,* God begins, helps, promotes, and fulfills good actions: St. *Paul* says, *it is God, which works in you, both to will, and to do of his good pleasure. Secondly,*

God is not alone pleased with good actions, but he rewards them also graciously both here and hereafter. Therefore said St. *Paul* in another place, *godliness is profitable unto all things, having promise of the life that now is, and of that which is to come.*

The bad actions stand likewise under the providence of God; not that God will, or consents to them, much less directs and commands them; for on the contrary he hates, forbids, and punishes evil; so says the Psalmist; *You are not a God, that has pleasure in wickedness, neither shall evil dwell with you: The foolish shall not stand in your sight, you hate all workers of iniquity:* Therefore if God sometimes permits evil, yet has he no pleasure therein; none should think that God beholds the evil that happens in the world, as an idle spectator, without any regard how it goes: No, God has such even eyes with hardened sinners, that he,

1st, Let them do what they will, he upholds nature, and hinders them not in their wickedness.

2ndly, He sees and knows, what they intend to do; as our Savior saw the treachery of *Judas*, and knew all what his enemies had concluded and resolved against him.

3rdly, He lets them go on, as a just judge and revenger over committed sins, after their own inclinations in wickedness, and does not assist them, to withstand the Devil, the world, and their own flesh and blood; but for their former contempt of his grace, draws away from them his Holy Spirit, by which they might be enabled to withstand all temptations. The *Jews* did despise the grace of God therefore did God take away his grace from them, *so that they should not see with eyes, neither hear with their ears:* King *Ahab* would not obey the advice of *Micaiah* the true prophet, therefore did the Lord put a lying Spirit in the mouth of the false prophets, for to deceive them.

4thly, When it comes so far, that a sinner shall commit a wicked action, then has God his reason, why the evil befalls another, then the sinner had purposed: The king of *Babylon* had drawn his sword to war, but was doubtful, either to war against the *Ammonites* or the *Jews*; but God made it so, that he left the *Ammonites*, and fell upon the *Jews*; because the Lord would punish them for their sins.

5thly, Sometimes God hinders the wicked, that they cannot fulfill their evil propositions. *The Lord plagued* Pharaoh *and his house with great plagues*, and thereby hindered him from gratifying his wicked intention, *with Sarah Abraham's wife:* God came to *Laban* the *Syrian* in a dream by night, and said unto him, *take heed, that you speak not to* Jacob *either good or bad:* We can find many more examples hereof in the Holy Scripture.

6thly, Sometimes can a wicked person have a bad intention against an innocent, but God delivers the innocent, and it falls either on a guilty, or the contriver himself. The accusers of *Daniel* brought it so far, that *Daniel* was cast into the lion's den; but God delivered *Daniel*, and the accusers were themselves cast in the den, and devoured of the lions. *Haman* had erected a high gallows, to hang *Mordecai* on, but he was himself hanged thereon, and *Mordecai* was honored. Then goes it, as *Solomon* says; *the righteous is delivered out of trouble, and the wicked comes in his stead.*

7thly, Sometimes can an opportunity be offered, whereof the wicked can take cause to do evil against the will and pleasure of God, yet speaks the Scripture thereof, as if God did it, not because he does it, or brings any to the doing thereof, but because he knows that it happens, and he permits it, though he has no pleasure in it. The king in *Egypt* and his subjects were envious against the children of *Israel*, because they increased greatly in the land, and wanted therefore to suppress them; yet says the Scripture: *That God turned the hearts of the* Egyptians, *to hate his people:* Shimei being of the family of king *Saul*, had an inward and secret hatred to *David*, who was crowned king; and also preferred before the family of *Saul*; but was afraid to show his anger publicly, as long as *David* had the power; but afterwards having an opportunity, and seeing that *David* was drove from his kingdom by his own son, he began publicly to curse *David*; though says *David, the Lord has said unto him, curse* David. The question is, how had the Lord commanded *Shimei* to curse *David?* Not by an outward command, for we do not read thereof in the Scripture, neither by an inward instigation; *For God cannot be tempted with evil, neither tempted be any man:* But the right sense hereof is, that, when *Shimei* saw, that he had now an opportunity to vent his anger against *David*, who had lost his kingdom and power, took thereof cause to curse *David:* Whereto God consented, in order to try the faith and patience of *David*, though God had no pleasure herein.

8*thly*, God observes, likewise, the bad actions thus; that they must come to the end and purpose God wills; but not as the wicked intended. *Joseph* was sold of his brethren through hatred, but God directed it otherwise than they intended, namely, for to preserve, not alone *Joseph* and all his family, but also all *Egypt* in the time of the famine. Satan intended to bring *Job* to despair, and to curse God; and therefore plagued him so sorely; but the patience of *Job* was thereby provided, and shone the brighter; and Satan became an impostor and liar.

9*thly*, God prescribes the bad actions a certain time, when they shall begin, and a certain length, how far they shall go. The *Jews sought often to take Christ, but no man laid hands on him, because his hour was not yet come*; therefore said he to the multitude, that took him on the Mount of Olives: *This is your hour, and the power of darkness:* King *Senacharib* did intend evil against King *Hezekiah*, and the city of *Jerusalem, but the Lord did put a hook in his nose, and a bridle in his lips, so that he was not able to shoot an arrow in the city.*

In *supernatural*; God often shows his care and providence with wonders and miracles, as Lord and Master of the whole nature; who can do what he will, not being bound to nature, or natural causes; in order to show his almighty power, for thereby to comfort the faithful, and to punish the ungodly. The sun stood still in the time of *Joshua*, went back in the time of *Hezekiah*, was darkened three days in *Egypt*, and three hours in the sufferings of Christ. These and many other such miracles, that we read of in the Scripture, are plain proofs of God's almighty power over the whole nature; so that nature itself would be altered before God should be disappointed in his purpose. Can God do such supernatural things, much more, and easier can he govern all things by the natural course: Though, should we not think, that God has more and harder work in the one than the other? No, for we can see, that the earth, the sea, and all things were created of nothing by his word. Although God is not bound to nature, or natural causes, yet has he bound us men to them, and chooses that we should use natural means, when we can have them, and leave the event to God; and they that use the means God has ordained shall be helped; but they, that condemn the same, tempt the Lord, and cannot expect help from him: *Jacob* had promise of God, that God would be with him, and help him in all places whither he went; yet did he all that he could, to obtain the friendship of his brother *Esau*. God could himself have kept his Son without means, yet uses he *Joseph*, who went into *Egypt* with the mother and young child: Our Savior in the time of his incarnation, could easily have walked always on the sea; yet he chose the ships, when there was any to be had; but when no natural means or help do appear, then must we depend alone on the providence of God, as *Esther* said, *I will go in unto the king, which is not according to the law, and if I perish, I perish; Abraham* did not know what to offer in the room of his son, but the Lord knew where the ram was caught in the thicket by his horns. We should therefore with the greatest reverence consider the providence of God, and honor him in all things, since he governs all things wisely to the honor of his holy name, and the salvation of the faithful.

Should any particular accident happen, we must therefore not think that God's providence is therefore diminished, and that God was not concerned, neither knew what happened: No, for the Lord knows and sees the least thing that happens, although they seem to us, to be but mere trifles, yea, even the cast of the lot is disposed of the Lord; neither should we think, that because God knows and fees a thing before, that therefore the same thing must absolutely happen thus, and not otherwise, by reason that God shall not be mistaken or disappointed in his decree; No, we must not have such abominable thoughts and conclusions of God; for thereof would follow, that God was the cause and author of all sin and evil in the world, since he knows and sees all things before. Likewise would follow thereof, that the wicked, who die in their sin, could not otherwise than die therein, because God had seen and known it before; such thoughts and opinions are the greatest blasphemy against God: On the contrary, according to such opinions, the faithful never could fall from their faith, which can happen, as the Spirit of the Lord convinces us of, and therefore admonishes us; *Take heed brethren, left there be in any of you an evil heart of unbelief, in departing from the living God:* you should be careful, *that you receive not the grace of God in vain: Beware left you fall from your own steadfastness. Work out your own salvation with fear and trembling.* As an astrologer is not the cause and author of an eclipse, because he has seen the same before; so is God neither the cause of sin, because he has seen it before in his all-seeing and all-knowing wisdom.

It is a very false opinion, that some have, and say therefore, when any misfortune befalls them, it was so fore ordained, or decreed; or else, it was so my fortune; wherewith they will throw the fault on God, as if he instigated, and secretly brought them to sin; *Sirach* answers such, saying, *say not you, it is through the Lord, that I fell away, for you ought not to do the things that he hates; say not thou, he has caused me to err, for he has no need of the sinful man: The Lord hates all abomination, and they that fear God, love it not; be himself made man from the beginning, and left him in the hand of his council, if you will keep the commandments, and do perform acceptable faithfulness; he has set fire and water before you; stretch forth your hand unto whither you will.*

As sure as we can see and behold everything in the world, as sure God upholds everything to that end and purpose, that we should seek the Lord, as the apostle says in our text. This is the final cause, wherefore God has created the world and all that is therein, and governs and preserves the whole nature yet daily and continually; namely,

First, that we should seek the Lord, if happily we might feel after him, and find him: Man is blind in many cases, and has hands and ears, but no eyes: When a blind man walks about in a house feeling for himself, and he comes and finds a harp hanging against the wall, which gives a sound when touched, then concludes the blind man, that there must be a master, who has made this instrument, and can play upon it; but when he hears the master play, then is he astonished and charmed, although he cannot see him; Thus run all men on against the creation, and the created things, and finding such harmony and and complete order therein, concludes thereof, that there must certainly be an artful and cunning master, who has made and ordered it so complete, and preserves it yet daily. Hereby are the heathens come in the knowledge of God: *For of the things that are made, could they understand the invisible things of God, even his power, and Godhead:* Though this their knowledge alone was not sufficient to salvation, wherefore the apostle sets an *if* by. It is a difficult thing come to in the true knowledge of God; and must we learn this of the word of God alone, and herein was St. *Paul* now willing to instruct the blind *Athenians* in our text.

Secondly, that we and all the creatures shall have our uphold, God lets sometimes mis-growth come in one thing or in another, yet his providence upholds us; whereof we have many examples, as well in the Holy Scripture, as of daily experience; we should therefore not think, that anything happens by chance or mere accident, as if nature could do of itself, what it would; no, God is the only Lord and master over the whole nature, and the same stands under his absolute command, to give forth as much or as little as the Lord pleases.

Thirdly, that we should have the eternal life. This is the end and purpose whereto we were created, preserved, redeemed, and sanctified; our meditations are led hereto by the sight of the creatures, for they convince us, that all what is in this world is vanity, and subject to vanity, and we can find no true comfort or rest in anything that is created, but must therefore lift up our thoughts higher and seek after another world, the heavenly *Jerusalem*, where we shall have full satisfaction in eternal joy.

The Lord be gracious unto us, and grant us at last the eternal life, and in that life the everlasting joy, for the sake of our blessed Savior Jesus Christ. AMEN.

14

Predestination

The text EPHESIANS, Chap. 1:3, 4, 5, 6 ver.

Blessed be the God and Father of our Lord Jesus Christ, who has blessed us with all spiritual blessings in heavenly places in Christ: According as he has chosen us in him before the foundation of the world, that we should be holy, and without blame before him in love: Having predestined us unto the adoption of children by Jesus Christ to himself, according to the good pleasure of his will: to the praise of the glory of his grace, wherein he has made us accepted in the Beloved.

INTRODUCTION

NONE can say otherwise, than that it is a very comfortable, gracious errant, that the bountiful God offers unto all repenting sinners, through the mouth of the prophet *Ezekiel*, in his book of prophecies, Chap. 33:11 ver. *As I live, says the Lord God, I have no pleasure in the death of the wicked; but that the wicked turn from his way, and live.* In these words are two things presented for our meditation: *First,* the misery of man; And, *second,* the mercy of God.

208

First, the *misery of men* is comprehended in the word *death*, which must be understood here, of the external death in hell; for the temporal death, no sinner can escape, although he be converted, and turn from his wickedness. Who can fully describe the miserable condition wherein sin has brought men? For, besides the many temporal miseries, whereto men are subject as long as they live, on account of sin, which miseries are likewise called death; so is this the worst of all, that the unconverted must suffer after their temporal death, in eternal pain and punishment in hell; *where they shall seek death, and shall not find it; and shall desire to die, and death shall flee from them.* In such misery and death has sin brought men; and it could not be otherwise, since the justice of God requires absolute punishment for sin; *The Lord did not spare the angels that sinned, but plunged them into hell, where he has reserved them in everlasting chains under darkness, unto the judgment of the Great Day.* Men had deserved the same wrath and punishment; but, that such is not befallen us, so that we are become wholly and eternally miserable, is through the great mercy of God; by which the Lord himself testifies here, saying;

Second, I have no pleasure in the death of a sinner: This gracious will of God is,

1. *Serious.* God confirms it with an oath, saying; *As I live:* he that swears, must swear by a greater than himself. Now God is the highest and greatest, and swears therefore by himself: He swears here not because he is not to be believed by his Words alone; *For God is not a Man, that he should lie, neither the Son of Man, that he should repent:* But he swears here on account of our infirmity, that we should believe him surer and firmer; for since God saw, and knew before, that men should be tempted mostly with these thoughts; *Our transgressions and sins are upon us, and we pine away in them; How shall we then live?* Therefore assures he unto them with this oath; *That he does not will the death of a sinner:* Oh, how happy are they who believe

209

in him; and on the contrary, how unhappy and eternal miserable are they who will not believe in him: *He that believes not God, has made him a liar.* God swears sometimes in anger and sometimes in grace: It was an oath in anger, when the Lord swore, that none of the men that came out of *Egypt*, should go into the land of *Canaan*, on account of their *murmurings in the wilderness.* It was an oath in grace, that God swore unto *Abraham*, saying, *By myself have I sworn, say to the Lord, for because you have done this thing, and have not withheld your son, therefore will I bless you, and multiply your seed.* We must always believe the Lord, he either swears in wrath or grace; *For all what he has spoken, will he also bring to pass*; God assures us of this his gracious and serious will, in many places in the Scripture, both with words and deeds.

With words, so says the Lord by the prophet *Isaiah*; *I have spread out my hands all the day unto a rebellious people, which walks in a way that was not good, after their own thoughts; a people that provokes me to anger continually to my face.* What can be said more comfortable? Our Savior and his apostles, have likewise assured us in the New Testament, *that God wills not the death of a sinner.* What is the meaning of the parable of the royal feast, whereto everyone was called and invited, than that God wills that all men should repent and be saved?

With *deeds:* He sent his Son to seek and to save that which was lost; herein has God opened his bosom, and showed, that he has no pleasure in the death of the wicked; and this is preached to all. Therefore is his will,

2. Revealed for all. None, let him be the wickedest sinner, is here excluded: All, all, whosoever have part in this promise, except they exclude themselves through unbelief and obstinacy. God is not as false men, who speak one thing with the mouth, and mean another in the heart; no, but the mouth, hand and heart of God follow always

together. *God is faithful, and it is impossible for him to lie.* The will of God is likewise,

3. *Conditional.* God has included his will within certain conditions, which we must follow, if we will enjoy the gracious promise of everlasting salvation. This condition is conversion. *The wicked shall turn from his way.* This conversion shall not consist in words alone, nor in outward appearance and gestures, but in a hearty sincere conversion from wickedness and vices, to good and virtues; and everyone shall search his own heart and conscience, to know what way he has walked upon till now, and then return again, with the prodigal, to his father's House; *If you return unto the Lord with all your heart, then prepare your hearts unto the Lord, and serve him only.* By a true and sincere conversion, there must be a living faith in Jesus Christ, that we thereby embrace the gracious promises of the remission of our sins, and attribute them unto us, being fully assured, that God will forgive us all our transgressions of grace, for the sake of Jesus Christ; thereupon will follow the bettering of our lives, which is the fruit of a true conversion: For he that is really grieved in his heart for his sins, and abhors them as an abomination, will not consent again to sin; and he that, with a true faith, embraces the merits of Christ, and depends alone thereon, lives in Christ, and Christ lives in him; and where Christ lives and reigns, there sin cannot reign; and where sin has no power, there is life; and then follows; *That the sinner shall live.*

But, as it is the gracious will of God, *That the wicked shall turn from his way, and live*; so is it likewise his just will, *that all unconverted sinners shall die the eternal death:* Which is not two wills in God, one contrary to another, but is one will: As a ruler of a city wills not, that any of his subjects shall be punished, if they live according to the law; but if they transgress the law, he will therefore punish them, although he has no pleasure in it: Since God has foreseen from eternity, who should believe in Christ and remain steadfast; and who should not believe, so he has likewise decreed from eternity, to save the believers and condemn the unbelievers. The last is called ejection, and the first election: The apostle St. *Paul* speaks of this election in our text, whereof we will discourse here on these two heads,

FIRST, *Of the election in itself.*

SECOND, *To what end God has chosen us.*

EXPLANATION of the TEXT

I. We will discourse of the election in itself.

The apostle begins his preaching of the election, with praises and thanksgiving, saying; *Blessed be the God and Father of our Lord Jesus Christ:* We must likewise praise and thank God, for this his grace, that he has chosen us in Christ to the eternal salvation of his own grace and mercy without our own merits. Hereof have we to consider,

1. Who it is, that has chosen us; *it is the God and Father of our Lord Jesus Christ:* The same Almighty God, who created man, has likewise chosen him to salvation; all the three persons in the blessed Trinity have created men, so have they likewise all three chosen men; and although the election is here attributed to God the Father, the first person, yet should not the Son and the Holy Spirit be excluded, for they are one God, and of one godly essence with the Father: There is mention made in our text of all the three persons, *God the Father of our Lord Jesus Christ, has chosen us in his Son Christ.* This is the two first persons, the third person the Holy Spirit is mentioned in these words, *That we should be holy, and without blame before him in love, and we should be received unto the adoption of children.* It is the work of the Holy Spirit to sanctify us, *and he hears witness with our spirit, that*

212

we are children of God. God the Father, the first person, has chosen us; Jesus Christ, the Son of God, the second person, has merited our election; and the Holy Spirit, the third person, seals and confirms our election.

2. *What election is.* Election is the purpose and conclusion of God's well-pleasing will, wherein he from eternity, before the foundation of the world, has of his great mercy and grace in Jesus Christ, decreed to save all them, that hereafter his godly foresight has seen and known; would by the preaching of the gospel, and the power of the Holy Spirit, believe in Christ, and remain steadfast unto their lives end, that the praise of his glorious grace could thereby be revealed.

One might now think, who can know what God has decreed from eternity concerning the salvation of men; yes, this can we know and learn, of what God has done afterwards in time: For, as none can know what is transacted in the king's council, before it is manifested by publication; when we then can conclude, that there has been such transacted, so can we likewise conclude of the things God has made in the time, what he had before concluded and ordained in his godly wisdom from eternity; for God is immutable in his will and purpose, and does nothing in time, but what he has decreed from eternity. God did send his Son into the world, born of a woman in time, that he should make the power of Satan to naught, and raise up men from the fallen condition, wherein the disobedience of *Adam* had brought them. Thereof we can conclude, that God had decreed from eternity, to send his Son into the world; who by his obedience should satisfy for the disobedience of *Adam*, in whom we were all become sinners. Again, since God lets his grace be offered to all by the preaching of the gospel, and he promises, to increase faith in the hearts of them, who receive and believe the gospel, and graciously to forgive their sins, and to adopt them unto children, and seals this promise with the holy sacraments; so we can conclude thereof, that God has decreed from eternity, that they, who receive the gospel, believe in Christ, and lets the Holy Spirit govern and guide them, shall not be lost, but have the eternal life. Our Savior says, *This is the will of him that sent me, that everyone which sees the Son, and believes on him, may have everlasting life: The others on the contrary, who would not receive the word, neither believe in the Son, the wrath of God abides on them:* Whereupon will follow eternal damnation; *for he, that believes not, is condemned already.*

The right meaning of election, according to the Scripture, is this: That God decreed from eternity to save the poor lost mankind, and free them from the eternal death and damnation, wherein *Adam* had brought them by his disobedience, since God saw and knew before, that man would fall from his holiness, he therefore placed on one side all men, and found them corrupt with sin, and thereby guilty to eternal death and damnation; and on the other side he placed his Son Jesus Christ, on whom he laid the sins of the world, with these words, as a short summary of the fore-ordination of God. *He that believes on the Son, has everlasting life, and he that believes not the Son, shall not see life, but the wrath of God abides on him.* None should think, that as God has graciously ordained the means, by which the faithful receive salvation, he has likewise in his wrath ordained sin and unbelief, by which the ungodly are condemned: No, for this would make God the cause and author of sin. All men are, on account of sin fallen under the judgment and wrath of God, and are guilty to the eternal death and damnation; but God of his infinite mercy in Jesus Christ, has ordained gracious means against the eternal damnation; which gracious means, some accept through faith, but others refuse and condemn through unbelief. Hence comes it, that they who believe are chosen, predestined and received in the eternal salvation; but the unbelievers remain in their corrupted condition, and are eternally damned, because they would not receive the grace of God offered to them. Hereby we can now lightly understand them words, in the explanation whereof a great many do mistake: *As many as were ordained to eternal life, believed*: that is, as many as followed the order, and used the means that God had ordained for the obtaining of the eternal life, and received the word, were baptized; did believe that Jesus Christ was the Son of God, and the Savior of the world, and did let the Spirit of God guide them; they were ordained to eternal life.

St. *Paul* calls the election in our text *predestination*; above which there is again two parts; namely, the first is *prognosis*, a foreknowledge of what we will ordain, or else was election blind, if God had not foreseen, who should believe in Christ; then comes *prothesis*, a conclusion or decree founded on Christ, and manifested in the gospel, to save them through faith in Christ; thereupon follows *proorismos*, predestination, wherein is comprehended both the end of election, which is the eternal life, and the means of obtaining the same, which are to be baptized, to receive the word, by the word faith, by faith Jesus Christ; and again by him, and through him, the everlasting salvation.

We can best include all this in a syllogism: God had ordained that they, who believe in Christ and remain steadfast, shall be saved; (that is, the decree of God) Now God has seen from eternity, that *Abraham, David*, and others should believe in Christ, and remain steadfast; (that is, the foreknowledge of God) therefore shall they be saved, (that is, the predestination of God.)

Although the Scripture makes no difference between these two words election and predestination, for the apostle uses them both in our text, saying, first, *God has chosen us in Christ*, and afterwards, *he has predestined us unto the adoption of Children by Jesus Christ*; yet they can according to the opinion of some, be also separated. That election has regard to the persons, that are chosen, and predestination comprehends the means thereof. Election is a roll of muster; Predestination is as a squadron standing in battle, and following the orders, and using the means prescribed by the commander. We can now easily conclude hereof,

3. What sort of men are chosen: They are sinful men, whom God had foreseen, that, by the preaching of the Gospel, should believe in Christ, and by the power of the Holy Spirit, remain steadfast in this faith, unto their lives end. For since the apostle says, in our text, *That God has chosen us in Christ, and has predestined us unto the adoption of children by Christ*; then follows thereof, that the election is not made without Christ, but in and by Christ; and since we have received the adoption to children by Christ, then were we without him, children of wrath, and a sinful generation: Though, by such sinful men whom God has chosen, shall and must be found, these two conditions: *First*, that they believe in Christ, and are assured, that Christ has redeemed them, and that God will receive them through faith of his mere grace: *Secondly*, that they shall remain steadfast in the faith until their lives end.

But since all they who hear the word of God, do not believe in Christ, but many are offended in him, and despise the word; and many who have once received faith, fall away again in unbelief and die therein; then follows thereof, that all who hear the word, are not chosen, but alone some few who remain steadfast in the true faith; as our Savior said, *few are chosen.*

Now since *faith is a gift of God*, and therefore not everyone, *for all men have not faith*, should God then seemingly be the cause that all are not chosen, because he does not give them this faith? No, God is not the cause hereof, but men themselves; for some will not hearken to the word, *but contradict and blaspheme* the same, as the *Jews*; some hear it, but loosely and in slumber, as *Eutychus*; some *to hear new things as the* Athenians; some for to despise and mock it, as the enemies of Christ; some do not understand it, and therefore *the Devil takes the word out of their hearts*; some will not receive the word, either through ambition or vain-glory, and worldly honor, as the *Pharisees*; some for to please their relations or patrons; some for fear of hatred and persecution, as the parents of the blind born; some cannot forbear the ministers, and therefore do not care to hear the word preached by him, as the hearers of the prophet *Ezekiel*; some are hindered by riches, wealth, or worldly care; some are so hardened in sin, that they despise the word; some are offended in the mean person, or appearance of the minister, as the countrymen of Christ; some when they have their Crimes and favorite vices corrected, grow angry, and will therefore not hearken further to the word; some seek but after wisdom and eloquence, despising the simplicity of the word; some are come so far that they have received faith, *but in time of temptation fall again.* By such, and many more, but to us unknown ways, is the fruitfulness of God's word hindered, so that men cannot receive faith. We can see hereby, that God is not the cause, but men themselves. Further have we to observe.

4. When this election is made. The apostle says in our text, *before the foundation of the world*; hereby we can conclude, that the election is of grace, immutable, and sure.

The election is of grace. For since it is not made in time, but from eternity, when there was no man, who could believe, so is all what God has done herein, of mere grace and mercy, without any merits or worthiness of men. *God called us with a holy calling, not according to our works, but according to his own purpose and grace, which was given us in Christ Jesus, before the world began.* This is certainly a great comfort, that one man has no preference before another; or else the poor and miserable would think, that God did love the rich and wealthy above them. God loves the elect all alike from eternity, yea, he loves them as his only Son, who is the head of the elect.

The election is immutable. Since God cannot err, neither be deceived in his providence or foresight, and has foreseen from eternity, who should believe in Christ, and remain steadfast, and has thereupon made his conclusion to choose them; then is it certain, that the election is immutable, and cannot be altered, neither on the side of God, nor on the side of the faithful. Not on the side of God, *For the foundation of God stands sure, having this seal; the Lord knows them that are his.* Hereby we can say, that the elect are written in the Book of Life, which book cannot like other books be blotted, but all what is written therein, stands immutable. Therefore does our Savior reckon it among the impossible things, *that the elect should be deceived*, and brought in error; namely such error, that continues unto their lives end, nor on the side of the faithful can the election be altered: For if they could lose their faith, and die in unbelief, then could they not be said, *to be chosen:* They well can commit such sins, by which they drive away the Holy Spirit, and lose their faith. But they repent, and become converted before they die; as we can see of the examples of *David, Peter, Thomas*, and others in the Scripture.

The Scripture makes mention of some, *that are blotted out of the Book of Life*; but the right meaning is, that they were never wrote in it. The Scripture uses these words, *blot out of*, because there are so many hypocrites in Christendom, who seem to others to be written *in the Book of Life*, and are often of the same conceit; but they are not: And therefore, since they fall away from their seeming faith, and die in unbelief, they are said, *to be blotted out of the Book of Life*, that is, they were never wrote in it, therefore did God refuse unto *Moses* his request, when he desired *to be blotted out of the Book of Life*.

The election is likewise sure both in name and number by God; and in heart and conscience by the elect. God knows the names of the elect; *I knew you by name*, said the Lord unto *Moses: Christ calls his own sheep by name,* and *will confess their names before his*

Father and before his angels. This confession of Christ, comprehends a loving affection, continual remembrance, fatherly commiseration, gracious acknowledgment, and eternal salvation. God knows the number of the elect likewise; for, since their names are written in Heaven, and God knows them that are his, so knows he likewise the number of them, though the number of the elect was not so immutably decreed by God, that there could not have been more chosen than they that are chosen. No, if more would have believed in Christ and remain steadfast, God would have foreseen that too, and likewise chosen them in Christ. It is one thing to know an affair, and another to decree it. God knows the number of the elect; but, therefore, he has not decreed before how high this number should go: *He that believes in Christ and remains steadfast, shall be saved.* They themselves can be sure of their election, as a Son is sure of heirship after his Father; if he is, and continues obedient; for, although the Spirit of God makes no mention no where of, that such or such a One is chosen, yet we can make this conclusion: He that has a true and living faith, and remains steadfast, him will Christ keep as a Good Shepherd, and none shall pluck him out of his hands. I, who am regenerated, will believe in Christ, and cleave unto him to my life's end; therefore will Christ, the Good Shepherd, not let me be plucked out of his hands: Will our reason say, yes, the regenerated can lose the grace of God? Then our faith should answer; They themselves have lest Christ, and are turned from him, but I will cleave to him, and he will never leave me; and if I should fall, the Lord is able to raise me up again. I will rely on the promises of God; whereof St. *Paul* says; *God is faithful, who has called us unto the fellowship of his Son Jesus Christ our Lord, and shall confirm us unto the end. God is faithful, who will not suffer you to be tempted above that you are able: It is God which works in you, both to will and to do of his good pleasure. God is able to keep that which I have committed unto him against that Day. The*

Spirit himself, bears witness with our spirit, that we are the children of God.

5. The ground of this election is Jesus Christ. The apostle says in our text: *God chose us in him*, that is, Jesus Christ. Christ is not alone the effectual cause of our election; since he, as a true God, with the Father and the Holy Spirit, has chosen us; but he is likewise the meritorious cause, ordained of God from eternity, to be the Redeemer and Propitiator of mankind; who, by his obedience and innocent death, has procured us the grace of election: For if Christ had not reconciled us to God, God could not have chosen us, since his wrath was kindled against us; and if God was angry with us, how could he choose us? But the righteousness of Christ has justified the justice of God; therefore, said St. *Paul, that Christ might reconcile us unto God, in one body by the cross, having slain the enmity thereby.*

Also the Father has had regard, in the election, alone to Christ and his merits, which he, in time, as the only High Priest from heaven, should offer upon the cross, as a sweet smell unto God; wherefore Christ is justly called, *the Lamb that bore the sins of the world.* God had regard to Christ, not alone so far as he should suffer and die for all, and by his death satisfy for the sins of the world; for therein all men are alike, since Christ bore the sins of all; but in particular, God has regard to Christ, so as he should be accepted by men. Now Christ is not accepted otherwise than by faith, therefore is election concluded on faith; namely, that all who believe in Christ, and remain steadfast till their lives end, shall be saved, and have life everlasting. We can prove this with the following conclusion; The same way that God justifies, sanctifies, and saves us in time, the same way has he decreed from eternity to justify, sanctify and save us, since he is immutable in his godly essence and does nothing in time, but what he has decreed from eternity: Now God justifies, sanctifies and saves us in time, through the merits of Christ embraced by faith; therefore has he likewise decreed from eternity, to justify, sanctify, and save us through Christ, whom we must embrace by faith; for he cannot be received otherwise than by,

6. *Faith*. This is the cord that ties Christ and us together, it is the hand wherewith we lay hold on Christ; it is the eye, wherewith we behold Christ; and it is the mouth wherewith we kiss Christ. But, since we can fall away again, and lose our faith that we have once received, therefore is a steadfast faith required. We shall not alone begin well, but we must also continue and end well: Our Savior says; *He that endures to the end, shall be saved.*

Should a child of God be doubtful of himself, and be afraid, that he should not remain steadfast in the faith to the end, then must he ground the steadfastness of his faith on the love of God, and on the intercession and power of Christ.

He should ground it on that love of God, which God bears to him in Jesus Christ; which is not grounded on any slight imagination, but on the faithful promises of God, and on the meritorious death of Christ; and, he may depend, that God, who has begun to love him in Christ, and for Christ sake, shall not leave him, neither take his grace from him, but will give him strength and power to remain steadfast; For God is so merciful, that he will not take his grace from anyone, except they condemn and despise the same: Therefore admonishes St. *Paul: Work out your own salvation with fear and trembling:* And St. *Peter*; *Brethren, give diligence to make your calling and election sure: For if you do these things you shall never fall. For so an entrance shall be administered unto you abundantly, into the everlasting Kingdom of our Lord and Savior Jesus Christ.*

He should likewise ground his faith on the intercession of Christ for the faithful. Our Savior says; *I pray not alone for these, but for them also which shall believe in me through their word.* We do profit by this intercession of Christ, when we pray therefore, and comfort us thereby. What said Christ unto *Peter? Satan has desired to have you, that he may sift you as wheat*; *but I have prayed for you, that your faith fail not.*

He must also ground his faith on the power of Christ. A child of God cannot of himself withstand the temptations of the Devil, the world, and his own flesh and blood; therefore we should no the discouraged: For, as we cannot of our own strength believe in Christ, so can we neither of our own strength remain steadfast, but it comes alone of the power of Jesus Christ, and the effect of the Holy Spirit. Christ himself says: *None shall pluck my sheep out of my hands:* And St. Peter says; *We are kept by the power of God through faith unto salvation.*

II. To what end God has chosen us.

The final Cause wherefore God has chosen us, has regard to God, and to us men.

First, to God. Our text says: *To the praise of the glory of his grace.* God has plainly shown herein, his great mercy and grace, that he has accepted us poor lot sinners, for Christ's sake, has adopted us unto children, and chosen us to be heirs of his heavenly Kingdom: *Behold what manner of love the Father has bestowed upon us, that we should be called the sons of God.* Although we had tongues of angels and men, and understood all mysteries and knowledge, yet we could not praise the grace of God enough. St. *Peter* says; *That we should show forth the praise of him who has called us out of darkness, into his marvelous light.* It was a marvelous light that God kindled for us, after we had extinguished the light, when he did let the light of his countenance shine over us, and ordained his only Son as a Savior; who with his preaching and miracles should shine for us, and instruct us how to believe, and afterwards with his death bring us out of darkness. It was a marvelous light God called us to, when by the preaching of the Gospel, he called us to his gracious kingdom, and therefore sent his apostles in the world as a light, by which the world could be instructed to find out the true light. Faith is a marvelous light, that shines in our hearts, to give the light of the knowledge of the glory of God, in the face of Jesus Christ; which light God enlightens with his word and Spirit, nourishes it with the holy sacraments, and *cleanses* it with crosses and affliction, and brings us at last thereby through this valley of darkness to the marvelous light in Heaven. Are we then not obliged to praise the glory of God's grace herefore?

Second, to us men: First, in this life, that we should be blessed: In *Adam* we were cursed, but God took the curse from us and laid it on Christ, that we through him should be blessed. He has given his blessings unto us, as a great prophet, since he has blessed the means by which the heavenly gifts shall be distributed unto us; namely, *Baptism and the Lord's Supper.* As a high priest, that as *Aaron did bless the children of Israel*, with stretched out hands, so has Christ at his ascension, blessed his apostles with stretched out hands, and also qualified them to the office of the New Testament, as a mild king: That as, *Melchizedeck*, king in *Salem*, blessed *Abraham*, so are we blessed of God in Jesus Christ, the King of Righteousness. Further,

That we should receive the adoption of children. *Adam* was the first child of God, but lost, through disobedience, the right of a child, and became a child of wrath, and made us all like unto him. God had no need of children, but we had great need of a Father; therefore must we, *being by nature children of wrath*, and having not a child's right, be adopted to children; and this adoption is of grace in Christ, whom God did send in time; *That we through him, should receive the adoption of children. As many as received him, to them gave be power to become the sons of God.* And, that we should be holy, and without blame before him in love, we must show our faith with a holy and blameless life before God, and love towards men. None shall think, that, since God has chosen us, we therefore may and should live as we please. No, our faith must shine forth in a holy and blameless life for God, and in love to all men. St. *Paul* says therefore: *Put on as the elect of God, holy and beloved, bowels of mercy, kindness, humbleness of mind, meekness, long-suffering, forbearing one another, and forgiving one another.* For since we can lose our faith, therefore should we always be careful that nothing, by which God can be offended, the Holy Spirit vexed, and the grace of God lost. We should listen faithfully to the saying of the Spirit of God through the mouth of St. *John* the divine: *Hold that fast which you hast, that no man take your crown.*

Secondly, after this life glorification. *For whom he has predestined,* (from eternity to be heirs of life-everlasting): *Them has he also called,* (in time by his word): *And whom he has called, them has he also justified,* (by faith in Jesus Christ): *And whom he has justified, them will be also glorify.*

The Lord strengthen us in all what is good, that we can prove our election with a holy, blameless and godly life, and remain steadfast in the true faith to our lives end; and at last receive the end of our faith, which is the salvation of our souls, alone for the sake of our blessed Savior, Jesus Christ. AMEN.

15

The Person of Christ

T he text ST. JOHN, Chap. 1:14. ver.
The Word was made flesh, and dwelt among us, and we beheld his glory, the glory as of the only begotten of the Father, full of grace and truth.

INTRODUCTION

THE apostle St. *Paul* gives us a short summary of the whole life of Jesus Christ, from the time of his birth until his ascension, when he says in his first epistle to *Timothy*, 3:16. Ver. *Without controversy, great is the mystery of godliness: God was manifest in the flesh, justified in the Spirit, seen of angels, preached unto the gentiles, believed on in the world, received up into glory.* These words are all words of salvation, and gives us three things to consider. *First*, a mystery. *Second*, the explanation of the mystery, and *third*, the manifestation of the mystery.

1. The mystery whereof St. *Paul* speaks here, he calls a mystery, a great mystery, a mystery of godliness, and a mystery without

controversy.

A mystery is a thing that is hid and secret, and cannot be apprehended with human reason, without special revelation and manifestation from God; as the great image king *Nebuchadnezzar*, beheld in his dream, is called *a secret*. The wonderful writing that was wrote on the plaster of the wall for king *Balshazzar*, is called *a hidden thing*. The incarnation of our Lord Jesus Christ, is called here by the apostle *a mystery*, because it is not alone hid and secret, from natural reason, but also far exceed the apprehension of human reason, although we might meditate thereon ever so much; and therefore it is called,

A great mystery. Great, since it concerns the great God, *who is great above all gods*. The whole blessed Trinity has here made such an action, that never can be compared. Great, for the great profit and benefit, that flows therefrom to us men. Therefore is it *a mystery of godliness*; because it is not alone in itself a godly mystery, whereof our salvation depends, but also teaches us true godliness, by which we can *deny ungodliness and worldly lusts*.

A mystery without controversy. Never could anyone comprehend, much less believe it, if it had not been manifested; and none in the whole Christianity can contradict it. But what is the explanation?

2. The explanation of this mystery is, *God is manifested in the flesh*. The evangelist St. John explains it also, *the Word* (that is, the second person in the Holy Trinity) *is made flesh*: For neither the Father, the first person, nor the Holy Spirit, the third person, is made *manifest in the Flesh*, and made man, but alone the Son of God. In these words we have a description of the true incarnation of Christ, of the two natures in Christ, and of the personal union of the two natures.

Of the true incarnation of Christ. Christ did often appear in the time of the Old Testament, to the old fathers in human form; but he laid always this form off again: But here is such a manifestation in

226

the flesh, that the Son of God is become a true man, and shall never lay off this human nature again.

The two natures in Christ. The divine nature is called God, and the human nature is called flesh; in this flesh is God made manifest, that is, Jesus Christ, the Son of God, *took part of our flesh and blood as other children.*

The personal union of the two natures. The two natures are so united in Christ, that he who saw and handled the flesh of Christ, *saw and handled* likewise the Word of Life, that is, the Son of God, as the Apostle St. *John* explains it. And this is,

3. The manifestation of the mystery. Since the Son of God did appear so mean, suffered hunger, thirst, poverty, and despise, so that none ever could have believed him to be the Son of God; therefore it was absolutely necessary, that he should be manifested unto the world in the following ways and manner.

He was justified in the Spirit. The *Jews* did despise him, and called him an impostor, *that was not worthy to live*; but at last did his righteousness and innocence appear by his miracles that befell at his death, according to the confession of his enemies; by his resurrection, ascension, and sitting on God's right hand.

He was seen of angels. The angels saw Christ in his birth, temptations, sufferings, death, ascension, and resurrection: And they never saw him, but they found something by which they were astonished. wherefore St. *Paul* says, that *the manifold wisdom of God is made known unto the principalities and powers in heavenly places.* This mystery was afterwards,

Preached unto the gentiles. The *Jews*, and even the apostles wondered that Christ should be *preached unto the gentiles.* The *Jews* were of opinion, that since the Messiah was promised unto them, he therefore should be preached unto them alone. The apostles themselves thought it wonderful that Christ should be *preached unto the gentiles* St. *Peter* was instructed hereby by a heavenly vision. St. *Paul* did account it a particular blessing, that *the grace was given unto him to preach among the gentiles the unsearchable riches of Christ.* Thereupon was Christ believed on in the world. The world did in the beginning despise and persecute Christ and his word; but afterwards they received him and his Gospel, and believed on him, being convinced by the many miracles, wherethrough the Word was confirmed. This may well be reckoned for a great miracle, that the unfaithful world was convinced, and did believe; wherefore old *Bernardus* said: The almighty God has made three wonderful things in the incarnation of Christ, that never happened before, nor after; that is, God and man; mother and virgin; faith and man's heart. Thereupon follows, that *he was received up into glory.* Thereby was manifested, that Christ had fully satisfied the justice of God for the sins of all. Therefore may now all tongues confess, that Jesus Christ is a Lord to the glory of God.

The evangelist St. *John*, speaks in our text of this mystery; whereof we will, in simplicity, consider the incarnation of the Son of God under these three heads.

FIRST, *The two natures in Christ.*

SECOND, *The personal Union of these two natures.*

THIRD, *The properties and Fellowship of this personal union.*

EXPLANATION of the TEXT

I. We have to consider the two natures in Christ.

When we in a godly meditation do consider the article of Christ, then should we not only behold him as a person without body, so as he has been from eternity, a true God alone; but we should also behold him as he is *manifested in the flesh*; that is, a true man. For as he is

228

a true God from eternity with the Father, and has his godly nature from eternity, as a person in the Holy Trinity; so has he in time taken on the human nature, and is born a man, and is now also true God, and true man in one person. It could not be otherwise, for there *cannot be any forgiveness of sins without bloodshed*, and God could not suffer nor die; by which the work of redemption could be completed. Since God cannot die, neither has he flesh and blood, and a simple man could not satisfy the severe justice of God, and reconcile the vengeance of God; therefore was it absolutely necessary and needful, that the Redeemer should be both God and man; and this is it that St. *John* means, when he says in our text: *The Word was made flesh.* Here mention is made of both the divine and human nature.

The divine nature is called here, *the Word.* Jesus Christ the Son of God is called here, *the Word*, in regard to his divine nature, and in regard to his office.

In regard to his divine nature. That as the words are conceived in our thoughts and mind, without hurting the thought; so is God the Son born from eternity of the Father, though without any diminution of the Father's person.

In regard to his office. The words are the interpreter of the mind, and with words we make known what we will: So has the Son of God been the interpreter from the Father, and has revealed unto us his Father's will. This Word is our *advocate with the Father*, and *intercedes for us by the Father*. If it was not for this word, we would all despair in temptation and prayers, and not be able to dare appear before the tribunal of God.

St. *John* convinces and proves, that this *Word* is true God, by the godly attributes that he mentions in the foregoing part of our text's chapter, as that it is eternal. *In the beginning was the Word*, that is from eternity; for before the beginning of time, there was no other beginning, but all eternity. And *the Word was God:* Christ is called

God in other places of the Scripture; as, *God over all, blessed forever: the true God and eternal life.* And,

By him were all things made. St. Paul says, *By him were all things created, that are in heaven and on earth.* Not as by a dead tool or instrument, but as a Creator: Therefore says the Scripture, *that Christ has created all things.* And,

He gives life. In him was life. He gives us the life of nature, grace and honor: He enlightens all *Jews* and *gentiles:* And this is the divine nature, that took on the human nature, which in our text is called *flesh*, for the following reasons: Because the Son of God, *the Word*, has not taken on the human person, but human nature, whereof St. *John* says, *The Word was made flesh:* This flesh was no person before, for then there would be two persons in Christ; but the divine nature of Christ, who was a person, and was called the *Word*, took on the human nature wholly, both in body and soul, which is called *flesh:* And these two natures now are so united with one another, that they are become one person, God and man. And,

Because the Son of God was a true natural man, like another man. This we can prove of his conception, birth, life, death and resurrection. Therefore said Christ of himself to the apostles, *A spirit has no flesh and bones, as you see me have:* And because the Son of God was a complete man, having both soul and body: The Scripture uses here the word *flesh*, of the one part of man; that is, the body; but excludes not the other part, that is, the soul. The body of Christ is called here *flesh*, and must be understood of both body and soul; for there is often mention made of his soul, as *my soul is exceeding sorrowful*, and many other places in the Scripture. All the qualities that can be found in man, essential or accidental, in soul or body, was found in Christ, sin excepted. Essential qualities are they, whereof human nature consist, and cannot be separated from it; as, the essential qualities of the soul are these, to be invisible, not to be of any stuff, to be wife, and to have a will: And of the body are, to have a bigness, form and shape, that can be seen and handled. All these natural essential qualities were in Christ, like in another man. Accidental qualities are they that can be separated from man; which were likewise in Christ; as, natural lifts. In the soul, that *be waxed strong in spirit, filled with wisdom*, and gathered knowledge like another child, to refuse the evil, and choose the good. In the body, that he grew up daily, and became a full grown man. The natural infirmities, sin excepted, as, in the soul; Ignorance in some things, grief and sorrow. In the body, eating and drinking, hunger and thirst, weeping, sleep, bloody sweat, and other such infirmities, whereto human nature is subject: Yet we must observe, that the body of Christ was not subject to all the infirmities that other human bodies are subject to; for there are some infirmities that do not proceed from nature, but from other causes, as either of a fault in the conception, or of an irregular life; and they were not in the body of Christ; for he was conceived of the Holy Spirit, and lived always regular, and was therefore never sick nor ailing. There are likewise some infirmities that proceed from the sinful corruption in nature, as desire to evil, sickness and deformity, and many others: The body of Christ was neither subject to these or such like infirmities, but alone to them that cleaves to nature, and cannot be separated from nature.

II. We have to consider the personal union of both natures in Christ.

Since there are two natures in Christ, the divine and human, and these two natures make but one person, which is Christ; then must there be a knot, by which these two natures are tied together in one person, and this is called the personal union. Here shall we observe,

What a union is. Union is, when two or more things are so united together that it becomes but one thing, and this is either natural or super natural: Natural union is, when some natural things are united together, as the foundation and the building, mortar and stone, the tree and branches. Supernatural union is, when several things become one above nature; as the three persons in the holy godly essence, are one God; also are the two natures in Christ but one person. The union of the godly and human natures in Christ is personal, and not of persons, for there is but one person in Christ, neither is it a natural union, but a union of natures; for these two natures are in a super natural way united. The personal union is, that the two natures in Christ are so united together, that of them both is become one person; though so, that one nature is not mixed in the other, as we can mix water and wine together; neither, that one nature is altered into another, as the water was altered into wine in *Canaan*; neither is one nature separated from the other, as the clothes from our bodies; but they are so united, that the Son of God *took part of flesh and blood as other children:* And *in him dwells all the fullness of the Godhead bodily.* As a man, consisting of two parts, body and soul, is but one man; so are the two natures in Christ but one person, not though from eternity; for before Christ was made man, then was the person of Christ the property alone of his divine nature; but after he was made man in time, then was the union made of the two natures; this union of natures in Christ is the highest, marvelous,

232

gracious, and eternal union.

It is the highest union, and cannot be compared in the whole nature. There is nothing in nature nearer unto the Son of God, than flesh. The old fathers have invented many similitudes, by which they would explain this union, a soul and body, sun and light, and many others; but there has always been some unlikeness in their comparisons.

It is a marvelous union. We must be astonished and wonder that God, who is eternal, and man who is mortal, could be so united in one person: God is a consuming fire, and man is as straw and chaff. It is a wonder, that straw put into the fire, is not consumed; much more is it to be wondered at, that God and man could be so close united in one person.

It is a gracious union. Since the divine and human nature are united together in Christ, then is God and man, who before were enemies, now reconciled, as St. *Paul* says, *God was in Christ, reconciling the world unto himself.*

It is an eternal union. Never will Christ lay off the human nature; neither shall the human nature be separated from the divine nature; for where we find the divine nature, there is likewise the human nature; and what is united together, remains always together: Therefore, since the two natures are so united together in Christ, then follows by consequence, that where one nature is, there is likewise the other.

The reason of this personal union of the two natures in Christ, is, that Christ should be a *mediator between God and man.* For none could satisfy the justice of God than one that was a true God, and none could die but one, that was a true man. Had Christ been a true man alone, he could not have satisfied the justice of God; had he been a true God alone, he could not have suffered and died; but Christ was true God and true man in one person, and has reconciled men unto God.

III. We have to consider the properties and fellowship of the personal Union.

Of this personal union flows fellowship; for where these is a union, there is likewise a fellowship. St. *John* says in our text, *the Word was made flesh*, that is, the Son of God became man, and took on with the human nature, human frailties; but he says just after: *We beheld his glory, as the glory of the only begotten of the Father, full of grace and truth.* The evangelist shows hereby, that Christ did in the midst of his humiliation, let shine forth some streams of his Godhead, which was communicated to his human nature; and this is the union or fellowship that followed on the personal union. We may in some manner explain this with the fellowship between the soul and body. When soul and body are united into one essence, then must there be a fellowship between the properties of both parties; but when the soul makes no longer use of the properties of the body, nor the body is longer partaker of the properties of the soul, then has there certainly been a separation of both parties, though it is not needful, that soul and body communicate to one another all their respective properties without exception. The soul communicates to the body the powers to move, hear, think, talk, and understand, but not to be immortal, invisible, and a spirit; they are properties, which the body cannot receive. The same way and manner is it with the two natures in Christ, that, since there is a union between them both unto one person, so is there likewise fellowship between the properties of both natures, though not all without exception. For to understand this better, how the two natures have fellowship in each others properties, we must observe the following four particulars.

First, some properties, which one of the natures has for itself, are attributed to the whole person, God and man: As, to be born, to suffer, to die, are such properties that belongs to the human nature;

234

though they are ascribed to the whole person, God and man: As, Christ has suffered in the flesh, Christ is born of the seed of *David*, according to the flesh; likewise are the properties of the divine nature ascribed to the whole person, as, to create, to be Lord of Heaven; and several others.

Secondly, some properties that the human nature has for itself, are attributed to the Son of God after both natures; as, *God has purchased a church with his own blood.* To have blood is the property of human nature, though it is attributed to the Son of God in both natures, and is called the blood of God, in regard to the Godhead, in the communion of which the human nature is received. *The Son of God loves me, and gave himself for me.* To give one's self in death is a property of human nature, though it is attributed to the Son of God in both natures. *God was manifested in the flesh:* To be manifested in the flesh, is a property of human nature; yet it is said of Christ, after both natures.

Thirdly, some properties which the divine nature has of its godly essence, are attributed to the human nature after the personal union; as, to give life, to take away sin, to forgive sin, to raise from the dead, to know men's thoughts, and to heal sicknesses; are properties belonging to the divine nature; yet is it attributed to the flesh of Christ, the power to cleanse from sins. Christ, so far as he is the Son of Man, can forgive sins. The voice of Christ has power to raise from the dead; the spirit of Christ can know the thoughts of the heart; the spirit and touch of Christ can heal the sick. All these properties are godly, whereof the human nature of Christ is made partaker, and is called a mysterious fellowship, since the manhood of Christ is exalted thereby in the communication of the Godhead by the personal union. The godly attributes whereof the manhood of Christ is made a partaker, are six.

1. Almighty. The man Jesus Christ is almighty. *I saw*, says the

prophet *Daniel, in the night-visions, and behold one like the Son of Man came with the clouds of heaven, and came to the Ancient of Days, and they brought him near before him, and there was given him dominion, and glory, and a Kingdom, that all people, nations, and languages, should serve him.*

2. Omniscience. Christ could in the time of his incarnation, *perceive in his Spirit the thoughts of men.* On him, *a Rod out of the stem of* Jesse *shall rest the Spirit of wisdom and understanding.* Well says Christ, that *the Father only knows all things.* But this word only is not mentioned nor meant here in respect to the Son and Holy Spirit, for they are of one divine essence with the Father, but alone in respect to the angels and men; and when Christ says, that *the Son knows not the day to come*, namely the Day of Judgment, then must we understand it, that Christ being then in the state of his humiliation, and not always using in this state the properties of his divine nature, did not know it.

3. Omnipresence. Not to be understood, that the body of Christ was so big or greatly extended that it could reach to all natural places; but as the omnipresence of the Father is Godly, by which he fills heaven and earth, and cannot be comprehended, so is the omnipresence of Christ's human nature after the personal union likewise; for all things depend on him, and we live, move, and have our being in him, as a true God and true man. We can prove the omnipresence of Christ's human nature by the following.

First: Of the properties of the personal union. *The Word* is made flesh, and wholly flesh, since the Godhead cannot be parted. *The Word* is omnipresent; then follows, that the flesh being the human nature is likewise omnipresent, and that wholly, since the natures in Christ cannot be separated.

Secondly, of the Scripture. Our Savior speaks of himself in several places of his omnipresence, according to both natures. *Where two or three are gathered together in my Name, there am I in the midst of them. Lo, I am with you always, even unto the end of the world.* This Word includes both the natures which Christ had, when he spoke them: He says in another place, *no man has ascended up to heaven, but he that came down from heaven:* Christ explains this of his human nature, when he says just after; *even the Son of Man, which is in heaven.* The same Son of Man, who then was upon earth teaching *Nicodemus,* said himself to be in heaven, namely, with the personal union, by which his flesh was participated in the divine nature: Also is then the human nature of Christ omnipresent; but in an incomprehensible manner. The apostle St. *Paul* affirms the omnipresence of Christ's human nature with these words, *he ascended up far above all heavens, that he might fill all things:* Christ ascended according to the human nature, and according to the same, he fills all things through the personal union. We can hereof form this conclusion, that the nature in Christ, which fills all things, is omnipresent; the human nature of Christ fills all things, therefore is the same omnipresent. St. *Paul* speaks of the same in another place, saying, *it pleased the Father, that in him should all fullness dwell.* Since now the fullness of the Godhead dwells in the body of Christ, and we know that the Godhead is omnipresent; then is certainly the body of Christ likewise omnipresent.

Thirdly, Of the sitting of Christ on the right hand of God. The personal union assures us, that when the Son of God was in the state of his humiliation, there had he always his human body with him, since the two natures are inseparably united: But the fitting of Christ on the right hand of God assures us, that the Son of God has not alone his human body over all with him, but also governs all things in heaven and earth with the same. Of the personal union has the human nature of Christ its omnipresence; but of the seat on the right hand of God has he his majesty, and governing over all, as a mighty

Lord over the whole world, and a gracious Lord over the Christian Church. For *God has put all things under his feet, and gave him to be the head over all things, to the church, which is his body, the fullness of him that fills all in all.*

4. Power to forgive sins, and to judge the quick and the dead, is likewise communicated to the human nature of Christ. These are the words of Christ himself; *the Son of Man has power on earth to forgive him sins. The Father has given him authority to execute judgment also, because he is the Son of Man.*

5. To give live, and to quicken. Christ says himself, *I am the living bread which came down from heaven; if any man eat of this bread, he shall live forever, and the bread that I will give, is my flesh, which I will give for the life of the world. Except you eat the flesh of the Son of Man, and drink his blood, you have no life in you. Whoso eats my flesh, and drinks my blood, has eternal life, and I will raise him up at the Last Day; for my flesh is food indeed, and my blood is drink indeed.*

6. The honor of adoration belongs to the human nature of Christ: This we can prove of the following,

First, of prophecies. It was prophesied of Christ, that he, as the Son of Man, should be worshiped of angels and men. *All the kings shall fall down before him, all nations shall serve him*, said the Psalmist. *Unto him every knee shall bow*, says the Prophet *Isaiah*. The apostle St. *Paul* explains this of Christ, when he says, *God has highly exalted him, and given him a name, which is above every name, that at the name of Jesus every knee should bow, of things in heaven, and things in earth, and things under the earth.*

Secondly, of commands. God has commanded, that everyone should worship Christ after both natures, and has promised thereby to hear and help them. *Worship him all you gods.* This does the apostle St. *Paul* explain of Christ, saying, *Let all the angels of God worship him*: and Christ says, *all men should honor the Son, as they honor the Father.*

Thirdly, of many examples. The wise men from east; the leprous; the centurion; the *Cannaitish* woman; *Jairus*; the blind man by *Jericho*; the apostles; and the church triumphant.

These are the divine attributes, whereof the human nature of Christ is made a partaker; and wherefore the evangelist says in our text, *We beheld his glory, the glory of the only begotten of the Father, full of grace and truth.*

Fourthly, both natures in Christ are alike acting in the work of our redemption. Hereto belongs all the actions of the offices of Christ, as he is our Mediator, our High Priest, our Prophet, our King and Judge, our Shepherd and Propitiator. That he has redeemed us from the curse of the law, freed us from sin, bruised the head of the Serpent, brought the blessing of *Abraham* over us, justified, and reconciled us unto God. These and other actions are divine, and no creature can do them; but Christ has effected them all in both natures: On the contrary, to become subject under the law, to be made a curse, to be made to sin, to be bit of the Serpent, to shed blood, to suffer, and to die; are actions which cannot be said of the divine nature alone: yet says the Scripture; *God sent forth his Son made of a woman, made under the law. The blood of Jesus Christ his Son cleanses us from all sins. God reconciled the world unto himself in Christ.*

We should learn rightly to understand this article, since it concerns our salvation and the eternal life, to *know God, and Jesus Christ whom he has sent.*

To whom, and the Father and the Holy Spirit, be all honor, might and majesty, now and evermore, AMEN.

16

The Offices of Christ

T he text stands in PSALM 45:7 ver.
God, your God has anointed you with the oil of gladness,
above your fellows.

INTRODUCTION

WHAT is more precious than gold? Jasper: What is more precious than jasper? Virtue: What is more precious than virtue? Jesus; He is the example of all virtues, in origin and effect; in name and practice. So says the singer of him in his first song, the 3rd verse, *Your name is as ointment poured forth.* Remark here, 1*st*, the name. 2*nd*, the sweetness of the name.

First, the name is Jesus, a name above all names. We can count the letters in this name, but who can describe the effect and power of the same name. In this name Jesus, lays concealed his person, his office, and his merits.

His person is true God and true man, and according to both natures, he is Jesus. He could not suffer and die without the human nature;

and without the divine nature he could not reconcile us to God.

His office is to be prophet, priest and king; all these three offices lay concealed in the name Jesus. He officiated the prophetical office, as Jesus, in bringing to us the Gospel from the bosom of his Father, which is, *the power of God unto salvation, to everyone that believes:* He officiated the sacerdotal office on the cross, as Jesus, in offering up himself a sacrifice for us, and in saving us with his own death; He officiates this office yet daily, in interceding for us by God. He officiates the royal office, in governing the world, and saving his people from their enemies, and freeing them from temporal and eternal evil. All the benefits that Christ has procured for us, according to his triple office, lay concealed in the name, Jesus; for this name, Jesus, comprehends a short summary of all the names which in the Scripture are given to him, according to his person and offices.

Second, the sweetness of the name is explained with a comparison; *An ointment poured forth.* What is sweeter than ointment? Ointment and perfume rejoice the heart. Ointment is used to *heat wounds:* The name Jesus heals the wounds of conscience. *Oil makes faces to shine:* The name Jesus makes our souls shine before God. Ointment rejoices the heart; the name Jesus comforts the conscience. How overjoyed was the woman who anointed the feet of Jesus, when he said unto her; *Your sins are forgiven; your faith has saved you, go in peace.* By the power of this name did the blind receive their sight, the deaf their hearing, the sick their health, and the dead their lives. The name Jesus, is an ointment poured forth in heaven and on earth. In heaven this name Jesus was poured forth as an ointment, when God chose us in him from eternity, before the foundation of the world; wherefore the apostle St. *Peter* says of him; *He was fore-ordained before the foundation of the world.* On earth, this name Jesus is become an ointment poured out at sundry times, in sundry places, for sundry persons.

At sundry times, both in Old and New Testament. In the Old Testament by promises, sacrifices and types. In the New Testament in his conception, birth and circumcision.

In sundry places, with preaching and miracles in the world, with bloody sweat in the Mount of Olives, and on the cross, where his name was put up, being an offence to the *Jews*, but a sweet savor for the faithful.

For sundry persons, both *Jews* and *Gentiles*. St. *Peter* was called to preach the gospel to the *Jews*, St. *Paul* to the *gentiles*.

The name *Jesus* is an ointment poured forth in the whole Scripture, in the whole Christendom, and in the heart of every faithful person.

In the whole Scripture. For *there is written in the law of* Moses, *in the prophets, and in the Psalms, concerning Christ.*

In the whole Christendom, where the Gospel is preached, is this name become an ointment poured forth; and poor lost sinners can be comforted, and saved thereby.

In the heart of every faithful one. *By faith dwells Christ in our hearts.* As the holy oil wherewith *Aaron* was anointed, had a sweet savor; so is the name Jesus an heavenly comfort in the hearts of them that in faith seek and love it.

And since the triple office of Christ, lay concealed in this name, so will we in the same name, with all simplicity, discourse in the three in Christ,

FIRST, *As Prophet.*

SECOND, *As Priest.*

THIRD, *As King.*

EXPLANATION of the TEXT

I. We will discourse of the office of Christ as prophet.

Christ came into the world for to save his people from their sins. It was
not enough that he saved them from their sins, except he restored to
them their lost salvation; as a good physician removes not alone the
sickness, but also restores the patient to his former health; And this
has Christ done with so many offices, as the salvation of men needed
for. Now, man was become in *Adam* stinking and filthy before God,
wanted therefore a priest, who could sacrifice a sweet savor, and
thereby reconcile men unto God. Men were dead from the grace of
God, and went astray in sinful ways from the heavenly kingdom;
therefore needed they a king, who could free and save them from
their enemies, and restore them again to the heavenly kingdom. Men
were blind in the knowledge of God, and ignorant in the cause of
their salvation, therefore needed they a prophet and a guide: Here
is the triple office in Christ. For he was to offer himself up a sweet
savor to God, to save us from our enemies, and instruct us in the will
of God.

Christ is not come to these three offices of himself, but he is
lawfully called and anointed thereto of God, as three sorts of persons
were, namely, kings, prophets, and priests. The ointment of Christ
was no outward oil on the body, but the Holy Spirit was itself the
oil, wherewith the human nature was anointed. Therefore says the
Psalmist in our text, *God, your God has anointed you with the oil of
gladness, above your fellows.* The apostle St. *Paul* repeats the same
words, and shows it to be said of Christ. Observe here,

1. Who has anointed? Your God. The first word *God*, must be
understood of Christ in both natures, as if the Psalmist would say; O!
holy Messiah, who are one God with the Father and the Holy Spirit,
and has taken in time the human nature, and is also true God and true
man; you has your God anointed. The second word God, *your God,*

must be understood of God the Father, who has anointed Christ: That Christ calls him "my God," is in regard to his human nature, which is anointed. We will understand the last word *God*, of all the three persons in the Godhead. That is likewise according to the Scripture, for Christ, as God, has anointed himself as man.

2. The ointment is called the oil of gladness, that is, the Holy Spirit; that as oil always swim at top, and will not sink, so works the Holy Spirit, holy thoughts and desires for heavenly things. Oil mollifies a thing that is apt to receive it; the Holy Spirit enters into men's hearts, that do not resist him, and operates both to will and to do good; though Christ was not anointed therefore by the Holy Spirit, since he was without sin. But when we say, that Christ is anointed, must be thereby understood, that the infinite properties of his divine nature are communicated to his human nature.

3. The person that is anointed, is Christ according to his human nature; his divine nature needed no anointing, since that is of one essence with the Father and the Holy Spirit.

Christ is anointed as often as his old father King *David*, who was anointed three times; he was anointed first time privately *in Bethlehem*; second time publicly *of the men of* Judah *in* Hebron; and the third time with grandeur *of all* Israel, Likewise is Christ anointed three times; first time in his conception by the *overshadowing of the Holy Spirit*; second time in his Baptism, by the *descending of the Holy Spirit as a dove*: the third time in his ascension, when *God made him both Lord and Christ.*

4. This anointing is made in an uncommon way; for our text says, *above your fellows.* prophets, kings and priests, are in this case, fellows of Christ, since they are likewise anointed: But there is a great difference, they are anointed with oil prepared according to the art of apothecary, but Christ is anointed with the Holy Spirit; they in their anointing receive gifts for themselves, but Christ was

anointed for to procure heavenly gifts for lost men. The faithful are likewise fellows of Christ, who are anointed likewise with the Holy Spirit to be kings and priests for God, everyone in his own measure; but Christ is anointed without measure.

Of the prophetical office of Christ, we shall observe following:

1st, That the Messiah, whom God had promised to the forefathers, should be a prophet. The words of the Lord, through the mouth of *Moses*, are; *I will raise them up a prophet from among their brethren, like unto you, and will put my words in his mouth; and he shall speak unto them, all that I shall command him, and it shall come to pass, that, whosoever will not hearken unto my words, which he shall speak in my name, I will require it of him.* The apostle St. *Peter* convinces us in his sermon to the Jews, just after the ascension of Christ, that this is said and prophesied of Christ: Our Savior applies these words to himself, when he says to the Jews; *Had you believed* Moses, you *would have believed me, for he wrote of me.* Hereof we can see,

2ndly, that Christ is the greatest prophet. *Moses* was a great prophet, for the Lord says himself; *There arose not a prophet since in* Israel *like unto* Moses, to be understood in the Old Testament: But Christ was yet greater, and also the greatest; *Moses* was but a type of Christ: As *Moses* brought out the children of *Israel* out of the bondage out of *Egypt*, so has Christ brought and freed us from the bondage of sin, and the kingdom of Satan. *Moses* was a mediator between God and the children of *Israel*: Christ is a mediator between God and man: *Moses spoke with God face to face*, and acquainted the children of *Israel* with the will of God; yet saw he but the back parts of God: But Christ has seen God in his full glory, for he is in his bosom, and has revealed unto us the will of God; *No man has seen God at any time, the only begotten Son, which is in the bosom of the Father, he has declared him.*

3rdly, what the prophetical office of Christ is: That is, that Christ

245

has learned of the clear beholding of God, and the anointing of the Holy Spirit, all the godly mysteries, according to his human nature; which mystery he has afterwards declared unto men, and has revealed unto them the will of God concerning their salvation; in particular, he has preached the gospel of the grace of God, and the remission of sins; and has confirmed his doctrine with many miracles, and thereby prays daily to his Father for the progress of his saving doctrine, although few receive the same. Hereof we can lightly conclude,

4thly, wherein the work of Christ's prophetical office consist; namely,

First, that he has declared unto us the will of God concerning our salvation, and has made known unto us all things that he had heard of his Father. Christ says himself; *My doctrine is not mine, but his that sent me. If any man will do his will be shall know of the doctrine, whether it be of God, or whether I speak of myself.* We must not think that they who lived before the time of Christ's incarnation, did not know the way and doctrine of salvation through Christ; no, for they had Christ in promises, sacrifices and prophesies. The first promise of Christ was in the Garden of *Paradise*; *The seed of the woman shall bruise the Serpent's head.* This promise was afterwards repeated to the Patriarchs, with some alteration of words; *In your seed shall all the nations of the Earth be blessed.* The Apostle St. *Paul* applies these words to Christ, when he says; *Now to* Abraham *and his seed were the promises made: He says not, "and to seeds," as of many; but of one, and to your seed, which is Christ.* The sacrifices in the Old Testament, were all types of Christ, as the Apostle St. *Paul* learns us, in his epistle to the *Hebrews*. The prophets have all prophesied of Christ, but in particular the prophet *Isaiah*. Hereof we can conclude, that the doctrine of Christ was not new, but the same that the forefathers had: Therefore said St. *Peter* in the synod in *Jerusalem*; *We believe, that through the grace of the Lord Jesus Christ, we shall be saved even as our fathers.*

Second, that he has confirmed his doctrine, not alone with sufficient proofs of the Old Testament, but also with many miracles; whereof the four evangelists are full. All these miracles are plain proofs, that the Lord Christ was the great prophet whom God had promised; that the human nature of Christ was made partaker after the personal union of the godly properties; and that he was a spiritual physician, who should heal not alone the sick and infirm in the time of his incarnation, but also men from their spiritual sickness and wounds; therefore says the Evangelist St. *Matthew*, after he has given us a narration of Christ healing the sick; *That it might be fulfilled, which was spoken by the prophet* Isaiah, *saying, He took our infirmities, and bore our sicknesses.*

That Christ did forbid sundry whom he healed, not to speak thereof; therefore are the following reasons. *First*, Since such miracles should be preached in the world, after his exaltation to the right hand of God, by the apostles alone, who were evidences chosen of God. *Second*, because Christ would not have his miracles spread about without his doctrine, whose testimony and seals they were; and they who were healed, were neither chosen nor instructed in the doctrine of Christ. *Third*, because there should be no suspicion, that he intended to erect a worldly kingdom; and therefore wanted not such a concourse after him. *Fourth*, because he did not seek any worldly honor and praise, much less testimony. *Fifth*, that he would fulfill the prophecy of *Isaiah, He shall not cry, nor lift up, nor cause his voice to be heard in the street.*

Third, that he has always prayed to God for the progress of his doctrine; whereof the four evangelists do testify, in the history of Christ.

II. We have to discourse of the sacerdotal office of Christ.

Hereof we shall observe following.

1. What high priest Christ is, not after the order of *Levi*, but *after the order of* Melchizedech. *Aaron* and *Melchizedech* were both high priests, but Christ far exceeds them: They were men alone, but Christ is both God and man: They were types, but Christ is the person himself, and therefore is he the greatest and holiest high priest. *The* Levitical *priests were all sinners, and by reason hereof they ought as for the people, so also for themselves to offer for sins*; but Christ is such *a high priest, who is holy, harmless, undefiled, separate from sinners, and made higher than the heavens.* The *Levitical* priest offered daily sacrifices according to the law of *Moses*; but Christ has offered himself, and *by his own blood he entered in once into the holy place, having obtained eternal redemption for us*: The Levitical sacrifices could not make anyone *perfect, as pertaining to the conscience*; but Christ through the offering of his body, has taken away sins, and procured thereby eternal salvation for us. The *Levitical* sacrifices were offered on earth in certain places, and at certain times; but Christ began his sacerdotal office on earth, and has completed the same in heaven: The *Levitical* priests died one after another, but Christ remains high priest in eternity.

2. The temple of Christ is not the tabernacle of *Moses* nor the temple of *Solomon*, but is *a greater and more perfect tabernacle, not made with hands.* And it is his body, his Church militant, and his Church triumphant.

His body is called a temple, wherein the fullness of the Godhead dwells. So said Christ himself of his body: *Destroy this temple, and in three days I will raise it up.*

His Church militant is his temple, whose glory is greater than that in *Jerusalem*: There was all earthly things made with men's hands, but here is Jesus Christ; there was a pot full of manna, wherewith the children of *Israel* were fed in the wilderness; but here is *the bread of life, of whom if any man eat, be shall live forever*; there was the tables of the law, but here is *the end of the law for righteousness to everyone that believes*; there was the blooming rod of *Aaron*, but here is *the rod come forth out of the stem of* Jesse.

His church triumphant is his temple, wherein Christ entered at his ascension, and seated himself on the right hand of God, after he had fulfilled the offering of reconciliation unto God with his body.

3. The sacrifice is Christ himself. The apostle St. *Paul* says, *Christ offered up a sacrifice once, when he offered up himself. Christ appeared once in the end of the world, to put away sin by the sacrifice of himself. So Christ was once offered to bear the sins of many. We are sanctified through the offering of the body of Jesus Christ once for all.* This sacrifice of Christ was offered up for the whole world, yea given for the wickedest sinners who are condemned. As Christ died for *Abraham*, who is saved, so did he likewise die for *Judas*, who is damned, for was Christ not dead for *Judas*, then was he wrongfully condemned for refusing and rejecting the grace that never was offered unto him. So far as the disobedience of *Adam* did extend, so far extends the obedience of Jesus Christ. *He died for all, that they which live, should not henceforth live unto themselves, but unto him, which died for them, and rose again. There is one God, and one Mediator between God and man, the man Christ Jesus, who gave himself a ransom for all. He is the propitiation for our sins, and not for ours only, but also for the sins of the whole world.* What can be plainer said then, *that Jesus should taste death for every man*, where-under, certainly, they who are damned must be reckoned; yet Christ died even for them who sin against the Holy Spirit; for they are also described of the apostle St. *Paul, Who were once enlightened, and have tasted of the heavenly gifts, and were made partakers of the Holy Spirit, and have tasted the good word of God,*

and the powers of the world to come. They have been made partakers of the Holy Spirit, who is the Spirit of Truth, whom the world cannot receive. And they crucify yet daily Christ on a new, and tread the blood of the covenant underfoot. Are they not then themselves the cause why they have no benefit of the death and merits of Christ. Besides these testimonies, there are yet three evidences, by which we can prove, that Christ died for the sins of the whole world. The apostle St. John speaks of these three evidences, saying, *There are three that bear witness in earth, the Spirit, the water, and the blood.* By the Spirit is understood the ministerial office, which is called the *ministration of the Spirit*: By the water is understood baptism, and by the blood the Lord's Supper. Was it now, that there was a man, for whom Christ did not die? Then, as often as the minister pronounced the absolution, or baptized, or administered the Lords Supper, might he be afraid that he would tell a lie; or, if there was any, who is excluded from the communion of Christ's death and suffering, then would the minister in pronouncing the absolution, or administering the sacraments, lie unto them in the Lord's name. That many therefore are damned, is not because Christ died not for them, but, because they themselves will not receive the gracious means, believe in Christ, and show their living faith in a godly life; and thereby obtain the benefits which Christ procured for them, namely, the eternal salvation. Hereof we can lightly conclude,

4. What the sacerdotal office of Christ is. That is, that Christ has with the holiness of his undefiled life, fulfilled the law of God in our stead, and with the sacrifice of his body on the cross, has perfectly satisfied for our sins, and by his intercession procures us the grace of God and the Holy Spirit, and all what we need for, to the obtaining of life everlasting.

5. Wherein the work of Christ's sacerdotal office consists, namely, herein,

First, that he with his holy and undefiled life has fulfilled the law of God, and has taken away the curse of the law, being made a curse himself.

Second, that he has offered up his body on the cross, and has thereby satisfied the wrath of God, and has made a full satisfaction for our sins.

Third, that he intercedes daily for us by his heavenly Father, and is therefore called an advocate with the Father, not to be understood in a human way, as if Christ prayed to his Father.

The children of God can be greatly comforted hereof, since they know that they have such a faithful mediator and advocate, who intercedes for them. Let the Devil accuse us before God; let the law curse us, and let our own hearts and consciences condemn us. We have a faithful advocate with the Father; *Who shall lay anything to the charge of God's elect? It is God that justifies. Who is he that condemns? It is Christ, that died, yea, rather that is risen again, who is even at the right hand of God, who also makes intercession for us.*

Third, we will discourse of Christ's office as King.

Whereof we shall observe the following.

1. Why is Christ become our King? On account of our sin. Our first parents were in the beginning under a gracious kingdom, having God for their king; but through disobedience, became under the dominion of the Devil; for, *of whom a Man is overcome, of the same is he brought in bondage:* As long as they were under the dominion of God, they had their honor; but when they became servants of Sin, they lost their honor and glory; not they alone, but also their whole posterity came under the power of darkness, and we should have never been relieved, if God had not sent his Son, who was to conquer Satan, and free us from his power and tyranny. The Psalmist says, *I have set my king upon the holy Hill of Zion.*

2. That Jesus Christ is a King after both natures. According to his

251

divine nature he is a King from eternity; and according to his human nature he is anointed King in time.

Christ is a sovereign King, having absolute power over all things in heaven, in earth and under the earth, and is therefore called, *King of Kings, and Lord of Lords.* There are three ways by which earthly kings come to their kingdoms; some are born kings as *Solomon*; some are chosen as *Saul*; and some by conquering with the sword. Christ is a king in all the three ways; he is born a king, so says the wisemen from the East, *Where is the newborn king of the* Jews: He is chosen king; so says the Psalmist, *I have set my king upon my holy hill of* Zion, he has conquered and purchased his kingdom, not with sword, but with his own blood, Christ is an eternal king; so says the evangelist *Luke, he shall reign over the house of* Jacob *forever, and of his kingdom there shall be no end.* The prophet *Daniel* prophesied of the kingdom of Christ. *This kingdom shall not be left to other people, but it shall break in pieces, and consume all the kingdoms, and it shall stand forever.*

Christ is a spiritual king, and his kingdom is in the world, but not of the world: His kingdom, namely the Christian church is therefore called, *a royal priesthood*; and his subjects, namely, the faithful, are called *the children of the kingdom.*

Christ is a peaceable king. The Prophet *Isaiah*, calls him, *the Prince of Peace. Of the increase of his government and peace there shall be no end.* He has procured us peace with God, peace in our conscience, and peace from the Devil; and this peace has he made *through the blood of his cross.*

Christ is a gracious king. He has not in his coat of arms a lion, but a lamb; although he is both a lion and a lamb: A lion against his enemies, and a lamb against his subjects. Christ constrains not his people, as *Pharaoh* constrained the children of *Israel*, and after all, *he gives us a more exceeding and eternal weight of glory.*

Christ is a righteous king. *Justice and judgment are the habitation of his throne, righteousness shall be the girdle of his loins, and faithfulness the girdle of his reins.*

3. What the royal office of Christ is. That is, that Christ, as Lord of heaven and earth, and in particular as king and head of the Christian church, governs and rules all things to the glory of God and the salvation of the faithful.

4. Wherein the royal Office of Christ consists, namely,

First, that he calls us by his gospel, to come and be received under his banner, which cannot be done, except we repent, and are converted, and *denying ungodliness and worldly lust, do live soberly, righteously and godly in this present world.*

Second, that he governs and rules all things in heaven and earth, and gives unto his subjects all what is needful for their temporal and eternal life, and descends them from all their enemies; though we must observe here, that Christ shares of his temporal blessings both to the just and unjust, and often a larger portion to the unjust than the just.

Third, that he at the Last Day shall judge the quick and the dead, the faithful and unfaithful; and then shall he bring the righteous into life-everlasting, but the ungodly shall go away into everlasting punishment.

Let us therefore humble ourselves before this our king, priest and prophet, and always strive to be obedient unto his command, then will be certainly defend us from our enemies, and at last receive us into his glorious kingdom. The Lord grant us this, for the sake of Jesus Christ. AMEN.

17

The Humiliation and Exaltation of Christ

T he text PHILIPPIANS, Chap. 2:6, 7, 8, 9, 10, 11. ver.

Jesus Christ being in the form of God, thought it not robbery, to be equal with God, but made himself of no reputation, and took upon him the form of a servant, and was made in the likeness of man; and being found in fashion as a man, he humbled himself, and became obedient unto death, even the death of the cross; where God also has highly exalted him, and given him a name, which is above every name, that at the name of Jesus every knee should bow, of things in heaven, and things in Earth, and things under the Earth; and that every tongue should confess that Jesus Christ is Lord, to the glory of God the Father.

INTRODUCTION

AMONG all the names which are given to Christ our Savior, this is the most principal, that he is called Jesus. This name is,

First, his proper name, and was given to him in the circumcision according to the command of God by the angel *Gabriel.* We read in the Scripture of three very remarkable men, who likewise bore this name Jesus, namely *Joshua* the son of *Nun, Joshua* the high priest in the time of the prophet *Zachariah*, and *Hosea* the prophet: But they were only figures to our Jesus, who in all justice is so called, since he is the Savior of the world. St. *Peter* says therefore, *there is no other name under heaven given among men, by which we must be saved:* He is also a true Jesus, both in name and deed.

Second, this name is very remarkable; Jesus signifies a Savior, for he was to save his people from their sins; but his people must be understood not the Jews alone, who are called a chosen people of God, and the faithful, who are called the children of the Kingdom, but also of all mankind; for this word people, is explained in another place, with *all people.* All men were under sin, the wrath of God, and power of Satan, and needed a Savior: The apostle St. *Paul* says: *"He is the Savior of all men, especially of those that believe."* The salvation which Christ has procured consist in, that he has freed and saved us from all evil, but especially spiritual evil, and that he has again procured for us amity with God, righteousness for God, peace in our conscience, adoption to children, the gift of the Holy Spirit, and comfort in crosses and affliction, and at last the eternal salvation.

Thirdly, particular is this name. When God gives a name, the same is always of a particular signification to the person to whom such a name is given. *Abraham* signifies a father of a great multitude, and was given of God to the old patriarch of the *Jewish* nation, who became likewise a Father of a great multitude, and was not alone according to the flesh, but also to the Spirit. *John* the Baptist was so called, since he was to begin to preach of the grace of God, which was to be manifested in the doctrine, miracles and sufferings of Christ, for *John* signifies grace of God; likewise is Jesus called so, which name signifies Savior, for he was to save his people from their sins.

Fourthly, it is a name that brings salvation. All blessings, help, comfort and salvation flows out of this name as from a fountain of salvation. *To him give all the prophets witness, that through his name whosoever believes in him, shall receive remission of sins.*

Fifthly, it is a holy name. The angels in heaven and saints adore and honor this name. The Devil in hell and the condemned are afraid thereof and tremble, and all the faithful on earth are rejoiced thereover, and embrace the same through faith; yea, the knee of all things in heaven, on earth, and under the earth, must bow down at this name; and every tongue must confess, that Jesus Christ is, *Lord to the glory of God the Father,* as the Apostle St. *Paul* says in the words of our text, wherein he describes Jesus Christ of his two states, namely,

FIRST, *The State of his Humiliation.*

SECOND, *The State of his Exaltation.*

EXPLANATION of the TEXT

I. Describes the Apostle St. Paul, Jesus Christ of the State of his Humiliation.

The law of retaliation is, as the damage is, so must the satisfaction be; *eye for eye, tooth for tooth, hand for hand, foot for foot, burning for burning, wound for wound, stripe for stripe.* If we could not know or understand the greatness of *Adam's* Fall in *Paradise,* then we can learn it of the sufferings and death of Christ, who did fully satisfy for their disobedience: *Adam* was proud, and would become like unto God; but Christ being in the form of God, thought it not robbery to be equal with God: Consider here,

1. Who humbled himself: Jesus Christ, true God and true man, in one person. The apostle speaks here of Christ, not according to his divine nature, for God is immutable, and can neither be exalted nor

256

humbled; and how can anything be given or taken from the divine nature, who is Lord of all things? Therefore, according to the same nature, Christ is exalted; according to the same is he humbled, and that is the human nature; which in the moment of conception, was through the personal union, made partaker in divine majesty and glory; but Christ did not always make use of this godly majesty and glory; for then the *Jews* could have not taken and crucified him; and also the work of our redemption would not have been completed.

Second, how Christ humbled himself. The apostle says in our text,

1. He *thought it not robbery to be equal with God*. Although his human nature was by the power of the personal union, made partaker of divine majesty and glory; yet he did not boast nor brag thereof, as they who have got a stately booty, commonly does; or as they who strive after great things, are proud thereof; as *Absalom*, who wanted to force his own father from the kingdom, and to be made king in his stead; or as our first parents, who wanted to bereave God of his honor, and become like unto him. Christ could have well boasted of his Godhead, but he evacuated himself from the godly excellencies, and did not constantly use them, except when the honor of God did require it: He had always the communicated divine attributes in his manhood, but did not show them, except when he saw it was needful; as he showed his almighty power in the raising of the dead, and healing the sick and infirm: He showed his quickening power in the conversion of sinners: He showed his omniscience in perceiving men's thoughts: He showed his omnipresence in seeing the absent things, as if present; as *Nathaniel* under the fig-tree: He showed his riches in feeding so many thousand men and women, with few bread and fish: He showed his power, in commanding the wind and weather.

2. *But made himself of no reputation, and took upon him the form of a servant, and was made in the likeness of men.* He was Lord of heaven

and earth, and yet was pleased to take on the form of a servant for our sake: He was handled, sold, taken, condemned, and at last, crucified as a servant.

3. *And being found in the fashion, as a man, be humbled himself, and become obedient unto death, even the death of the cross.* This was the lowest degree of Christ's humiliation, that he would suffer a shameful death on the cross, for to show his obedience to the will of God, and to procure a ransom for our sins, and is made a curse. We have a glorious figure of Christ in *Isaac:*

1st, in the name. *Isaac* signifies laughter; Christ is our only comfort and joy.

2ndly, in the conception. *Isaac* was conceived of *Abraham* and *Sarah*, in their old age, in a supernatural way; Christ was conceived in a supernatural way of a virgin without the knowledge of a man.

3rdly, in the circumcision. *Isaac* was the first that was circumcised after God had ordered this holy covenant: Christ was last circumcised in the Old Testament, and by consequence the first in the new, for the New Testament began with him.

4thly, in sufferings. *Isaac* was obedient to his father to be offered up, he bore himself the wood for to burn, and was willing and silent, when his father bound him and laid him on the altar; Christ was obedient to his heavenly Father, he bore his own cross, whereupon he was to be circumcised, and opened not his mouth, but went as a lamb to the butcher's stall.

5thly, in the resurrection. *Isaac* was dead in the thoughts and heart of his father, the three days they were on the road to the land of *Moriah*, where he was to be offered up; but on the third day, when the angel of the Lord withheld *Abraham* from offering up *Isaac*, then arose *Isaac* again as from dead in his father's thought: Christ was three days dead, and rose again on the third day.

II. The Steps of Christ's Humiliation are Nine, to wit.

First step is his conception in his mother's womb, by the overshadowing of the Holy Spirit, where he laid nine months like another child.

Second step is his birth, when he was born in a stable, and wrapped up in swaddling clothes, and laid in a manger.

Third step is his circumcision on the eighth day, according to the command given to *Abraham*, and the custom of the *Jews*.

Fourth step is his exile into *Egypt*, where *Joseph* fled with the mother and the child for fear of *Herod*.

Fifth step is his growing up like other children, in years and in wisdom.

Sixth step is his fasting and temptation in the wilderness.

Seventh step is his ministerial office; in which time he was blasphemed, despised, hated, and persecuted.

Eighth step is his sufferings and pain from his bloody sweat in *Gethsemane*, until on the cross, where he died and fulfilled the prophecy, and satisfied the wrath of God.

Ninth step is his burial, when he like another dead body was buried and laid in a grave.

The foregoing nine steps belong to the state of Christ's humiliation, and comprehend the whole course of Christ's life, which St. *Paul* calls *the days of his flesh*. We must understand this humiliation alone of the human nature, although it concerns likewise the whole person; for Christ has not alone taken on the human nature, but also the accidents and mutations of human nature; so that we can well say: That God, the second person in the Godhead, died for us: But we cannot say that the Godhead died.

III. Describes the apostle St. Paul the state of Christ's exaltation.

The state of the exaltation of Jesus Christ began after his death and burial, and did continue after his ascension in the sitting on the right hand of God, when he entered into his glory. Consider here again:

1. Who is exalted. Jesus Christ true God and true man in one person; since this person consists of two natures the divine and the human, then can we ask, according to which nature is Jesus Christ exalted? Not according to the divine, for that is immutable, and cannot be humbled nor exalted, but the right meaning of St. *Paul* according to the Scripture, is, that Jesus Christ is exalted according to the human nature, that he ascended to heaven according to his human nature, that he sits on the right hand of God according to his human nature; and that a name above all names is given to him according to his human nature.

2. How Christ was exalted, the apostle says in our text.

First, wherefore God has also highly exalted him. The word wherefore signifies, not a cause *wherefore God has exalted him*; as if Christ had earned this exaltation through and with his humiliation; but it is an order, that upon the humiliation followed the exaltation, not through merits, but of grace, as the word in the *Greek* text signifies. This exaltation of Christ is wonderful, and exceeds far the apprehension of human reason. St. *Paul* cannot find words to express it with, and says therefore not alone exalted, but highly exalted.

Secondly, and given him a name, which is above every name, that at the name of Jesus every knee should how of things in heaven, and things in earth, and things under the earth, and that every tongue should confess, that Jesus Christ is Lord to the glory of God the Father. By this name we should be admonished.

1st, of the name Jesus itself: That it is gracious; for we have grace by God through this name: That it is saving; for *there is no salvation in any other name:* That it is precious; for it is the *pearl of great price,* which the merchant bought: That it is powerful; for the apostles wrought many miracles in this name; yea the devils tremble for this name. That it is the water of life, the light for the blind, a strength for the weak, a comfort for the afflicted, and life for the dead. And that this name is excellent, and the excellency thereof is by the preaching of the gospel spread over the whole world for all men, in heaven for all the holy angels, and in hell for the devils.

2nd*ly*, of the power of the kingdom of Christ: That he is Lord, God, and the Son of God, under whose subjection everything is laid. For the word name signifies not alone the case, but also the work in itself, which is signified in this name. *According to your name, O God, so is your praise unto the end of the world.* This name signifies here the godly honor, glory and majesty, and likewise the godly dominion in heaven and earth, into which Christ according to his human nature entered, and took full possession thereof. This name was happily given to Christ in the state of his humiliation, but was then looked upon as in another person, who can have his own name; but in the state of his exaltation it is given to him, as a glorious name, whereof all could know, that he was Jesus a Savior.

3rd*ly*, of the divine adoration we must pay unto this name: *That all knees shall bow at it,* by which is understood, that we must adore Christ's both natures after the personal union; for since the apostle says in our text, *that God has highly exalted him, and given him a name, which is above every name,* then can we lightly conclude thereof, that the human nature of Christ must be adored and worshiped by us as well as his divine nature. *At this name shall every knee how, of things that are in heaven;* the holy angels and the elders, who worship him as true God and true man, for they are all made subject unto him. *Of* *things on earth*, that is, all men, both good and bad, righteous and unrighteous, high and low; yea, *all kings shall fall down before him, all nations shall serve him.* The *Jews, Muslims,* and *heathens,* do not bow their knees for the Lord Jesus, but they rather despise and mock him; but the meaning of the apostle in our text, is not what they do, but what they ought to do; and at the Last Day, when he shall come to judge the quick and the dead, then shall they bow their knees for him, and adore him. *And of things under the earth*; that is, the devils and evil spirits in Hell; they were obliged to adore Jesus in the state of his humiliation, much more now he is in the state of his exaltation.

4thly, of the confession of his name: *That every tongue should confess, that Jesus Christ is Lord to the glory of God the Father.* Christ is made according to his human nature a Lord, the Lord of Glory, the Lord of Lords, and King of Kings. *All men should honor the Son, even as they honor the Father*; *he that honors not the Son, honors not the Father, who has sent him.*

Christ is Lord to the glory of God the Father, for God has gotten him through Christ, glory of mercy, he had compassion on lost mankind, and sent his Son to be a Savior, who under his manhood should conquer the great old serpent, that had deceived our first parents, God has got in Christ glory of truth, in fulfilling his promise, which he had made concerning the seed of the woman, that was to bruise the head of the serpent. God has got in Christ glory of justice, in not sparing his only and beloved Son, who should fully satisfy the justice of God, and also reconcile us again unto God, in whose disgrace we all were fallen through the disobedience of *Adam.* God has got in Christ, glory of wisdom and majesty, in the personal union of the two natures in Christ, which is the greatest miracles, and far exceeds the apprehension of man's reason; yea, is a great mystery even for the angels. In Christ was united the highest and lowest, the most majestic and the most despised, the strongest and the weakest, the holiest, the best and the worst; for what is higher, stronger, holier, and better than God; and what is weaker, lower, and worse than man; though these two are united here in one person.

3. The steps of Christ's exaltation are four.

First, his descending into Hell. On the third day after his burial, when he had conquered the pain of death, and soul and body were again united, then did Christ descend into hell, before he appeared on earth, and shewed the evil spirits in hell, how grossly they had abused him, and through that, had lost their right and claim on mankind, and that he had now fulfilled what was promised by the prophet; *I will ransom them from the power of the grave, I will redeem them from death; O death I will be your plague, O grave I will be your destruction. He preached also unto the spirits in prison*; that is, he upbraided them with their unbelief, and disobedience, and convinced them, that now were all the promises fulfilled, which they in their lifetime had so obstinately rejected. Thereupon followed,

The *second* step, his resurrection. On the third day he rose again from the dead: Which is a plain proof of his victory and triumph over sin, death, the Devil and hell. The resurrection of Christ is attributed to all the three persons in the Holy Trinity.

God the Father raised him from the dead, after he had made full satisfaction for us, and had fulfilled the promises.

Christ raised the temple of his body himself, on the third day, after the *Jews* had destroyed him; then did it plainly appear, that he was *the Son of God with power, according to the Spirit of holiness, by the resurrection from the dead*. The Holy Spirit, *the Spirit of God raised him from the dead*. The body of Christ was the temple and habitation of the Holy Trinity, and it is therefore a quickening body.

The enemies of Christ are very willing and desirous, to make the resurrection of Christ suspected, and therefore gave large money to the soldiers, who were to watch over his grave, that they should say, his disciples came by night, and stole him away while we slept; but as darkness must give room to light, so likewise this abominable invention and lie, must give room to the truth. The resurrection of Christ is confirmed by his appearing ten times afterwards at different places, and at different times, for different persons.

First, appeared he to *Mary Magdalene, out of her he cast seven devils.*

Second time, to the women, who went early to the grave to anoint him.

Third time, to *Peter* the apostle, who had denied him.

Fourth time, to the two disciples who went to *Emmaus*, of whom one was *Cleopas*, but the other is uncertain.

Fifth time, to the eleven, when *Thomas* was not there.

Sixth time, to the eleven when *Thomas* was by.

Seventh time, by the sea *Tiberias*.

Eighth time, on a hill in *Galilea* to more than five hundred.

Ninth time, to the apostle St. *James*.

Tenth time, when he took leave from them. And,

The *third* step, ascended to heaven on the fortieth day after his resurrection, in the sight of them all.

The heaven whereto Christ ascended cannot be explained in this world with words, neither be apprehended with human reason; though we can say according to the Scripture that it is *far above all heavens*, and that Christ is *made higher than the heavens*; and that it is not described so much of a certain place, as of the joy and glory; and that it is *a building of God, a house not made with hands, a greater and more perfect tabernacle not made with hands, that is to say, not of this building.* Lastly, that the heavenly glory is so great, that *eye has not seen, nor ear heard, nor has entered into the heart of men.*

There is great difference between the ascension of Christ, and that of *Enoch* and *Elijah*, Christ ascended by the power of his own Godhead, they by the power of God. They ascended so, that they

264

are no more here on earth, Christ is over all after his ascension, especially in his church, a comfort for the faithful, but a punishment for the wicked. They ascended, and were received into everlasting joy: Christ ascended, and sat himself on the right hand of God.

Fourth step is his sitting on the right hand of God. We must not understand here by the right hand of God, any limb on a body, nor any certain place, but the almighty power of God by which he governs all things. It is a comparison taken of a human way of speaking, that as a man has all his strength mostly in the right hand, wherewith he does everything; so signifies the right hand of God, the glorious and almighty power of God, wherewith and by which he governs and rules all things in heaven and earth, and everywhere.

When we therefore say, that Christ sits on the right hand of God; that signifies, that Christ governs all things in a godly way, according to his human nature. After the same nature, that Christ was exalted, after the same sits he likewise on the right hand of God. God raised Christ from the dead, and *he is gone into heaven, and is on the right hand of God, angels and authorities, and powers being made subject unto him.* Christ sits not idle on the right hand of God; no, but he governs all things, especially he has great care over his church, which he has purchased with his own blood, and sends faithful pastors and teachers, intercedes for them by his Father, defends them from their enemies, and at last brings them into everlasting salvation.

Which salvation the Lord grant us, for Christ's sake. AMEN.

18

The Law

T he Text ST. MATHEW, 22:37, 38, 39, 40. ver.
You shall love the Lord your God with all your heart, and with all your soul, and with all your mind: This is the first and great commandment: And the second is like unto it: You shall love your neighbor as yourself. On these two commandments hang all the law and the prophets.

INTRODUCTION

AS God is alone Lord over all things, and is himself a law, so will he that everyone should acknowledge him to be Lord, and therefore be obedient unto his law and commands. Therefore wrote he in the creation a law in man's heart, and gave afterwards his law, after which man was to regulate himself, and show his obedience to his Lord and Creator; but when man did transgress the outward law, then became the inward law corrupted and darkened, wherefore God gave another complete law on Mount *Sinai*; whereof *Moses* gives us a full description in *Exodus* 20 wherein he shows us, 1. The giving of the law with all its circumstances. 2. The division of this law.

1. The giving of the law with all its circumstances. Observe here,

First, the *giver* of the law. It is the Lord God, the same God who sent *Moses* to *Pharaoh*; who told unto *Moses*, when *Moses* asked him, who he was? *I am that I am*; who had wrought so many miracles for *Pharaoh* and his people; and who had brought the children of *Israel*, out of bondage out of *Egypt* with a mighty hand. It is the Lord Jehovah, maker of heaven and earth.

Secondly, the place where the law was given, was the Mount *Sinai*, lying in *Arabia*, where the Lord appeared the first time to *Moses*, and afterwards gave the law from thence, whereof it is called a holy hill, a hill of God.

Thirdly, the way and manner, how the law given, was dreadful, for there happened seven terrible tokens, the mountain shook, and were smoking, wherefore the law is called a *fiery law*; there was thunder and lightning; there was a thick cloud on the mountain; there was a great storm; there was the sounding of trumpets; and there was the loud voice of God heard.

Fourthly, the people to whom this law was given. It was given to the *Jews* whom God had chosen among all the nations to be his people. wherefore the *Psalmist* says of them, *that God has not dealt so with any nation.* This law was given, since the natural law written in man's heart was darkened through the disobedience and transgression of *Adam*, for to enlighten and clear up again the natural law.

267

2. The division of this law. Besides the natural law written in man's heart, God gave here on Mount Sinai to his people, the written law, which is a threefold sort.

First, the moral law, of the Ten Commandments, which mostly agrees with the natural law.

Secondly, the ecclesiastical law concerning the church ceremonies, and offices of the *Jews*.

Thirdly, the temporal law, being an appendix to the moral law.

Moses comprehends these three sorts under these words, *These are the commandments:* (The moral law:) *The statutes:* (The ecclesiastical law.) *And the judgment:* (The temporal law:) *Which the Lord your God commanded to teach you.*

The two last sorts, namely, the ecclesiastical and temporal law, did oblige the *Jews* alone; but the first, that is the moral law, or the Ten Commandments, obliges all men, of what nation or profession whatsoever; and that under pain of temporal and eternal punishment. Our Savior Jesus Christ chooses out of these laws the moral law, and gives us in our text, a short Summary of the Ten Commandments. We will before we come thereto, discourse first of the other three sorts; and the heads of this discourse will be,

FIRST, *Of the natural law.*

SECOND, *Of the ecclesiastical law.*

THIRD, *Of the temporal law.*

FOURTH, *Of the moral law.*

EXPLANATION of the TEXT

1. Of the Natural Law.

The natural law is a knowledge, that God did in the first creation print in the heart and mind of man, and plants it daily in the thoughts and hearts of everyone, by which we know that there is a God, whom we must honor and worship; and that we must do good and shun evil. It is called a natural law, because it is born with everyone in their nature; and without any foregoing instructions, learns us, what we shall do or not, and consists mostly in these articles according to the Scripture.

First, that there is a supreme being, whom we must honor and worship; which can be learned of beholding the visible things.

Secondly, that we must do what is good and honorable, and shun what is evil and dishonorable.

Thirdly, that our *conscience accuses us* when we do evil, *and excuses us* when we do good.

Fourthly, that it is the *judgment of God, that they which commit evil are worthy of death, not only do the same, but have pleasure in them that do them.*

Fifthly, that *whatsoever we will that men should do to us, we do even so to them.*

Upon these articles is our conscience grounded, which shows us inwardly what must be done, and judges all our actions; if we do good, our conscience excuses us, but if we do evil, the same accuses us. We have therefore no need to seek a testimony of our actions from outward, for we have the surest testimony inward in us, and we must behold the admonition of our conscience as a voice from God, and it can well therefore be said: He that is not afraid for his conscience, is neither afraid for God.

This natural law is alike by everyone, who is by his right senses: For, as the natural law is written in the heart of everyone, so is it

269

alike by all. St. *Paul* says therefore of the *gentiles*, who had not the law, *that they by nature do the things contained in the law, and having not the law, are a law unto themselves, and show the work of the law written in their hearts.*

God has planted this natural law in man's heart for three reasons.

1*st*, That they who do not know God of the word, can by the natural knowledge be encouraged *to seek him, if happily they might find him.*

2nd*ly*, That worldly business and conversation can be kept in order, and they that do not know the law of God, can have a certain rule to live after.

3rd*ly*, That idolaters, and all they who sin against their own conscience, shall *be without excuse.* Let us now look into,

II. The Ecclesiastical Law.

The ecclesiastical law of the *Jews* were the statutes, which God had given to the *Jews* concerning their ceremonies and worship, which they were to observe, partly that they should be figures to the spiritual things, partly that they should show them their spiritual uncleanness, and partly that they should be a guardian into Christ.

The things which God had ordered to be observed according to the law, did concern, *First*, the priests; *Secondly*, the holy places; *Thirdly*, the high feast; *Fourthly*, the sacrifices; *Fifthly*, the sacraments; *Sixthly*, concerning clothing, eating, washing, and others.

1*st*, Concerning the priest, we can read of fully in the third Book of *Moses* called *Leviticus.*

2nd*ly*, The holy places were two, namely, the tabernacle in the time of *Moses*, and the temple in the time of *Solomon.*

The tabernacle in the time of *Moses*, was built according to the command of God; and the description thereof *Moses* gives in his book called *Numbers.* This tabernacle lasted until the time of King

Solomon, who built likewise by the command of God, a temple in *Jerusalem*.

3rdly, The high feast, according to the law, were, the *Sabbath* kept holy every seventh day in the week; the *new moon feast*, when they blew with the trumpets; the *Paschal Feast*, in remembrance of their deliverance from *Egypt*; the *Pentecost feast*, in remembrance of the giving of the law; the *Feast of Atonement*; the *Feast of the Blowing of Trumpets*; the *Feast of the Tabernacles*: the *Feast of Harvest*, after they had gathered in their fruits; the *Feast of the Lands-Resting-Year*, which was to be kept every seventh year; the *Jubilee Feast*; then returned everyone to his possession and his family: This feast was kept every fiftieth year.

The feasts, according to the church ordinances, were, the *Feast of Purim*, in remembrance of their deliverance from *Haman*'s wicked intention; the *Feast of the Dedication and Cleansing of the Altar*: This feast was kept holy, and celebrated in the time of Christ's incarnation; The *Feast of the Victory over Nicanor*.

4thly, The sacrifices; they were many, namely; the *burnt offerings*, which were to be burnt with holy fire on the altar; the *meat offering* of the fruits of the earth; the *offering of thanksgiving*; the *sin-offering of ignorance*; the *trespass offering*; the *consecration offering*; the *purification offering*, for women and others; the *reconciliation offering*, and the *daily offering*.

5thly, The sacraments; these were two, the circumcision, and the Easter lamb.

6thly, Concerning clothing, eating, washing and others, we can read of in the books of *Moses*, where he gives us a plain description of the ecclesiastical law, and the ceremonies of the Jewish church. All these Levitical ceremonies and sacrifices, were alone figures to Christ, and are therefore no more used in the New Testament, since Jesus Christ, to whom they were figures, is come, and has fulfilled the law.

Let us speak also.

III. Of the Temporal Law.

This law was as an appendix to the moral law, or the Ten Commandments; and *Moses* gives us a complete narration and explanation
thereof in his books: This law is likewise no more in force, in the
time of the New Testament, except so far as they agree with the
natural law written in our hearts, and the moral law, or the Ten
Commandments. Lastly, we will discourse,

IV. Of the Moral Law.

The moral law, commonly called the Ten Commandments, is nothing
else but an explanation of the natural law, and was given publicly
on Mount *Sinai*, to the children of *Israel*, after they were come out of
Egypt. It was written with the finger of God on two tables of stone; in
which law we can see and behold, as in a glass, the corruption of our
sinful nature, how we ought to be, and what we ought to commit and
omit; the same obliges all men to perfect obedience, both inward
and outward, and threatens the transgressors with temporal and
eternal punishment.

None should think, that what is comprehended in the Ten Commandments was unknown to men, till it was given publicly on
Mount *Sinai*; no, for it was known unto them from the beginning,
and it was written in their hearts in the creation, since man was
created in the image of God, which consists in righteousness and
true holiness: And we may see this righteousness and holiness in
the Ten Commandments. The forefathers, who lived before the law
was given on Mount *Sinai*, knew by the natural law written in their

hearts, the will of God, by which they could regulate their actions and living, and also become pleasing in the sight of God; but since this natural law was darkened by the disobedience of our first parents, and the nature of man was become corrupted, and inclined to evil and mischief; therefore it did please the gracious God, to give this moral law, by which the natural law is become enlightened again; and we can learn thereby the will of God.

Our Savior gives us a short summary of the Ten Commandments, in the words of our text, wherein he divides the Ten Commandments in two tables, and reckons to the first table the commandments, which speaks of our love towards God; and to the second table, them which treat of our love towards our neighbors, Christ calls the two tables, the two great commandments. That the fourth commandment is the first in the second table, we can prove by the words of St *Paul*, when he says: *Honor your father and mother, which is the first commandment, with promise.* We will follow the order of the Ten Commandments, and give a short explanation of them.

The First Commandment

I am the Lord your God; You shall have no other gods before me. In this commandment is not alone forbidden all sorts of outward idolatry, but also the trusting in anything else but the living God, who created heaven and earth. And this commandment can be transgressed in manifold ways; both in words, thoughts and deeds.

The Second Commandment

You shall not take the name of the Lord your God in vain, for the Lord will not hold him guiltless, that takes his name in vain. We can transgress this commandment in three ways:

First, With our hearts, when we put a little value on the Name of God, and do not consider rightly the great blessing we have of the manifestation of the name of God, nor acknowledge the same as we ought.

Second, with our mouths, with swearing, cursing, blaspheming, lying, and enchanting.

Third, with our actions; when they who are placed in authority, not alone let the transgressors of this commandment escape, but also have pleasure in their doings.

The third commandment

Remember the Sabbath Day, to keep it holy. The Sabbath Day is not instituted of men, but of God, and is therefore called the Lord's Day: This commandment we can transgress with absenting ourselves from the public worship of God, and with neglecting the gracious means offered to us in the word of God and the Holy Sacraments, and all charitable actions.

The Fourth Commandment

Honor your father and your mother, that your days may be long upon the land, which the Lord your God gives you. This is the first commandment in the second table. Under the name of father and mother, must be understood all they, who are in authority over us, either in church or state.

The Fifth Commandment

You shall not kill. This commandment defends the life of our neighbors, and can be transgressed in words, thoughts, or deeds. It defends likewise our own life, which we neither must destroy, but seek to preserve the same.

The Sixth Commandment

You shall not commit Adultery. This commandment defends the honor of our neighbor, and can likewise be transgressed in many ways, in thoughts, words, or deeds.

The Seventh Commandment

You shall not steal. This commandment defends the goods and fortune of our neighbors, and can also be transgressed with thoughts, words, or deeds.

The Eighth Commandment

You shall not bear false witness against your neighbor. This commandment defends the reputation of our neighbors, and we can transgress the same in many ways with thoughts, words, or deeds.

The Ninth Commandment

You shall not covet your neighbor's House. This commandment forbids the actual desire, that we should not strive after to obtain and gratify our evil and wicked desires and lusts.

The Tenth Commandment

You shall not covet your neighbor's wife, nor his servant, nor his maid, nor his ox, nor his ass, nor anything that is your neighbor's. This commandment forbids the original desire, which is the secret fault of the heart, and derives from our inbred sin, and corrupted nature, which we ought to endeavor to subdue and resist.

This law given of God on Mount *Sinai*, and repeated in the New Testament is,

First, holy. The Lord said himself to *Moses* and the children of *Israel*; *Be you holy, for I am holy.* If the giver be holy, then must certainly the gift be holy likewise. Besides, it instructs us how we should live, and serve God in holiness, not alone in actions but also in thoughts.

Secondly, the law is immutable. God is immutable, so is likewise his Law. *It is easier for heaven and earth to pass, than one tittle of the law to fail.*

Thirdly, the law is perfect. We are commanded to love God with all our heart, with all our soul, and with all our mind. Hereby we can see, that God will not be worshiped in part; but he requires the whole man both soul and body.

Fourthly, the law is spiritual, for it is given of God, who *is a Spirit*; and it requires of us, not alone outward bodily obedience, but also inwardly spiritual. *Luther* said, "Every commandment is so spiritual, that it forbids and commands not alone the action, that is, the

275

branches, leaves and fruit, but even also the desire, that is, the root and nourishment." Thereof follows,

Fifthly, that the law is impossible to be kept now. Who can love God with all his heart, with all his soul, and with all his mind? We must confess here with the mouth, what we find to be true in our heart. That *the flesh lusts against the Spirit*, and that *the law of our members war against the law of our mind.* Therefore have all the saints publicly confessed, and complained, that they were sinners before God and his tribunal; and it is certain, that where sin is, there can the law not be kept. The pious *Job*, of whom the Spirit of God testifies, that he was a man *perfect and upright, and one that feared God, and eschewed evil*, confesses himself, with these words, his own unrighteousness; *I know it is so of a truth, but how should man be just with God? If he will contend with him, he cannot answer him one of a thousand. Behold be puts no trust in his saints, yea, the heavens are not clean in his sight, how much more abominable and filthy is man, which drinks iniquity like water.* The Psalmist King *David*, whom the scripture calls a man after the heart of God, confesses likewise his own unrighteousness, saying, *If you Lord should mark iniquities, O Lord, who shall stand? O Lord enter not into judgment with your servant, for in your sight shall no man living be justified.* His son King *Solomon* makes the same confession, saying: *Who can say, I have made my heart clean? I am pure from my sin.* Could a man fulfill the law, then could he likewise be justified and saved thereby; but now, *by the deeds of the law, there shall no flesh be justified.* Then follows, that none can fulfill the law: And could man keep the law perfect, then was Christ come needless in the world, to procure us *the righteousness of God*; for, *what the law could not do, in that it was weak through the flesh, God sending his own Son, in the likeness of sinful flesh, and for sin condemned sin in the flesh, that the righteousness of the law might be fulfilled in us.*

But since man cannot perfectly keep the law, why then has God given the law? The reasons thereof are following,

1st, That it should be a bridle on sin, by which sin and wickedness can be hindered, and the wicked can be kept in awe; that they should not do what they will, and please themselves, because the conversation, modesty and tranquility of all societies should not be disturbed. *Luther* said, "The first use of the law is to subdue wickedness; for the Devil reigns in the whole world, and instigates men to wickedness: Therefore has God ordered, magistrates and authority, and has given a law, after which the magistrates are to rule and govern, and hinder wickedness."

2ndly, That it should be a glass wherein we can behold the corrupted nature, which lays concealed in our flesh, wherefore the Apostle St. *Paul* says, in several places of his epistles. *By the law is the knowledge of sin: The law works wrath: The law entered, that the offence might abound: I had not known sin but by the law, for I had not known lust, except the law had said, you shall not covet: The Scripture hath concluded all under sin.* We are oftentimes conceited, and imagine that we are holy, and say like the *Pharisees, I thank you, O God, that I am not like other men.* We should all be innocent, and just, thinking when we go but to church, receive the sacraments, and practice such outward good actions, that we are good Christians, and God must be contented with us; but when we come to prove ourselves by the law, and do behold ourselves in the clear shining glass of the law, then do we find, that all our outward good actions are but hypocrisy, and that we cannot be justified by them. God requires more of us, namely, a perfect obedience, which, although we cannot show it, is yet required of us, since he had once given and granted full power and strength to man in the creation, which our first parents shamefully lost by their transgression.

3rdly, That it should be a rule of our life, wherein the faithful, who are regenerated, are instructed, which are the good actions, that they must do in order to become well-pleasing in the sight of God: The wicked and hardened sinners are kept in awe by the law, as an unruly and wild horse by the bridle, that they should not do and act according as they think proper, and complete the wicked designs of Satan, who goes round, seeking whom he may devour.

The Lord raise in our hearts by his Holy Spirit, a true will and desire, to walk all our lifetime on the path of his holy command, and that we may walk here according to his law in our imperfection, until we come to full perfection in his Kingdom, for the sake of our blessed Savior, Jesus Christ. AMEN.

19

The Gospel

T he Text ROMANS, 1:16. ver.
The gospel is the power of God unto salvation, to everyone that believes.

INTRODUCTION

IN the night when Christ was born, appeared an angel of the Lord unto the shepherds abiding in the field, and said unto them: *Fear not, for behold, I bring you good tidings of great joy, which shall be to all people; For unto you is born this day a Savior.* As we can read in the Gospel of *Luke* 2:10, and 11. ver. Point your thoughts here,

1. On the person who brought this glad tiding. It was an angel of the Lord, without doubt, according to the opinion of the old church fathers, the angel *Gabriel,* whom God had used for the annunciation of Christ's conception. This angel appeared not in such glory as *Moses, the skin of whose face shined so when he came down from Mount* Sinai, *that* Aaron *and the children of* Israel *were afraid to come nigh to him;* But in the glory of the Lord, wherein laid concealed the person of

Christ, who, although born now in the greatest poverty like another child, was notwithstanding the eternal Son of God, *the brightness of his glory, and the express Image of his person.*

2. On the words of the angel, wherein we can find,

First, the introduction: *Fear not.* It is no wonder that these shepherds were afraid, for we have examples, that even holy men have been afraid in such like case. *Zacharias* was a priest, who was executing his priestly office before God; but when an angel of the Lord appeared unto him, *he was troubled, and fear fell upon him.* This dread follows man naturally, and is occasioned for the sake of sin; for sin brought fear into the world, as we can see of the example of our first parents, and will never be removed before sin is removed; but the Lord be praised, who has caused it so, that we have no cause to be afraid, therefore says the angel, in

Secondly, the preparation: *For behold I bring you good tidings of great joy, which shall be to all people.* When the glory of the Lord appeared on Mount *Sinai,* in a thick cloud, smoke, thunder and lightning; then became the children of *Israel* fore afraid, and stood afar off; but *Moses* said unto them, *fear not, for God is come to prove you:* The fear of the people could not be wholly removed by this saying; for since the Lord would prove them, then might they be afraid, if they were not fully prepared; and so holy as they ought to be. On the contrary, the angel of the Lord, who appeared here in the glory of the Lord removed all fear and dread from the shepherds; for the Lord, would not prove, but comfort them: They had therefore cause to say, *Sing O heavens, be joyful O earth, and break forth into singing O mountain, for the Lord has comforted his people, and will have mercy upon his afflicted.* The hearts of the people were become saint under the dominion of the *Romans,* and likewise under sin, and the law. In the same is brought a *good tiding,* whereover they should be rejoiced, *according to the joy in harvest, and as men rejoice when they divide the spoil, for the yoke of their burden, and the staff of their shoulder, and the rod of their oppressor is broken:* And he who was to do this, was now born, as

3. The tiding of the angel shows: *For unto you is born this day a Savior:* This was the first gospel of Christ preached after his birth, and the meaning thereof is thus: "O you miserable and lost mankind be rejoiced, and fear not longer, for this day is born unto you the promised seed of the Woman, who shall save you from sin, death, devil and hell, and restore again to you the grace of God, and eternal salvation." This is the meaning of the apostle St. *Paul*, when he says in our text, *the gospel is the power of God unto salvation, to everyone that believes.* In which words are laid before us the following two heads;

FIRST, *What the Gospel is.*

SECOND, *The Power of the Gospel.*

EXPLANATION of the TEXT

I. What the Gospel is,

The gospel has not been known naturally to men as the law, but it is a mystery concealed by God from eternity, and would never have been manifested if *Adam* had not sinned; for otherwise, *Adam* had enough in the one part of the heavenly doctrine, namely, the law, which he might have kept easily: But when *Adam* became, through disobedience and transgressing the law and command of God, unable hereto, then needed he another means for the obtaining of everlasting salvation, which is the gospel: This we can prove by these, that God, willing to be merciful unto *Adam* and his posterity, did manifest and reveal the first gospel, of the *seed of the woman, who should bruise the head of the serpent.* Afterwards the law and the Gospel were always preached together; and therefore follows the gospel in order after the law; that they who are terrified with the thunder and lightning of the law, can be comforted with the gracious promises of the Gospel, and they who are broken in their consciences by the hammer of the law, can be again cured and healed by the balm of the gospel. Observe here,

First, the signification of the gospel. It signifies a good saying, or a glad tiding; as, when an enemy is conquered, and there is peace a glad tiding; as we read of the *Philistines, who published in the house of their idols, and among the people*, what a glorious victory they had obtained over *Israel*; for the gospel proclaims to us the victory Christ has obtained over our spiritual enemies; or, when the enemy, who blocked up a city is fled away, and has left a great booty; as happened in the camp of the *Syrians* before the city of *Samaria*, which was found out by the four leprous men, who therefore called that day a day of good tidings; for the gospel annunciates, that the hellish enemies, who blocked up the souls of men, are fled for Christ, who has *led captivity captive, and gave gifts unto men*; or, when a father receives news *of a child being born unto him*; for the Gospel convinces us, that *unto us is a child born, and unto us is a Son given*, who *has given power to all them that believe on his name, to become the sons of God.* The gospel contains in common the divine doctrine comprehended both in the law and the gospel, but in particular the gracious preaching of grace and good tidings of Christ, and of his merits, which are the forgiveness of sins, righteousness, and eternal life, which are offered to all them who believe in Christ. In this way have the fathers in the Old Testament had Christ in promises, prophecies, sacrifices and figures. wherefore the gospel is described by several

Secondly, names in the Old Testament, which have all regard to Christ and his merits: As, that he should be *the seed of the woman who was to bruise the head of the serpent:* That he should be born of the seed of *Abraham*, wherein *all the nations of the earth should be*

blessed: That he should be born of the tribe of *Judah, unto whom the gathering of the people should be:* That he should be a great prophet like unto *Moses, who should speak to the people in the name of the Lord:* That he should be *the Immanuel,* that is, God and man, who should justify us, and bear our iniquities: That he should be a *Rod of the Stem of Jesse,* and a branch of the house of *David,* who should be called *the Lord our Righteousness:* That he was to finish the transgression, and to make an end of sins, and to make reconciliation for iniquities, and to bring in everlasting righteousness: That he should be *a ruler in* Israel: That he should *subdue our iniquities, and cast our sins into the depth of the sea:* That he should be *the desire of all nations: A just King having salvation: A fountain opened for sin and uncleanness:* And, *the Son of Righteousness with healing in his wings.*

In the New Testament the gospel is described with plainer and clearer words. That Christ is a savior, and *shall save his people from their sins:* That it is a good tiding for the poor in spirit, and sinners, for Christ *is come into the world to call sinners to repentance:* wherefore Christ calls them *that labor, and are heavy laden, and he will give them rest:* That he is *the Lamb of God, who bore the sins of the world:* That he is *the only begotten of the Father, full of grace and truth:* That he is therefore sent of God into *the world, that whosoever believes in him, should not perish, but have everlasting life:* That he is *the resurrection and life, he that believes in him, though he were dead, yet shall he live, and whosoever lives and believes in him shall never die.* Hereof we can perceive, that the Gospel is of a heavenly

Thirdly, origin, and is come from God; therefore it is called in our text, *a power of God.* The all-knowing God seeing from eternity that *Adam* and *Eve* should fall in sin and transgression, foreordained, Christ, who is the heart and kernel of the Gospel, to be a mediator, and *chose us in him,* and gave us in him, *hope of eternal life, before the world began:* For this is the Gospel called, a *mystery, which was kept secret since the world began: A mystery, which from the beginning of the world hath been hid in God: A mystery, which has been hid from ages, and from generations, but now is made manifest to his saints.* But although the gospel is from heaven, yet God uses to the.

Fourthly, preaching of the same, men on earth. In the Old Testament the patriarchs did preach the gospel according to the promise made of the seed of the woman, and the promise made unto *Abraham,* that in his seed should all the nations on the earth be blessed. The priests and the prophets did likewise preach the gospel of Christ to come, the priests in their sacrifices, which were all figures to Christ, and the prophets in their prophecies. In the New Testament the apostles and disciples did preach the Gospel, first for the *Jews,* and afterwards for all nations; after them are the faithful ministers and servants of God called and ordained to preach the gospel, though we must not forget to mention here the faithful servant of God, *Martin Luther,* whom God did use in the last days, to cleanse the doctrine of the gospel from all human traditions and superstitions, and to place it on the apostolic candlesticks, that it should shine forth again, and we thereby be instructed in the right way to salvation. We may therefore well apply to him the vision of St. *John* the Divine: *I saw another angel fly in the midst of Heaven, having the everlasting gospel to preach unto them that dwell on the earth.* Of the foregoing we can conclude,

That the same gospel, which was preached in the Old Testament, is the same that is preached now in the New Testament; so that all they who were saved before the incarnation of Christ, are saved through faith in Jesus Christ, which is preached and manifested in the gospel.

By faith Abel *offered unto God a more excellent sacrifice than* Cain, *by which he obtained witness, that he was righteous, God testifying of his gifts: By faith* Enoch *was translated, that he should not see death, for before his translation be had this testimony, That he pleased God: By faith*

Noah *became heir of the righteousness, which is by faith.* Our Savior says of *Abraham, your father* Abraham *rejoiced to see my day, and he saw it, and was glad;* namely, in faith. We can hereof be convinced, that they were all saved, and *died in faith, not having received the promises, but having seen them afar off, and were persuaded of them, and embraced them, for without faith it is impossible to please God.* The prophets are full of the doctrine of the Gospel of Christ: *They testified before hand the sufferings of Christ, and the glory, that should follow: They all gave witness to him, that through his name, whosoever believes in him, should receive remission of sins.* And as the prophets did preach of Christ to come, so did the apostles preach the same of him, who was come, not for the Jews alone, as in the Old Testament, but for all nations, and over the whole world.

II. The Power of the Gospel.

Let us now hear of the power of the gospel, since our salvation is concealed and hid therein. If we would have the kernel, we must first break the nut. The power of the gospel is not.

Of eloquence, like the worldly philosophical arguments, by which the ears of men can be tickled, and their hearts be persuaded to believe, as *the Orator* Tertullius *would inform the governor against* Paul, *and persuade him to believe, that* Paul *was a pestilent fellow, and a mover of sedition: The preaching of the Gospel is not with enticing words of man's Wisdom, but in demonstration of the Spirit, and of power.* The power of the gospel is neither.

Of the letter; as if there was a particular power or virtue in the bare words of the gospel according to the letters, against calamities and misfortunes, as many superstitiously imagine, and therefore abuse it, using the same to their abominations. *Brentius* has a comparison here taken of the history of *Esther, That whosoever, whether man or woman, shall come unto the king into the inner court, who is not called, there is one law of his, to put him to death, except such to whom the king shall hold out the golden scepter, that he may live.* This scepter, although made of gold, had no power as long as it was not in the king's hand but when the king had it in his hand, and held it out to the person who approached him, then was the scepter in its right use, and saved them who touched it from death. Likewise is it with the gospel, when it is in its right use, then is it a heavenly means, by which the Holy Spirit operates in the elect of God, true faith and salvation. But the power of the gospel is godly, and is grounded on the promises of God, and on the merits of Christ; is operated by the Holy Spirit, is received by faith, is sealed by the sacraments, is shewed in several godly effects, and is concluded of the final causes.

The promises of God are all the Scripture. Texts called, which treat of the grace and mercy of God towards sinners, that he wills not their death, but that they should repent and believe in Christ, and be saved, and obtain everlasting salvation.

Christ and his merits is the kernel of the gospel. Under the merits of Christ must be reckoned, not alone all good that he has procured for us but also all evil that he has redeemed us from. The good things, which Christ has procured for us are, the perfect fulfilling of the law in our stead: For *Christ is the end of the law for righteousness, to everyone that believes:* Reconciliation unto God, *God has reconciled us to himself by Jesus Christ:* The adoption to children, *as many as received him, to them he gave power to become the sons of God:* The gift of the Holy Spirit, *because you are sons, God has sent forth the Spirit of his Son into your hearts:* And the eternal Life, *Grace reigns through righteousness unto eternal life by Jesus Christ our Lord:* The evil wherefrom Christ has redeemed us, are sin and iniquities, *God has made him to be sin for us who knew no sin,* and the punishment for sin, *for if when we were enemies, we were reconciled to God by the death of his Son, much more being reconciled, we should be saved by his life: Christ has redeemed us from the curse of the law, being made a curse for us: Through death Christ destroyed him, that had the power of death, that is, the devil.*

The Holy Spirit is powerful by the word of the gospel in man's heart. For as the manna fell down with the dew, so is the dew of the grace of God, and the power of the Holy Spirit mixed with the manna of the gospel, and it is therefore called in our text, *the power of God unto salvation, to everyone that believes.*

Faith receives the word of the gospel, and in the gospel the grace of God, and Jesus Christ, with all his merits; which we can see of the examples of the *Jews*, who heard the preaching of St. *Peter* on the Day of *Pentecost*; of the *chamberlain, Cornelius, Lydia*, and others.

The sacraments seals and confirms to us the promises of God preached and manifested in the gospel; for all what is promised in the gospel is sealed and confirmed by the sacraments.

Several godly effects convince us likewise of the power of the gospel, namely, that it *reveals to us the council of God concerning our salvation*, and is therefore called *the revelation of the mystery:* That it increases faith in the heart, and confirms the same, and is therefore called, *the word of truth:* That it assures us of the grace of God, and reconciliation unto God, and is therefore called, *the gracious word:* That it regenerates us, and therefore called, *the good seed:* That it gives *knowledge of salvation by the remission of sins*, and therefore called *the good word of God:* That it assures us of the adoption unto children, and the eternal life, and therefore is called, *the word of life:* That it gives comfort and peace to the conscience, and therefore called, *the gospel of peace:* And that it brings us at last to life everlasting, and is therefore called, *the gospel of salvation.*

The final causes, why the gospel is made manifested, and revealed, are the glory of God, and the salvation of mankind.

The glory of God we can see in the miracle of the personal union of the divine and human natures in Christ, which is called in the Scripture, *a great mystery*; and likewise in his great mercy, that he would rather give his only Son to die for us, than that we should be lost.

The salvation of man is also a final cause of the manifestation of the Gospel; for, since we could not be justified by the law, therefore was God so gracious to reveal to us in the gospel, his secret counsel concerning our salvation, that *through Christ is preached unto all, the forgiveness of sins, and by him all that believe are justified.* Thereof we can see that the power of the gospel, is

Conditional, and the faithful alone have good thereof. God lets his gospel be published for all men, and it is his serious *will*, that *all men shall be saved, and come unto the knowledge of the truth.* And he has likewise promised, that he will give power unto his word, to convert the heart of men. Christ is a Savior for all, and the promises of the gospel are universal; but there is a condition, by, namely, that we should believe. The power is hid and concealed in the gospel like the milk in a woman's breast, but faith must draw it out, like the child the milk out of its mother's breast: As we are condemned through. Unbelief, so are we likewise saved through faith. Hereof we can see why all they who hear the gospel, are not saved, but the most part are damned; the fault thereof is not in the gospel, but in men themselves, who will not obey the gospel, nor embrace the gracious means offered in the gospel; and therefore becomes the gospel to them through their own disobedience and unbelief, *the Savior of death unto death.*

Although the law and the gospel are not one, yet are they not against one another, but they go as hand in hand, and agree in origin, and in their final causes.

They agree in origin. The same Lord and God, who gave the law, has likewise given the gospel. If now they two were against one another, then would follow thereof, that God was against himself, since he has revealed his will in them both.

They agree likewise in the final causes. The doctrine of the law and the gospel promise us both the everlasting salvation; the law through works, the gospel through faith, *for what the law could not do, in that it was weak through the flesh, God sending his own Son, in the likeness of sinful flesh, and for sin condemned sin in the flesh, that the righteousness of the law might be fulfilled in us, who walk not after the flesh, but after the Spirit:* Yet notwithstanding, there is great difference between the law and the gospel, as we can see of the following.

First, of the manner of revelation. The law is partly known by nature, since it was *written* in the creation *in man's heart*; but the gospel is a mystery hid for human reason, but *declared* and revealed *of the Son of God, who is in his Father's bosom.*

Secondly, of the subject. The law prescribes good works with commands and threatenings; the gospel prescribes faith, that we by the same must embrace Jesus Christ, and by him the remission of sins, justification, and salvation; the law commands, the gospel shows reward.

Thirdly, of the conditions. The promises of the law are with such conditions, that we must fulfill the same in all its commands and not depart therefrom in the least: The promises of the Gospel are of grace, and will be fulfilled if we will but receive the same through faith, and believe.

Fourthly, of the effects. The law punishes and terrifies a sinner; the gospel publishes the forgiveness of sins, and with powerful comfort raises up, wherefore it is called the word of salvation, and the gospel of peace: The knowledge of the law shows the evil of sin; the comfort of the gospel rejoices the heart: The law is a hammer, which breaks down the sinful hearts; the gospel is an ointment, which heals the wounded consciences.

Fifthly, of the persons. *The law is made for the lawless and disobe-dient, for the ungodly, and for sinners, for unholy and profane;* but the gospel must be *preached to the poor in spirit, and to the broken hearted,* who feel the wrath of God in their consciences, and are afraid thereof.

It is very needful for us to know these differences between the law and the gospel, on account of the following.

1st, in the article of justification. We are not justified by the law, for that is weak through the flesh; but by the gospel, which is *a power unto salvation, to everyone that believes.* The law must be preached, that we can learn thereof to know the works which we ought to do, but in the work of justification must we know, that there is always war between the merits of the law, and the grace of the gospel, for we can deserve nothing with our good works.

2ndly, in the right use of the keys of heaven. The remission of sins shall not be proclaimed to unconverted sinners, but on the contrary, the wrath of God by the law; *that tribulation and anguish shall be upon every soul of man, that does evil:* But unto the poor, and of a contrite spirit, and they that tremble at the word of the Lord, shall the gracious promises of the gospel be proclaimed.

Let us thank and praise God for the glad tidings of his grace offered to us in the gospel, and let it be our only comfort in all afflictions, and at last in death, that we may hereafter receive the eternal life in Jesus Christ our blessed Savior. AMEN.

20

The Old and New Testament

The Text, HEBREWS 9:15, 16, 17, 18, 19, 20, ver.
Christ is the mediator of the New Testament, that by means of death, for the redemption of the transgressions that were under the first testament, they which are called might receive the promise of eternal inheritance: For where a testament is, there must also of necessity be the death of the testator: For a testament is of force after men are dead, otherwise it is of no strength at all, whilst the testator lives: Whereupon neither the first testament was dedicated without blood: For, when Moses had spoken every precept to all the people, according to the law, he took the blood of calves and goats, with water and scarlet wool, and hyssop, and sprinkled both the book and all the people, saying, this is the blood of the testament, which God has enjoined unto you.

INTRODUCTION

THE Lord commanded *Moses: You shall make two cherubim of gold, of beaten work shall you make them, in the two ends of the mercy seat:* These two cherubim were figures to the two testaments, which we call the Old and the New. The first was made with the *Jewish* nation, the latter with all nations on earth; the Lord speaks himself of these two testaments by the prophet *Jeremiah*, saying, *Behold, the days come, says the Lord, that I will make a new covenant with the house of* Israel, *and with the house of* Judah: *Not according to the covenant that I made with their fathers in the day that I took them by the hand, to bring them out of the land of* Egypt, *which covenant of mine they broke, although I was a husband unto them, says the Lord. But this shall be the covenant that I will make with the house of* Israel, "*after those days,*" *says the Lord,* "*I will put my law in their inward parts, and write it in their hearts, and will be their God, and they shall be my people.*" The two cherubim stood over the mercy seat, which was the cover over the ark. The ark was a figure of Christ; the two testaments have likewise regard to Christ: The Old Testament showed him afar off, and to come; the new shows him present, and come: The faces of the cherubim looked one to another; the Old and New Testament likewise look one to another: The Old Testament is made manifest in the New; and the New lays concealed in the Old: The Old contains the promises and prophecies of Christ; the New shows us the fulfilling of the promises and prophecies: The Old is illustrated by the New; the New is founded on the Old: And the same Jesus, who appeared often in human shape to the forefathers in the Old Testament, is now in the New, manifested in the flesh, and is become a true man.

God used to give answers from between the two cherubim. We can find godly answers in both testaments. We will according to our text, speak here of these two testaments, and thereof hear,

FIRST, *What the Old and New Testament is.*

SECOND, *Wherein they both do agree, and disagree.*

EXPLANATION of the TEXT

I. What the Old and New Testaments are.

We cannot rightly understand a thing, except we know before hand what the words signifies. Although "testament," according to the word has several significations, and signifies, 1st, a covenant made between two parties, which comprehends what must be done, and is confirmed with oath, sacrifices and eating together; as *the covenant of* Abraham *and* Abimelech: 2ndly, the covenant that God promised with oath to send the Messiah to the world, whereof *Zacharias* the priest, says in his song, that *God will remember his holy covenant*; in regard to this did St. *Peter* call the *Jews, children of the covenant*; 3rdly, The last will of a person concerning the disposal of his estate among his heirs after his death; of which St. *Paul* says, *a man's covenant, if it be confirmed, no man disannuls, or adds thereto:* Yet notwithstanding the most agreeable and principal signification here, is, that the testament signifies a covenant between God and man, wherein God promises his spiritual gifts unto men, and confirms it with certain seals, by which men promise and oblige themselves to obedience: Such two testaments has God made with men, the first in the Old, the Second in the New; and although there is but one faith, one way to Salvation, and one manner how to be reconciled unto God; yet are there two testaments, the first made with the *Jews* in the Old, the second with all nations on earth in the New: Which can be proved by the following,

First, by Scripture texts, which speak of the two testaments, the Old and the New: *Behold the days come says the Lord, that I will make a new covenant with the house of* Israel, *and with the house of* Judah: *Not according to the covenant, that I made with their fathers in the day that I took them by the hand, to bring them out of the land of* Egypt, *which my covenant they broke, although I was an husband unto them, says the Lord: But this shall be the covenant that I will make with the house of* Israel, *After those days says the Lord, I will put my law in their inward parts, and write it in their hearts, and will be their God, and they shall be my people.* The two testaments are mentioned in these words; the first made with the Jews, whom God brought out of the land of *Egypt,* and gave his law unto them on Mount *Sinai:* This Testament was grounded upon the justice of God, and the perfect obedience of the Jews: The second is made with all people on earth, and is grounded on the mercy of God, and faith of men.

Secondly, by the names which is given to these two testaments: They are called, the *less* and *the better; the letter* and *the Spirit; the two covenants, the one from the Mount* Sinai, *which genders to bondage, and the other from* Jerusalem, *which is above, and genders to freedom.*

The Old Testament was a covenant of command, which God made with the children of *Israel* four hundred and thirty years after the promise made to *Abraham,* when they were brought out of the land of *Egypt,* with giving by his servant *Moses* on Mount *Sinai,* the laws after which they should live, and promising unto them all temporal and eternal blessings, if they obeyed and fulfilled the law. This covenant was written in a book, by which the people did promise to obey, and to live accordingly; whereupon this covenant was confirmed on both sides with *the blood of calves and goats,* and sealed with the two sacraments; the circumcision, and Easter-lamb. The Apostle describes this testament also in our text, *Neither was the first testament dedicated without blood: For, when* Moses *had spoken every precept to all the people, according to the law, he took the blood of calves and goats, with water, and scarlet wool, and hyssop, and sprinkled both the book, and all the people, saying, this is the blood of the testament which God has enjoined unto you.*

Observe, God made a covenant before with *Abraham,* of which he speaks himself often to the children of *Israel*, though, when there is mention made in the Scripture of the Old Testament, thereby must be understood the covenant which God made with the children of *Israel*, after they were brought out of *Egypt*, as we can see by the Words of *Moses*, when he said to the People: *The Lord our God made a covenant with us in* Horeb; *the Lord made not this covenant with our Fathers, but with us, even us, who are all of us here alive this day.*

But, that we may better understand the nature of this testament, we will explain it with the comparison of a covenant, since the apostle calls it so in our text: When a covenant shall be erected, then must there be observed these four following articles. 1. The persons who make the covenant with one another. 2. The covenant itself in all its clauses and points. 3. The confirmation of the covenant with hand and seal: And, 4. The cause why such covenant is made. These four parts are all found in the Old Testament.

1. The persons are, on one side, the holy God, whom the apostle calls in the foregoing verse before our text, *the living God.* On the other side, the children of *Israel*, whom God had brought out of the land of *Egypt.* These two parties were properly concerned in this covenant, as *Moses* said, *Behold the blood of the covenant, which the Lord has made with you concerning all these words.*

2. The covenant in itself, was this: That God gave unto them his law, and promised thereby, *If you will obey my voice indeed, and keep my covenant, then you shall be a peculiar treasure unto me above all people; for all the earth is mine, and you shall be unto me a kingdom of priests, and an holy nation*: That is, they should have the blessed and promised land of *Canaan* for an inheritance here, and eternal life hereafter. On the other hand did the children of *Israel* promise, and say, *All that the Lord has said, will we do, and be obedient.*

3. The confirmation of the covenant was: That *Moses*, who was a mediator between God and the children of *Israel*, wrote all the words

of the Lord in a book, and *sacrificed oxen, calves and goats, and took of the blood with water, scarlet wool and hyssop, and sprinkled it on the book, and on the people for a testimony.* The words *Moses* used, were, *Behold the blood of the covenant, which the Lord has made with you concerning all these words;* in general the glory of God, and their own salvation in particular.

4. The cause why God made this covenant with the children of *Israel*, was, that if they were obedient, and fulfilled their part of the covenant, then would God likewise fulfill his part and give them temporal and eternal blessings; but if not, then should they expect temporal curse and eternal damnation.

All this had regard to the covenant, which God would make afterwards in the New Testament. By the *blood of calves and goats*, was signified the blood of Christ, which was to be shed for the ransom of the whole world; *That by means of death, for the redemption of the transgressions that were under the first testament, they which are called might receive the promise of eternal inheritance.*

The meaning hereof is that as the blood of the sacrifice (in respect to Christ) which was sprinkled in the Old Testament, could redeem men of the transgression which they had committed under the Old Testament; so should the blood and death of Christ reconcile the sins of all them who had lived under the Old Testament before his incarnation, and likewise of them under the New Testament after his incarnation.

This covenant, with all its laws and ceremonies are now at an end, and do not concern us Christians, for it should not last longer than till the coming of Christ, as the Lord said, *Behold the days are coming, says the Lord, when I will make a new covenant:* The apostle St. *Paul* explains this word new, also; *In that he says a new covenant, he has made the first old. Now that which decays, and waxes old, is ready to vanish away.*

The moral law, or the Ten Commandments, which were likewise made a part of the Old Testament, is nevertheless in full force in the New; for, before they were given on Mount *Sinai*, and also made a part of the Old Testament, they were written in the creation in the heart of men, and they therefore can not be looked upon as alone belonging to the Old Testament made with the *Jews*, but also to the New made with all people and nations on earth.

The New Testament is a gracious covenant made by God with all men, and grounded on Jesus Christ, and his merits, who put away the Old Testament, and erected a new, which he began in his baptism, preached and proclaimed in his ministerial office, and confirmed the same with his innocent blood on the cross. God offers in this covenant to all men all heavenly and spiritual blessings in Christ, namely, the grace of God, the forgiveness of sins, the Holy Spirit, justification and eternal life; but he confirms and seals them alone unto the faithful.

As there was four parts in the Old Testament, so is there likewise four parts to be observed in the New, namely,

First, the persons are on one side, God; and one the other side, the whole world, or all men in the whole world. The Old Testament was made alone with the *Jews*, but in the New *is the grace of God, that brings salvation, appeared to all men.*

Second, the covenant in itself, is; That God has sent his Son into the world, and offers to all men in the same, his Son, his grace, the forgiveness of sins, the Holy Spirit, justification, and all the benefits which Christ has procured with his birth, sufferings and death; and all to the end, that we should have the eternal life of grace, wherefore God demands nothing else of us, than that we should believe and be baptized; by which he, that is baptized, promises to deny the Devil and all works, to believe in God the Father, Son and Holy Spirit, and to live a godly life.

Third, the confirmation is made with the own blood of Jesus Christ: *For where a testament is, there must also of necessity be the death of the testator*. Hereto was the *blood of calves and goats*, wherewith the Old Testament was confirmed, a figure; wherefore Christ uses in the institution of the Lord's Supper, mostly the same words as *Moses*, only, that he calls his testament, *the New Testament*, for to discern it from the Old; and he mentions *his blood* instead of *the blood of the sacrifices*. These are his own words: *This*, (namely, what is in this cup, and which I give to you,) *is my blood of the New Testament*. As *Moses*'s words should be understood, as they were spoken, and the Blood wherewith the Old Testament was confirmed, was the blood of the sacrifices, and not a sign or token of blood; so must likewise the words of Christ be understood as they are spoken by Christ himself, namely, that the blood wherewith the New Testament is confirmed, and which is given in the Lord's Supper, is not a signification or token of the blood of Christ, but the blood of Christ himself, though to be understood in a spiritual and sacramental way.

Fourth, the final cause why God has made this New Testament, is on the side of God, this: That he will give us his grace, the forgiveness of sins, justification, and at last everlasting salvation. On our side it is, that we should believe, therefore he let this gracious covenant be proclaimed by the preaching of the gospel to all, and he seals and confirms the same in the faithful by the sacraments of baptism and the Lord's Supper: The *Jews* had the promises in the Old Testament of the land *Canaan*, and the eternal life, but they should obey and keep the law: We Christians in the New Testament have it easier, for there is alone required of us, to believe in Jesus Christ, and remain steadfast in this faith, then shall we be saved by grace for Christ's sake.

As loving as the eternal life is to us, as loving must likewise our faith be, and as circumspectly ought we to walk, and let our faith shine forth in a godly life, not with unbelief and wickedness, brake the covenant, but honor the same, and *serve God with fear in holiness and righteousness before him all the days of our life.*

God will on his side, never broke the covenant; for so faith he himself by the prophet *Isaiah: The mountains shall depart, and the hills be removed, but my kindness shall not depart from you, neither shall the covenant of my peace be removed, says the Lord, that has mercy on you.* Princes and lords make often covenants with one another, and for a little misunderstanding, and sometimes no cause, break their covenants: But the covenant of God stands unalterable; and even if we through frailty or ignorance break the covenant on our side, yet, when we repent and confess our faults by prayer and supplications, God will remember his holy covenant. Thereof says the Lord, by the prophet *Jeremiah, If a man put away his wife, and she goes from him, and become another man's, shall be return unto her again? Shall not that land be greatly polluted? But you have played the harlot with many lovers, yet return again unto me, says the Lord.* We will now hear the second part, which is,

II. Wherein the Old and New Testaments agree and disagree

Of what has been said before, we can easily judge wherein they both agree, and disagree.

They agree in the following four articles.

1. In the instituter. God has instituted and made them both.

2. In the moving cause; namely, the mercy of God.

3. In the subject. The Old showed us Christ to come, the New shows us Christ come.

4. In the good promises. God had promised to the *Jews*, if they were obedient, all temporal and eternal blessings: God promises to

us the eternal Life, if we believe in Christ.

They disagree in the following.

1. In the persons to whom they were given, and through whom they were given. The Old Testament was given alone to the *Jews* and their proselytes: The New is given to all of what nation, country and language whatsoever, if they will but believe, and be baptized. *Moses* was a mediator between God and the children of *Israel* in the Old Testament: Christ is Mediator between God and men in the New Testament: As great difference as there is between *Moses* a servant, and Christ the Son, as great difference is there between the two testaments.

2. In the time, place and manner. The Old Testament was given just after the children of *Israel* were brought out of the land of *Egypt*: The New was given in the last time, when Christ came into the world. The Old went out from Mount *Sinai:* The New went from *Jerusalem*, wherefrom the apostles were sent to preach the Gospel everywhere. The Old Testament was given with terrible thunder and lightning: The New was given with meekness: Christ did preach with a meek spirit, and the Holy Spirit was sent in the shape of cloven tongues like as of fire, and as the rushing of wind.

3. In promises. St. *Paul* says, that *the New Testament is established upon better promises than the Old:* Not as if the Old did promise alone earthly and temporal blessings, namely, the multiplying of their seed, the land *Canaan*, and the *Levitical* offerings, (for they had likewise gracious promises which lay concealed under the earthly figures;) but, that St. *Paul* calls the *promises of the New Testament better than these of the Old:* Therewith has he regard, first to the clearness thereof: The New shines clearer than the Old. What lays concealed in the old under dark figures, is revealed in the New; therefore is the Old Testament compared by the night, and the new by the day, that as the moon and stars shine in the night, and the sun

in the day, so did *Moses* shine in the Old Testament as the moon, and the other prophets as the stars, until the Son of Righteousness rose up in the New Testament; and did shine over the whole world with his doctrine and miracles. Second, to the presence. Salvation is nearer to us in the New Testament, then it was to them in the Old: We believe in Christ already come, they believed in him, who according to his human nature was absent, and afar of; they had him alone in hopes, but we have him as between our hands; Third, to the excellency. The Old Testament had promises of spiritual blessings, but under condition, that they should keep and fulfill the law perfectly; whereto the law neither promised, nor gave any power: But the promises of the New Testament flow out of mere grace without any condition of our own merits, or obedience. All they who believe in Jesus Christ, and remain steadfast till their lives end, shall have the eternal life; whereto the Gospel gives power by the assistance of the Holy Spirit, both to believe in Christ, and to live according to the will of God.

4. In the consecration. The Old Testament was consecrated with the blood of creatures, as oxen, calves and goats; but the New Testament is consecrated with the precious blood of Jesus Christ the Son of God.

5. In the writings. The Old was written on tables of stone, but the New is written by the Spirit of God in tables of flesh, namely, the hearts of the faithful.

6. In the continuation. The Old Testament should last until the coming of Christ, who should put the same away; but the New shall last unto the world's end, according to its officiating manner; and unto eternity, according to its power and profit; therefore it is, called the blood of the everlasting covenant, and Christ is called a priest forever. I will conclude this discourse with the words of St. *Paul* to the *Hebrews: Now the God of peace, that brought again from the dead our Lord Jesus, that great Shepherd of the Sheep, through the blood of*

the everlasting covenant, make you perfect in every good work to do his will; working in you, that which is well-pleasing is his sight, through Jesus Christ. To whom be glory forever and ever. AMEN.

21

Repentance

The Text, 2 SAMUEL, 12:13. ver.

And David *said unto* Nathan, *I have sinned against the Lord: And* Nathan *said unto* David, *The Lord also has put away your sin, you shall not die.*

INTRODUCTION

WHEN the Kingdom of Christ was daily expected, and his coming was near, that he should proclaim the Gospel of his Kingdom unto all people, then came a little before, *John* the Baptist, as the forerunner of Christ, according to the prophecies; and preached repentance, saying, *Bring forth fruit meet for repentance. The ax is laid unto the root of the trees; therefore every tree, which brings not forth good fruit, is cut down, and cast into the fire:* as we can read in the Gospel of St. *Matthew*, 3:8, and 10. verses. These words contain two things, namely, 1. An admonition to repentance, and 2. A threatening, if we do not repent.

1. The admonition to repentance is this, *Bring forth fruit meet for*

repentance. The admonition is concerning fruits, that must come forth of repentance; for repentance is as a tree, whose root is true sorrow and grief, the leaves are hearty confession, the flowers are the comfortable attribution of the merits of Christ by a true faith, the fruits are Christian virtues and a new life. As the tree can be known by its fruits, so can likewise repentance be known by works. The *Jews* were of opinion, that they were holy enough, and that the baptism of *John* was too mean for them, who were of a noble branch planted, *of the vine which the Lord had brought out of* Egypt. Abraham *was their father, they were the children of the prophets, and of the covenant, which God made with their fathers. They were* Israelites, *to whom pertains the adoption, and the glory, and the covenants, and the giving of the law, and the service of God, and the promises.* But *John the Baptist,* shows them, that all such glorious leaves without fruit is vain: and, if they would become well-pleasing in the sight of God, then ought they to *bring forth fruit meet for repentance.* A tree standing on a fruitful place, and not bringing forth fruit, is good for nothing: Our Savior cursed the fruitless fig-tree. *Not everyone, that says unto me, Lord, Lord, shall enter into the Kingdom of Heaven, but he that does the will of my Father, which is in heaven.* God requires fruit of us, therefore has he planted us. *Who plants a vineyard and eats not of the fruit thereof? Solomon* says, *the root of the righteous yields fruit.* By the fruit we can discern a saint from a hypocrite. A hypocrite has fine leaves, but the root of the righteous yields fruit. The fruits are sure demonstrations of faith. God requires of us not alone fruit, but also much fruit. *Herein,* says our Savior, *is my Father glorified, that you bear much fruit*; on the contrary is laid and made,

2. A great threatening on the fruitless. *The ax is laid unto the root of the trees, and therefore every tree, which brings not forth good fruit, is cut down, and cast into the fire.* By the ax is understood the just punishment of God, wherewith he punishes the wicked

and unconverted, and fruitless Christians; as war, plagues, dearth, famine, and all such calamities. *John the Baptist*, says, that this *ax is laid unto the root of the trees*; for God is a long-suffering God, and bears long-suffering with us. He bore three years with the fruitless fig-tree, and suffered it to stand even the fourth year, before he commanded the dresser of the vineyard, to cut it down. He spared the first world one hundred and twenty years, before he sent the flood. He bore four hundred years with the iniquity of the *Amorites*, before he punished them. He gave the *Ninevites* forty days to repent, and be converted. But, when the long-suffering and forbearance of God cannot lead anyone to repentance, then he cuts him in his justice, though not entirely from the root; as we can see of the tree in *Babylon* by the prophet *Daniel, whose branches were cut off, the leaves shaken off, and the fruits scattered; but the stump and the roots remained in the earth. For in the midst of wrath the Lord remembers mercy.* If we will not be moved and repent by such, then follows; *That every tree, which brings not forth good fruit, is cut down, and cast into the fire.* When the long-suffering of God turns to wrath, then is there no longer salvation for the tree; the everlasting fire is prepared in Hell, for all such fruitless trees, where they shall burn, and not be consumed: *Their worm shall not die, neither shall their fire be quenched.*

That we may not be like trees, who are full of leaves, and have no fruits, let us, according to the example of *David*, be encouraged to repentance, and out of our text behold the tree of repentance.

FIRST, *In its Root.*

SECOND, *In its Branches.*

THIRD, *In its Fruits.*

EXPLANATION of the TEXT

I. We will look at the Tree of Repentance in its root.

Heaven is free from sinners. *For there shall in no wise enter into it anything that defiles.* If we imagine, that they alone who have never sinned, should come in there, we would all be poorly off: But it is our only comfort, that the Lord, according to his great goodness, has promised repentance and forgiveness to them that have sinned against him; and of his infinite mercy has appointed repentance unto sinners that they may be saved. This appointment of God is,

1. Needful. We fall through sin and transgression out of the grace of God into his wrath, which is fearful; we depart thereby from the promises, which we made in our baptism, and are translated out of the Kingdom of God's dear Son into the power of darkness; we loose our peace and rest with God, and likewise the Holy Spirit, and become troubled and frightened in our conscience; and we also do lose by sin and iniquity, faith, love, grace, and eternal salvation. He that rightly considers this miserable condition, can easily judge how needful repentance is. Upon sin follows punishment, both temporal and eternal, from which nothing can help us but repentance; which is the only means by which we can come again into the grace of God, and escape the punishment of sin. Sin is a deep pit, but repentance is a ladder, by which we can climb out of this pit, and come into the grace of God. Sin is a lion, but repentance is *Sampson*, who by the power of the Holy Spirit, can destroy this lion. And since we sin daily, then must we repent daily. The daily bread is not so needful for our bodies, as repentance is for our soul; therefore has our Savior placed these two petitions after one another, *Give us this day our daily bread, and forgive us our trespasses.* Repentance ought to be our daily work.

2. It is of grace, without any of our merits. Wherewith have we deserved this of God, that he has been so gracious, and appointed repentance unto us for our good and salvation? Hence shines forth,

306

that *the Lord is long-suffering to us-ward, not willing that any should perish, but that all should come to repentance.* Besides, God fore-comes us with his grace, and gives us godly thoughts, and enlightens the eye of our knowledge, so that we can see our error, and thereof be convinced, and abhor all sin and evil. As one who in the dark goes into a room full of poisonous vermin, and lays himself down to rest, is terrified, and runs therefrom, if another brings in a light, by which he can behold his dangerous condition; so is it with a sinner, he understands not of himself his miserable condition, before God through his mercy and grace, enlightens him, and he thereby perceives, his miserable condition, and repents.

3. It is godly. Repentance *comes neither from the east, nor from the west, nor from the south, nor from the mountains in the wilderness;* neither is it wrought after men's will in their heart, but it has an heavenly origin. God himself is the effecting cause in our repentance. The Lord says himself, by the prophet *Ezekiel: A new heart also will I give you, and a new Spirit will I put within you, and I will take away the stony heart, out of your flesh, and I will give you a heart of flesh.* God effects the conversion in us by the preaching of his word, and by his ministers.

The word comprehends the law and the Gospel. The law terrifies our heart, and brings men to the knowledge of his sins, and shows us the wrath of God over sin; and is therefore compared, *by a hammer, that breaks the rocks in pieces,* and by a two edged sword, that pierces through the conscience. The gospel effects faith and comfort in our heart, in pointing out to us Jesus Christ the mediator, who has satisfied for the sins of the world; and in assuring us, that God will forgive all repenting sinners for the sake of the merits of Christ. This is a great comfort.

The ministers help likewise to promote our conversion, and are therefore called *laborers together with God,* and *ambassadors for Christ.*

Nathan was sent to *David, Ananias* to *Paul,* and *Peter* to *Cornelius. Paul* was sent to the *gentiles, to open their eyes, and to turn them from darkness to light, and from the power of Satan unto God, that they may receive forgiveness of sins.* God uses also cross and affliction to the promoting of our conversion; for what is cross and chastisement but visible preaching of the wrath of God over sin. As *Absalom* did set on fire the barley field of *Joab,* when he would not come to him; so sends God likewise crosses, when we will not turn to him.

4. It is universal; Repentance is not for *David* alone, neither for the righteous, for *they that be whole, need not the physician.* But *God commands all men everywhere to repent.* What the prophet *Nathan* said unto *David, You are the man,* may everyone of us say unto himself, you are the man that must repent. Everyone put with *Moses* his hand in his own bosom, and he shall find that it will come out again leprous; for *who can give a clean thing of an unclean thing?* A contrite heart is needful and suitable for rich and poor, high and low. The whole man, consisting of soul and its faculties, and body and its members, must all be converted: The mind, which was corrupted, full of darkness, ignorance and vanity, must be altered and become inclined to God and the godly things: The will, which was alone inclined to evil, must also be altered, and become likewise inclined to all good, and to obey, and follow the commands of God. Therefore is true conversion described in the Scripture with these words, *to turn from sin, from wicked ways, from darkness to light,* and from *the power of Satan unto God;* which cannot be done without entirely altering the will and mind. The body with all its members are full of sin. *The whole head is sick, and the whole heart faint, from the sole of the foot even unto the head, there is no soundness in it, but wounds and bruises, and putrefying sores.* They must all show token of conversion; the heart must sigh, the eyes must weep, the knees must bend down, and the mouth must confess with *David, I have sinned against the*

Lord.

II. We are to behold the Tree of Repentance in its branches.

We can lightly conclude hereof, what repentance is in its branches, namely, a spiritual alteration in the whole man, effected by the Holy Spirit, by the service of the law and the gospel. In which alteration man does seriously grieve over his sins, and despairs not, but with a true faith cleaves to the promises made in the gospel concerning the forgiveness of sins, alone for the sake of Christ, after which he endeavors, by the grace of God, to live a better life.

The tree of repentance has two branches, namely, contrition and faith.

Contrition being the first branch of repentance, contains these six following parts, namely,

First, knowledge of sin. None can rightly repent and be grieved over his sins, if he does not know them. A patient cannot be grieved over his sickness, as long as he does not know that he is sick. The Lord requires such knowledge of repenting sinners. *Acknowledge your iniquity, that you have transgressed against the Lord your God.*

Secondly, the perceiving of God's wrath against sin. He that knows his sins rightly, perceives at once that he by his sins has provoked God, and has brought the wrath of God with all temporal and eternal curse and damnation over him; for, on the pleasing trees of sin, grows always deceiving fruits of punishment.

Thirdly, terror of conscience. He that feels and perceives the wrath of God, must certainly be terrified in his conscience, for the check of conscience is a post-errant from the justice of God, and is therefore called, *spiritual poverty, spiritual captivity and bands,* and *hearty sorrow.*

Fourthly, submission for the majesty of God. He that knows and understands how greatly he has provoked God, which is the highest good, and the greatest majesty, humbles himself before God; since he perceives, that if God would do with him according to his justice and power, he would be destroyed in a moment.

Fifthly, confession of sins. He that rightly knows his sins, and repents, will certainly confess with the mouth as *David, I have sinned against the Lord.* God requires such confession of all repenting sinners, and promises forgiveness, *if we confess our sins, he is faithful and just to forgive us our sins, and to cleanse us from all unrighteousness.*

Sixthly, hatred and aversion for sin. He that seriously repents, and perceives how he has provoked God, and has brought the wrath of God upon himself, he has afterwards aversion and hatred to sin, and abhors to do the least wickedness, or anything against the command of God.

In these six foregoing parts consist a true contrition, which cannot be effected of men by their own natural power, but the Holy Spirit must effect the same, or else it is but a hypocritical conversion. For there is great difference between a true, and a hypocritical contrition. A true repenting sinner looks mostly to God, whom he has offended, and is grieved thereover: A hypocrite seeks most to human laws, judgment, and punishment, and is afraid therefor. A true repenting sinner knows not alone his outward crimes and sins, but also the secret faults of his heart: A hypocrite beholds alone his outward wickedness, and if he finds none, he conceits himself to be innocent. A true repenting sinner looks not alone on the temporal but also eternal punishment, and is afraid therefor; but he is risen again by faith in Christ: A hypocrite is alone afraid for temporal punishment, and if the eternal enters into his thoughts, it brings him often into despair.

But, that none should think that since contrition is the effect of the Holy Spirit, he must not be concerned thereabout, but leave it entirely to the Holy Spirit, (who knows his own time and will effect it when he sees fit,) and that in the meanwhile he may live as he pleases: he must learn to know, that the Holy Spirit works true repentance in men, though not without means, but by means, *to wit*, by the preaching of the law; by which he shows us our sins, knocks on our hearts, as with a hammer, and lays the wrath of God before our eyes. As the children of *Israel* were terrified in the giving of the law, and were afraid of the thunder and lightning, and the sounding of trumpets, and the voice of God, so that they not alone removed far off, but even said, *Let not God speak with us, lest we die*; so likewise is a true repenting sinner terrified by the preaching or the law. Thereupon follows the inward testimony of the conscience, which accuses and condemns them. The Holy Spirit uses often the examples of God's vengeance and wrath over sin; as the first world, *Sodom* and *Gomorrah, Jerusalem*, yea, even the Son of God himself, who is the greatest example of God's vengeance over sin.

Faith is the second branch on the tree of repentance, and comprehends these three following parts, namely,

First, knowledge; that we know by God's word, Jesus Christ, according to his person and offices. *This is life eternal, that they might know you the only true God, and Jesus Christ, whom you have sent.*

Secondly, consent, that we not alone know by the word of God, what Jesus Christ is according to his person and offices, but likewise consent in the same, and acknowledge the same to be true, which is called in the Scripture, the *obedience of faith: The word mixed with faith*, and *a sure demonstration*.

Thirdly, a sincere and hearty embracing of Christ and his merits: For since Christ and his merits are graciously offered unto us in the gospel, on God's side, then it is just, that we on our side embrace and receive him with a true faith; and then it can be said, *Whosoever*

believes on him, shall not be ashamed.

In these three parts consist a true faith; but the last part is the most principal. For there is none among Christians, who does not know Christ, who he is according to his person and office, and acknowledges it to be true what is written of him: But there are few, who embrace him and his merits; which we can see by their living. By a true faith must be a new obedience, by which a Christian proves his conversion to be sincere. New obedience consists in, to hate evil, and to strive after good. This is called in the Scripture, *crucifying of the flesh*, and *the renewing of the Spirit*. We must first crucify our flesh, and all its lusts, and then be daily renewed in the Spirit; and when the old man, the old *Adam*, is crucified and overcome, then the new man receives life in us; and therefore, since the old *Adam* arises so often again in us, so that there is always *war between the flesh and the spirit*, it ought to be our daily work, and we shall be assisted herein by the following, namely. 1. By hearing, reading, and meditating on the Word of God; for it is *the helmet of salvation, and the sword of the Spirit*; and it is *like the tower of* David, *built for an armory, whereon there hang a thousand bucklers, all shields of mighty men.* 2. By subduing the first wicked thoughts. When any evil thought arises in our hearts, we ought not to harbor them, but subdue and resist them. We cannot hinder a bird from flying over our head, but we may from lighting thereon, and much more from making a nest among our hairs. Bad thoughts are as the *Serpents root, whereof comes a cockatrice.* 3. By shunning all opportunities. He that will guard himself from sin, must likewise shun all opportunities of sin: He that comes too nigh to the fire, will burn himself.

III. We should behold the tree of repentance in its fruits.

As *David*'s repentance was true and sincere, so had he the fruits thereof, and receives,

First, the forgiveness of sins. The prophet said in our text, *the Lord has put away your sins.* We must not understand it so, as if there should not be sound any more sin in *David*; but that his sins should not be reckoned unto him to damnation. The word, *put away*, has regard to Christ who has born all our iniquities. This is the first benefit we have of conversion, that we receive the remission of sins. As the prophet *Nathan* said to *David* in God's stead, *The Lord has put away your sins*, so God forgives yet daily all repenting sinners their sins, in the absolution, through the mouth of his servants; for none can forgive sins of their own power but God only. Therefore said not the prophet, *I have put away your sins, but the Lord.*

Should anyone ask, how God annunciates the forgiveness of sins? He must know, that God did it himself to *Adam* and *Eve*, and uses afterwards the prophets and priests in the Old Testament: But in the New, Christ did it himself in the time of his incarnation, and afterwards gave such power to his disciples. But now, God uses the ministers of the Gospel thereto, and has therefore given unto them the keys of Heaven. They are men in their persons as others, but in their office they are men of God, ambassadors of Christ, *servants of Christ; and stewards of the mysteries of God.*

When therefore a minister absolves, or annunciates a true repenting sinner, who has a true faith in Christ, and alone depends on the grace of God, and the merits of Christ, he may then be as sure of the forgiveness of his sins, as if Christ had done it himself; according to the words of our Savior, *Whosoever sins you remit, they are remitted unto them, and whosoever sins you retain, they are retained.*

It is required of a true repenting sinner, that if he has offended his neighbor in anything, either in words or deeds, he must give him satisfaction, and be reconciled with his neighbor, before he can expect any fruit of his repentance. Therefore faith our Savior, *if you bring your gift to the altar*, (that is, when you wilt worship God, or use the Holy Sacrament, which are now in the New Testament, instead of the *Levitical* sacrifices in the Old,) *and there remembers, that your brother has ought against you, leave there your gift before the altar, and go your way, first be reconciled to your brother, and then come, and offer your gift.* The words, *be reconciled to your brother*, signifies, according to the grounds of the text, to satisfy your brother, and give him something for something, against what you hast offended him in, or with. *David* received,

Secondly, the removing of the punishment, *You shall not die.* Hereby must we understand, 1. The spiritual death. When a man sins, he loses thereby the grace of God, and also the spiritual life in God; for the grace of God is the life of the soul, as the soul is the life of the body. But when he receives the forgiveness of sins, then begins he to live again in God. 2. Eternal death, whereto all sinners are liable, as long as they remain in their sinful condition. *And death and Hell were cast into the lake of fire, this is the second death.* 3. The temporal death, whereto everyone is subject by nature; for death is unto the faithful, and a repenting sinner, as but sleep, a departing and entrance into eternity in everlasting joy.

David received this grace of God, not because he repented, and was converted, for thereto was he obliged; but alone for the sake of Jesus Christ and his merits, to whom *David* had his refuge through faith, as the 51st *Psalm* convinces us of. We cannot deserve the forgiveness of sins by any of our actions, or conversion, but Christ is the meritorious cause, whom we must embrace in a true faith. *David* received,

Thirdly, the mitigation of crosses and affliction. *David* met with many crosses; as the child's death; his son *Absalom* killed his brother

Amnon, and wanted to deprive *David* himself of his kingdom and life; *Seba* made the children of *Israel* fall off from him; and his kingdom was plagued with three years famine; and with three days plague. But they were all fatherly chastisement. They were not laid on *David*, that he thereby should make satisfaction for his sins, and also become the forgiveness of them: No, for Jesus Christ alone has made full satisfaction for the sins of the world, by his suffering and death. *Christ has redeemed us from the curse of the law, being made a curse for us. Jesus delivered us from the wrath to come.* When the Scripture would describe our reconciliation to God, it says: *All his transgressions, that he has committed, they shall not be mentioned unto him. God has cast all my sins behind his back. I have blotted out as a thick cloud, your transgressions, and as a cloud your sins.* If God should punish them who are reconciled unto him, then remembers he their sins: If he punish their sins, then has he not blotted them out, and he will call them to an account therefor, and has not cast them behind his back. But the temporal chastisement, which were laid on *David* after his conversion, should admonish *David*, that he should not put too little value on his sins, and forget them. The Lord had put away his sins, and forgiven them and the punishment thereof, yet he intended to send some temporal punishment, which *David* was to look upon as fatherly chastisement; for God is so gracious, that when we repent, and are reconciled unto him through faith in Christ, then alters and turns he the curse to blessing, and temporal punishment to chastisement. *Eve* was punished in child-bearing, yet it is a blessing for a faithful woman; for so says St. *Paul: Notwithstanding she shall be saved in child-bearing.* Labor was laid upon *Adam* as a punishment, though faith the Psalmist: *Blessed is everyone that fears the Lord, that walks in his ways. For you shall eat the labor of your hands.*

There are several reasons why God visits the converted with crosses, namely,

1. That they should be public testimonies of God's vengeance over sin. *If judgment begins first at the house of God, what shall the end be of them that obey not the Gospel of God?* When *Moses* did beseech the Lord for his sister *Miriam*, who was punished with leprosy, then said the Lord unto *Moses: If her father had but spit in her face, should she not be ashamed seven days?*

2. That they should be an admonition of former sins, and warning for sins to come. When a child falls in the fire, it gets not alone a scar and mark thereof, but also a dread of fire for time to come.

3. That they should serve to increase abhorrence for sin, and our love to God. Crosses and afflictions are also a fan, wherewith all wickedness and bad desires are fanned off from us.

4. That they should be an exercise of our daily repentance, the trying of our faith, the watchman of our obedience, and a motive to prayers and hope; if God would either mitigate them, or entirely remove them; if not, then do *we know, that all things work together for good, to them that love God:* Crosses is as a brush, wherewith God brushes off our sins.

5. That they should guard us, and keep us from the conceit of our own holiness and worthiness above others, and bring us to an humble confession, that in our flesh dwells yet the remnant of sin, which must be subdued with crosses and afflictions.

On the contrary is the punishment over the ungodly and unconverted, not a fatherly chastisement, but a just curse, and warning of greater punishment to come: neither can they have any comfort thereof, since they are yet in the disgrace of God.

Since the bountiful and merciful God, has been so gracious to us, and has appointed repentance to Salvation, then let us not neglect the gracious time, but repent and be converted; whereto the following reasons should move and persuade us.

First, the serious command of God. *Turn O backsliding children, says the Lord, turn you to me with all your heart. Turn you unto me, says the Lord of Hosts, and I will turn unto you, says the Lord of Hosts.* The Holy Scripture both in the Old and New Testament is full of such commands; by which we can plainly see the grace of God, that he delights not in the death of a sinner.

Second, the shortness of our life. None can lengthen his life. *What is your life? It is even a vapor, that appears for a little time, and then vanishes away.* Therefore, since nothing is surer than death, and nothing more unsure than the hour thereof, how dares then anyone, to put off his repentance, and continue in such a dangerous condition, wherein the eternal state of their soul runs such a great hazard. God has promised his grace today, but not tomorrow; neither do we know, if we shall live till tomorrow, nor *what shall be on the morrow.*

Third, the profit we have, if we repent in time, namely, a gracious God, deliverance from the power of Satan, the removing of punishment, and the obtaining of life everlasting.

Fourth, the damage we have thereof, that we put off our conversion, namely, the hardness of heart, the offending of the holy angels, and our neighbors, the driving away of the Holy Spirit, the losing of all spiritual comfort, the wrath of God, and eternal damnation.

Lord God Heavenly Father be gracious unto us, and by the power of your Holy Spirit effect and work in us a true conversion; and heal the sores of our hearts, for the sake of the precious wounds of your beloved Son our Savior Jesus Christ. AMEN.

22

Faith

T he Text, HEBREWS 11:1. verse.
Faith is the substance of things hoped for, the evidence of things not seen.

INTRODUCTION

THE favor and grace of worldly lords is happy, but likewise danger-ous, for it is not firm, and to be depended upon. On the contrary, the grace and favor of God is saving and everlasting, by them that love God. *My kindness shall not depart from you, neither shall the covenant of my peace be removed, says the Lord.* We can by our own merit procure the king's favor; *For the king's favor is towards a wise servant:* But the grace of God we cannot procure with any of our own merits, but we receive the same alone through the merits of Christ, which we must embrace by faith; for, as St. *Paul* says in his epistle to the *Hebrews,* 11 the 6. verse. *Without faith it is impossible to please God.* The apostle shows us in these words, two things. 1. The necessity of faith; and 2. The excellency thereof.

1. The necessity of faith. We can see thereby, that it is *impossible to please God without it.* *Adam* and *Eve* our first parents could please God before the Fall without faith; they knew nothing of faith in the merits of Christ, but lived after the manner as the elect in heaven do, who please God without faith. But after the Fall, faith was so needful, that we could not please God without it; and that for the following reasons.

The *first*, on the side of God, his eternal decree and purpose. When God concluded from eternity, to receive the fallen mankind again into grace, in Jesus Christ, then he made this condition, that all they who believe in him, should not be lost, but have the eternal life: As God is immutable in his essence, so is he likewise in his decree; therefore *it is impossible to please God without faith.*

The *second*, on the side of man; the embracing the gracious promises of God. Since faith is the only means by which we receive Christ, and all his merits, then do we see thereby, that *it is impossible to please God without it.* As *Judah* said of his father *Jacob: That his life is bound up in* Benjamin's *life:* So we can say, that the soul of the faithful is bound up in Christ. This shows us,

2. The excellency of faith. To please God thereby, it must be the desire of everyone to please God, *but without faith it is impossible.* We may say of faith, what *Solomon* said of a virtuous woman. *Many daughters have done virtuously, but you excel them all:* A man can be adorned with many virtues, but faith excels them all. Therefore is it called, *most holy faith: more precious than gold.* Faith makes us accepted in the Beloved; so that, if we ask anything, God hears us. Therefore said our Savior always unto them whom he healed, *as you have believed, so be it done unto you,* or else, *your faith has made you whole.*

If it is a great happiness to please an earthly Lord or King, who can exalt us to worldly honor and dignity, and who are but mortal and of earth and dust, much greater, yea the greatest happiness it is to please the heavenly monarch, who is Lord of Heaven and earth, and can exalt us to eternal honor and glory in Heaven, which shall last without end. Since then faith is so needful and excellent, that *it is impossible to please God without it*, so will we discourse hear of faith under these two heads.

FIRST, *The Causes, Power, and Effect of Faith.*

SECOND, *The Division and Accidents of Faith.*

EXPLANATION of the TEXT

I. The Causes, Power, and Effect of Faith.

As the eye is the light of the body, so is faith the light of the soul. Our bodily eyes behold the present things that appear in our sight, but faith beholds the absent things as present; wherefore the Apostle says in our text: *Faith is the substance of things hoped for, the evidence of things not seen.* The Apostle uses hear these two words, *substance* and *evidence.*

Substance signifies a thing, which stands sure and firm in the mind and heart of a man, so that it cannot be moved, having a sure foundation, which is the promises of God. As they are substantial, so is likewise faith, built upon the same substance. Hence faith is called by several names in the Scripture, as strong faith, comforting, bold, immovable, glorifying, apprehending, and several more names.

Evidence signifies a powerful conviction, by which the conscience is so conquered and overcome, that it has nothing to say against, but must become a captive captivated under faith; therefore all what is promised in common to all, can everyone apply to himself in particular.

These two words *substance* and *evidence*, contain the three following parts, which belong to faith.

The *first*, is knowledge. If we would believe a thing, then must we have knowledge thereof beforehand. We cannot believe a thing, whereof we have no knowledge. *How shall they believe in him, of whom they have not heard?* Knowledge bears the light of faith. *I know whom I have believed*, says St. *Paul*. Knowledge is the eye of faith; an eye without light, is as good as faith without knowledge: As faith without works is dead, so is faith without knowledge blind. We can see how needful knowledge thereof is, that the Holy Scripture calls faith sometimes *knowledge*. Faith must have knowledge of the word of God, according to the three articles of our belief.

The *second*, is consent; not a loose and waggling, but sure and firm, without doubting. This consent comes thereby, that we in all manner and way are assured, that the word, whereto we consent, is the very word of God, which never deceives. Natural things we do believe, because they have cause in nature, but supernatural things we must consent to, because God has said so in his word, without enquiring, or seeking any other cause.

The *third*, and most principal, is a hearty and sincere confidence in God, by which a Christian trusts in God, and is assured of, that he shall be saved for Christ's sake. A child of God makes such a conclusion in himself, when he perceives by God's word, that God is faithful in his promises, since God is so gracious, that he wills not the death of a sinner, and has therefore sent his only beloved Son into the world, to seek that which was lost, and lets this grace be preached publicly in the gospel; then do I depend upon it, that God wills not the death of me, and that he has sent his Son to seek me, therefore am I sure, that *Christ died for my sins, and was risen again for my justification*, has reconciled me to God, and has saved me from sin, the curse of the law and Hell.

That faith is such a sure confidence in the mercy of God, and the merits of Christ, and that every Christian ought to have the same, we can prove by the Scripture. God commands that all they who will be justified and be saved, shall believe. *Whosoever believes that Jesus is the Christ, is born of God, He that believes, and is baptized, shall be saved.* Of this we can be convinced, that faith is an absolute confidence in the merits of Christ, which everyone that will be saved, must have.

The word of God is compared in the Scripture by *meat and drink.* Faith is the mouth by which we receive this meat and drink, and are made partakers of this heavenly food. As it is not enough, that he who is hungry and thirsty, touched alone the meat and drink, for that will not satisfy him, except he eats and drinks thereof; so must everyone attribute to himself by faith, the promises of God, and the merits of Christ, if he should be satisfied in his desire to life-everlasting. A man cannot work and effect such faith in himself of his own power. But,

God is the original effecting cause of faith, or which is the same, the Holy Spirit, to whom the work of regeneration is attributed; from which work the Father and the Son cannot be excluded. Therefore is faith called, *the work of God.* Christ is called, *the author and finisher of our faith*: And the Holy Spirit is called, the *Spirit of faith.*

God does not now use apparitions, dreams, and revelations, as in the old times, to promote faith in the heart of men, but he uses thereto,

1. The ordained means, namely, the hearing, reading, and med-itating on the word of God; for of the light of the word comes the light of faith. As the natural light came forth in the first creation by the word of God, so comes forth the spiritual light, faith, in the regeneration of the word of God; of which *Paul* says, *For God who commanded the light to shine out of darkness, hath shined in our hearts, to give the light of the knowledge of the glory of God, in the face of Jesus Christ.* The Holy Spirit stirs up faith in baptism in the heart of them

322

that are baptized, and seals and confirms faith in the Lord's Supper.

2. The ministers are also promoters of faith in men's heart, and are therefore compared by gardeners, and sowers, who sow the word of God in the heart of men. *Who then is* Paul, *and who is* Apollos, *but ministers by whom you believed?*

When also the word of God is preached, then offers God not alone unto all in the gospel, the merits of Christ, which he has procured with his death and suffering; but he promises likewise, that he will be powerful, and increase faith in the heart of them that do not resist obstinately; therefore must every child of God be concerned for the means, by which faith is received. He must have due attention and reverence for the word of God, believe it in simplicity, and keep it in a pure heart; then will his faith increase, and shine forth in holiness of life, until it becomes perfect, and obtains its.

Full object; namely, the thing which God has revealed in his word. The apostle calls them in our text, *the things not seen, though hoped for.* What are the things, which are not seen? They are God and his grace, Jesus Christ and his merits, the Holy Spirit and his gracious work, angels and devils, heaven and hell, and all such things, which we cannot see, yet must we believe them, since the word of God commands it. What are the things hoped for? They are, deliverance from need and sorrow in this world, the resurrection of the body, and life-everlasting. These we must hope for, since God has promised them in his word.

Not alone full grown people, but also small children, and even infants, have this faith; for although they cannot discern the right hand from the left, neither have sense to hear and understand the word of God whereof faith comes, neither know what sin is, though as full grown people receive faith by the hearing of the word of God; so has it pleased the gracious God to communicate faith to little children in the baptism, which is *the washing of regeneration; and renewing of the Holy Spirit.* Hereby is ascribed unto children an effecting faith. Our Savior says, *Whoso shall offend one of these little ones, which believe in me.* And that we should not think, that it was a big child, of whom Christ said it, since *he called it unto him, and set him in the midst of them*, namely, the apostles; the evangelist St. *Mark* explains it, saying, *He took him in his arms.* Our Savior says in another place: *Suffer the little children to come unto me, and forbid them not, for of such is the Kingdom of God*; and we know, that none can come in the Kingdom of God without faith, for *without faith it is impossible to please God.* Little children are regenerated, and renewed in baptism, which cannot be done without faith, for *faith purifies the heart.* Hereby is attributed unto little children the properties of faith; as the praise of God, and spiritual joy, as we can see by the example of *John*, who *leaped in his mother's womb.* Which leap since it was not occasioned by any natural cause, convinces us, that children can have faith, and the spiritual motions of faith, and are therefore, called, *heirs of the Kingdom of Heaven*, who are planted or grafted in the blessed vine Jesus Christ, to draw strength and power from him. The full grown people, as well as the little children, live the same life in God; for *the just shall live by his faith.*

The little children who die without baptism, must not be excluded from this grace, for God can effect faith in them by the power of the Holy Spirit; they were bound in the Old Testament to the circumcision, as much as we are in the new to baptism. Who will, or dare now condemn all the children that died in the wilderness, when they could not perform this covenant? We cannot find, neither can we suppose, that the child of *David* with *Bathsheba*, was circumcised before it died, since it died before it was eight days old, yet says *David, I shall go to him, but he shall not return to me.* In short, none is condemned, because he is deprived of the sacrament of baptism; but better for those that does not condemn, nor despises the same.

This brings me to discourse of,

The power and effect of faith, which are the following,

Faith cleanses the heart from sin; it has a clean and heavenly nature; it is in the soul, as the light in the air, to cleanse it; as fire to the gold, to try it; and as medicine to the body, to drive away sickness. It is an heavenly plant that will not thrive in unclean earth, and we can thereby draw from Christ, with the woman who *had the bloody issue*, power to stop the fountain of our sinful flesh and blood.

Faith justifies us, not as an effecting cause, but as a tool or instrument by which we embrace Christ, and *receive of his fullness, grace for grace.* In regard to this, it is called a *precious faith;* the worth and preciousness is not to be found in faith itself, but in Jesus Christ, who is the mark where faith aims; therefore, says St. *Paul, By grace are you saved through faith,* but not for the sake of faith.

Faith adopts us to be children of God: *As many as received him, to them gave he power to become the sons of God, even to them that believe in his name.* A father loves his child, because it is generated of his seed: God loves the faithful, *being born again, not of corruptible seed, but of incorruptible, by the word of God.*

Faith sanctifies us; it purifies not alone from committing sins, but guards also against sin and wickedness: It effects as long as men live by justification in heaven, and by demonstration of a holy life on earth, and is therefore called *most holy faith.* St. *Paul* says, and admonishes us therefore; *Above all take the shield of faith, wherewith you shall be able to quench the fiery darts of the wicked.*

Faith reconciles us to God; *As the girdle cleaves to the loins of a man, so have I caused to cleave unto me the whole house of Israel, and the whole house of Judah, says the Lord.* Faith is the girdle by which we cleave unto God, more firm than one friend is bound to another; for a friend is not always present by his friend, but God is always present by the faithful: yea, he even dwells in them.

Faith makes us spiritually living: *The just shall live by his faith* when we begin to believe, then do we begin to live; for faith is in the soul, as the pulse-vein is in the body.

Faith makes our actions pleasing in the sight of God: *By faith* Abel *offered unto God a more excellent sacrifice than* Cain, *by which he obtained witness that he was righteous, God testifying of his gifts.* Faith made his sacrifice pleasing; and his gift testifies of his faith.

Faith pacifies our conscience: St. *Paul* says, *being justified by faith, we have peace with God, through our Lord Jesus Christ.* Faith is the dove of *Noah*, who brings an olive leaf, and assures us, that we have peace with God.

Faith confirms our hearts and souls. *Paul* and *Barnabas confirmed the souls of the disciples, and exhorted them to continue in the faith.* The faithful are as *Joseph*, of whom the patriarch *Jacob* says, *the archers have sorely grieved him, and shot at him, and hated him; but his bow abode in strength, and the arms of his hands were made strong by the hands of the mighty God of Jacob.* Faith draws power and strength from Jesus Christ, as the bee the honey from the flowers. *I can do all things through Christ, who strengthens me.*

Faith stirs up in us hope, that we, through patience, expect the fulfilling of the promises. Since faith is the substance of things hoped for, then we can conclude thereby, that faith comes before hope; for faith must first understand the promises, before we can hope for them. Hope is the daughter of faith; faith beholds as well the things past, as to come, and believes the birth, suffering and death of Christ, which are past, as well as his coming to judgment, which is to come. Hope beholds alone the things to come: faith is as the cable, and hope is as the anchor, and both serve to keep our souls, that they should not be cast away upon sinful rocks, and be entirely lost forever. Faith saves us here, both in the gracious kingdom, and hereafter, in the glorious kingdom.

326

Here, in the gracious kingdom: The faithful are *made partakers of the divine nature*; and are *blessed with all spiritual blessings in Christ. The Holy Spirit dwells in them.* And, *the Kingdom of God is within them.*

Hereafter, in the glorious kingdom; where our salvation shall be perfect and without end; and then shall we sing this song; *We have a strong city, salvation will God appoint for walls and bulwarks.*

II. The Division and Accidents of Faith.

As there is but one life after this life, and one door to go through to it, namely, Jesus Christ; so is there but one way to go to this door, which is faith, therefore is there but *one faith*, as St. *Paul* says.

Faith is one, not in number, for everyone must have his own faith; neither in degrees, for it is in some strong, and in others weak, *according as God has dealt to every man the measure of faith*; and oftentimes faith can be first strong, then weak in the same man. But faith is one in regard to Christ, and his merits, which must be received by faith. *There is no salvation in any other; for there is none other name under heaven given among men, by which we must be saved.* Hereof is faith called, *common faith*. St. *Peter* says of the faithful: That *they have obtained like precious faith with us*, namely, the apostles, so that they who lived under the Old Testament had the same faith as we under the New. They believed in Christ, who was to come: we believe in Christ, who is come, yet faith is different, and of many sorts, namely,

1. Living and dead faith. Living faith is a doubtless hearty confidence in Christ shining forth in good works. A dead faith is as St. *James* says, *it has not works, is dead, being alone*, and is called by our Savior, *a corrupt tree bringing forth evil fruit.*

2. Wavering and steadfast faith. Wavering faith, is *when a man bears and receives the Word, but endures for a while: For when tribulation*

or persecution arises because of the word, by and by be is offended, and falls off. Steadfast faith is, when a man remains steadfast in his faith, unto his life's end.

3. Ones own and strange faith. One's own faith is the confidence of every person in the promises of God and merits of Christ: Strange faith is, when we bring forth the need of others, and by our faith procure temporal blessings for them. When *Christ saw the faith of them, who brought the sick of the palsy on a bed*, he healed him. They who were in the ship with *Paul*, were all saved by the faith of *Paul*. But none can receive any spiritual blessing by the faith of another, except he believes himself.

4. Historical, miraculous and justifying faith. Historical faith is, when we believe all what God has revealed in his word to be true, though without having any confidence therein. This faith is not alone found by the wicked, but even by the devils themselves. Miraculous faith is such faith, by which they who are gifted, could, by the power of God, do miracles as the apostles. This gift of doing miracles is sometimes found in the wicked: Our Savior says therefore, *Many will say to me in that day, Lord, Lord, have we not prophesied in your name, and in your name have cast out devils, and in your name done many wonderful works? And then will I profess unto them, I never knew you, depart from me, you that work iniquity.* Justifying faith is a sincere and hearty confidence in the mercy of God, and merits of Jesus Christ.

5. Strong and little faith. Strong faith is combined with such strong confidence that nothing can move it, but cleaves always to the mercy of God, even in the greatest calamities and misfortunes and temptations. Such faith had *Jacob, Moses, Job*, the *Centurion*, and the *Canaanite* woman. Little faith is mixed with doubt, as the disciples, who said to Jesus when they were in the storm, *Lord save us, we perish*: And *Peter, who was afraid, and began to sink when he saw the wind*. The apostle St. *Paul* compares himself in the beginning of his faith

to a child, saying: *When I was a child, I spoke as a child, I understood as a child, I thought as a child; but when I became a man, I put away childish things.* As we grow from childhood to youth, and from youth to manhood, so grows likewise faith by degrees; yet where faith is, there is it whole, although it appears not always wholly through the infirmity of the flesh; for as a child is whole man, both soul and body, but has not full strength before it is grown up, so is it likewise with faith; it is first a suckling faith, which must be suckled *with the sincere milk of the word, and grows thereby.* It is first as a mustard-seed, and grows afterwards to a big tree: And it is as the corn, which is *first the blade, then the ear, after that the full corn in the ear.* Hereby we can see, that

Faith is not always alike strong. The faith of *Peter* was once so great, that he dares to walk upon the sea with Christ, and even offered to go in death and die with Christ; but a few hours after, his faith became so little, that he denied Christ. They of little faith should be comforted thereby, that a little faith pleases God also, and embraces Christ and his merits, as well as a strong faith. A little hand is a hand, and sparks is fire. The promises of God is mostly for them of little faith; for he says not, He that has such a faith that he can remove mountains, or walk upon the sea shall be saved; but alone, *He that believes shall be saved,* although their faith might be little. We must observe in the preaching of Christ on the mountain concerning salvation, that his promises has regard to them of little faith: *Blessed are the poor in spirit, for theirs is the Kingdom of Heaven. Blessed are they that mourn, for they shall be comforted. Blessed are the meek, for they shall inherit the earth. Blessed are they which do hunger and thirst after righteousness, for they shall be filled.* Hereby we can see, that a little faith can likewise be sure of heaven; for, since it embraces Christ and his merits, as well as a strong faith, then has it likewise part and lot in Christ and his merits.

In the meantime, shall every child of God be careful and concerned for his faith, that the same may increase more and more; and should be diligent in reading and hearing the word of God, using the sacrament of the Lord's Supper, walk circumspectly, that he sinned not willfully against his own conscience; and pray with the disciples; *Lord increase our faith.* If we are not careful, and supply constantly the lamp of our faith with the oil of the word of God, the same will soon be quenched and entirely lost.

Men can lose faith again, so that they can never receive it again: But this can be understood alone of them who are regenerated, but not chosen. The elect can lose their faith, but not until their life's end, for then they were not chosen. They who are alone regenerated, can lose their faith entirely, to their life's end, and never receive it again; this we can prove from several places of the Scripture; as, *When a righteous man turns away from his righteousness, and commits iniquity, and dies in them for his iniquity that he has done, shall he die.* St. *Paul* testifies, that the converted gentiles can, through unbelief and pride, lose the grace of God, and be broken off, although *the gifts and calling of God are without repentance.* That the regenerated can by their works, defile the temple of God, and thereby lose their salvation, and be destroyed, and that they who were once made partakers of the Holy Spirit, can so fall away that they are eternally lost; St. *Peter* says, that, *If after they have escaped the pollution of the world, through the knowledge of the Lord and Savior, Jesus Christ, they are again entangled therein, and overcome; the later end is worse with them than the beginning.* Therefore admonishes us the Spirit of God so seriously in several places, saying; *Watch ye, stand fast in the faith; quit you like men; be strong. Work out your own salvation with fear and trembling. Be you faithful unto death; exhort one another daily, while it is called today lest any of you be hardened through the deceitfulness of sin. Beware lest you fall from your own steadfastness. Cast not away your confidence, which has great recompense of reward. He that shall endure to the end, the same shall be saved.* We must therefore be cautious and careful, that we do not lose our faith. It is as the holy fire, that must always burn upon the altar of our hearts, enlightened by the Holy Spirit, and nourished by the gracious means God has ordained.

The Lord be gracious unto us, and by his Holy Spirit, stir up faith in all unbelievers; increase it in them of little faith, and strengthen all the faithful: That we may all carry away the end of our faith, even the salvation of our souls; for the sake of our Blessed Savior, Jesus Christ. AMEN.

23

Justification

T he Text, ROMANS 3:24, 25, ver.
We are justified freely by his grace, through the redemption that is in Jesus Christ. Whom God has set forth, to be a propitiation, through faith in his blood; to declare his righteousness for the remission of sins that are past.

INTRODUCTION

THAT man is always afraid, who knows himself guilty, and has nothing wherewith to make satisfaction, when he is called to an account. We see how terrified the servant was, who owed ten thousand talents, and had nothing to pay with. We are all greatly indebted to God, and have nothing of ourselves to pay with. The day of account is certain, and uncertain: certain it is in its coming, and uncertain in the time when it shall come; therefore we must be always prepared for it, and say with *David*, in his *Psalm* 143:2. *Enter not into judgment with your servant; for in your sight shall no man living be justified.*

The Psalmist remembers here in the over-haling of his sinful debts, three things. 1. The severe justice of God. 2. His own, and all men's unrighteousness. And, 3. The grace of God: For the first he is terrified: Of the second he complains; and by the third he is comforted.

First, the justice of God expresses *David* with these words; *Enter not into judgment with your servant.* God has his judgment seat in two places, on the earth and in heaven.

Here on earth God judges three ways; namely, with his word; with punishment, and with destruction. The first is called the judgment of God's mouth; the second, the judgment of his hand; and the third, the judgment of his destruction. God admonishes us with the first; he corrects us with the second, and destroys us with the third. God had declared and pronounced the first judgment, by the prophet *Nathan* to *David*, who was thereby terrified, and was afraid of the other two judgments, and therefore prayed: *Enter not into judgment with your servant.*

Hereafter will God keep judgment on the Last Day; *Then shall we all appear before the judgment seat of Christ, that everyone may receive the things done in his body, according to that he has done, whether it be good or bad.* The Psalmist is likewise afraid of this judgment, and prays, that God will not enter into judgment with him; and thereby acknowledges,

Second, his own and all men's unrighteousness; *For in your sight shall no man living be justified.* The inbred unrighteousness, which we have of *Adam*, is as a poisonous fountain in us, from which flows out all unrighteous works and wickedness: *How should man be just with God? If he will contend with him, he cannot answer him one of a thousand.* And although we could, by the grace of God, live such a life, that we could say with the apostle St. *Paul, I know nothing by myself:* Yet, we cannot be justified thereby before God, but we must

333

always and daily pray to God for the forgiveness of our Sins, and rely on the merits of Christ, and have our refuge to,

Third, the grace of God. *Enter not into judgment.* We must appeal from the judgment seat to the mercy seat of God; from the justice of God to his mercy, which he promises to all who believe in Christ. For, since Christ is the only man, who is likewise God, and who is in grace with God, and God has given him, that he should be our righteousness, and that we by faith should attribute unto ourselves his righteousness, as there is no other by which we can be justified, but through. Faith in Christ; the apostle St. *Paul* speaks here in our text, of the work of this our justification; from which we will draw these two heads,

FIRST, *How it goes with the justification of men before God.*

SECOND, *What profit and comfort we have of justification.*

EXPLANATION of the TEXT

I. How it goes with the justification of men before God.

Justification is the same as forgiveness of sin, though with this difference, that justification comprehends the whole process, how it goes with a sinner before the tribunal of God. Remission of sins is the conclusion of the sentence: As it goes before a worldly judgment seat, that, first, the guilty is accused; the accuser brings forth the cause, and shows the other's guilt, then speaks the Judge the sentence. If then anyone be bail for the guilty, and pay for him, then becomes he free: but if none will answer for him, then must he himself pay or suffer therefor. Likewise is it with the justification of men before the tribunal of God: The sinner is accused, and is guilty, his debts are his sins and transgressions; the accusers are the law of God and

Satan, the judge is the just God, and the evidence is the conscience: Then comes Christ, and answers for men, and shows that he has satisfied for them, has fulfilled the law, has taken upon himself the curse of the law, has cleansed and purged their conscience with his own blood, and has bruised the head of the Serpent. The poor sinner attributes to himself through faith, these merits of Christ, and is justified before God, and receives the forgiveness of his sins. This is the right meaning of St. *Paul* in the words of our text; of which we will consider the following.

1. What justification is. Justification is the work of God the Father, Son and Holy Spirit, by which he of mere grace and mercy, for the obedience and perfect satisfaction of Jesus Christ the Mediator, forgives sinful men, who believe in Christ, their sins freely, and imputes to them the righteousness of Christ, and accepts them unto the heirship of eternal life to the glory of his grace, and the salvation of the faithful.

2. Who is the effecting cause in our justification? All the three persons in the Holy Blessed Trinity. Of God the Father St. *Paul* says: *Who shall lay anything to the charge of God's elect? It is God, that justifies.* Of God the Son says the prophet *Isaiah, By his knowledge shall my righteous Servant justify many.* Of both the Son and the Holy Spirit says St. *Paul, you are justified in the name of the Lord Jesus, and by the Spirit of our God.*

3. What the moving causes are, by which God is moved to justify us. They are on God's side; His mercy and grace, and on our side; our miserable condition; so says the Psalmist, *The Lord looked down from heaven upon the children of men, to see if there were any that did understand, and seek God. They are all gone aside, they are all together become filthy,* (as a carrion, according to the signification of the text:) *They were dead in trespass and sin,* and *under the power of darkness: There was none that does good, no not one.* God had compassion over

335

this miserable condition of men, and therefore sent his beloved Son to be a Savior, that they should be quickened through him from sin, and be delivered from the power of darkness, and the bondage of Satan. He alone is,

4. The meritorious cause of our justification. And Jesus Christ is called, *true God and true man in one person*, and has merited and pro-cured our justification according to both natures. We can observe the righteousness of Christ in two ways, partly belonging to his person, and partly to his office. In regard to his person, his righteousness is both according to the divine and human nature. According to his godly nature, he is essentially just, and is therefore called, *a just God and Savior*. According to his human nature, he is naturally just, for he was conceived and born without sin. This righteousness was required to the completing the work of redemption. The righteousness of his office was, that he gave himself under the law, to satisfy the justice of God, and suffered the shameful death on the cross, although he had never sinned in thoughts, words, nor deeds: This righteousness Christ communicates to us, who have none of our selves. It is called in the Scripture, *the righteousness of God*, in regard to the effecting cause, which is God: *The righteousness of faith*, since faith is the means by which we embrace the same: And, *the righteousness of the gospel*, as it is offered to us in the gospel. The apostle calls it in our text, *Justification through the redemption that is in Jesus Christ, whom God has set forth to be a propitiation through faith in his blood*. The meaning hereof is, that, since God is not alone merciful, but also just, and hates and punishes sin and iniquity; so was it absolutely necessary, that the justice of God should be satisfied. This could not be altered, or else men could not, who were polluted with sin, be received in the grace of God: Therefore has God of his infinite mercy, sent his Son Jesus Christ, who should take upon him the sins of men, and fully satisfy the justice of God with his death and bloodshed. For,

without shedding of blood is no remission, as St. *Paul* says.

5. The form of justification consists in these three parts, namely, 1. Sins are forgiven. 2. The righteousness of Christ is imputed. And, 3. The sinner is received to be heir of eternal life. These three parts happen all at once, and it goes with the sinner, as it did with *Joshua* the High Priest, who was clothed with filthy garments, which *were taken from him, and was clothed again with change of raiment.*

First, the sins are forgiven; not alone the original, but also the actual, as sin dwells in us as long as we live, and can never be rooted out; but then God is said to forgive sins, when he accounts them not to us for punishment, but beholds us in Christ as righteous as if we had never sinned.

Second, the righteousness of Christ is imputed. All what Christ has done and suffered is imputed to a converted sinner, by the grace of God, as fully as if he himself had suffered. God not alone forgives him the sins he has committed, but he gives him likewise the righteousness of Christ, and adorns him with a glorious garment, wherewith he can stand in judgment before the face of God. That this righteousness of Christ is not imagined, but real, and in truth imputed to repenting sinners, we can prove by the following, namely,

1*st*, That it is grounded upon the mercy and gracious will of God, by which he has decreed from eternity, not to account to them, who believe in Christ, their sins and transgressions.

2nd*ly*, That it is grounded upon the obedience of Christ. Why should Christ, who was holy and innocent, have suffered and died, if he had not taken our sins upon him? In the same manner, as it is said, *that Christ is become sin for us*, in the same manner we are said, *to be justified before God.*

3rd*ly*, It is grounded upon the working of grace by the Holy Spirit. When a child of God has through faith made the righteousness of Christ to be his own, then is he nearer united with Christ, than with

337

himself, and then lives he not himself, but Christ lives in him, and when Christ lives in him, and he abides in Christ, then *brings the same forth much fruit.*

Third, the sinner is received to be heir of eternal life. It is the final cause why God justifies us, *That the righteous nation, which keeps the truth, may enter in*; into the Kingdom of Heaven, St. *Paul* says hereof, *Now being made free from sin, and become servants to God, you have your fruit unto holiness, and the end everlasting life.*

6. The means which God uses for the promoting of our justification, are the ministers who preach, the word that is preached, the sacraments which are the seals, and faith by which we are made partakers thereof, and which embraces Christ and his merits.

Everyone that will be justified must have this faith for his own person. Therefore faith the prophet *Habakkuk*; *The just shall live by his faith*, and where this faith is, the faithful can say, *Who shall separate me from the love of Christ?*

Either faith is little or strong, yet it is a *precious faith*, in regard to Christ who is thereby embraced, also men can be saved by a little faith. As a gold-ring remains in its value, either if it is worn by a full-grown person, or a child; so is faith either strong or little like precious, since they both embrace Christ and his merits.

Away therefore with all doubts, by which a Christian can be brought, to despair of his justification and salvation. A child of God, who has made a true and sincere repentance, and has received of the gospel, faith and the Holy Spirit, and cleaves to the gracious promises of God, and the merits of Christ, can in all manner and way be assured of the forgiveness of his sins, and of the grace of God, and also of his justification before God. Which we can prove by the following.

First, of the faithful promises of God. God has promised in the gospel, that he will be gracious, and forgive the sins of all them who sincerely repent, are converted, and believe in Christ. Of all these promises, the principal is that which we find in the evangelist St. John: *God so loved the world, that he gave his only begotten Son, that whosoever believes in him, should not perish, but have everlasting life.* God has fulfilled the first part of this promise, by giving his Son; and he will likewise fulfill the second part, and give to all them who believe in his Son the everlasting Life.

Second, of the oath of God. God does not alone promise his grace, forgiveness, of sins and everlasting life, to the faithful, but he confirms it also with an oath, in order to remove all doubts of the heart of men. So faith the Lord by the prophet *Ezekiel, As I live says the Lord God, I have no pleasure in the death of the wicked, but that the wicked turn from his way and live.* Our Savior says by St. John: *Verily, verily, I say unto you, if a man keep my saying, he shall never see death.*

Third, of the sacraments. God has not alone promised unto repenting sinners his grace, and confirmed the same with an oath, but he seals them also with the sacraments. In regard to this, the apostle St. *Paul* calls circumcision, *A seal of the righteousness of faith*, because they who were circumcised should be assured of their justification through faith in the *Messiah*, that was to come. In the New Testament the sacrament of baptism and the Lord's Supper do assure, and seal to us the grace of God, and the remission of sins through faith in Christ.

Fourth, of the inward testimony of the Holy Spirit in our hearts. God has not alone promised to repenting sinners, his grace and forgiveness of sins, has confirmed the same with oath, and sealed with the holy sacraments, but he also assures the faithful thereof, by the inward testimony of the Holy Spirit in their hearts. *After that you believed*, (says St. *Paul*) you *were sealed with that Holy Spirit of promise*. A child of God can then be assured, that he is in the grace of God, since he has the Spirit of Christ. This Spirit is *not the Spirit of bondage, again to fear, but the Spirit of adoption, by which we cry, Abba, Father.*

Fifth, of the certainty, that we are heard. Our Savior has promised and confirmed with an oath, that we shall be heard, saying; *Verily, verily I say unto you, whatsoever you shall ask the Father in my name, he will give it you.*

Sixth, of the properties of faith. Faith is a substance, full of assurance, confidence, and comfort: These names cannot subsist where there is doubt. The apostle St. *Paul* says: *Shall tribulation or distress, or persecution, or famine, or nakedness, or peril, or sword, separate us from the love of Christ:* And afterwards he declared his confidence, saying, *For I am persuaded, that neither death, nor life, nor angels, nor principalities, nor powers, nor things present, nor things to come, nor height, nor depth, nor any other creature, shall be able to separate us from the love of God, which is in Christ Jesus our Lord.* This is not a false imagination, nor unsure conceit, but a certain conclusion, proceeding from the inward testimony of the Holy Spirit in the heart.

Seventh, of the abhorrence of all doubts. Doubt is a sin against the first commandment, and bereaves God of his glory, and honor of truth; and, on the reverse, accuses God with lies and perjury. Doubt is absolutely against faith, whose property is a sure confidence; It drives away the rest and peace of our conscience, the comfort of the Holy Spirit; the grace of God, and our firmness in crosses and afflictions. Doubt comes by our corrupt nature: For, since the Fall, it is natural to men to flee from God, and to doubt of his will. The Devil strives always to increase this doubt in the hearts of men, that they can be brought to despair. A Christian who has made a true and hearty repentance, has received faith and the Holy Spirit, and cleaves to the gracious promises of God, and the merits of Jesus Christ; can be assured that his sins are forgiven, and he is justified before God. And this brings me to the second head of my discourse, which is,

340

II. What Profit and Comfort we have in Justification.

The profit and comfort we have of justification is, namely, reconciliation to God, adoption to be sons of God, a good and peaceable
conscience, sanctification, the Holy Spirit, freedom from the obedience of the law, redemption from the curse of the law, patience
in crosses and afflictions, and a certain hope of eternal salvation.
And thereupon is a child of God daily striving after a new life: When
man believe in Christ, then is he justified in two ways, which is,
notwithstanding, but one Justification, and cannot be separated,
namely,

1. He is absolved from his sins, which are forgiven. The righteousness of Christ is imputed to him, and he is adopted to be a Son of
God, and heir of the heavenly Kingdom, alone for the sake of Christ,
whom he embraces through faith. For, since God has not spared his
own Son, but gave him for our sake, how should he not then give
us graciously all good things in him. Therefore he that embraces
Christ, whom God has given, through faith, he receives likewise the
forgiveness of sins, the righteousness of Christ, the adoption to be
a child of God, and assurance of life-everlasting. This justification
lasts as long as we live, and are in this world, if we do not ourselves
obstinately reject the same.

2. The second, way is that a man, who believes in Christ, and has
the Holy Spirit, who renews him daily, and works and effects in him
works of justification, so that he subdues and crucifies the flesh and
its desires, and lives not longer according to the flesh, but according
to the Spirit; this is a renewing that that must not be separated from
the foregoing justification: For he that is justified through faith in
Christ, is stirred up by the Spirit of God, not alone to abhor the works
of the flesh, that is sin, but also to practice the works of justification,

and to walk circumspectly. This justification, although effected in men by the Holy Spirit, is notwithstanding imperfect in this life; therefore we must always see to the former justification, by which all our sins are forgiven by grace through faith in Christ.

Since we can come at such easy and cheap rates to the grace of God, and our own justification in Jesus Christ; then let us step forth, and humble ourselves before this mercy seat, and pray for the remission of our sins, and purge ourselves from all worldly and fleshly filthiness, perfecting holiness in the fear of God, that we may come at last to the perfect righteous spirits in the new heaven and new earth, where righteousness dwells.

Grant us this, O merciful Father, for Christ's sake. AMEN.

24

Good Works

T he Text, EPHESIANS 2:10. verse.

We are God's workmanship, created in Christ Jesus unto good works, which God has before ordained, that we should walk in them.

INTRODUCTION

AS there follows always upon great heat in the summer, thunder and lightning, so follows likewise upon the abusing of the grace of God great punishment; which our Savior will learn and instruct us of in the parable of the fig-tree, whereon there was found no fruit; saying by the Evangelist St. *Luke*, 13:6, 7, 8, and 9. vers. *A certain man had a fig-tree planted in his vineyard, and he came and sought fruit thereon, and he found none. Then said he unto the dresser of his vineyard, behold, these three years I came seeking fruit on this fig-tree, and find none: Cut it down, why cumbers it the ground? And he answering said unto him, Lord, let it alone this year also, till I shall dig about it, and dung it; and if it bear fruit, well, and if not, then after that you shall cut it down.* In this parable we have to observe,

1. The diligence of the certain man. He had a vineyard, and planted a fig-tree in the same, and chose certainly a fruitful and convenient place for it, and took great care and pains therewith, according to the nature of such trees, and came constant seeking fruit thereon. All this has God done with men in a high degree. He, as the heavenly Lord, has planted us by baptism in his vineyard, the Christian church, has watered us by the Holy Spirit, the word, and the Lord's Supper, and has not spared anything in order to make us fruitful. But what fruit was found on this fig-tree, our Savior complains of.

2. The bad nature of the fig-tree. *And he came and sought fruit thereon, and found none.* Every person is a tree in the vineyard of God; but that this unfruitful fig-tree stood in a fruitful vineyard, signifies, that there are many fruitless Christians in the Christian church, who live in all manner of wickedness and fleshly lust, without repentance and true faith; by which they provoke God, and offend their neighbors. They have some glorious leaves of outward, pious and charitable actions, but no true fruit is found on them.

The fruits which a Christian ought to bear, are both inward and outward. The inward fruits, *are love, joy, peace, forbearance, gentleness, goodness, faith, meekness, temperance:* These are the fruits of the Spirit, and *the soul of the Lord desires them.* The outward fruits are a godly and Christian life, and the practice *of good works*; and likewise timely fruit; namely, in the time of temptation, fruits of faith; in prosperity, fruits of thanksgiving; in misfortunes, fruits of humbleness; in poverty, fruits of hope; in sickness, fruits of prayer and patience: And where such fruit is not found, there will follow,

3. A severe judgment. Cut it off; the branches shall not alone be cut off, and the stump with the root remain in the earth, as it happened with the big tree by the prophet *Daniel*; but the whole tree shall be cut down, and the roots be rooted out, that the same shall not longer incumber the earth. God has several ways to cut down

344

such unfruitful trees; as 1. By punishment on themselves or their children; for *wickedness shall be broken as a tree: Their children shall not take root, and their branches shall bring no fruit.* 2. By withdrawing of the grace of God, that he, in his justice, takes away his Holy Spirit and grace from the fruitless, so that the word of God has no power upon them: And 3. By death, when they die suddenly in their sins, and have no time to repent. And if such trees are suffered to stand longer, it is alone by grace through,

4. The intercession of the dresser of the vineyard. Jesus Christ the dresser of the vineyard of God, intercedes, that God would not cut down in his wrath such fruitless trees, *let it alone this year also.* So says St. *Paul: Christ entered into heaven itself, now to appear in the presence of God for us. He is at the right hand of God, making intercession for us.* This intercession of Christ is so powerful, that many unfruitful trees are spared, and bear afterwards fruit. As we can see of king *Manasseth, Mary Magdalen, Paul,* and others.

He that will bear good, and much fruit, is a God-pleasing tree, and shall be removed at last from the earthly into the heavenly vineyard; but he that will not, shall be cut down. Therefore encourages the apostle, all men to the practice of good works in the words of our Text: Of which we will discourse upon these two following heads, namely,

FIRST, *Of good works, and their nature.*

SECOND, *Why we should practice good works.*

EXPLANATION of the TEXT

I. Of good works and their nature.

The apostle does encourage the Christians to the practices of good works. He first sets forth these two things to consider, namely,

First, their miserable condition, wherein they were before their conversion; *They were dead in trespasses and sin,* and could as little convert themselves, as the dead can raise themselves up, by which their daily life and doings could testify; for, *They walked in time past, according to the course of this world.* They followed the instigation of the Devil, and did all what he gave them in their hearts to do; whereof the following were three causes; 1st, the Devil; *The Spirit that now works in the children of disobedience.* 2ndly, the bad conversation and examples of others: And, 3rdly, their own flesh, and the desires and lusts thereof.

Second, the apostle sets forth, *The great mercy and love of God,* that he made us partakers of all the blessings of Christ, and *has quickened us together with Christ: Has raised us up together, and made us fit together in heavenly places in Christ Jesus.* When a Christian considers such great grace, then he will certainly strive after the practicing of good works, and meditate upon what he has been, namely, a stinking and filthy sinner, who never could do any God-pleasing action, although the same was done ever so well; and remembers what he is now, namely, a new man, and a child of God, who is pleasing in the sight of God, in Christ Jesus; and can now, by the grace of God, and the assisting power of the Holy Spirit, act to the glory of God's holy name: Our text makes mention thereof, and we shall observe,

1. **What good works are.** What the heathens used to call virtues, the Holy Spirit calls good works, and comprehends all the obedience, which a child of God can, through the whole course of his life, show to God and his neighbor, according to the command of God: So that good works, are the works of a regenerated child of God, both in his outward and inward living and conversation, according to the commandments of God, by the assisting grace of the Holy Spirit through faith, to the glory of God, to his own gratitude, and to the profit of others.

346

Works are called in general, all what we do; and are either natural, as to eat, drink, sleep, and such like; or moral, as to live soberly, keep house and rule it; or works of Christianity, as to church, to receive the Sacrament, to read the word of God, to pray, to give alms, and all other charitable actions. All these actions are called good works, since they seemingly agree with nature, modesty and honesty, and cannot be found fault with; though they are not the right good works which God demands, if true faith is not joined with them, and the same be acted by a pure and sincere intention; for hypocrites can likewise do outward good actions, though *they have no reward of the Father which is in heaven:* Therefore must good works of Christianity go further, and contain in particular, true holy motions in the heart, faith, joy and peace in the conscience, love, purity of heart, and such like. Therefore are good works called in the Scripture, The *fruits of the Spirit; fruits of righteousness; armor of light; sacrifices of righteousness; Works made in God.* And to practice good works, is called in the Scripture; *Let your light so shine before men, that they may see your good works: Do works meet for repentance:* To *do good, and be rich in good works: To be zealous of good works:* To *maintain good works:* To *bear fruit.: To be fruitful in every good work: Not to be slothful and unfruitful to the knowledge of our Lord Jesus Christ.* Of these and more other such like names we can see, that good works proceed mostly from inward, and not from outward appearances alone.

2. Why are they called good works? They are called so in regard to,

1*st,* Regard to the effecting cause, which is the Holy and Blessed Trinity. *God the Father makes us perfect in every good work, to do his will, working that which is well-pleasing in his sight, through Jesus Christ.* God the Son, Jesus Christ, is the true vine; he that remains in him bears much fruit. The Holy Spirit regenerates and renews us, and makes us fruitful to all good works. Hereto God uses his servants, who are called, *laborers together with God*; and they preach to us, and declare to us the will of God.

2ndly, The instrumental cause on God's side, is the law and the gospel: The law commands us, the gospel draws us to do good works.

The law commands us thereto, as the Lord says himself; *Whatever I command you, observe to do it; you shall not add thereto, nor diminish from it.* The law threatens besides, *Cursed be he that confirms not all the words of this law, to do them.*

The gospel draws us to do good works: It regenerates man, and makes him a new creature in Christ, and quickens him to the practices of good works; therefore faith Christ; *The words that I speak unto you, they are Spirit, and they are life.* The gospel shows us likewise, how our actions can be made *acceptable to God, by faith in Jesus Christ.*

3rdly, The instrumental cause on men's side, is faith. Faith is the soul, and foundation, and root of all good work: As the body without soul is a dead corps, so is likewise good work a dead image without faith. *By faith we live in Christ, and Christ lives in us.* Where now faith is, there are the fruits of spiritual life, good works.

The reasons why good works, take its value of faith, are following.

First, by faith we are reconciled unto God, grafted in Christ, and united with him. He that is now reconciled unto God, grafted in Christ, and united with him, his actions are looked upon, not as they are in themselves, but in Christ Jesus, who has purged and cleansed us with his precious blood.

Second, good works are the fruits of faith: Through faith we are justified, and through faith dwells Christ in our hearts; therefore, take good work, its true and intrinsic value of faith, where through Christ is received.

4thly, The person that must do and practice good works, must therefore be regenerated, and a faithful Christian; for what is not of faith is sin: Therefore calls the apostle in our text such persons,

God's workmanship, created in Christ Jesus. The works, and the persons that do the works must agree. A bitter fountain cannot bring forth sweet water; neither can a corrupt tree bear good fruit. The person that will do any God-pleasing work, must first be reconciled to God, and become well-pleasing in the sight of God, which comes through faith in Christ, the only Mediator. Our Savior explains this before the apostles, when he says; *As the branch cannot bear fruit of itself, except it abides in the vine; no more can you, except you abide in me. I am the vine, you are the branches: He that abides in me, and I in him, the same brings forth much fruit, for without me you can do nothing. If a man abide not in me, he is cast forth as a branch, and is withered, and men gather them, and cast them into the fire, and they are burned. If you abide in me, and my words abide in you, you shall ask what you will, and it shall be done unto you.*

5*thly,* The works, in themselves, that should be good works must be regulated and done according to the word and command of God; for God has no pleasure in anything, except what he commands himself, or at least is agreeable thereunto: In regard to this says St. Paul; *Brethren, whatsoever things are true; whatsoever things are honest; whatsoever things are just; whatsoever things are pure; whatsoever things are lovely; whatsoever things are of good report; if there be any virtue, and if there be any praise, think on these things, and do them.* In another place the same apostle includes all good works in these three words, *Soberly, righteously, and godly.* Soberly towards ourselves; righteously towards our neighbors, and godly towards God. *Luther* comprehends it in these three words: *Believe, love, suffer.*

Although a child of God regulates all his actions and works, after the word and command of God; yet he cannot attain in this world to such a perfection that they can stand before the judgment of God: All saints must pray unto God for the remission of their sins; and say with the prophet *Isaiah; We are all as an unclean thing, and all our righteousness are as filthy rags.* This is the complaint of the pious Job; *If I wash myself with snow-water, and make my hands ever so clean, yet shall you plunge me in the ditch, and mine own clothes shall abhor me:* The Psalmist makes this humble confession; *If you, O Lord, should mark iniquities; O Lord, who shall stand?* And in another place he says; *O Lord, enter not into judgment with your servant, for in your sight shall no man living be justified.*

The reasons why the works of the regenerated and faithful children of God are imperfect in this world, are: *First,* the condition of regeneration, which must daily increase by the children of God; and can never be fully perfected before the soul is separated from the body; *And this mortal shall have put on immortality.* The apostle St. *Paul* had attained mostly to the prize; yet he confesses; *I follow after, if that I may apprehend that. Secondly,* the remnants of sin, which cleaves always to the children of God, as long as they live. *The law is spiritual,* says St. *Paul, But I am carnal, sold under sin.* Thereof comes: *Thirdly,* the continual war between the flesh and the Spirit, *which are contrary one to another, so that the children of God cannot do the things that they would.*

God is notwithstanding so gracious, that he, in regard to the merits of Jesus Christ, is well-pleased with that little good we, by the assistance of his Holy Spirit, can perform; and looks upon it, as if it was quite perfect: Yea, he attributes to us, poor sinners, all the good which he effects himself in us, and ascribes it to our faith, as if that was the effecting cause thereof. We can as little boast of our good works, as that if we had created ourselves; for the Apostle says in our text; *God has created us in Christ Jesus, unto good works.* We ought therefore daily to practice good works, because it is,

First, the command of God. *Let your light so shine before men, that they may see your good works, and glorify your Father, which is in Heaven.* If a tree whereof a gardener has been careful with digging and dunging could speak, it would thank him for his trouble, and promise him much fruit; but many men are so corrupt and wicked, that they do not alone omit all what is good, but even commit all what is evil.

Second. Our obligation. A child is obliged to obey its parents, likewise are we obliged to obey the commands of God, and to show ourselves loving and serviceable to our neighbors. Faith shows itself in love, and love serves our neighbor in all what we can perform.

Third, promoting the peace of our conscience. With good works we *make our calling and election sure.* The apostle says in our text, *that we should walk in them*; namely, good works. The word here used (*walk*) signifies to walk round about, as in a circle. The beginning of our works should be good; likewise should be the end thereof. It is not enough to begin well, but we should also end well. *Be you faithful unto death, and I will give you a crown of life.* Take away constancy, then has obedience no reward, good works no praise, and righteousness no crown to expect.

And since our best works are unclean and imperfect in the sight of God, then none can deserve anything from God thereby, much less the eternal life. Our Savior says himself, *When you shall have done all things, which are commanded you, say, we are unprofitable servants, we have done that which was our duty to do.* St. Paul says, *Not by works of righteousness, which we have done, but according to his mercy he saved us.* What comparison is there between our works, which are finite and imperfect, and the eternal life, which is infinite and perfect? Well are the righteous and faithful said, *to be worthy to walk with Christ* in everlasting life: But this worthiness is not of themselves, but is partly of the merits of Christ, which they have embraced through faith; and partly thereof, that they by the assistance of the Holy Spirit have followed the means of God, prescribed in his word, for the obtaining of life-everlasting; therefore has God thought them worthy to walk with Christ in white raiment.

Every child of God that will do any good works, which may and can please God, must observe the following rules,

First, he should do such works which God has commanded; for self-invented actions are an abomination to the Lord. Christ says, *In vain they do worship me, teaching for doctrines the commandments of men.*

Second, he should regulate his works by the word of God, as the Psalmist says, *Your word is a lamp unto my feet, and a light unto my path.* They must not alone be good in outward appearance, but they should also proceed from inward sincerity of heart.

Third, he should do them by faith; not alone such faith that he knows and believes, that they are commanded by God, but also, that he knows and is assured of: Both his own person and his works are pleasing in the sight of God, for the sake of the Mediator Jesus Christ.

Fourth, he should do them of love. When they are committed of love, then are they likewise of faith, for these two can never be separated from one another. The four living creatures, which the prophet *Ezekiel* saw, had wings and under their wings hands. A Christian should not alone have wings of faith, but also hands of love to serve and assist his neighbor.

Fifth, he should seek thereby the honor of God. Which ought always to be the mark whereat our good works aim. A candle shines not for its self, but for them that are in the house. A Christian must therefore likewise not do his good works for himself, but to the glory of God, and to the profit of his neighbors.

The heathens did endeavor to practice all sorts of virtues, because they knew of no other good works: But, since their actions were not so commanded by God, neither were regulated after the word of God, nor did proceed from a true faith in Christ, whom they did not know, neither were effected of the Holy Spirit to a good end and purpose: Therefore were their virtues but shadow of virtues, or properly speaking, splendid vices. For, although they could be good according to nature and outward morality, yet could they not be reckoned for good works in the sight of God, as wanting the true root, Jesus Christ and the living faith in him.

II. Why we should practice Good Works.

God has called us with a holy call, has chosen us in Christ, and has *purified us unto himself a peculiar people, that we should be zealous to all good works,* and walk in them. All our works should have regard to God, to ourselves, and our neighbors.

To God, that we show unto him, 1. Glory. 2. Obedience, and 3. Gratitude.

1. Glory will God have of our works. Therefore has he created, redeemed, and grafted us in Christ Jesus, and *has made us a chosen generation, a royal priesthood, an holy nation, a peculiar people, that we should show forth the praise of him who hath called us out of darkness, unto his marvelous light.* As a gardener is praised, when the trees in his garden bear much fruit; so is the name of God likewise glorified by our good works which are the fruits of our faith.

Should anyone be concerned thereover, that he has not done many good works in his lifetime, since Christ will sum up at the Last Day all our good works, and reward everyone accordingly; he must be comforted thereby, that a tree, whereupon is found but one single fruit, cannot be called dead. Besides, Christ called all the ground that bore an hundredfold, sixty fold, and thirty fold, by one name. And the servant, who gained two talents, is called as well a good and faithful servant, as he who gained five talents.

2. We show our obedience to God with our good works. *This is the will of God, even your sanctification, that you should abstain from*

fornication: That everyone of you should know how to possess his vessel in sanctification and honor. It is the will of God, that *we should be Holy, as he is Holy,* not in perfection, but in imitation.

3. We show gratitude and thankfulness to God, when we practice good works: Therefor has *God created us in Christ Jesus unto good works, that we should walk in the same.* Therefore has *Jesus Christ given himself for us, that he might redeem us from all iniquity, and purify unto himself a peculiar people, zealous of good works:* Therefor has the Holy Spirit renewed and regenerated us in Baptism, that *we should put on the new man, which after God is created in righteousness and true holiness,* which are the fruits of the Spirit: Therefor has God, *saved us from our enemies, and from the hands of all that hate us, that we might serve him without fear in holiness and righteousness before him all the days of our life:* Therefore has God chosen us, and promised, that he will be our God and Father; that we should *cleanse ourselves from all filthiness of the flesh and Spirit, perfecting holiness in the fear of God.*

Our works should also have regard to ourselves that our faith might show itself to be living: None can see faith in our heart; but from good works, the same can be known to be living, like the feeling of the pulse convinces the physician of the condition of his patient. Let a garden be adorned ever so much with flowers, yet can they not be seen without light. If the heart of a Christian be filled and adorned with faith; yet can the same not appear except by the light of good works. And that the gifts of the Holy Spirit may increase daily more and more in us, as the priests in the Old Testament were obliged to keep the holy fire always burning, that it should not extinguish, so must we likewise daily increase the gifts of the Holy Spirit, by the practice of good works. For this end admonishes St. *Paul, That we should stir up the gifts of God, which is in us. By diligence we make our calling sure.*

354

Our works should have likewise regard to others, both to angels and to men.

The angels converse among us, although we do not see them. They observe our actions, if we do good, they are rejoiced, and if we do evil, they are grieved. On the contrary the bad angels are rejoiced, when we do evil, and sore vexed when we do good, though they cannot oppose us in good works.

Our neighbors can by our good works and good examples, be encouraged to the practice of good works also; for as one hungry is increased in his appetite, by seeing others eat, so is man likewise encouraged to good, by seeing the good works of others. If they are wicked and evildoers, then shall they, by beholding our good works, be ashamed, and obliged to stop their mouth from slander, *and glorify God in the Day of Visitation.*

The Lord of his grace make us fruitful in all good works, that we could be filled with the fruits of righteousness, which are by Jesus Christ, unto the praise and glory of God. AMEN.

25

The Christian Church

T he Text, PSALM 87:1, 2, 3. ver.

His Foundation is in the holy Mountains. The Lord loves the gates of Zion more than all the dwellings of Jacob. Glorious things are spoken of you, O city of God. Selah.

INTRODUCTION

WHERE God is seen or heard, there everything appears majestic, holy and glorious. When *Jacob* went from his father *Isaac* in *Bersheba*, to *Padan-Aram*, in *Syria*, unto his uncle *Laban*, then tarried he all the night in the field, and had the heavens for his canopy, the ground for his bed, and the stones for his pillows; and in his sleep, he saw a ladder set upon the earth, and the top of it reached to heaven, and behold the angels of God ascending and descending; and behold the Lord stood above it, and spoke to him. In the morning, *Jacob awoke from his sleep, and be said, surely the Lord is in this place, and I knew it not; and he was afraid, and said; How dreadful is this place! This is none other but the house of God; and this is the gate of heaven;* as we

356

can read in *Gen.* 28:11, 12, 16, 17.

Of this vision we can take: *First,* a glorious description of the Christian church here upon earth; and, *Second,* a short summary of the doctrine taught and preached in the Christian church.

First, the Christian church can be described, according to this sight, by three names; and then be called,

1. The place of God's presence. *Surely,* says *Jacob, the Lord is in this place, and I knew it not. Jacob* knew full well, that God is omnipresent, and over all; For *he is not far from everyone of us.* He is, *a God that filled heaven and earth. The heaven is his throne, and the earth his footstool.* But that God should be in such manner with him here in a lonesome place, where he was a stranger, and with his gracious presence, comfort him as a Father, guide and protector: this *Jacob* knew not. And therefore, when he found the presence of God, and heard the gracious promise of the seed of the woman preached here, by which he was instructed before in his Father's house; then he said: *Surely the Lord is in this place, and I knew it not.* We see here that God is nearest to his children when they least expect it. He is not bound to any certain place, but he appears in what place or manner he will: Therefore we must, wherever we are, have holy thoughts and devout hearts, especially, when we are in the place of the worship of God; which we may call with *Jacob,*

2. The house of God: *This is none other but the house of God.* There was no house in this place where *Jacob* slept and dreamt, yet he calls the same the house of God; because where God and the word of God is, there is the house of God. We honor a house on account of the person who dwells therein, much more should we honor the house of God, which is called here,

3. The gate of heaven: From the church militant here on earth do we enter into the church triumphant into heaven; and none can enter into heaven, except he has been in this life, a true member of

357

the Christian church. *Blessed is the man who you chose, and causes to approach unto you, that he may dwell in your courts.*

Second, the doctrine that is preached and taught in the house of God. The Christian church lies concealed in this vision; and consists principally in these four articles. 1. *Of God.* 2. *Of Christ.* 3. *Of the angels.* And, 4. *Of men.* All these four articles are found here: God stood above the ladder, and spoke. Christ is compared to the ladder: The angels were ascending and descending: And *Jacob* laid upon the ground, and slept. Of this house of God speaks the Psalmist in our text, and calls the same, *the gates of Zion*, and the *city of God*; and praises likewise the *glorious things* which *are spoken* and preached there. Of this text we will observe these two parts, namely,

FIRST, *The Christian Church as a City.*

SECOND, *The Right Token, or Sign of the Christian Church.*

EXPLANATION of the TEXT

I. We shall consider the Christian church as a city.

What we love, we keep and defend the same always. There is nothing here upon earth which God loves more than his church; therefore he keeps and defends the same as a well founded city; for as our text says; *His foundation is in the holy mountains.* The Christian church is described here, 1st, Of its constancy. 2nd. Of its excellency.

1. *Of its constancy.* It has a foundation. The constancy of a city depends upon the foundation thereof. A house built upon sand cannot stand against wind and weather. The foundation of the Christian church, is Jesus Christ, and the doctrine of him: And this foundation is,

Eternal: *For God has chosen us in Jesus Christ, before the foundation of the world*; as St. *Paul* says.

Godly: It was laid and fore-ordained by God himself in his decree from eternity; and afterwards in the time he was sent into the world, to be the foundation of our salvation, and the beginner and finisher of our faith: That, as *the hands of Zerubbabel laid the foundation of the Lord's house, and his hands finished it also*; so has Christ likewise laid both the first and last stone of our salvation.

Unmoveable: The Devil with all his power, cannot shake it; *And the gates of hell shall not prevail against it.*

Living and quickening: *He that believes on me*, says our Savior himself, *has the everlasting life.*

Glorious: *The stone which the builders refused, is become the head-stone of the corner*; and is *crowned with glory and honor*. This is the foundation of the Christian church; by which we can see,

2. *Its excellency.* It is built *in the holy mountains.* By these mountains we can understand the prophets in the Old, and the apostles in the New Testament, who are called the foundation of the Christian church, not by origin, but by service, for they were the first that laid this foundation in the world, by preaching the doctrines of Christ.

After the foundation is laid, then is the building raised. Here we have to observe, 1. *The builder.* 2. *The workman.* And, 3. *The builder himself.*

First, the builder, who is the holy and blessed Trinity, Father, Son and Holy Spirit; and therefore is the Christian church called *the city of God.*

God the Father has built this city, *The Christian church.*

1. In that he, from eternity, since he foresaw that men would fall in sin, *has ordained Christ* to be a mediator and savior; and *has chosen in him*, as many as he foresaw would believe in Christ, and remain steadfast in their faith.

2. In that he, in the beginning, gathered himself a church in *paradise.* And although our first parents lost the holiness wherein

359

they were created; God has, notwithstanding, constantly had his church of the *patriarchs* and *prophets*, until the time was come; then sent he his Son into the world, that he, by his doctrine, and preaching, should gather and establish a church.

3. In that he placed Jesus Christ as a king upon his holy hill, and ordered us in the Baptism of Christ, to hear and obey him.

4. That he has exalted Christ unto his right hand, and *made him to be the head of the body, the church.*

God the Son has built this city the Christian church.

1st, As a prophet: In that he has declared to us the will of God concerning our salvation; for just after the Fall, our first parents did receive the gracious promise, *Of the seed of the woman, who should bruise the head of the Serpent.*

2ndly, As a priest: In that *he has purchased unto himself a church with his own precious blood,* and *has given himself for us an offering, and a sacrifice to God, for a sweet smelling savior.*

3rdly, As a king: In that he governs, maintains and defends his church, against all its spiritual enemies.

God the Holy Spirit has likewise built this city the Christian church; and he builds yet daily upon the same.

First, In that he sends faithful ministers and laborers, and inspires them with all heavenly gifts, in order to preach the gospel.

Second, In that he sanctifies the means, by which this building is finished, namely, the word of God, and the holy sacraments.

Third. In that he comforts and upholds the faithful, in crosses and afflictions, that they should not despair, and is therefore called, *the Comforter; a free Spirit*; a Spirit of power and strength; and *the earnest of our inheritance.*

2. The workmen are the ministers, by whom God gathers his church: Therefore are they called in the Scripture: *the builders, laborers together with God, God's mouth, ambassadors for Christ,*

ministers of Jesus Christ. Some of these workmen are called by God himself, as the prophets and apostles; who, although they lived at different places and times, do notwithstanding agree in their doctrine, and points all as with one finger to Jesus Christ. Some are called by means, as the ministers in our days; they do not lay any foundation, but they build upon the foundation laid by the prophets and apostles. The means that these workmen use towards the building of the church of God, are the word of God, and the holy sacraments. When our Savior did send his apostles into the world, then commanded he them to use these two means, saying, *Go therefore, and teach all nations, baptizing them.*

3. The building itself is called, *the Christian church* of Christ, who is the head and Lord thereof. They that believe in Christ, and confess themselves to be of his church, are called *Christians*, and this was the name used first in *Antioch*, there the believers in Christ were called before, *disciples, brethren, congregation.* This name should admonish us of our honor, that God has thought us so worthy as to call us by his own Son's name. The believers in Christ did not take this name upon themselves, but the Lord gave it unto them according to the prophecy of *Isaiah, The Lord shall call his servants by another name. And you shall be called by a new name, which the mouth of the Lord shall name.* Therefore we should be careful, that we do not disdain this holy name, after which we are called, through unbelief and wickedness: But, *let everyone, that names the name of Christ, depart from iniquity.*

The name of church in the *Greek*, signifies, the Lord's house, not a house built of stones and timber, but of men: For the Christian church is a visible congregation of men, whom God of his grace and mercy calls together to the Kingdom of Christ, by the preaching of the gospel, and the administration of the sacraments; among whom there are some, who remain steadfast in the true faith in Christ, unto

ARTICLES OF FAITH

their lives end. And again, others who are hypocrites, consenting to the doctrine of Christ with their mouths, but their hearts are afar off, and therefore do not live as they ought to do.

The materials whereof this building consist, are men, whom the apostle St. *Peter* calls, *lively stones.* In the Old Testament were the *Jews*, and some *heathen* proselytes, alone-belonging to the church of God; but in the New Testament, the gates of *Zion* are opened, more, and now everyone of what country, nation or tongue whatsoever can enter into the city of God; though under this condition, That they should believe, and be baptized. And there is no respect of persons before God, For *in every nation, he that fears him, and works righteousness, is accepted with him.* And since there is so many sorts of Christians in the church, therefore is the same compared to a field, wherein grows wheat and tares; to the ark of *Noah*, wherein was both clean and unclean creatures; and to a net cast into the sea, wherein is gathered of every kind of fish, both good and bad.

In the house-church of *Adam*, there was a hypocritical *Cain:* In that of *Noah*, there was a cursed *Ham:* In that of *Abraham*, the despising *Ishmael:* In that of *Isaac*, the hateful *Esau:* In that of *David*, the ambitious *Absalom:* And even in that of Christ, the treacherous *Judas.* Therefore they are not all of the Christian church, that are in the Christian church.

The Christian church is both visible and invisible. Visible it is not, in regard to persons, whom we see; but in regard to the visible service and doctrine, whereto the persons confess themselves, either they are believers or unbelievers, elect or hypocrites, as many as hear the word, and use the sacraments, in the outward visible congregation. Invisible it is, in regard to the persons, for we cannot know who believes in Christ, and shall remain steadfast unto their lives end, for that is alone known unto God, who *knows them that are his:* Therefore are the elect called, *the hidden of the Lord*, because they are hid from

362

the world and the vanities of the world, and *their lives is hid with Christ in God.* Hereby comes the spiritual fellowship between Christ and the faithful, so that they become one with Christ, and the temple and habitation of the Holy Spirit; which is unknown to the eyes of men.

Spiritual fellowship between Christ and the faithful, is a wonderful and inward connection, which exceeds the apprehension of human reason and nature; by which men becomes, by the hearing of God's Word, and the right use of the holy sacraments, through faith and the assisting power of the Holy Spirit, increased in Jesus Christ, and by him united with God himself, to be partaker of the death and honor of Christ, and to obtain life-everlasting.

The Foundation of this spiritual fellowship is Jesus Christ, who by his incarnation, sufferings, obedience, satisfaction and merits, hath reconciled us unto God, and has procured us this gracious fellowship; although this gracious fellowship belongs alone to the faithful, who are the invisible church. The means that God uses hereto are on God's side, the word and the sacraments; and on our side, our faith. Of the word we receive faith by the effecting power of the Holy Spirit. *By faith Christ dwells in our hearts*, and when Christ dwells by faith in our hearts, then do we become *the temple of God*, and the dwelling place of his Spirit; and this faith makes a child of God, not alone *a member of Christ*, but also *partakers of his divine nature*, by which he becomes Holy both in soul and body.

This fellowship consist therein, *that God is in them of a truth. Christ lives in them*, and they in Christ: And *they are joined unto the Lord, and are one Spirit with him.* Therefore are the faithful called in the Scripture by such glorious names, as: *The saints and the excellent, the betrothed of Christ, God's friends, God's house, lights in the world, sons of God: a royal priesthood.* And many more such glorious names, which would be too tedious to sum up here. This fellowship is not

363

dead and idle, consisting only in the bare name; no, but the same is effecting and powerful, showing itself in

First, the communion of the death and life of Christ. Of the death of Christ, that since the faithful are united with Christ, who is crucified, dead and buried for them; so are they by the power and merits thereof reconciled unto God, redeemed from the curse of the law, and saved from the dominion of sin. Of the life of Christ; in that they by the power of the resurrection of Christ, *are blessed in heavenly places, should walk in newness of life*, and shall at the Last Day, *be fashioned like unto the glorious body of Christ.*

Secondly, the fellowship with Christ. Where this union is, there is likewise fellowship: The faithful are united with Christ; by conse-quence they have also fellowship with him, and such a fellowship, that Christ has taken upon himself all the sins of them, and the whole world, and gives again unto them his righteousness through faith: In regard to this spiritual union of faith, it is said of the prophet: *He that touches you, touches the apple of God's eye.* And our Savior says, *Verily I say unto you, in as much, as you have done it unto one of the least of these my brethren, you have done it unto me.* When *Paul* persecuted the Christians, then took Christ their cause upon himself, and said unto him, *Saul, Saul, why do you persecute me?* Of this fellowship and union flows love on both sides; for since the faithful are united with Christ, and have received his Spirit, so do they love Christ, and Christ loves them again with a particular love; for *God loves the gates of* Zion *more than all the dwellings of* Jacob. And since the faithful have received the Spirit of Christ, which is the Spirit of love, *so have they the mind of Christ.*

Thirdly, the inward communion of the faithful among themselves. Since the faithful have all received the Spirit of Christ, and are members of the same spiritual body; so are they not alone united with Christ the head of the body, but also inward with one another: Faith binds the children of God to Christ, and likewise to their neighbors. In regard to this faith the apostle St. *John, If we love one another, God dwells in us, and his love is perfected in us. Hereby we know, that we dwell in him, and he in us, because he has given us of his Spirit: And we have known and believed the love that God has to us. God is love, and he that dwells in love, dwells in God, and God in him.*

This spiritual union is a deep mystery hid in this Life; but the same shall appear at the great Day of Judgment. It is a treasure, whereof we can take comfort in crosses and affliction. How should he value the world and all the troubles thereof, who presses toward heaven and the heavenly Joy? *I count all things but loss,* says St. *Paul, for the excellency of the knowledge of Christ Jesus my Lord, for whom I have suffered the loss of all things, and do count them but dung, that I may win Christ, forgetting those things, which are behind and reaching forth unto those things, which are before, I press toward the mark, for the prize of the high calling of God in Christ Jesus.* It is likewise a powerful encouragement to thank and praise God for his grace and mercy, to pray for the continuance thereof, to keep ourselves from sinning, and to live a Christian life, that we should not lose this great grace of God. For, although Christ promises, That *no man shall pluck his sheep out of his hands*; yet the faithful can pluck themselves, be cause of the breaking of this union, through willful sins, against their conscience and unbelief. Our Savior says therefore, *If a man abide not in me, he is cast forth as a branch and is withered*: Therefore must every child of God walk circumspectly, and be diligent in hearing and reading the word of God, using the sacrament of the Lord's Supper, praying devoutly, abhorring sin, and in living a Christian and godly life. And as long as this spiritual union lasts, as long shall the Christian church stand fast and sure. For *his foundation is in the holy mountains.*

The Christian church is called in the third article of our faith, A holy, catholic church: *A,* signifies one, because it has but one Lord and head, Jesus Christ: *Holy*, not alone because the members are called with a holy vocation, and separated from the wicked dross of the world; but also, because Jesus Christ, their head, is holy, and has purged them from their sins, with his own precious blood: *Catholic*, because it is not bound to any certain place or nation, but is found over the whole world, where the word of God is preached, and the sacraments are rightly administered.

II. The right token, or sign of the Christian church.

Every city has its own coat of arms or mark, by which the same can be known and distinguished from another. The Christian church, the city of God, has likewise its own certain token or sign, by which it can be known. Thereof speaks our text, saying: *Glorious things are spoken of you, O city of God.* What glorious things are they? They are, 1. The pure and true doctrine of the word of God: And, 2. The right and faithful administration of the sacraments.

First, the pure and true doctrine of the word of God. What is more glorious than the word of God? The Psalmist says; *The law of the Lord is perfect, converting the soul. The testimony of the Lord is sure, making wise the simple. The statutes of the Lord are right, rejoicing the heart. The commandment of the Lord is pure, enlightening the eyes. The fear of the Lord is clean, enduring forever. The judgments of the Lord are true and righteous altogether: More to be desired are they than gold, yea, than much fine gold; sweeter also than honey and the honey-comb. The law of God's mouth is better unto me, than thousands of gold and silver.* And our Savior says; you *are my friends, if you do whatsoever I command you.*

Second, the right and faithful administration of the sacraments. What is more glorious than the sacraments of baptism and the Lord's Supper? They are the two lips, wherewith the heavenly bridegroom,

Jesus Christ, kisses his bride, the Christian church; and they are as two breasts of comfort, wherefrom we draw the sincere milk of consolation. Baptism opens the door for us to heaven; the Lord's Supper makes us eager, and assures us of our coming in there.

We could explain this better after all the articles of faith, and thereby show what glorious things are spoken of in the city of God: But that these two before-mentioned tokens are the proper marks of the true Christian church, we can prove by the following:

1. When the Spirit of God's will describes the true church, he mentions no other tokens of the same than these two: The preaching of the word of God, and the administration of the sacraments. Of the preaching of God's word, says St. *Paul: you are no more strangers and foreigners, but fellow citizens with the saints, and of the household of God; and are built upon the foundation of the apostles and prophets; Jesus Christ himself being the chief cornerstone.* Of the sacrament of baptism, says St. *Peter*, after he had preached to the Jews; *repent and be baptized everyone of you, in the name of Jesus Christ, for the remission of sins.* And of the sacrament of the Lord's Supper, says St. *Paul, The cup of blessing which we bless; Is it not the communion of the blood of Christ? The bread which we break; Is it not the communion of the body of Christ. For we being many, are one bread and one body; for we are all partakers of that one bread.*

2. The church of the Old Testament, was also distinguished from all others, by these two tokens: So says the Psalmist of the *Israelitish* church; *The Lord shows his word unto* Jacob; *his statutes and his judgments unto Israel. He has not dealt so with any nation.* The Christian church, in the New Testament is also distinguished from others, by the word and the sacraments; for when Christ did send his apostles, then he commanded them to preach and baptize.

3. God uses no other ordinary means than these two, for the gathering and upholding of his church. He gathers the same by

his word, and nourishes and upholds the same by the sacraments.

4. The Christian church is bound to the words of God, which is the only rule of our faith and life; as Christ says; *He that is of God, bears God's words.* Hereof follows, that the sincere preaching of God's word, and the right administration of the sacraments, are the true and undeceivable token of the Christian church. And where these tokens are in purity, there is the true church of God. Hereby everyone may easily conclude, that

The evangelical church is the true Christian church: For there is nothing preached but the pure word of God, wrote by the prophets and apostles. There is no other foundation laid to salvation than Jesus Christ: There is no other sacraments used than those two which Christ himself has instituted; and that according to the meaning of the express words of the institution. The beginning, progress and end of our salvation is not ascribed to any of our own worthiness or good works, but to the grace of God alone, and the merits of Jesus Christ. In the meantime the practice of good works is absolutely required, being the fruits of a living faith, though not such works as men can invent, but as God has commanded.

The merciful God, who of his grace, has called us to his church, strengthen and confirm us by his Holy Spirit, in faith and love; that we, above all things, may love the word of God, and use his holy sacraments worthily; that when our days, in his church militant here on earth, shall come to an end, we may be made members of the triumphant church hereafter in heaven; Grant this, O Lord, for Christ's sake. AMEN.

26

The Ministerial Office

T he text, MATTHEW, 28:18, 19, 20, ver.
All authority is given unto me in heaven and on earth. Go therefore and teach all nations, baptizing them in the name of the Father, and of the Son, and of the Holy Spirit; teaching them to observe all things whatsoever I have commanded you: And lo, I am with you always, even unto the end of the world.

INTRODUCTION

AS the office is, so must likewise the ministers of the office be. God had commanded *Moses*, that he should choose of the people, *wise hearted men, whom he had filled with the Spirit of Wisdom, to make* Aaron's *garments.* Much more ought they to be filled with the Spirit of Wisdom, who should make the holy and heavenly garments wherewith the souls of men should be clothed and adorned before God. The ministers of the gospel have the administration of a holy office, therefore must they likewise strive after holiness, and give their hearts to resort early to the Lord; and pray to him with humble supplication, that he will send his Spirit of Wisdom, of his holy heaven, and from the throne of his glory, who can be present, and labor with them, that they may know what is pleasing unto the Lord. Therefore the Lord himself admonishes by the prophet *Malachi*, 2:7. saying, *The priest's lips should keep knowledge, and they should seek the law at his mouth, for he is the messenger of the Lord of Hosts.*

The priests are described here, by three things: *First*, by their names. *Second*, by their office, and *third*, by their freedom.

First. By their names. God honors them with three names, and calls them: *priest, God's mouth, and the messenger of the Lord of Hosts.*

1. *Priests* were they, who in the Old Testament did administer the sacrifices, and other holy ceremonies; although this name is not given to the priests in particular, in the New Testament, but also to the faithful in common: Whom *Christ has made kings and priests unto God.* Other ways are they, who are called and ordained to the ministerial office, called *priests.* They are called in the New Testament with several other names, as, *laborers together with God, servants of the Word, servants of God, shepherds, teachers, overseers, preachers, leaders, elders, stewards over the mysteries of God, and ambassadors for Christ.*

2. *God's mouth.* As there is no respect of persons with God, so must neither a priest have respect to persons; but he must preach the word of God, and follow the saying of *Balaam, If you would give me your house full of silver and gold, I cannot go beyond the word of the Lord my God, to do less or more.*

3. *The messenger of the Lord of Hosts.* Angel signifies as much as messenger, for they are ministering spirits sent forth by God. The priests also are like the angels; they are willing to obey their Lord, and execute his commands, and be watchful over them, for whose service they are sent forth. The priests must

take heed unto themselves, and to all the flock, over which the Holy Spirit has made them overseers, to feed the church of God, and that *not by constraint, but willingly, not for filthy lucre, but of a ready mind.*

Second, their office consists in,

1. *Knowledge in God's word. The priest's lips should keep knowledge.* God has committed to their trust his word, which they must keep, *avoiding profane and vain babblings*, and preach the same in all sincerity and integrity of heart. Hereto is required three things: namely, prayer, reading and meditating. By prayer they must prepare themselves to reading, and upon reading shall follow meditation. The priest's lips should so keep the knowledge, that his discourses be not trifles, but as *the words of the wise*, which *are as goads and as nails fastened by the masters of assemblies.*

2. *Doctrine. They should seek the law at his mouth.* A priest ought to be well versed and expert in the word of God, in order to resolve and instruct them who are willing to be instructed in the way to salvation, and therefore consult with him. We cannot borrow anything from him that has nothing, much less can we seek wisdom and doctrine by him that has none. Since they are ambassadors for Christ, then have they also glorious,

3. *Freedom.* God takes them under his protection, for where is an earthly Lord, who would suffer his servants, especially on his errand, ashamed; Examples of which we have in king *David*, who revenged the shame done to his servants by *Hanun*, king of the children of *Ammon*: Much more will God take on the cause of his faithful servants, when they are ashamed or injured by anyone. Therefore, after our Savior had in our text, given unto

his apostles, a full instruction of their office, then promised he, for their security and progress, his gracious presence. We will, according to our text, speak here of these three following parts.

FIRST, *Of the Origin of the Ministerial Office.*
  SECOND, *Of the Ministerial Office itself.*
  THIRD, *Of their Reward and Comfort.*

EXPLANATION of the TEXT

I. Of the Origin of the Ministerial Office.

The ministerial office is a holy office, not instituted of men, but of God himself, whereto certain able persons are lawfully called, that they should preach the word of God, administer the sacraments, pray for the flock that they are made overseers of, and exercise church discipline according to the word of God; that the glory of God and the salvation of men may be promoted thereby. Here we have to consider the following,

1. Who has instituted the ministerial office. God the Holy and blessed Trinity. Our Savior says here in our text, *All power is given unto me in heaven and on earth.* This power is given unto him by the Father, *who has put all things under his feet, and gave him to be the head over all things to the Church.* The Father did send the patriarchs and prophets in the Old Testament; Jesus Christ the Son of God, did send his apostles and disciples to preach; the Holy Spirit inspires the priests with power and heavenly gifts, and *makes them also able ministers of the New Testament.* He *gives them wisdom and a mouth to speak* with; and is therefore called, *the Spirit of Wisdom and Understanding, the*

Spirit of Council and Might, the Spirit of Knowledge, and of the fear of the Lord.

2. Who must officiate the ministerial office? They must be men, lawfully called and ordained.

They must be men and not women, for so says St. *Paul, It is a shame for women to speak in the church*; and in another place he says, *Let the woman learn in silence with all subjection.* Besides, our Savior did choose all the men whom he sent to teach all nations. We find examples in the Holy Scripture, of women who have taught publicly; as *Priscilla*, whom St. *Paul* called, *my helper in Christ Jesus*; And of the four daughters of *Philip*, the evangelist, we read, that they *did prophecy*. But of these examples, which are extraordinary, we cannot make a general conclusion, that the ministerial office may be entrusted to women.

In the persons who officiate the ministerial Office, must be found the following three articles, 1. Wisdom. 2. Delivery. 3. Morality.

First, wisdom, and deep knowledge in the Scripture. Our Savior calls it *wisdom*, for he that shall instruct another in the right way to salvation, must know himself the same.

Second, delivery. It is not enough that a minister knows and has knowledge of God and the godly things, but it is likewise required, that he should be able to instruct others rightly, and in a proper way; and that with proper, intelligible and significant words: For they who use in their sermons moving words of human wisdom, whereof their hearers have no Good to salvation, are as the fig-tree who was full of leaves, but there was no fruit found upon it; their sermons are good for the brain, but not for the heart. The Lord commanded the prophet *Isaiah: Take you a great roll; and write in it with a man's pen.* To write with a man's pen is to set forth the godly mysteries with simple, true, and intelligible words. We can ourselves see by the sermons of Christ on the mountain, how intelligible he brought forth his heavenly doctrine, with simple words, and parables. All ministers ought to let this be the only pattern of their discourses.

Third, morality in their life and conversation. He that should be an example for others, and instruct them in the true way to salvation, must live accordingly, and show the truth of the doctrine which he preaches in living a good life; for so says St. *Peter: Be examples to the flock.*

They should be lawfully called to the ministerial office. *No man takes this honor to himself, but he that is called of God.* The persons whom Christ commanded to go and preach to all nations, were all lawfully called. In our days the ministers are called by the authority of church vestry, examined by the clergy, and received by consent of the whole congregation, and although they are called by men, yet we can say, they are called by God. St. *Paul* had *called the elders, and overseers in* Ephesus; yet he says that *the Holy Spirit had made them overseers over the flock.* We can also observe, that they who are called in our mediate days, are as lawfully called, as they who were immediately called in the old days.

In the calling of a minister, the following must be observed,

1st, There should be made sincere supplication to God for able and faithful ministers. We see that our blessed Savior himself, before *he called his disciples, and chose of them the twelve apostles, went out into a mountain to pray, and continued all night in prayer to God.* And he commanded himself to pray for good ministers, saying, *Pray the Lord of the Harvest, that he will send forth laborers into his harvest.*

2ndly, It should be done to the glory of God alone. He that has right to call a minister, should put away all fleshly affection, friendship and relation, and consider alone the glory of God, and the edifying of the flock, and not any worldly interest or gain; and he that is called should not use any ceremony, which is so called by *Simon* the

Magician, who offered the apostles money for to have the gift of the Holy Spirit.

3rdly, The person who is to be called, must be examined, for to know if he is able, and understands himself what he is to instruct others in. St. *Paul* says; *Let them first be proved, then let them use the office.* An unlearned minister, is like a bird without feathers, and a ship without a rudder.

They should likewise be ordained to the ministerial office. The ordination of a minister, is a public confirmation and testimony, by which the person who is lawfully called and examined is ordained to the ministerial office, with prayers, and laying upon of hands; by which the ministerial office, and the authority thereof, is delivered to him and he is admonished by his duty, how he should behave both in doctrine of truth, and in his exemplary way of living: Whereupon he that is ordained gives his hand to him who ordained him, as a pledge and sure token, that he, with a godly purpose, will do and act according to the grace God has given him.

This ceremony of ordination, is not so absolutely necessary as if it was a help to the office; but the same is used in our days, to show the worth of the ministerial office; and to foresee, that not everyone that please, shall run to it, and thereby bring it to contempt or abuse.

The authority which is given to the ministers in their ordination, is no worldly authority, which is executed with the sword; for this belongs to kings and rulers, *who exercise lordship, and are called benefactors:* But the same is,

Spiritual; and agrees with the nature of Christ's Kingdom, which is spiritual, not exercised with outward force, but with inward conviction in the conscience, by the *work of God, which is quick and powerful, sharper than any, two edged sword, piercing even to the dividing asunder of soul and spirit; and of the joints and marrow; and is a discerner of the thoughts and intents of the heart.* Of this authority did the prophets speak so bold to the kings and nations, whereto they were sent; as we can see of *Nathan, Elias, Michael,* and the others; and likewise of *John the Baptist:* Though the ministers should use prudence and cautiousness in their preaching of punishment to the persons, according to their station. They should make difference between persons and their posts: The persons must be corrected and rebuked, but his post must be honored. The prophet *Samuel* rebuked King *Saul* for his disobedience, but he honored him for the elders and people. We can likewise see how cautious the prophet *Nathan* was, when he was sent to king *David* with a death's errand for his crime.

They have likewise the authority of the keys of heaven, according to the words of our Savior to his apostles; *Whatsoever you shall bind on earth, shall be bound in heaven; and whatsoever you shall loose on earth shall be loosed in heaven.* Hereby has a minister spiritual power and authority to declare unto a sinner, who truly repents, and is grieved of his sins, thereby alone trusting in the merits of Jesus Christ, and promising a better life; the remission of his sins for Christ's sake, to the glory of God, and the salvation of his soul.

They have hereby likewise, spiritual power to excommunicate all public sinners, who either with false doctrine or wickedness, are an offence and bad example to others in the congregation: But the minister must be herewith careful, and act according to the rule prescribed by our Savior; *If your brother shall trespass against you, go and tell him his fault, between you and him alone; if he shall hear you, you have gained your brother. But if he will not hear you, then take with you one or two more, that in the mouth of two or three witnesses every word may be established. And if he shall neglect to hear them, tell it unto the church; but if he neglect to bear the church, let him be unto you as a heathen man, and a publican.* This must be done, that the whole congregation should not be blamed for such wicked and offensive person's sake; neither the Holy Sacraments be abused, nor others be deluded by their bad examples; and likewise, that such excommunicated persons may be made shame of, and thereby come again to rRepentance, and to the confession of truth.

II. Of the Ministerial Office Itself.

As there belongs to the ministerial Office a lawful vocation, ordination and power; so belongs to the officiating of this office, the following five parts, wherein the ministerial office consists: For the ministers must not be slothful, feeding themselves more than their flock. Their Office consists therein, that they should,

1. Preach and declare the word of God. Our Savior says in our text; *Teach all nations, teaching them to observe all things, whatsoever I have commanded you.* This is the most principal part in the ministerial office, by which the Holy Spirit effects the conversion and salvation of men; therefore requires St. *Paul* of a minister, that he should be *apt to teach.* His doctrine for children he should take from the Catechisms, as it is the most simple manner of instructing children in the way to salvation: This is the meaning of the apostle St. *Peter,* when he said; *As newborn babes desire the sincere milk of the word:* And of St. *Paul,* who says; *Everyone that uses milk, is unskillful in the word of righteousness, for he is a babe:* And in another place he says; *I have fed you with milk, and not with meat.* The meaning is, that as milk is the best and most agreeable food for babes, by which they can grow, and become able to digest meat, and other hardy victuals; so is catechizing the best doctrine for children in years and knowledge, by which they can get a good. Foundation to build the whole Christian doctrine and faith upon. He must

take his doctrine from the Scripture, for those who are already grounded therein, and have experienced mankind to discern between good and bad. A minister should always explain his text in the right meaning, and to the right use.

In the right meaning, according to the explanation of God's Spirit in the Scripture, and not according to human invention, with adding there to, or diminishing therefrom: For, *the prophecy of the Scripture is not of any private interpretation.* The Scripture must be explained and interpreted by the Scripture; *Not in words which man's wisdom teaches, but which the Holy Spirit teaches, comparing spiritual things with spiritual.*

And to the right use. A minister must, after the explanation of his text, always show the doctrine which arises therefrom, and exhort his hearers to the believing, doing and following the same; and likewise show to his hearers, the punishment which shall follow the evildoers and disobedient; and on the contrary, the comfort and blessings which the faithful shall enjoy in Christ.

1. They should administer the sacraments, according to the institution of Christ; for Christ commanded his apostles, not alone to teach all nations, but also to baptize them; therefore they are called *stewards of the mysteries of God.*
2. They should pray for their hearers; that God will be present with his Holy Spirit, by the preaching of *the word*, that the same *shall not return void: For, neither is be that plants anything, neither he that waters, but God that gives increase.* The hearers should likewise pray both for themselves and for the ministers, according to the admonitions of the apostle St. *Paul: Continue in prayer, and watch in the same with thanksgiving: With all, praying also for us, that God would open unto us a door of utterance, to*

speak the mystery of Christ.

3. They should forego their hearers with good examples, or else there might be said of them; *You therefore which teaches another, you do not teach yourself.* They who teach others, and do not live accordingly, are as the bells, who called and warned others to come to church, but they themselves remain hanging in the steeple; or as they who show to others a good lodging or shelter, and remain themselves in the storm or rain; or as they who built upon the ark of *Noah*, but came not in it, neither were saved therein.

4. They should be careful of the poor and sick. By the poor are not understood alone they who are needy and want charity and assistance, either old or infirm, or young, and unable to maintain themselves; to these should the ministers show mercy, and see that the alms are justly distributed, and assist them with their own, according to their abilities; but also they who are poor in Spirit: The ministers must visit the sick, and comfort them. The shepherds in *Israel* were blamed, because they had *not strengthened the diseased, nor healed the sick, nor bound up the broken.*

III. Of the Reward and Comfort of the Ministers.

When the ministers and their hearers, everyone on his side, do as they ought to do, then will God do on his side, all what he has promised; which is, that they shall be favored with,

1. His presence and protection; *Lo, I am with you always.* These words are full of comfort, both for the teachers, as also for the hearers.

379

These words were first spoken to the apostles; for they were to go out into the world, as sheep among the wolves, the greatest part of the people to whom they were sent to preach the gospel, being to persecute, and even deprive them of their lives; as was prophesied to them by Christ: Therefore did Christ arm them with this letter of protection, *I am with you always.* The meaning hereof is; I, according to both natures, both God and man in one person, am with you: I, as Priest, Prophet and King, am with you. As Priest, have I purchased my church with my own blood, and of this church I make you overseers, and *am with you always:* As Prophet, have I declared unto you my heavenly Father's will and counsel, concerning men's salvation; and you must teach all nations what I have commanded, and be not afraid; for, *lo, I am with you always:* As a King, all power in heaven, and on earth is given unto me, by which I am enabled to protect and defend you; therefore be encouraged, for, *lo, I am with you always.*

This promise concerns all other preachers and ministers, who are come in the room of the apostles; for the apostles could not live unto the end of the world; therefore was this promise made likewise to their followers in that office. They have also no cause to be afraid, since they have this gracious promise of the presence of Christ: For, *If God be for us, who can be against us?* And this promise of Christ shall be the only comfort to the ministers in their office, in what trouble whatsoever that might come to them.

The hearers shall likewise be comforted by this promise of Christ, *lo I am with you always, even unto the end of the world.* What profit or fruit would the preaching of the minister bring forth, if God was not present by the hearers? The Lord must enlighten their mind, that they may understand the words which are preached, and open their hearts, that they may receive the word, and keep it, and meditate upon it. And then shall the prophesy of *Isaiah* be fulfilled in them,

As the rain comes down, and the snow from heaven, and returns not thither, but waters the earth, and makes it bring forth and bud, that it may give seed to the sower, and bread to the eater: So shall my word be that goes forth out of my mouth; it shall not return unto me void, but it shall accomplish that which I please, and it shall prosper in the thing whereto I sent it.

1. The gift of faith. Of God's word comes faith. Faith is the fruit of the Spirit, and grows both by the preachers and hearers. The more diligent a minister is in his study, and careful in his office, the more grows his faith, and the gifts thereof; for *unto everyone that has, shall be given, and he shall have abundance.* Also by the hearers, the more devout they are in the hearing of God's word, the deeper impression it makes in their hearts, and the more the Holy Spirit effects and operates faith in their hearts. And then will it go as the Spirit of God says, *He that is righteous, let him be righteous still, and he that is holy, let him be holy still.*

2. Reconciliation unto God. *I am with you.* God will not, nor can be with anyone, except they are reconciled unto him. Our Savior says, *He that is not with me, is against me.* God offers to us in his word, reconciliation; and it is therefore called, the *word of reconcilation.* He that hears the word, and receives the same, to him is attributed,

3. The remission of sins and justification. *I am with you.* Where the light appears and comes, there must darkness depart, *For what fellowship has righteousness with unrighteousness? And what communion has light with darkness?* Therefore said Christ to *Paul* in the apparition on the road to *Damascus, I now send you unto the gentiles, to open their eyes, and to turn them from darkness to light, and from the power of Satan unto God, that they may receive forgiveness of sins, and inheritance among them, which are*

sanctified by faith, that is in me. Upon the remission of sins and justification follows,

4. The eternal life. This is the final cause and purpose why God lets his word be preached, and therefore is the gospel called, *the power of God unto salvation, to everyone that believes.* Of the preaching of St. *Peter,* said the angel of the Lord to *Cornelius, He shall tell you words, by which you and all your house shall be saved.*

Of all what has been said, we can see,

First, the honor of the ministerial office. Since the ministers are ambassadors for Christ, and laborers together with God, then ought the congregations to honor them: Their person and appearance may be mean, yet must their office be looked upon as holy and high, since our Savior himself has officiated, and thereby glorified this office. The congregations must likewise love them. *We beseech you brethren,* says St. *Paul, to know them which labor among you, and are over you in the Lord, and admonish you; and to esteem them very highly in love for their works sake.*

Second, the patron and defender of the ministerial office. Our Savior says in our text, *I am with you always, even unto the end of the world.* The ministers are called, *fathers* of the church, because they shall beget spiritual children in Christ by the gospel. And the *kings and queens* are called, *its nursing Fathers, and nursing Mothers.* Also we do see that the worldly Magistrates are the visible Protectors of the ministerial Office, and even if they should fail, so can they be sure, that God will protect and defend them in their lawful calling and administration. So says the Lord to the prophet *Jeremiah, Behold I have made you this day a defensed city, and an iron pillar, and brazen wall against the whole land, against the kings and princes thereof, and against the people of the land, and they shall fight against you, but they shall not prevail against you, for I am with you, says the Lord, to deliver you.*

Third, the reward of the ministers. Besides the temporal reward, which the hearers, or the congregation are obliged to give them, whereof St. *Paul* says, *Even so has the Lord ordained, that they which preach the gospel, should live of the gospel;* the ministers have to expect an eternal reward, whereof our Savior says, *Well done good and faithful servant, you have been faithful, enter you into the joy of your Lord.*

The Lord make both the preachers and hearers, partakers of this heavenly joy, for Christ our Savior's sake. AMEN.

27

The Sacrament of Baptism

The Text, MATTHEW 3:13, 14, 15, 16, 17, ver.

Then comes Jesus from Galilee to Jordan unto John, to be baptized of him. But John forbid him, saying, I have need to be baptized of you, and you come to me? And Jesus answering, said unto him, suffer it to be so now: For thus it becomes us to fulfill all righteousness: Then he suffered him. And Jesus, when he was baptized, went up straightway out of the water; and lo, the heavens were opened unto him, and he saw the Spirit of God descending like a dove, and lighting upon him. And lo, a voice from heaven, saying: This is my beloved Son, in whom I am well pleased.

INTRODUCTION

WHEN kings and lords would have their will and pleasure published, then do they give out their proclamations under their royal hands and seals; so likewise has the heavenly King and Lord, revealed and declared his will unto men in his word; and confirmed the same, with his two heavenly seals, which were in the Old Testament, *The circumcision, and the Easter Lamb.* And after these two sacraments were put away in the New Testament, he gave in the room of them two others, namely, *baptism,* and *the Lord's Supper:* Not because God is mutable in his purpose or decree; but, because the New Covenant, being better and more excellent than the Old, is established upon better promises. The Old Testament did assure the forefathers of Christ, who was to come in the flesh: The New assures us of Christ manifested in the flesh. The Old should only last until the coming of Christ, who should put the same away, with all the Levitical offerings and ceremonies, which were all figures to Christ: But after Christ was manifested in the flesh, he instituted the sacrament of baptism in the room of the circumcision; and the Lord's Supper, in the room of the Easter Lamb, according to the explanation of the apostle St. *Paul,* who calls *baptism, a circumcision made without hands,* and the *Lord's Supper,* the Passover.

Concerning circumcision. This was the first covenant in the Old Testament, in which God had commanded, under curse and punishment, that every male-child of the seed of *Abraham,* and the whole Jewish nation, should be circumcised on the eighth day after its birth; but the full-grown persons, who were heathens, and became proselytes, should be circumcised, although they were advanced in years. God made this covenant with *Abraham* and his seed, that the Jewish nation should be hereby separated from the other nations; and mostly, that the circumcision should be a powerful means by which men, who were otherwise strangers to God, should come in the gracious covenant with God, be regenerated, and assured of the justification of faith, and of God's gracious and merciful help and assistance in all adversities. In this circumcision we have the following to observe,

First, the necessity thereof. God had commanded that every male-child, and all men, should be circumcised; and they who were not, should be cut off from the people. *Abraham* was obedient hereto, and the same day that he received this command, did circumcise himself in the ninety-ninth year of his age; and likewise his son *Ishmael*, who was thirteen years old; together with every male in his house, born therein, or bought with money of the strangers, were circumcised with him. The females were not circumcised, though they were not excluded from this covenant of God, which did extend to all the seed of *Abraham:* For as *Abraham* is called, *a father of all them that believe*; so is *Sarah* called, *a mother of all them that do well.* It was not allowed that anyone who was not circumcised, should marry a Jewish woman, or cat the Passover; but he that was not circumcised, should be cut off from his people.

Second, the essential parts in the circumcision were two, one earthly and one heavenly. The earthly was the foreskin of the flesh, whereon they were circumcised: The heavenly was the gracious covenant, whereof the circumcised were made partakers for the sake of the Messiah, who was to be born of the seed of *Abraham*, in whom all the nations of the earth were to be blessed.

Third, the operation was made thus: The friends and neighbors came together in the parent's house, to be present by the circumcision of the child. The minister operated the office with a sharp knife or flint, according to the command of God; thereupon the name was given to the child: For as God changed the name of *Abraham*, when he made this covenant with him, so have the *Jewish* nation always followed this custom, and give the children their names at the time when they are circumcised.

Fourth, the profit of the circumcision were both temporal and spiritual blessings.

The temporal blessings were, that they who were circumcised should be God's people, and partakers of the covenant, which God had made with *Abraham* and his seed, concerning the land *Canaan*.

The spiritual blessings were, that they should be members in the church of God, assured of the remission of their sins, faith and justification, and at last the life everlasting. These blessings are all comprehended in these words and promises, *I will establish my covenant between me and you, and your seed after you, in their generations, for an everlasting covenant, to be a God unto you, and to your seed after you.*

As the circumcision was the first entrance to the true church in the Old Testament; so is baptism in the New, the first entrance into the communion of saints, and the Christian church, which Christ himself instituted and consecrated with his own baptism; whereof our text makes mention. According to which we will discourse of,

FIRST, *The necessity of baptism. And,*

SECOND, *The holiness of the same.*

EXPLANATION of the TEXT

I. The Necessity of Baptism.

As *Aaron* was, in many respects, a figure to Christ, so was he likewise particularly herein; That he, when he was to be consecrated to the office of High Priest, should be washed first with water in the door of the tabernacle of the congregation. Jesus Christ was also baptized publicly by St. *John* in the river *Jordan*, when he was to begin his ministerial office. In our text, mention is made,

1. Of the time when Christ baptized. Our text says, *Then,* that is, when *he began to be about thirty years of Age.* None must hereof make a conclusion, that none must be baptized before they come to that age. No, for this would be a false and groundless conclusion: The reason why Christ was not baptized in his infancy, is, that the sacrament of baptism was not then as yet instituted. We can form a

387

better conclusion of the circumcision of Christ, which was performed the eighth day after his birth, since the baptism is come in the room of the circumcision. Besides, there is great difference between Christ and other men; for he was God and man in one person, and needed for his own person no baptism, and could therefore be baptized. It is absolutely necessary therefore that our children be baptized, that they may be grafted in Christ, and become instead of children of wrath, children of God.

2. Of the place wherefrom Jesus came, was *Galilee*, and from *Nazareth* into *Galilee*, where he had been with his parents; but now he leaves them, and will betroth his Bride the church, and cleave to her, in order to beget spiritual children with her in his ministerial office. The place whereto Christ came was *Jordan*, (a famous river in *Judea*,) where *John the Baptist* did baptize publicly: Hereto came Christ for to be baptized in *Jordan*. This river is in many parts a figure to the baptism. The children of *Israel* went through this river into the promised land *Canaan* baptism is a door to heaven, which is the blessed land God has promised us. The river *Jordan* parted *Judea* and *Galilee*; Baptism parts Christians from non-Christians.

3. Why Christ came to *Jordan, to be baptized of him.* There is mention made in the Scripture of four sorts of baptism:

First, of baptism of the cloud and the sea, by which the children of *Israel* were baptized, when they, by the help of the pillar of cloud and fire, went through the Red Sea, which St. *Paul* calls *baptism,* saying, *Our fathers were under the cloud, and also passed through the sea, and were all baptized unto* Moses *in the cloud, and in the sea.* We can see, that thereby is signified holy baptism. For 1. as the children of *Israel* were saved, by the passing through the Red Sea from the heavy yoke and slavery of *Pharaoh:* So are the Christians saved by baptism, from the power of Satan and bondage of sin. 2. *Pharaoh* and all his hosts were drowned in the Red Sea: The old *Adam*, and all its lusts and desires are drowned in baptism, as in a sea made red with the blood of Christ. 3. The children of *Israel* were assured by the cloud, who guided them through the sea, of the gracious presence and help of God, and likewise obliged to show unto *Moses*, God's faithful servant, obedience; as we can read, *And the people believed the Lord, and his servant* Moses. So are we assured by baptism of the grace of God, for it is the *answer of a good conscience towards God*, and we are thereby bound to obey Christ our Savior.

Secondly, of the baptism of blood. Herewith was Christ baptized in his sufferings, when he *trod the winepress alone*, and not alone his garment, but even his body was sprinkled with blood. The sufferings of the apostles and holy martyrs, who suffered for Christ's sake, is likewise called a baptism, though there is great difference between them: for the sufferings of Christ had an infinite power, and could pacify the wrath of God, and satisfy for the sins of the world: But the apostles and other martyrs could not satisfy even for the least of all our sins, and they did receive the martyrs crown, not through merits but of grace. But their sufferings is called a baptism, 1. Because their sufferings were sanctified by the suffering of Christ, whom they embraced through faith. wherefore St. *Paul* says of them, that *they obtained a good report through faith*, because they honored Christ by their sufferings, since they suffered for the sake of his name, and did seal their preaching of his doctrine with their blood: As our Savior said to St. *Peter, that he should glorify God by his death.* In regard to this faith the *Psalmist; Precious in the sight of the Lord is the death of his saints.*

Thirdly, the baptism of the *Holy Spirit and fire.* Herewith were the apostles baptized on the day of *Pentecost*, when the *Holy Spirit* descended *upon them in the shape of cloven tongues like as of fire.*

Fourthly, of the doctrine of baptism. The doctrine which *John the Baptist* preached, is called a *baptism*. As one being baptized is sprinkled over with water, so did *John* sprinkle or spread his doctrine over his hearers, and sealed the same afterwards with the baptism. Therefore is the doctrine of the Lord called, *water, rain, dew, small rain, and showers.*

But, why would Christ be baptized by *John*, since he did baptize to repentance and the remission of sins, when Christ needed none, neither repentance nor remission of sins? Christ needed no baptism for his own person; but since he had taken upon him the sins of the world, therefore would he be baptized for men's sake. The principal reasons why Christ would be baptized, are the following,

1st, That he would show and prove, that baptism was instituted by God. If the same had been an human invention, our Savior would never had suffered himself to be baptized; neither would the Holy and Blessed Trinity, have honored and confirmed the same with their presence, much less would Christ have commanded to baptize, in *the name of the Father, and of the Son, and of the Holy Spirit.* Therefore are the *Pharisees and lawyers*, said, to *have rejected the council of God against themselves, being not baptized. John* was the first who baptized, but he took not this honor and authority of himself, but, *he was sent from God*, as St. *John* the evangelist says; therefore would Christ be baptized of him, that the people should be convinced, that the baptism of *John* was from God, that his doctrine and testimony was to be depended upon.

2ndly, That he would show that he was a Savior both of *Jews* and *Gentiles*; therefore was he first circumcised for the sake of the *Jews*, and afterwards baptized for the sake of the *gentiles*, and for that is Christ called, *The chief cornerstone.* That as a cornerstone frames two sides of the building together; so has Christ bound the *Jews* and *gentiles* together in his spiritual building.

3rdly, That he, by his baptism, would consecrate and sanctify our baptism. Never could the water have had the effect of regeneration and renewing, if it had not been sanctified by the baptism of Christ.

4. Of the person who baptized Christ: *John* who was sent and ordained by God, to *preach the baptism of repentance for the remission of sins*, whereof he is called, the *Baptist*. The sacrament of baptism must be administered by persons ordained thereto, whose hand and mouth God uses thereto.

5. Of the dialogue between *John* and Christ. Our text says, *John forbad him*, not through obstinacy, neither for compliment sake; but of a true and sincere humbleness of heart: For the higher knowledge men have of Christ, the greater humbleness is found by him. Hereof we can conclude, that *John* knew Christ, although he had never seen him; he could know him when he was yet in his mother's womb, by the inspiration and operation of the Holy Spirit; much more could he know him now by the inspiration of the same Spirit. As he confesses himself, saying, *I knew him not, but he that sent me to baptize with water, the same said unto me, upon whom you shall see the Spirit descending, and remaining on him, the same is he which baptizes with the Holy Spirit.* But since *John* knew Christ, why did he then forbid him?

The reason why *John* forbid Christ, we can see by the following words, when *John* said, *I have need to be baptized of you, and you come to me? John the Baptist* confesses hereby,

First, the greatness and holiness of Christ, and his own unworthiness; and will say, I am the servant, you the Lord; I am a poor sinner, you just and Holy; I am earth and dust, you my heavenly Creator; I am mortal, you eternal; I am unworthy to loose the latchet of your shoes, much more of this great honor of baptizing you. Although *John* has the testimony in the Scripture, that *he is the greatest among them that are born of women*, yet he confesses himself, his own unworthiness here in our text.

Second, the necessity of baptism. *I have need to be baptized of you.*

As needful as the circumcision was in the Old Testament; as needful is the baptism in the New. Our Savior says: *Verily, verily I say unto you, except a man be born of water, and of the Spirit, he cannot enter into the Kingdom of God.* The apostle St. *Paul* calls baptism, *the washing of regeneration, and renewing of the Holy Spirit.* As needful as it is to be born into the world, if we would have the natural life; as needful it is to be regenerated by baptism, if we would have eternal life.

Though we should not condemn all the children which die without baptism; for, not being deprived of the baptism, but the contempt thereof, condemns. God has bound us men to baptism, when it can be had, but not himself, Christ said, *Except a man be born of water and Spirit, he cannot enter into the Kingdom of God.* But we must observe to whom Christ, spoke these words, namely to *Nicodemus,* who was a ruler among the *Pharisees,* which sect did despise baptism: Therefore is the meaning of Christ with these words; You and your sect despise and condemn the baptism of *John,* but I say unto you, and that under the confirmation of an oath, *except a man be born of water and of the Spirit, he cannot enter into the Kingdom of Heaven.* We must also understand these words of Christ, by them who ought to be baptized, can be baptized, and yet reject and despise the same, and thereby neglect this holy covenant and sacrament; for them, I say, it is impossible to enter into the Kingdom of God. Of this we can see, that this saying of Christ does not extend to little children, who are either dead-born of their mother's womb, or die just after their birth, and can also not be made partakers of this holy covenant; for as little as they can demand the baptism, as little can they despise the same. Besides, that parents should not be concerned for their children, who die without baptism, then must they rightly consider these words of Christ our Savior, *He that believes, and is baptized shall be saved, but he that believes not, shall be damned.* We see here that Christ makes no mention of baptism in the last part of these words; but says, *He that believes not, shall be damned.* Hereof we can conclude, that not the being deprived of baptism, but that unbelief in the word and command of God, condemns. This unbelief appears either in obstinacy or disregard, that we reject the gracious means offered to us for the obtaining of life-everlasting, or that we are careless and neglect the same, which both cannot be found by little children.

Upon the saying of *John,* Christ answered and said, *Suffer it to be so now, for thus it becomes us to fulfill all righteousness.* The meaning hereof is, I must do what becomes my office, and you must do what becomes your office; and we also do both fulfill all righteousness. My heavenly Father has sent me into the world, to be a Mediator between God and man; and by my death and sufferings, to procure unto mankind, the righteousness which they have lost in *Adam;* and likewise to sanctify the means by which also my righteousness shall be attributed unto them, and whereof the sacrament of baptism is one, and the entrance into my church: Therefore it well becomes me to receive the same; and you, who is sent from God to baptize to repentance, for the remission of sins, it becomes to administer the same. Herein is concealed a glorious comfort against sin and unrighteousness, that Christ has fulfilled all righteousness, *For God has made him to be sin for us, who knew no sin, that we might be made the righteousness of God in him.* He neglected not the least thing belonging to our salvation, even to his own shame and despise; for he is baptized here by *John* as a sinner, for a testimony that he had taken upon himself the sins of the world, because we should be pure and justified through faith, by grace before God.

When *John* had heard the reason, why Christ would be baptized, *then he suffered him;* most in the same manner as *Peter,* who first refused, that Christ should wash his feet; but when he heard that if Christ did not wash him, he should have no part with him, then said he, *Lord, not only my feet, but also my hands and my head.* Also is *John the Baptist* persuaded by the words of Christ, and did administer the baptism unto him. I come now to the second head of my discourse, namely.

II. The Holiness of Baptism.

We can perceive the holiness of baptism by these two things. 1. Of the matter, which is double, both earthly and heavenly, outward and inward. And, 2. Of the miracles which happened in the baptism of Christ.

   1. The outward matter is water. Our text says, *And Jesus, when he was baptized, went up straightway out of the water.* We must not use any other matter in baptism than water. The apostles did baptize with nothing else but water, and St. *Paul* called baptism, *a washing,* though it is all one, whether with well, sea, rain, or fountain water, either cold or warm. The inward matter in baptism is the Holy Spirit, *Except a man be born of water and of the Spirit.* The apostle St. *Paul* teaches the same, saying, *According to his mercy he saved us by the washing of regeneration, and renewing of the Holy Spirit, which he shed on us abundantly, through Jesus Christ our Savior.* We may suppose by the words in our text, That *Jesus went up straightway out of the water;* and that his whole body was dipped in the water, although all the Christian churches have since taken to throw, or sprinkle water on the head of the child who is baptized; because the dipping of the child, with his whole body in the water, would endanger the child's health, and even life: And it is besides alike, whether the whole body is dipped in the water, or but part of the body is made wet, as long as it is but administered with water on the person who is baptized.

   2. The miracles which happened in the baptism of Christ.

   First, the heavens were opened. This happened not in, but after the baptism of Christ. This brings into our remembrance the pain and honor, the humiliation and exaltation of Christ; who, after he was gone through the deep waters of his sufferings, was afterwards crowned with glory and honor. *The heavens were opened*, partly to show us the person and office of Christ: His person, that he was the Son of God, true God and true man, in one person; His office, that he was a teacher sent from God, to instruct men in the true way to salvation, and also to open the doors of heaven unto men, which was shut up against them; and partly to instruct us in the fruit and profit of our baptism. For as *the heavens were opened*, over Christ after he was baptized, so is likewise the heaven of grace opened for all who are baptized, that they can have free entrance into the mercy seat of God. Every person in the Holy Trinity officiates his part in our baptism. God the Father elects and makes a covenant with him that is baptized, and chooses and adopts him to be a child of God: God the Son cleanses and purges him that is baptized, and clothes him with righteousness and holiness: God the Holy Spirit effects and operates faith and regeneration in his heart, and seals his gracious covenant. wherefore he is called, *the earnest of our inheritance.* All the three persons in the Holy Trinity are mentioned by the apostle *Paul*, when he says, *According to his mercy he*, namely God the Father, *saved us by the washing of regeneration, and renewing of the Holy Spirit, which he shed on us abundantly through Jesus Christ our Savior.*

Here happens a new birth, or regeneration, which we can understand, and comprehend as little as *Nicodemus*, who said, *How can these things be?* We cannot apprehend the natural birth, much less the supernatural regeneration; though we can make this conclusion, that as the first man was created by all the three persons in the Trinity; so the whole Trinity, likewise effects and operates the regeneration in our baptism. We should not think, that the operation of the Trinity lasts but as long as the baptism is administered; no, for the

Trinity is always present with his grace by the person who is baptized, provided he does not depart from this covenant made in his baptism, with wicked and sinful actions against his own conscience, and the testimony thereof; but remains steadfast in his faith. *The Lord* our heavenly Father, *pities them that fear him, like as an* earthly *Father pities his children.* The Son of God acknowledges them to be *heirs and joint heirs with him*; and *the Holy Spirit himself bears witness with our Spirit, that we are the children of God.*

Second, the descending of the Spirit of God like a dove. Christ had the Holy Spirit before; for he was conceived by the Holy Spirit: But here it was needful, that the same Spirit should light visibly upon him, not alone for the sake of *John the Baptist,* who thereby should know him; but also for the sake of the people who were present, that they should be convinced, that he was to baptize with the Holy Spirit, as *John* had said of him; and likewise that he was the person, of whom the prophet *Isaiah* had prophesied and said, *The Spirit of the Lord God is upon me, because the Lord has anointed me, to preach good tidings unto the meek: He has sent me, to bind up the broken-hearted, to proclaim liberty to the captives, and the opening of the prison to them that are bound.*

The Holy Spirit would not descend and light upon Christ like fire, as upon the apostles in the Day of *Pentecost*; but like a dove, for to show; 1st, The meekness and mildness of Christ in his office towards all repenting sinners: For as *the sin-flood was a figure unto baptism,* so must the *dove* which *Noah sent forth out of the ark, and returned with an olive leaf in her mouth,* be a figure unto the dove which descended and lighted upon Christ; who assured us, that he would save us from the sin-flood of God's wrath, and procure unto us peace with God. wherefore he is called by St. *Paul, our Peace.* 2ndly, How the true Christians ought to be in their Christendom, namely, mild and meek like unto the nature of doves, which are without gall; and therefore

396

is the Christian church called, *a dove.*

Third, the voice of God the Father was heard from heaven, saying, *This is my beloved Son, in whom I am well pleased.* These words were not said for Christ's sake, but for the sake of the people who were present, that they should know, that Jesus of *Nazareth* was the Son of the Living God. There was likewise heard at another time, a voice from heaven for the people's sake, as Christ himself said, *This voice came not because of me, but for your sake.* When Christ was transfigured upon Mount *Tabor*, then was also this voice heard, with an addition of these words, *hear you him.* We must understand these words as if said and meant here in his baptism; for, therefore did God give this public testimony of his Son in the presence of the people, that they should hear him.

By the evangelists St. *Mark* and St. *Luke* we find, that God spoke these words to the Son, saying, *You are my beloved Son.* We can conclude hereof; That God the Father spoke first to the Son, and with this voice did confirm him in his ministerial office, which he was to begin then; and he afterwards spoke to *John* and the people, that they should hear and obey this heavenly teacher. We can learn hereof,

1st, That there is three persons in the divine essence. The voice of the Father was heard from heaven; the Son stood in the river, and was baptized, and the Holy Spirit descended like a dove. Therefore did our Savior command, to baptize in the *name of the Father, and of the Son, and of the Holy Spirit*; which words are likewise used by us, in the administration of this holy covenant of baptism.

2ndly, That Jesus the Son of *Mary*, is the Son of God; and therefore not alone true man born of the *Virgin Mary*, but also true God born of the Father from eternity. And since the Father spoke these words of Christ standing in his manhood for the eyes of the people, *this is my beloved Son*; then we can be convinced thereof, that Christ not alone according to his divine nature, but also according to his human nature, is the Son of God through the personal union.

3rdly, That Christ is our Mediator and Propitiator, and has reconciled us unto God. This we can conclude thereof, that he is called God's *beloved Son in whom the Father is well pleased. David* was a beloved man, *to whom God gave this testimony, and said, a man after mine own heart.* The prophet *Daniel* is called by the Lord, *a greatly beloved man: Benjamin* is called, *the beloved of the Lord:* But never was these words said of any man, *in whom I am well pleased.* Thereof we can conclude, that *Jesus Christ is the* only *Mediator between God and man. Neither is there salvation in any other; for there is none other name under heaven given among men, by which we must be saved.* We should therefore cleave unto him by faith, if we intend to be well pleasing in the sight of God, *for without faith it is impossible to please God,* as St. *Paul* says.

It is comfortable that Jesus is the beloved Son of God; but more comfortable it is, that God is well pleased in him: For thereof we can conclude, that the love which the Father has to the Son, shall extend to us, since he was well pleased in all what Christ suffered for our sake. The prophet *Isaiah* says, *It pleased the Lord to bruise him, he hath put him to grief.* So are we thereby *dear children of God accepted in the beloved.* And since the Son is a true God with the Father, then do we become thereby *partakers of the divine nature.* O! Abundance of comfort. In the old days God said, *it grieves me, that I made man:* But now says he, *this is my beloved Son.* When God beholds us and our sins according to the law, then he sees nothing else but Abominations, but when he beholds us, according to the Gospel in his beloved Son, so is he well pleased in us for the merits of Christ. The offerings of *Noah* was so pleasing to God, that he said and promised, *not to curse the ground again any more;* much more was God pleased with the sacrifice of *Christ,* who *gave himself for us an offering and a sacrifice to God for a sweet smelling savor;* and was thereby reconciled with us, and accepted us in the beloved.

The well-pleasing of God will be our shield against the temptations of Satan and the adversities of the world, *If God be for us, who can be against us? For if when we were enemies, we were reconciled to God by the death of his Son, much more being reconciled, we shall be saved by his life.* What would a child of God doubt on the friendship and well-pleasing of God, although the world goes against him, and he must suffer cross and affliction therein? Was not Jesus Christ the beloved Son of God obliged to suffer and undergo a great deal more, and that not for his own, but for our sake? Therefore should we not be feeble minded, for God will never leave off from loving his children, although they are troubled in this world; but, as he has received them to be his children in baptism, so will he always love them that remain steadfast until their end, for the sake of Jesus Christ his beloved Son, in whom he is well-pleased. *For whose sake the Lord strengthen our faith, and make us eternally happy.* AMEN.

28

The Lord's Supper

The Text, 1 CORINTHIANS, 11:23, 30. verses.

For I have received of the Lord, that which also I delivered unto you, that the Lord Jesus, the same night in which he was betrayed, took bread: And when he had given thanks, he broke it, and said, take, eat, this is my body, which is broken for you, this do in remembrance of me. After the same manner also he took the cup, when he had supped, saying, This cup is the New Testament in my blood, this do, as often as you drink it, in remembrance of me: For as often as you eat this bread, and drink this cup, you do show the Lord's death till he come; wherefore, whosoever shall eat this bread, and drink this cup of the Lord unworthily, shall be guilty of the body and blood of the Lord. But let a man examine himself, and so let him eat of that bread, and drink of that cup. For he that eats and drinks unworthily, eats and drinks damnation to himself, not discerning the Lord's body.

INTRODUCTION

AS the children of *Israel* had, in the Old Testament, two sacraments, namely, circumcision, and the Passover: So have we Christians in the New Testament, likewise two sacraments, namely, baptism, and Holy Communion. Baptism in the room of the circumcision, and the communion in the room of the Passover.

Of this Passover *Moses* gives a full description in his book called, *Exodus*, in 12 Chap. Hereof we shall see,

1. Who is the institutor of this Passover; God, who spoke to *Moses*, and sent him to bring the children of *Israel* out of *Egypt*, and who had wrought so many miracles, and who had answered unto *Moses*, when he asked for his name, *I am that I am*. None but God could institute a sacrament, since none else but God could give the heavenly things, which are concealed in the sacraments. Therefore God did order and command *Moses* and *Aaron*, how they should act in that holy office, and the administration thereof, that they should not alter anything therein; for God needed no reformation from men.

2. The description of the Passover. They should *take a male lamb of a year old without blemish, out from the sheep or goats, and kill it in the evening, and take of the blood, and strike it on the two side posts, and on the upper door-post of the house, wherein they should eat it: They should not eat it raw, nor sodden at all with water, but roast with fire, his head with his legs, and with the purtenance thereof; neither should they break any bones thereof: They should let nothing thereof remain until the morning, and that which remains thereof until the morning, they should burn with fire: They should eat it with their loins girded, their shoes on their feet, and their staff in their hand, and they should eat it in haste: They should eat the flesh that night with unleavened bread and with bitter herbs*; and *it was the Lord's Passover.*

3. The signification of the Passover. This Passover was a figure

unto Christ, and therefore says the apostle *Paul: Christ our Passover is sacrificed for us.*

The sacrament of the Passover is now put away in the New Testament, since Christ is come and manifested in the flesh; unto whom all the ceremonies of the Old Testament were figures. What should we do longer with the figure, since the Master himself is come, and has instituted in the room of the Passover, the sacrament of the Lord's Supper; wherein he gives us his body and blood to eat and to drink, which is more than the Passover? What could the Passover help the children of *Israel,* if God's command had not been by it? And what helps the Lord's Supper without a true faith thereby, depending alone on the merits of Christ? On the contrary; As they who did not keep the Passover according to the command of God, *should be cut off from* Israel; so do they likewise, who go unworthily to the Lord's Supper, eat and drink damnation to themselves: Therefore it can well and rightly be called, a *Holy Table.* We will in the name of our blessed Savior, discourse according to our text, of this holy sacrament, under the following heads.

FIRST, *What holy table the Communion is.*

SECOND, *The punishment of them, who receive it unworthily.*

THIRD, *How men should prepare themselves worthily.*

EXPLANATION of the TEXT

I. What holy table Communion is.

When you sit to eat with a ruler, consider diligently what is before you; says *Solomon.* We ought to observe this table-rule more at the Lord's Table. We ought to behave ourselves reverently, when we are honored and admitted to the table of a great Lord, much more by this holy table of God; who is Lord of Lord's, and King of King's, and for whose majesty, *the Seraphim do cover their faces*. We shall find the holiness of the Lord's Table, when we consider the following.

1. The Lord of this table, who has instituted this Sacrament, whereof our text says, I have received of the Lord that which also I delivered unto you, that is the Lord Jesus. This Lord is,

First, a glorious Lord. It is worth observing, that, when God would institute a sacrament either in the Old or New Testament, then placed he always before it his godly majestic title, for to show his own power, and the worth and honor of the sacrament; and to overcome human reason, who either should oppose, or alter the same. In the institution of circumcision, the Lord said to *Abraham, I am the almighty God.* In the institution of the Passover, God used his essential name, saying to *Moses, I am the Lord.* Likewise in the New Testament, when Christ did command his apostles to administer the sacrament of baptism, then said he first, *all power is given unto me in heaven, and on earth.* Christ will show with these words, that he, by his own godly power, has instituted baptism; and no cause is therefore lest for anyone to ask why, and for what reason must the same be administered with water, and how the Holy Spirit can be shed on men in the baptism with water. And of the sacrament of communion, says our text, *the Lord Jesus Christ.* The apostle *Paul* has regard here both to the person and to the office of Christ; according to his person he is our Lord, and likewise according to his triple office of Priest, Prophet and King. Jesus is our Lord.

Secondly, true and faithful. We may depend upon his words, and be assured, that he will give us, what he promised in this sacrament, and therefore not take upon ourselves to alter his words, or explain them according to the weak apprehension of human reason.

Thirdly, mild and good. He thought upon our welfare, in the same night that he was going to his sufferings and death, as a loving father, who when he is going to die, is concerned, that his children can and may farewell; for Christ knew full well what power and tyranny Satan would exercise against the faithful, in order to weaken, and if it was possible to quench their faith; therefore instituted he this sacrament, by which they could strengthen their faith.

Fourthly, the wisest. For *in him are hidden all the treasures of wisdom and knowledge.* Therefore knew he full well, what he did and said, when he instituted this sacrament. There is also no need for anyone to lend to Christ, any of human wisdom, or to alter his words either with taking from it, or adding to it.

The same night in which he was betrayed, he instituted this sacrament after he had eat the Passover with his disciples. The evangelist St John says, *he rose from Supper and laid aside his garment, and took a towel, and girded himself,* in order to wash the disciples' feet: And after washing their feet, then took he the bread that was on the table, and the cup, and instituted also this communion, which therefore is called the Lord's Supper; because the same is instituted of the Lord, and we receive in the same his body and blood.

We are therefore not bound to administer this sacrament at night: No, for the time is not fixed, or absolutely mentioned or commanded, as it was in the Old Testament with the Passover. The old fathers have rather chosen hereto the morning time, because men are then sober and also more apt to godly thoughts and sincere devotion: But, since it has pleased Christ, to institute this sacrament in the night, we can make these meditations: 1. That he did put away the Old Testament, which is compared by the night, and did institute the New, which is compared to the day. 2. That this Testament should be kept and administered according to his institution, since this was the last night of his visible living on earth, when he gave this his last will and Testament. 3. That as there is darkness in the night, so is there likewise darkness and ignorance in our human reason, concerning the apprehension of the high mystery of this sacrament: And he that will come to a true sense of the same, must not follow his own reason, but captivate his reason under the obedience of faith, and in simplicity cleave to the words of Christ. 4. That we were under the dark power of Satan; but Christ has, by the blood of his covenant freed us, and *turned us from darkness to light, and from the power of Satan unto God, and has made us partakers of the inheritance of the saints in light.*

2. What is brought forth on this table of the Lord?

Bread and wine, and therewith the body and blood of Christ. The bread and the wine, which are earthly, and the outward things, we can see; but the body and blood of Christ, which are heavenly, and the inward, we cannot see. The bread must be natural bread, baked and made of flour and water, either with or without leaven: The wine must be natural juice of grapes, either red or white. The old fathers have given several reasons, why Christ has instituted this sacrament under bread and wine: For, although his own free-will and pleasure was the most principal reason hereto, yet since Christ was the eternal wisdom of God, it cannot be doubted, but that he has through, and for particular considerations, chosen bread and wine for the administration of this holy sacrament. The reasons we have, and can suppose therefor, are the following,

First, in order to fulfill the figures of the Old Testament. *Melchizedech, King of* Salem, *and priest of the Most High God, brought forth bread and wine to* Abraham *and his soldiers.* When we, as spiritual soldiers, have been in battle with our spiritual enemies, then refreshes us, Jesus Christ the King of Righteousness, with his body and blood in this sacrament, under bread and wine; and strengthens us further to war and withstand all our spiritual enemies, and their temptations, by the power of the Holy Spirit.

Secondly, on account of the continual use of bread and wine. Among all eatables none is more common than bread, and likewise among liquors, none than wine. wherefore the Psalmist says, *Wine makes glad the heart of man, and bread strengthens man's heart:* Therefore has Christ chosen to give us his body and blood by these means, that we thereby, could be made partakers of what is immortal and supernatural.

Thirdly, for to unite himself with us. Nothing is nearer unto Christ, than his body and blood; and nothing is nearer unto us than what we eat and drink: Therefore Christ would use bread and wine, for the assuring us of the spiritual union between him and us.

Fourthly, for the remembrance of love. As of many grains is made one bread, and of many grapes one wine; so are we all fed in the Lord's Supper with one body and blood, and are all partakers of that one bread, for to be *one* spiritual *body in Christ, and everyone members one of another.* Whereof St. *Paul* says, *for we being many are one bread and one body, for we are all partakers of that one bread.*

Fifthly, for a perfect nourishment. We need for the support of our bodies, food and drink; whereof bread and wine are the most principal: Christ would acquaint us, with the bread and wine in the Lord's Supper, that he gives us there a perfect nourishment for our souls; for as he took on flesh and blood for our sake, and was sacrificed on the cross, so has he likewise freed us, with the giving of his body, and shedding of his blood, from the eternal death.

Under these two visible and earthly things bread and wine, lay concealed two invisible, heavenly things, the body and blood of Christ: Under bread, the body; and under wine, the blood of Christ.

That the body and blood of Christ are present and given in the Lord's Supper, we can prove,

First, by the institution of this sacrament. 1. What is given to eat and to drink in this sacrament, must absolutely be present: Now it is not alone the bread and wine which we see given, but also the body and blood of Christ, which we cannot see, except with the eyes of our faith, according to the words of Christ, *This is my body, This is my blood.* Thereof follows, that the body and blood of Christ is present. 2. The blood wherewith a Testament is sealed and confirmed, must be present. The Old Testament was confirmed with the blood of the sacrifices, which was present: The New Testament is confirmed with the blood of Christ, and it must therefore be present. 3. The same body and blood which Christ gave in death for us on the cross, is present in the Lord's Supper: For of the bread Christ said, *This is my body, which is broken for you*; and of the wine said he, *This is my blood, which is shed for you.* Now there was no figured nor signified body crucified, neither signified blood shed on the cross, but the very and true body and blood of Christ was crucified and shed: therefore must the body and blood of Christ be present in the Lord's Supper, and not a signification or token thereof. 4. The New Testament is not *a shadow of things to come, but the body is of Christ.* The Lord's Supper is the sacrament of the New Testament; therefore is the same not a shadow nor signification of the body and blood of Christ, but the body and blood itself. If Christ had instituted this sacrament of the Lord's Supper, under a shadow, that the bread should but signify his body, and the wine his blood, so that they should not be present; then needed he not to put away the Passover, since the killing, roasting, and eating thereof, the striking of blood on the posts of the door, and all the ceremonies thereof, were a plainer shadow and signification of the sufferings and death of Christ, than bread and wine in the Lord's Supper. 5. Jesus Christ calls in the institution, the blessed cup, *the New Testament in my blood, which is shed for you.* Did we now receive wine alone of this cup, then could the same not be called, *the New Testament*, since the same is not confirmed with wine, but with the blood of Christ, which then certainly must be present.

Second, by the words of the apostle *Paul, the cup of blessing, which we bless, is it not the communion of the blood of Christ? The bread, which we break, is it not the communion of the body of Christ?* If then the blessed bread be the communion of the body of Christ, and the blessed cup the communion of the blood of Christ, then must certainly the body and blood of Christ be present in the Lord's Supper. Was the body and blood of Christ, as far from the blessed bread and wine, as heaven is from earth, according to the wrong opinion of some, then could the blessed bread and wine not be the communion of the body and blood of Christ, but the apostle would have called it, the sign or token of the body and blood of Christ.

What communion this is, or how it can be, we cannot apprehend; but we must be satisfied with the words of Christ, and believe him: The bread is not altered, transubstantiated or turned into the body of Christ, neither the wine into the blood of Christ; for the apostle *Paul* calls the bread, *bread*, and the wine calls he *wine*, even after the blessing, though there becomes a communion between the bread and the body of Christ, and the wine and the blood of Christ: So that, when we eat the bread, we do eat the body of Christ, and when we drink the wine, we do drink the blood of Christ, in a spiritual and sacramental way, which we cannot understand or apprehend: Therefore we shall let it remain by the words of Christ, and put our whole confidence in him, *Who is able to do exceeding abundantly above all that we think.*

Third, of the confirmation of the apostle St. *John. This is he that came by water and blood, even Jesus Christ, not by water only, but by water and blood; and it is the Spirit, that bears witness, because the*

Spirit is truth: For there are three that bear record in heaven, the Father, the Word, and the Holy Spirit, and these three are one: And there are three that bear witness in earth, the Spirit, the water, and the blood, and these three agree in one. By the spirit is understood, the ministerial office, and therefore called, *the ministration of the Spirit.* By the water is understood the sacrament of baptism, and by the blood the sacrament of the Lord's Supper. Of these words we can make such conclusion, that what comes to us by Christ, and bears witness in earth, must absolutely be present: Now Christ comes to us by his blood, and bears witness of the same, therefore must it be present.

3. The holy ceremonies which Christ uses here, are,

First, the consecration. *He took the bread and gave thanks:* After the same manner *he took the cup and gave thanks.* In this Thanksgiving has Christ thanked his heavenly Father, who had given unto him power and authority to institute this holy sacrament; and also for the work of our redemption, that God would be so gracious and bountiful to us poor sinners, as not to spare his own beloved Son, but send him in the world, and delivered him up for us all, to save and free us from the power of Satan. The *Jews* had a custom, that after the eating of the Passover, they took a cup, and drink thereof, giving thanks unto their Heavenly Father, for their deliverance from the bondage in *Egypt.* When we ourselves use the sacrament, or see others use it, we should then give thanks unto God for this gracious work of redemption, which Christ has procured for us with his suffering and death: wherefore the apostle *Paul* admonishes, *as often as you eat this bread, and drink this cup, you do show the Lord's death till he come.* And by this thanksgiving did Christ separate this bread and wine from all worldly use, and made it also a holy means for the distribution of his body and blood: for this blessing and thanksgiving did not consist in bare words, but had a godly power in them, as well for the present time, as for the time to come.

Secondly, the distribution. *He broke it, and gave it.* That Christ did break the bread was to make it more apt to be distributed, since the Jews did make broad thin cakes for to eat with the Passover; and this sort of bread was on the table, whereof Christ took. But since the breaking of the bread is not an essential part of the sacrament, but alone a preparation for the distribution, so it is left to Christian freedom, either to break or not: Therefore if it is broken, or separated before, in convenient parts, for the distribution; what needs then the breaking thereof?

Thirdly, the reception thereof: *Take.* Whether the communicant receives the sacrament, with his hand, or his mouth out of the ministers hand, is all one, and even alike; for the word, *take*, is used as well in regard to the mouth, as to the hand; and it is likewise a Christian freedom.

Fourthly, the eating and drinking. *Eat, this is my body; drink, this is my blood.* There are three sorts of eating and drinking. 1. A natural eating, which we must all do, for the support of our bodies. 2. Spiritual eating: This is alone through faith, whereof our Savior speaks by the evangelist St. *John*, the sixth Chapter. 3. Sacramental eating and drinking, as here in the Lord's Supper. This mystery is too high for the apprehension of human reason, and therefore we must believe the words as they are said and spoken.

4. The guests were the disciples of Christ.

As they who were not circumcised, were forbidden to eat the Passover in the Old Testament; so must they who are not baptized, not be admitted to the Lord's Supper. It must be a disciple of Christ, who knows what it is to examine himself; Though, as there was among the twelve apostles one traitor, *Judas Iscariot,* who likewise received the body and blood of Christ, but to his own damnation; so do we likewise find many unworthy guests, who receive this sacrament with their mouth, but they eat and drink damnation to themselves.

5. The benefit which they, who receive it worthily, have, are the following.

First, the remission of sin, and the strengthening of the faith. If the body and blood of Christ, which is become a sacrifice and ransom for our sins, be eat and drank in the Lord's Supper; so can they who are worthily prepared with a true faith, be assured that they have part in all what Christ has procured with his death and sufferings, namely, the remission of sins, the grace of God, and the eternal life. Thereof Christ assured us with these words, *This is my body, this is my blood, which is shed for the remission of sins.*

Secondly, union with Christ. Since nothing is nearer unto Christ than his body and blood, and nothing is nearer unto us, than what we eat and drink; so we can conclude thereof, that Christ would unite himself with us in the nearest manner, as the branch is to the vine, whereof he draws power and strength to grow and become fruitful: And since the body and blood of Christ is quickening, and filled with heavenly gifts, so have we therein the true fountain of life; whereof we can draw the spiritual life here, in grace; and hereafter, in glory everlasting, Which is,

Thirdly, the eternal Life. Where true faith is, there is the remission of sins, life and happiness: For where ever the remission of sins is, there is life and happiness everlasting indeed.

II. We have to discourse of the punishment of them who receive the sacrament of the Lord's Supper unworthily.

Although they all receive the body and blood of Christ, yet they have not alike benefit thereof; for they who receive it worthily, have the remission of sins, life, and everlasting happiness; but they, *who eat and drink unworthily, they eat and drink damnation to themselves, not discerning the Lord's body.*

Here we must overlook, who are unworthy guests, and what makes them unworthy, so that they have damnation by this sacrament.

Not them of little faith; for a little faith is also faith, and God has most care for them of little faith. He has promised, that *he will not break a bruised reed, nor quench the smoking flax.* He has said, that *he will gather the lambs with his arms, and carry them in his bosom, and will bind up that which was broken, and strengthen that which was sick.* Therefore has Christ instituted this sacrament, that they of little faith could be strengthened thereby; like the preaching of the gospel, which stirs up, nourishes and confirms our faith. All they of little faith, should observe these means, and use them rightly, for they are the breasts, whereof faith draws strength and nourishment.

But the unworthy guests, are the unrepenting hardened sinners, who do not know their sins, much less are grieved over them; but live in all manner of wickedness, abominations, hatred and security, have no faith, neither a Christian purpose of bettering their life: If such should go to the Lord's Supper, they *eat and drink unworthily,* and they must expect great punishment, for they make themselves guilty thereby,

1. *Of the body and blood of the Lord.* He commits a great crime against the divine majesty of God, and loses thereby his eternal

welfare: Like one who attempts to lay violent hands on a royal diadem, or commits, *crim en læsæ Majestatis*, is liable to forfeit all his estate.

2. To judgment. *For them remains a certain fearful looking for judgment, and fiery indignation, which shall devour them*; for *he that believes not, is condemned already:* They bear their own judgment in their bosom, and at the Last Day they shall receive and find the execution of this judgment, when *they shall look upon him, whom they have pierced.*

3. To all temporal punishment, which are a chastisement to all repenting sinners, but a punishment to all unrepenting; and if they do not convert by times, they must expect a greater and more severe punishment. The reason of this is, that

First, they discern not the Lord's body. They do not consider, that they receive the body of Christ, *in whom dwells all the fullness of the Godhead bodily:* The body, *which takes away the sins of the world.* The things which God has sanctified, men must likewise keep holy; What is more holy than the body of the Lord? This discerning of the Lord's body, is not understood by them, who go to the Lord's Supper only through custom, or for ceremony sake.

Secondly, They eat and drink unworthily; and thereby *become guilty of the body and blood of the Lord.* Judas and the crucifiers of Christ became *guilty of the body and blood of the Lord:* The first, in betraying him with a kiss; and the others, in crucifying him, and shedding his innocent blood, though to no benefit for themselves: So do they, become *guilty of the body and blood of the Lord, who eat and drink unworthily,* for in so doing is shedding the Lord's blood on a new. As they who pierced the side of Christ, did not do it with an intent to drink his blood, but only to shed it on the ground; so do they, *who eat and drink unworthily,* shed the blood of Christ to no purpose, but they rather trample the blood of the covenant under their feet.

III. We have to discourse of, how men should prepare themselves worthily.

Since it is so dangerous to go unworthily to the Lord's Supper, then let us be more careful, and examine and prepare ourselves worthily thereto, that we may not eat and drink to our eternal damnation, which otherwise would be to our eternal salvation. A worthy preparation consists in,

1. Examining ourselves. The apostle *Paul* says, *let a man examine himself*; that is, let him go into his own conscience, and call himself to an account, and search all his actions and doings, and

First, make this question to himself: Do you know, and understand, that you have sinned, and thereby provoked God to wrath? There are many who do not know their sins, nor the greatness of them: Of such *Solomon* says, *there is a generation, that are pure in their own eyes, and yet is not washed from their filthiness.* These should take the glass of the law before them, and behold themselves, and they would see the stains in the face of their soul and conscience: The Ten Commandments, should be the touchstone by which they should try their hearts, and meditate upon, how often they have transgressed everyone of them with thoughts, words or deeds. Thereupon should follow,

Secondly, a sincere contrition of heart and grief over, as well what evil we have committed, as what good we have omitted: Herein the following example of the prophet *Daniel*, who says, *I set my face unto the Lord God, to seek by prayer and supplication, and with fasting, and I prayed unto the Lord my God, and made confession.* If we are not able of our selves to utter ourselves before God, then we may use the 6, 32, 38, 51, 102, 130, and 143, *Psalms* of king *David*, which are very proper and serviceable on such occasions.

Thirdly, this contrition of heart should be joined with a true faith in Christ, and a sincere believing in his words: For, since the apostle *Paul* requires, that *men should discern the Lord's body*, so should we look upon this sacrament to be a heavenly meal, wherein Christ is present, and feeds us with his body and blood under bread, and wine; that he, by this precious pledge for our redemption, might confirm in our hearts his gracious promise concerning the remission of our sins, and thereby strengthen our faith. This a communicant must believe, and not alone be assured of, that the body and blood of Christ is present, but also, that he is made a partaker of all the benefits which Christ has procured with his death and sufferings, according to the words of Christ, *this is my body, which is given for you; this is my blood, which is shed for you.* He that believes these words with a true faith is worthy and well prepared, for he has what these words promise, namely, the remission of sins: But whosoever does not believe, or doubts about them, he is unworthy and unprepared, because the word, *for you,* requires absolutely a heart that believes. The apostle *Paul* says, *he that doubts, is damned if he eats, because he eats not of faith, for whatsoever is not of faith, is sin.*

2. *Showing the Lord's death.* Hereof shines forth his abundant love, *that he gave himself in death for us,* by which we are strengthened in our faith, that we can expect from God for Christ's sake all good; and be assured of, that since *we are reconciled unto God by the death of his Son, when we were enemies, much more being reconciled we should be saved by his life.* Thereby we are encouraged to mortify sin; that, as Christ died for sin, so should we die from sin, and live unto him *which died for us, and rose again. To show the Lord's death,* signifies likewise, to praise and thank him for his death and sufferings, which he underwent for our sake: which should be done not alone with our mouth, but also with our actions; that we *being dead to sin do live unto righteousness:* For thereby we do show that we have always the death and sufferings of the Lord in our thoughts and meditations. This is

the meaning of our Savior when he says, *this do in remembrance of me.*

3. Brotherly reconciliation with our neighbor. He that rightly considers the death of Christ, shall find that he, through love, has forgiven us all our sins, and gave his life in death for us; therefore it is just, that we should forgive our brothers their trespasses. What are the *hundred pence,* which our neighbors owes us, to be compared to the *ten thousand talents,* which we owe to God? And yet he forgives us, when we sincerely crave his pardon and forgiveness: Our Savior says, *when you stand praying, forgive, if you have ought against any, that your Father also, which is in heaven, may forgive you your trespasses.*

This should we do not alone now and then, or as often as we intend to go to the Lord's Supper, but every day, as long as we live, until he comes either by death or judgment: *He that endures to the end shall be saved.* It is not enough to begin well, but we should also end well. This crowns our action, and brings us to a happy end.

God enlighten by the Holy Spirit, the hearts of them who will receive the Lord's Supper, that they may know and understand their own unworthiness, the grace of God, and the love of Jesus Christ; and thereof be strengthened in their faith, and at last receive the end of their faith, even the salvation of their souls, for the sake of Jesus Christ our blessed Lord and Savior. AMEN.

29

Prayer

T he Text, PSALMS 50:15, ver.

Call upon me in the day of trouble; I will deliver you, and you shall glorify me.

INTRODUCTION

THERE is nothing in religion more needful than to pray, and there is nothing we are more unwilling to do than the same; and even, when we come thereto, how cold and lukewarm are we? We need therefore well to observe the words of the apostle *Paul* in his 1 epistle to his beloved *Timothy*, the 2nd chapter, the three first verses, *I exhort therefore, that first of all supplications, prayers, intercessions, and giving of thanks, be made for all men: For kings, and all that are in authority, that we may lead a quiet and peaceable life in all godliness and honesty: For that is good and acceptable in the sight of God our Savior.*

In these words we have. 1. An exhortation to prayers. 2. A division of prayers. And 3. The benefit of prayers.

1. Concerning the encouragement, the apostle says, *I exhort therefore, that first of all.* We can see how needful that prayer is,

that our Savior in the time of his humiliation, exercised the same constantly. When he began his ministerial office, he began the same with prayer: In the progress of his ministerial office he did nothing without prayers; he began his sufferings with prayers, and ended the same with prayers: Everyone of what condition whatsoever, must listen to these words of the apostle. The Scripture uses commonly, exhortations in high, profitable and needful cases; faith is a weighty matter, therefore *exhorted* Barnabas *them all, that with purpose of heart they would cleave unto the Lord.* St. *Paul exhorted the disciples to continue in faith.* To serve God in spirit with sincere devotion is very needful and profitable, therefore exhorted the apostle *Paul* thereto saying, *I beseech you therefore brethren by the mercies of God, that you present your bodies a living sacrifice, holy, acceptable unto God, which is your reasonable service.* What is more weighty, profitable and needful than prayer? It is weighty in power and effect, it is profitable in the consequence, and needful in all conditions. What can a soldier do in the battle without arms, wherewith he must defend himself? Our life is a continual war, and that spiritual: If we are not armed with prayers, then are we soon conquered: Therefore ought we daily and momently to remember the words of exhortation of the apostle.

2. Concerning the division of prayers. There are four sorts accord to the words of the apostle; 1. *Supplications:* When we pray to God for the remission of sins, or moving away of any temporal or spiritual punishment, we must do it with supplications. 2. *Prayers:* That is, when we pray to the Almighty for what is needful, as well for the body as the soul. 3. *Intercession.* When we pray and intercede for others, we should not pray for ourselves alone, but also for others; it is natural to pray for ourselves, but loving to pray for others. And, 4. *Giving of thanks:* When we have received any blessing from God, then ought we to thank God therefor, otherwise it would be the greatest ingratitude. And since not one minute passes without our receiving

some blessings from God, then we must *give always thanks unto God and the Father in the name of our Lord Jesus Christ.* We must pray for all men, even our enemies, and for the ungodly, that they may turn from their wickedness and live. In particular, we should pray *for kings, and all that are in authority.* Let them be good or bad, yet we should pray for them: Are they good, we should pray that God may prosper their government, and give unto them a long life of peace and quietness, *that mercy and truth may meet together, righteousness and peace kiss each other:* Are they bad, we should pray that God will turn their hearts, and give them a better mind.

As for the prayers which *David* and the prophets have prayed against the ungodly, we should look upon to be either prophesies of the evil, which should befall them, or else wishes under condition, if they did not repent, and were converted from their ungodliness: They who are in authority, can do both bad and good: Are they inclined to evil, we should pray that God would hinder their evil design, and turn their bad intentions to good; are they inclined to good, we should pray that God will strengthen and confirm them in goodness, *that we may lead a quiet and peaceable life, in all godliness and honesty:* And this is,

3. The profit and benefit of prayers: This consists inwardly in a quiet conscience; and outwardly in peace with others. When we do what is acceptable in the sight of God, and profitable to our neighbors, then we have a clear and good conscience; When we pray for them that are in authority, we can have a quiet and peaceable life, serve God in peace, follow our lawful calling in peace, and expect in peace the grace of God, blessing in our doings, and prosperity in our calling. Peace and quietness is as the tree of king *Nebuchadnezzar, which stood in the midst of the earth, and had fair leaves, and much fruit for meat, and shadow for the beasts of the field.* Also is godliness and honesty the fruit of the tree of peace. The *first* has regard to God, the *second* to

our neighbor; the *first* concerns our faith, the *second* our conscience. And since we can obtain this by the protection of our magistrates that are in authority, then we ought to pray for them, *for that is good, and acceptable in the sight of God our Savior.* As parents are pleased to behold the obedience of their children, and the children are made thereby bold to crave and ask what is needful for them; so is it likewise *good and acceptable in the sight of God our Savior*, when we obey his commands, and can lay before him in our prayers, our wants and needs; and he will not refuse his children, what they pray for. Hereof the Lord assures us in the words of our text: Whereof we will consider the following.

FIRST, *The Nature of Prayers.*

SECOND, *The Effect and Power thereof. And,*

THIRD, *Of Thanksgiving in particular.*

EXPLANATION of the TEXT

I. We will consider the nature of prayers.

We love always precious things, as gold and jewels. What is more precious in all our doings and actions, than prayers? Is faith, which is the life of prayer, more precious than corruptible gold? Are the promises of God, whereof we pray, precious? Is the blood of Christ, wherewith our prayers must be sprinkled over, precious? Then prayer must be likewise precious, when the same proceeds of faith, is founded upon the promises of God, and sprinkled over with the blood of Christ: Of this prayer says the apostle St. *James*, that it *prevails much.* None should therefor regard prayer too little, for God himself has great regard to prayers. *It shall come to pass, that before they call, I will answer, and while they are yet speaking, I will hear,* says the Lord, by the prophet *Isaiah:* Thereof speaks the Lord likewise in our text, saying, *Call upon me in the day of trouble, I will deliver you, and you shall glorify me.*

These words contain, 1. A command, *Call upon me in the day of trouble.* 2. A promise, *I will deliver you:* this is the effect and power of prayer. And, 3. A duty, *and you shall glorify me:* this is the giving of thanks.

In the command, *Call upon me in the day of trouble*, is to be observed, 1. The description of prayer. 2. Who should pray. 3. How we should pray. 4. To whom we should pray. And, 5. When we should pray.

1. The description of prayer, we do find in this word *call*; which is not so much the work of the mouth, as of the heart: For what is prayer else than the lifting up of our hearts to God, either in thought or sigh? For, since *God is a Spirit, therefore will he be worshiped in Spirit and truth.* He observes mostly the heart, although there is no outward token near. The Psalmist says, *Lord you have heard the desire of the humble, you wilt prepare their heart, you wilt cause your ear to hear.* Here prayer is called *the desire of the heart*, and is placed together, on the one side, men's heart; and on the other side, the ear of God. If the ear of God hears the prayer, then must the same proceed from the heart.

Though it is not enough to pray alone in thought; we should observe time and place, and honor God also with our members, and follow the example of Christ, who *prayed with a loud voice.* We men are so frail and fickle, that without our heart is assisted with a loud voice in our prayers, it oftentimes goes astray upon worldly things; therefore have the saints used several gestures besides a loud voice; as, to fall upon their faces, as *Moses, David*, and others; to bend their knees, as *Solomon* and *Paul*; to lift up their eyes to heaven, as *David*; to beat upon the breast, as the *publican:* But among all these gestures they have used mostly the bowing of the knees, and lifting up of the hands: With the first, they showed their humility; with the second their devotion. We use now in our days, the bowing of knees, and folding together of the hands: With the bowing of the knee, we show our humility; with the folding together our hands, we remember the covenant made in our baptism; For, in common, a covenant or agreement is made and concluded with the giving of hands by the parties concerned, and to show, that we surely depend upon the promises of God, wherefore we pray.

2. Who should pray. *Call upon me*, is a word of command, and extends to all men whose duty it is to pray, and to honor their Creator; though they who will not obey this command, and pray with love, they will at last be obliged to pray for fear of worse to come: We ought not to be ordered nor forced to pray, but reckon it as a great honor, that God is so gracious, as to allow us to speak and converse with him in our prayers.

Yet God will not have this service of everyone; but he that will pray must be a regenerated Christian, a repenting and faithful, a spiritual priest. *God is a Spirit*, and he that will pray, must be regenerated and renewed by God's Spirit. As long as a man remains in his sinful condition, he cannot pray to any effect and purpose; but when he is regenerated of the Holy Spirit, then he can call, *Abba Father*; for prayer is nothing else but the breath of the soul, in his Father's bosom. *God is a light, and in him is no darkness at all:* Therefore must he, who will pray to God, first lay off all the unfruitful works of darkness, cleanse his heart through faith, let the Spirit of God guide and enlighten him, and walk circumspectly as a child of light. As the sacrifice is, so must the priest be; if the sacrifice is spiritual, the priest must likewise be spiritual, who has received the ointment of the Holy Spirit: The incense is a contrite heart, grieved over former sins; the altar is Jesus Christ, in whose holy name we should pray, if we will be heard.

3. How we should pray. When the Lord says, *Call upon me*, then

he is willing that we should call upon him according to what he has ordered in his word, and not otherwise: That is,

First, in repenting. Since *God hears not sinners*, then we must lay off all sin: The Lord says by the prophet *Isaiah, When you spread forth your hands, I will hide my eyes from you; yea, even when you make many prayers, I will not hear; your hands are full of blood.* A godly life is the best prayer, although we speak not one word. A sincere sigh of a repenting sinner, is more acceptable in the eye of God, than the long prayers of an unrepentant one: For such mock God when they pray *Our Father*; it is profane to say, *Our Father*, since God will be a Father only to them who honor him. How can they say, *hallowed be your name*, where they themselves pollute the holy name of God with their ungodliness? Needless do they say, *your Kingdom come*, when they themselves confound the gracious Kingdom of God in their hearts, and let the Devil, the world, and their own sinful flesh and blood reign there. How can they say, *your will be done*, when they always oppose and withstand the same in all their thoughts, words and deeds? Is it to pray for *daily bread*, when they will not wait the hour of God, but cheat and defraud their neighbors in order to procure themselves daily bread;—to pray for the *remission of sins*, when they will not leave off to sin, neither forgive *others their trespasses*;—to pray that God will not *lead them into temptations*, when they themselves in all their actions throw themselves in temptations;—to pray for *deliverance from evil*, when they draw all evil upon themselves with their wickedness and ungodly life? We can also see, that they who pray without repentance, are condemned by their own prayers.

Secondly, in faith. To pray in faith, is to pray in the name of Jesus. Faith is the life of prayer, having two hands; with one it takes hold of God's promises, and with the other it takes hold of Jesus Christ and his merits. When we therefore pray in faith, then we do pray in the name of Jesus, and can also be assured of, that God will give

423

us what is needful for the sake of Jesus Christ, on whose merits our faith depends.

Thirdly, in reverence. When we are admitted to speak to a great Lord, how humble and reverently are we, and careful of every word we speak; much more ought we to behave ourselves reverently when we appear before the throne of God with our prayers, *who is Lord of Lords, and King of Kings*, for whose godly majesty the seraphim do cover their faces.

Fourthly, with a clean conscience. When our conscience accuses us, and is guilty of any high crime, then becomes our heart disturbed, and is afraid to pray; thinking you yourself hast been the cause of your own sufferings. If you had obeyed the command of God, this would not have befallen you. Hereof can lightly arise despair.

Fifthly, with reasonable discretions. We should pray for spiritual things, which is necessary to salvation, without condition: for, if we would pray under condition for the grace of God, the remission of sins, the governing of the Holy Spirit, faith, love, hope, and patience; that would be, as if we doubted on the general promises of God, wherein he offers all this to them who will receive them: We should pray for temporal things with condition, if it pleases God, and it is to the glory of God, and our own happiness, otherwise God has not promised to hear us. And we must follow the example of the royal Psalmist, who said, *If I shall find favor in the eyes of the Lord, he will bring me again, and show me both the ark and his habitation; but if he thus say, I have no delight in you, behold, here am I, let him do so me, as seems good unto him.*

Sixthly, with perseverance. It is not enough to pray once or twice, or now and then, but it must be a continual work. The daily life of a Christian, must be a daily prayer. Thereto our Savior admonishes us, when he says, *ask, seek, knock.* This is, a comparison taken of a beggar standing at a door asking for alms, who when he is not heard in his asking, seeks, till he finds a hole or crack in the door, where through he calls, and if he is not heard then knocks he on the door: We should also remain constant in our prayers, and not leave off: As the thief dares not break in the house, as long as the good man of the house watches; neither can the Devil attack, but much more flees away from us, when we continue in prayer of a sincere and contrite heart. We should not lay off the arms of prayer, as long as the war of this life continues.

4. To whom we should pray. The Lord says in our text, *call upon me*. We should pray to God alone, who is one in essence, but three in person, *the Father, the Son, and the Holy Spirit*. By him we can find all the properties, which are required of him, whom we must pray to: For he is *all-knowing, almighty, and omnipresent*, he is the *highest wisdom, the highest goodness, and truth itself:* Therefore we can be assured, that he alone can hear, help and deliver us.

5. When we should pray. Our text says, *in the day of trouble*. Although it is the serious will and command of God, *that we should always pray*, yet is human nature so corrupt, that we are unwilling thereto, except when we are forced through trouble and need; therefore makes our text particular mention of *the day of trouble*, not to be understood, that we should not pray in prosperity and good days; but that we should not despair, and doubt of the help of God, *in the day of trouble*. We call upon them, that are far off: When our sins have parted us from God, so that he seems to be far from us; then we can call him back again with a sincere repentance, and serious and devout prayers. The prophet *Jeremiah* says in his *Lamentations, You drew near in the day that I called upon you, you said, fear not*. Although, *he that keeps* Israel, *neither slumbers nor sleeps*; yet shows he, as if he slept: Therefore should we pray to him, and say with the *Psalmist, awake, why do you sleep, O Lord, arise, do not cast us off forever*. Since we are daily subject to all misfortunes and trouble; therefore we must

always pray. A true Christian ought to speak oftener to God in his prayer, than even to men in his conversation. Thereupon follows,

II. The Effect and Power of Prayers.

The power and effect of prayers, consist in these words, *I will deliver you.* This is the promise of God, that he will,

1. Graciously hear us. God is not blind or deaf, as the idols of the heathens, *who have eyes, and cannot see, and ears, and cannot hear: He will regard the prayers of the destitute,* and *bear the groaning of the prisoner. Syrach* says, *the prayer of the humble pierces the clouds, and till it come nigh, he will not be comforted.* When we think, that he is farthest off, and hears not, then is he often nearest: *The Lord is nigh unto all them that call upon him, to all that call upon him in truth. He will fulfill the desire of them that fear him, he also will hear their cry, and will save them.* God hears in every place: The place sanctifies not the prayer, but the prayer sanctifies the place; *Abraham, Isaac, Jacob,* and others did pray in the open air; *Jonas* in the *whale; Jeremiah* in the *pit; Daniel* in the *Lion's Den*; and the three men in the *fiery oven.* When our heart is pure, and our prayer devout, then is it matterless, in what place whatsoever we pray, for God will hear us: We must always pray; we see our Savior prayed in the day, evening and night; King *David* prayed in the morning, noon, evening and night; and likewise the prophet *Daniel.* The *Roman* dictators had always their doors standing open, that everyone might have free access to them: The door of God's grace stands always open, so that everyone can have free access, by and through Christ.

It seems sometimes, as if God hears us not; this happens,

First, that we should pray more fervent and constant. *When there arose a great tempest, in-so-much, that the Ship was covered with the waves, the disciples cried heartily.* The Lord says of *Israel, I will bring her into the wilderness, and speak comfortably unto her.* When God brings us into the wilderness of crosses and afflictions, where no human help can be expected, then speaks he with us, and then arises many good thoughts in our hearts; and we pray more earnestly: and that is called, *a comfortable speech*, since the Lord does it with a good intention, *and will not try us above what we are able to hear.*

Secondly, to try our faith, hope, love, and patience. We could never have known the greatness of *Abraham*'s faith, *Job*'s patience, the perseverance of the *Caananitish* woman, and of the love of the great sinner, if the same had not been manifested by afflictions: The lily grows under the snow, so do the virtues of God's children shine forth under affliction.

Thirdly, to show his own godly freedom. God is not obliged to hear, when we pray; neither can we obliged him thereto, except when we lay before him his promises: But the Lord knows his own time, and shall and will hear us, when it is consistent with his godly will and pleasure. A faithful Child of God never prays but the Lord hears him; if not according to his will, yet according to God's will: And if not to his temporal benefit, yet to his eternal salvation; for the promises of the Lord have a sure foundation: wherein he assures us of,

2. His well-pleasing help, *I will deliver you.* This is the eternal word of God, which is truth; therefore we can and must depend upon, that he will deliver us, even if we had no more promises in the Scripture than this, that the Lord will hear and deliver us, that would be sufficient; but we can find a great many more both in the Old and New Testament: Therefore is the help and deliverance of God,

First, sure, for they are founded upon the truth and mercy of God. Upon the truth of God: As little as God can deny himself, so little can he depart from his word. Upon the mercy of God: God is of his nature compassionate, and willing to hear the children of men, whereof he testifies himself by the prophet *Jeremiah*, saying, *I will rejoice over them, to do them good:* Much more will he do it now he has commanded them to pray. O pray, pray everyone who can, and be assured, that God will hear, and deliver you.

Secondly, experienced. Look at the generations of Old, and see. Did ever any trust in the Lord, and was confounded? Or did any abide in his fear and was forsaken? Or whom did he ever despise, that called upon him? The time would be too short, were I to sum up the examples of the saints both in the Old, and New Testament; wherein a faithful child of God who prayed, was never spoken of but was heard and delivered.

Thirdly, bountiful. God frees and delivers us from all corporal need, trouble, sickness, poverty, and other calamities; from spiritual trouble; disturbed conscience, sorrow, *the bitterness of soul, and the pit of corruption*; and particular in the trouble of death, when we are forsaken by everyone, and cannot find help and relief by men; then *will the Lord preserve us unto his Heavenly Kingdom.*

III. Thereupon follows, the giving of thanks.

When God has heard and delivered us, then should we thank and praise him: *You shall glorify me.* This is our duty so to do. As many blessings and benefits, either corporal or spiritual, which we receive, so many causes it is of our praising and thanking him. All the rivers come from the sea, and run into the sea again; so must all the benefits, which come from God, as from a bottomless fountain, return to him again in praises, and giving of thanks. This must be done,

1. From the heart. We should praise and glorify God with our mouth and tongue; but if it comes not from the heart it is not acceptable

in the sight of God: For *the Lord looks on the heart.* The *Psalmist* understood this rightly, and said therefore, *I will bless the Lord at all times, his praise shall continually be in my mouth, my soul shall make her boast in the Lord.*

2. By faith. As our prayer must proceed from a true faith in Jesus Christ, if the same should be heard, so must likewise our praise and giving of thanks, proceed from faith; for *whatsoever is not of faith, is sin,* and displeases God. Therefore advises the apostle *Paul, be filled with the Spirit, speaking to yourselves in psalms, and hymns, and spiritual songs, singing and making melody in your heart to the Lord, giving thanks always for all things unto God and the Father, in the name of our Lord Jesus Christ.* And in another place, the same apostle faith, *let us offer the sacrifice of praise to God continually, that is, the fruit of our lips, giving thanks to his name.*

3. In truth and deed. The best giving of thanks consist in a Christian and godly life. God cares not for the praises of our mouth, when we dishonor him with our living: Then can be said to us, as *Moses* said to the children of *Israel, Do you thus requite the Lord, O foolish people, and unwise.* We should let the light of our faith, *so shine before men, that they may see our good works, and glorify our Father which is in heaven.* The apostle *Paul* says, *glorify God in your body, and in your spirit, which are God's.* He would say as much; Since you have from God both your mouth and tongue, which are members of your body, and also spirit, so praise and glorify him with both body and spirit.

The Lord be gracious unto us, and give us a mind and desire to pray; hear us when we call upon you, and deliver us from all need and trouble, that we may praise and glorify your holy name here in time, and hereafter in eternity, for Christ's sake. AMEN.

30

Christian Liberty

T he Text, GALATIANS, 5:1st, verse.

Stand fast therefore in the liberty wherewith Christ has made us free, and be not entangled again with the yoke of bondage

INTRODUCTION

WHEN men departed first from the noble worship of the gracious God, they become subject to many powers and lords, who are evil inclined; for so says our Savior by the evangelist St. *John*, 8:34. *Whosoever commits sin, is the servant of sin, and the servant abides not in the house forever, but the Son abides forever. If the Son therefore shall make you free, you shall be free indeed.*

Our blessed Savior speaks here in these words, 1st, Of an evil service of sin. 2ndly, of an evil reward for this service. And, 3rdly, of freedom from this service.

First, the service of sin is evil in its *beginning,* worse in its *progress,* and the worst in the *end:* It is a great honor to become from a servant, a Lord; but the greatest disgrace it is, to become from a lord, a servant.

It was a great honor for *Joseph*, when he was exalted from the prison to the royal dignity in *Egypt*. On the contrary, it was a great dishonor for king *Nebuchadnezzar*, when he was drove away, not alone from his glory and kingdom, but even from among men, and was obliged to take up his dwelling with the beasts of the field, and to eat grass as oxen. *Adam* our first father was a free lord, as long as he remained in the service of God, but when he became a servant of sin through disobedience, then he lost his honor, and came in the greatest shame and misery; for *whosoever commits sin, is the servant of sin.* This service is,

1. A shameful service. Sin and shame follows always as hand in hand together; therefore faith the apostle *Paul, when you were the servants of sin what fruit had you then in those things, whereof you are now ashamed?* Is he not foolish who will serve a lord that gives no other wages then shame and misery? And they, who serve sin, have an unclean office: For what is more abominable than sin? Therefore our Savior knew not how to describe the foolishness of the prodigal, by greater uncleanness, than that he *did eat husk with the swine.*

2. Hard, we may say of them who serve sin, as the Lord said of the children of *Israel, you shall serve other gods day and night, where I will not show you favor.* What did *Judas* the traitor receive by his service, than a bad conscience in his bosom, and a halter round his neck. A servant has his convenient rest, but a servant of sin hath no rest, *they sleep not, except they have done mischief, and their sleep is taken away, unless they cause some to fall.*

3. Hurtful: A servant serves in order to better himself, and to lay up some thing for his own good. He that serves sin, looses not alone what good he can have, but treasures up unto himself much evil, namely, a check in his conscience, the curse of the law, the wrath of God, the temptations of Satan, and at last eternal damnation, if he repents not in time, but continues in this service to his life's-end.

431

4. Horrible: He that serves sin, serves also the Devil: what can be more horrible? Sin and Satan have a like power over their servants: Satan is an *old Serpent, a liar, a murderer, and a fierce and roaring lion*; Sin is likewise the same, for it is as a serpent, and will bite, *and the teeth thereof, are as the teeth of a lion*, slaying the souls of men. Satan rewards his servants with eternal pain in hell, and likewise gives sin.

Second, an evil and bad reward. He pushes his servants out of the house: *The servant abides not in the house forever.* Misdemeanor and crimes drive servants away. When *Adam* had sinned, he was drove out from *paradise*, as a testimony, that he should also be excluded from the heavenly *paradise. Hagar* and her son *Ishmael*, were drove out of *Abraham's* house, because they mocked *Isaac.* A servant abides in the house for some time, but not forever; for when it comes to heirship, then must he depart. They who serve sin, can well remain for some time in the house of God, namely the Christian church; but when they die, then must they depart from the gracious house of God, and cannot enter into his glorious house, *but they shall be cast out into outer darkness.* How we can get rid of this miserable service, of sin, our Savior shows us, when he speaks,

Third, of the spiritual freedom, saying, *If the Son therefore shall make you free, you shall be free indeed.* What freedom is this? The spiritual freedom is a right, which Christ has procured with his own precious blood, therein, that all men are freed by him from the curse of the law, the service of sin, and the yoke of the *Levitical* ceremonies, and human commandments: Whereupon will follow hereafter, perfect freedom from sin, and the eternal death, to the glory of God, and the salvation of the faithful. This freedom, which Christ has procured for us, is,

1. Undeserved. Wherewith have we deserved this? A servant should serve in the Old Testament six years, and should go out free for nothing in the seventh year; but we could never have been freed

from the service of sin, if Jesus Christ, the eternal Son of God, had not freed us therefrom. Therefore this freedom is,

2. Precious. *We are not redeemed with corruptible things, as silver and gold, but with the precious blood of Christ.* What is more precious than the blood of Christ? Therefore this freedom is,

3. Highly valuable. A servant accounts it a great honor to be made free; we also must reckon it yet a greater, yea even the greatest honor, that the Son of God took on the form of a servant, in order to make us free; and we must therefore walk circumspectly, that we do not lose this freedom again: Whereto the apostle *Paul* admonishes us, when he says in the words of our text, *Stand fast therefore in the liberty wherewith Christ has made us free, and be not entangled again with the yoke of bondage.* We will here, according to our text, enquire into these three points, namely,

FIRST, *Who has freed us.*

SECOND, *Where from we are freed.*

THIRD, *How we shall stand fast in our liberty.*

EXPLANATION of the TEXT

Liberty is a noble thing, desired, but not obtained by everyone; neither would it be good, that everyone had liberty in temporal cases, for it would then go according to the proverb; 'When everyone may do as he will, then doth he as he is inclined to.' There are two sorts of freedom, namely, corporal and spiritual.

Corporal; which likewise is called political or worldly liberty. This belongs to kings and royal families, who do not stand under any command on earth. The subjects can likewise have liberty in their constitution, everyone according to his station and condition: But the same liberty is granted unto them by God, and the magistrates; wherefore they are oftentimes obliged to give money, as *Claudius*

Lysias, who with a great sum obtained the *Roman* freedom.

Spiritual or Christian liberty, whereof we speak here, is a gracious state, wherein God places us by Christ, in that he gives us a true faith, and frees us from the heavy yoke of the ceremonial service, and grants us freedom and liberty to use his spiritual good things: The same is called, *Christian liberty*, for the following reasons. 1st, Because Christ has purchased the same with his blood. 2ndly, Because the Christians use the same, as the apostle *Paul* says, *Brethren, you are called unto liberty.* This liberty belonged to the faithful in the Old Testament, who had received the Holy Spirit, which is called, *a free Spirit*, as well as to the Christians in the New Testament, though not so abundantly; wherefore they served God with a willing obedience, without force. For where the Spirit of God comes, there he operates a willing obedience to the law of God: though, since the same Spirit drove them to obedience, by the severe threatening of the law, who with fear brought their conscience in the knowledge of their sins, and threatened them with eternal curse and damnation; therefore are they said, to have *received the spirit of bondage to fear*: They were children and heirs, but lived under the yoke and service of the ceremonial law, like a child under the custody of a schoolmaster, or tutor. Against this the faithful and Christians, in the New Testament, have received *the spirit of adoption*, in order to show unto God a willing obedience, not by the terror and threatening of the law, but by the preaching of the gospel, which encourages our hearts to serve the living God, in joy *without fear*. Therefore is the church of the New Testament called *free*, in comparison to the *Jewish* church, which was under bondage, and therefore called, *the bondwoman:* by which we can see, that this liberty is rightly called, *a Christian liberty*, since it is proper to the Christians, and is used by them alone. Here falls now under our consideration the first part of my discourse, which is.

I. Who has made us free.

Of this, the apostle says, *Christ has made us free.* *Cyrus* king of *Persia,* made the children of *Israel* free from the *Babylonian* captivity, but Jesus Christ has made us free from the captivity of Satan, therefore he came into the world under the form of a servant, that he, by his birth, living, suffering and death should, confound the kingdom of Satan, and *bring out the prisoners from the prison, and them that sat in darkness out of the prison-house,* and procure us our liberty again: Though the Father and the Holy Spirit must not be excluded from this work. The Father sent forth his Son to redeem them that were under the law: The Son took on the form of a servant, in order to make us free, *for he that is called in the Lord, being a Servant, is the Lord's free-man; likewise also, he that is called being free, is Christ's servant.* The Holy Spirit is *not a spirit of bondage, but a Spirit of Adoption,* who assures the faithful of their liberty, for *where the Spirit of the Lord is, there is liberty.* But since God acts nothing with us without means, but by means, so has he ordained the ministerial office, which is called, *the ministration of the Spirit,* wherein he offers unto us the means of obtaining this liberty; and which means are both outward and inward.

The outward means are, 1st, The word and the gospel, which is the word of truth preached by Christ himself: God lets this liberty be proclaimed and offered to all who will receive and enjoy the same in his word and gospel; and therefore is the preaching of the gospel called in the Scripture, *the proclaiming of liberty to the captives, and the opening of the prison to them that are bound.* As in the Old Testament, when the trumpets of the Jubilee did sound, then did everyone return again to their properties, all debts were quitted, and all servants made free: So God proclaims by the sound of the gospel, liberty from the spiritual bondage under Satan, and the remission of sins. 2ndly,

435

The sacraments. In the baptism we receive first, entrance into this liberty, and become *fellow citizens with the saints, and of the household of God:* In the Lord's Supper we are assured of this freedom, for since he has procured us the same with his death and suffering, and we are made partakers of his body and blood in the Lord's Supper, then we have therein a strong confirmation upon our spiritual liberty, which we receive by,

The inward means, namely, faith: For *by faith we have access into the grace of God; by faith we become sons of God,* and they who are sons of God, are free: Therefore St. Paul says, *the law of the Spirit of Life,* (that is, the gospel of Jesus Christ, wherein is life and spirit, and which I embrace by faith,) *has made me free from the law of sin and death,* that is, has placed me in such liberty, that sin and death has no more power over me.

Thereof follows, that the spiritual or Christian liberty, is used alone rightly by the faithful, and none else. Christ has made all free from the curse of the law, the service and bondage of sin, and the tyranny of Satan; but none becomes partaker thereof, except the faithful, who will receive and embrace the same. As when a king, or any mighty lord publicly proclaims for his subjects, that they shall have such and such privileges, under condition, that they should seek for them according to the prescription of the king; so God lets this liberty be offered to men, but under that condition, that they should believe. The unbelievers boast likewise of, that the spiritual liberty belongs to them; but as long as they remain in their unbelief, they have no more benefit thereof, than a stranger has benefit of another's privileges, which he can read, but to no advantage. What benefit had the *Jews* in having *Abraham* for their father, and for his sake attributed to themselves great privileges by the adoption, the covenant, the giving of the law, and the promises? Nothing at all; because they had not *Abraham's* faith, much less shewed their faith

436

in their works. The liberties, which a faithful receives, are as *a garden enclosed*, wherein no stranger can come to gather the flowers, but the children of the house; but when an unbeliever is converted, he is not longer a stranger, but a child. *Ishmael* was the son of the bond woman, and had no right to the heirship and family of *Abraham*; therefore said *Sarah, cast out this bond woman and her son*. The unbelievers are not God's children, therefore do they not belong to the household of God; and shall receive at the Day of Judgment this sentence, *cast the unprofitable servants out into outer darkness, there shall be weeping and gnashing of teeth*.

II. Where from we are made free.

Let us now hear, what liberties Christ has procured for us, and wherein they consist. We can conclude by the nature of Christ's kingdom, how the liberties are: for since the Kingdom of Christ is spiritual, so must the liberties of the same kingdom, be likewise spiritual; and consist in these two parts, 1. A deliverance from what is evil. 2. A right and liberty to what is good.

1. Concerning the deliverance from what is evil. The evil where-from Christ has made us free, are,

First, the service of sin. *Being made free from sin, we are become servants to God:* For although *sin* is, and *dwells in us*, yet is the same forgiven through faith in Jesus Christ. Neither reigns the same in us, but is mortified more and more daily by the grace of regeneration, until it is entirely taken away in the hour of our death: Therefore, as Christ died once for sin, but lives afterwards unto God, so should we likewise be dead to sin, and live in Jesus Christ our Lord. Where man is dead from sin, there lives man unto God in Christ; Where man lives unto God in Christ, there man lets the Holy Spirit govern: And where the Spirit of God is, there is liberty.

Secondly, temporal death. Although *it is appointed to men to die*, either faithful or not, yet the death of the faithful is not a punishment for sin, but an end of all temporal calamities, a dissolution from all hard yokes, an entrance to life, and a door to eternal rest: In the mean while, the body is laid in the grave, till the coming of Christ to judgment; then shall it be raised up again with honor, and be crowned with immortality, and death shall then be destroyed.

Thirdly, the eternal death. Since Christ has made us free from sin, and has made death to naught; so has he also made us free from the eternal death, because the same is the wages of sin. By St. *John* the Divine, says the Lord, *He that overcomes, shall not be hurt with the second death.*

Fourthly, the tyranny and power of Satan. *He works with power in the children of disobedience*; but against the faithful and elect he cannot prevail, any more than him who has nothing in Christ. He has also nothing in them that by Christ are made sons of God: He can tempt us, and he walks about as a roaring lion; but in Christ we can bruise him under our feet.

Fifthly, the curse of the law. The law of God requires a perfect obedience of us, if we will be justified thereby before God, and obtain the eternal life, and be free from the curse pronounced against them that do not keep the law. But Christ has made us free from the force of the law to obedience, *for he is the end of the law for righteousness to everyone that believes*; and also from the punishment of the law to damnation. So says the apostle *Paul, Christ has redeemed us from the curse of the law, being made a curse for us*; though the law is not taken away, as is shewed in a former discourse.

Sixthly, the *Jewish* ceremonial and political law. All the *Levitical* ceremonies were figures to Christ, and are now, since the incarnation of Christ, of no signification; therefore it was concluded in the apostolic synod held at *Jerusalem*, not *to put a yoke upon the neck of the disciples*. The apostle *Paul* when he saw, that some thought the circumcision needful, because he had circumcised *Timothy* on account of some *Jews*, to whom he was to preach, says, *Behold, I Paul say unto you, that, if you be circumcised, Christ shall profit you nothing: For I testify again to every man, that is circumcised, that he is a debtor to do the whole law.*

Seventhly, the yoke of human commandments. Hereby is not meant the commands of our magistrates, and them that are in authority over us, founded upon justice and equity, for them we are obliged to obey; but such commandments, that are neither commanded nor forbidden in the word of God, which everyone, without a check in his conscience, can omit or commit, according to his own choice and pleasure; and they are called middle things, consisting either in general concerning men's living; or in particular, concerning our worship in the Church.

1. Middle things concerning men's living, are the things, that in themselves are neither good nor bad, and men can use well or evil; as, eating, drinking, clothing, matrimony, single life, and all other such like transactions; these things we can use, or not, without check of conscience, according to our own choice and pleasure: But the abuse of the same will become a sin, therefore we must be careful how we use the gifts of God, that the things which are given us as a blessing, do not become our damnation. Therefore says St. *Paul, every creature of God is good, and nothing to be refused, if it be received with thanksgiving.*

2. Middle things concerning our worship in the church are certain church ceremonies, neither commanded nor forbidden in the word of God, but used partly for order and decency sake, partly for edification, and can be used without check of conscience as long as until men imagine that they are part of religion, and absolutely needful; and

as if the true worship could not be without them. Such church ceremonies are with us, the confession and absolution, the sign of the cross, and Godfathers and Godmothers in baptism, certain evangelical and apostolical texts every Sunday, several holy days and fasting days, the surplice, the Communion table, the kneeling at the Lord's Supper, the administration of the Lord's Supper with unleavened bread, organs, ringing and tolling with the bell, and images or pictures: Such and other such like church ceremonies can be used or left off, according as it is thought proper, though not according to the fancy of everyone, but alone according to the command of the magistrates, with advice of the clergy as we can see of the examples of *Joshua, David, Hezekiah*, and others; neither must they be left off on account of the fancy of opposers. In regard to this says the apostle *Paul, neither* Titus, *who was with me, being a* Greek *was compelled to be circumcised: And that because of false brethren unawares brought in, who came in privily to spy out our liberty, which we have in Christ Jesus, that they might bring us into bondage: To whom we gave place by subjection, no not for an hour that the truth of the gospel might continue with you.*

III. How we should stand fast in our liberty.

Even in persecution we should not give place to the enemies of our Christian religion and liberties, but we must stand fast. The children of *Israel* acted foolish, in that they wanted to go back to *Egypt*, after they were made free, and brought out of the house of bondage. When we are once made free, then must we *not entangle ourselves again with the yoke of bondage*, wherefrom we are made free, but *stand fast in our liberty.*

This Christian liberty we should not use to *Epicurian* liberty: As if we could and might live according to the desires and lusts of our own flesh and blood, as the men did before the sin-flood, in the time of *Noah*; or as them of *Sodom*, in the time of *Lot*, who did alone seek their temporal and carnal satisfaction and lust. Neither should the Christian liberty be used to a libertinish liberty, consisting in, that they foolishly imagine, or rather maliciously and wickedly conceit, that nothing, of what kind or nature whatsoever, is evil and sinful of itself; but alone because men imagine them to be sinful: Such liberty profits nothing, and can better be called, a yoke and bondage, because they serve their own lusts and imaginations: But the true Christian liberty consists in the following articles,

1. That men serve and worship God in holiness and righteousness, obey his commands, is guided by the Spirit of God, for *where the Spirit of the Lord is, there is liberty.* He that worships God, has heaven for his treasury, God for his treasurer, the angels for his ministers and waiters, and the creatures for his servants. He that serves God, has right and liberty to all the treasures of God's grace, like a king's favorite, has free liberty to go over all the riches of his Lord: He can *come boldly unto the throne of grace, that he may obtain mercy, and find grace to help in time of need.* He has liberty to use all the creatures of God with a good conscience, for the faithful are *the heirs of the world*, and he has *boldness to enter into the holiest by the blood of Jesus.* Satan comes with his temptations, our flesh and blood with their allurements, the world with its persecutions, and our conscience with its desperations, and will deceive us; yet let us *stand fast in the liberty, wherewith Christ has made us free, and be not entangled again with the yoke of bondage.* The procuring of this liberty did cost our Savior his precious blood; let us therefore put a great value thereon, and not use the same, *for an occasion to the flesh*, as them who *while they promise them liberty, they themselves are the servants of corruption.* He who is begifted of a king with certain privileges, is always careful,

that his privileges and liberty should not be corrupted in the least; much more should a faithful child of God, *stand fast in the liberty wherewith Christ hath made himself free*, from Satan, the world, and his own sinful flesh and blood.

2. That we do nothing, whereon our conscience doubts, or against our own mind. When we do a thing, whereon we doubt, either to be right or not, that is sin, for *what is not of faith, is sin:* Therefore should we be fully assured in our mind, that a thing is allowed, before we do the same, and when we are not ourselves convinced thereof, than may we take the advice of another, who is better instructed therein.

3. That we do not use our Christian liberty to the offence of them of little faith. Love should rule our actions. God has forbidden, to curse the deaf, and to put stumbling blocks before the blind. We also should neither use our liberty in the presence of them who are offended thereover. The apostle *Paul* says, *all things are lawful for me, but all things are not expedient; all things are lawful for me, but all things edify not. It is good, neither to eat flesh, nor to drink wine, nor anything by which your brother stumbles, or is offended, or is made weak. wherefore, if meat make my brother to offend, I will eat no flesh while the world stands, lest I make my brother to offend.* The meaning of the apostle, we can see by the foregoing, when he says, That he dares himself to eat meat: But if he did perceive, that a brother, who had knowledge, and was scrupulous thereover, should thereby be obliged to eat against his conscience of the meat in the idol's temple, where he might find *Paul* eating, then would he rather let it alone, than cause his brother to offend. In such cases we should, through Christian love, resist from our liberty, and act so that our brother should not be offended.

4. That we should not give place by subjection to the enemies in anything: that they should not be confirmed and strengthened in their false opinions and constructions, and take thereby opportunity

to boast, that their opinion is the best, and most consistent with the Scripture. Therefore admonishes the apostle *Paul, be you not unequally yoked together with unbelievers.* What is it to be yoked together with unbelievers, but to consent to their wrong opinion and conceit. Therefore would he not give place by subjection to the false brethren, who came in privily to spy out the liberty of the Christians. *Moses* stood so much upon the liberty of the children of *Israel*, that he would not that there should be one hoof left behind. The prophet *Daniel* would not pray in private, but his *windows being open in his chamber towards* Jerusalem, *he kneeled upon his knees three times a day, and prayed*; that it should not seem, as if he gave place to his opposers and enemies.

Since then God has been so gracious, and has sent his Son, who has made us free from sin, death, Satan and hell, that we should serve him in holiness and righteousness all the days of our life, let us then pray to this bountiful God, that he will let his Holy Spirit guide us, so that we can stand fast in the liberty wherewith Christ has made us free, *and do nothing, but what is acceptable in the sight of God, and to our own salvation, until we obtain the heavenly and eternal liberty in his glorious kingdom.* AMEN.

31

Affliction

T he text, 2 CORINTHIANS 4:17, 18. ver.

Our light afflictions, which is but for a moment, works for us a far more exceeding and eternal weight of glory: While we look not on the things which are seen, but at the things which are not seen; for the things which are seen are temporal, but the things which are not seen, are eternal.

INTRODUCTION

WITH trouble man climbs to a high place, and with difficulty man comes to glory: The Kingdom of Heaven is compared in the word of God to a great city, and a royal palace built upon a high mountain, whereto is a difficult assent, full grown with thorns. Our Savior says thereof, *Straight is the gate, and narrow is the way, which leads unto life, and few there be that find it.* The apostles knew this full well, and therefore did confirm the souls of the disciples, and exhorted them to continue in the faith, for *we must through much tribulation enter into the Kingdom of God,* as the Spirit of God says, *Acts 14* chapter, 22 verse. In these words is described, 1. The difficulty of the way in many tribulations. And, 2. The glory of the mark in the Kingdom of God.

1. The difficulty of the way in many tribulations. Human life is compared in the Scripture, *by a way:* For as he, who walks upon a way comes farther and farther forth, and his way becomes shorter and shorter; so do we go forth daily upon the way of our Life, and come nearer and nearer to the mark: As soon as we enter into life, we begin to go out again, he that walks upon a way, leaves everything behind; *We brought nothing into this world, and it is certain we can carry nothing out.* Every way has its mark, wherefrom, and whereto; so our life hath its marks from our mother's womb unto our grave: He that walks on a way is in continual danger, first with the badness of the way under foot, then with storm and rain over head; so is our life full of labor and sorrow, outward strife, inward terror, tribulation in the body, tribulation in the soul: Who can sum up all the tribulations, which we must undergo? In particular the best children of God suffer the greatest afflictions. *We,* says the apostle, of himself and other faithful, *must through much tribulation enter into the Kingdom of God.* O could we rightly understand that affliction is a token of God's love, and the true color wherewith God marks his own; we should then endeavor to take hold thereof with both hands, and say with the apostle *Paul, We glory in tribulations.* Overlook the examples of the saints, and you shall find that none of them entered into the Kingdom of God without tribulation; for God proved them, and found them worthy for himself; as gold in the furnace has he tried them, and received them as burnt offerings. Who will then shrink away for this, wherewith the children of God have been tried? Since *we must through much tribulation enter into the Kingdom of God, many are the afflictions of the righteous.* It cannot be otherwise in regard to,

First, the will and ordination of God. God has not ordained any other way, wherethrough his children must enter into his heavenly

445

kingdom, than by afflictions and tribulation: In like manner there was no other way for the children of *Israel* to the promised land, than through the wilderness. Not that the Lord is pleased in troubling of men, but because that he is delighted in the patience of the children of men, just as a father is pleased with his child under his fatherly correction. In regard to this *Solomon* says, *Whom the Lord loves, he corrects, even as a father the son, in whom he delights.*

Secondly, the trial of our faith. When we try an earthen vessel, whether it is empty or full, whole or cracked, then we do knock on the same: When God knocks on men, who is compared with an earthen vessel, with the hammer of affliction, then can it be perceived whether they are full of the knowledge of God and Christian virtues, or not.

Thirdly, our own purification. Our Savior says, *Every branch that bears fruit, my Father purges it, that it may bring forth more fruit.* This purging is done with affliction. This comparison is taken of the vines, which are trimmed, and purged from dead limbs and branches, in order to make the same fruitful.

Fourthly, the likeness of the image of Christ. As our Savior says of his own sufferings, *Ought not Christ to have suffered these things, and to enter into his glory:* So may we say of afflictions? Ought we not to suffer them, since *we must through much tribulation enter into the Kingdom of God.* When a traveler has finished his journey, then does he forget all his troubles: The tribulations of God's children, shall also end in joy, their fighting in victory, and their affliction in a glorious crown: which is.

2. The glory of the mark in the Kingdom of God, whereunto they shall enter. Affliction is as a golden ladder, whereon we, through the merits of Christ, and the power of the Holy Spirit, can climb up to heaven, and enter into the Kingdom of God. Though we must not apprehend this also, as that affliction is the effecting cause

of our salvation, or that men do deserve the Kingdom of Heaven, by and through his patience in affliction: No, but when we have endured faithfully and patiently unto our lives-end; then do we become thereupon, and not thereby saved. He that will be crowned with honor and glory in the Kingdom of God, must endure patiently, fight and conquer manly here on earth. Hereof assures the Spirit of God, all them who are under affliction in the words of our text, whereof we will behold these two following heads, namely,

FIRST, *What affliction is under its several names.*

SECOND, *What Profit we have thereof.*

EXPLANATION of the TEXT

I. What affliction is under its several names.

Affliction is called in the Holy Scripture by several names, as,

1. *A cross*, in regard to the cross of Christ. That as Christ bore his own cross; so must likewise all his followers bear theirs: This name is a glorious comfort under affliction. Is it a great honor for a servant to have his Lord's gold chain round his neck? Then is it a greater honor for a Christian to bear the cross after Christ. Had *Simon*, of *Cyrene*, rightly known the condemned man who went before him, there would have been no occasion of forcing him to bear the cross of Christ.

2. *The yoke of Christ.* Our Savior says, *Take my yoke upon you:* This is a comparison taken of oxen yoked in a plough: The farmer yokes his oxen in order to try them, if they are strong and willing to work; God puts this yoke of Christ on his children, for to try how they are inclined, and if they will cleave to him, and not let any tribulation separate them from him. The oxen is made came under the yoke, and kept in the furrows; God tames his children under Christ's yoke, and

keeps them within the bounds of piety and charity. Therefore says the *Psalmist, It is good for me, that I have been afflicted, that I might learn your statutes.* The oxen is not always in the yoke, but is taken out and foddered; God lets his children suffer under Christ's yoke, but at last they shall be relieved, *that they may rest from their labor,* if the ox knew how he must labor and be beaten, he would not stand and be yoked so willingly: If a child of God had not better to expect under Christ's yoke than the same, then would he despair. *If in this life only we have hope in Christ, we are of all men most miserable:* But now we expect some thing better, namely the eternal joy, which no sorrow shall take from us. In regard to this our Savior calls, *his yoke easy, and his burden light*; in comparison to the wrath of God, and the burden of the eternal punishment, wherefrom Christ has made us free, and of the great joy, which shall follow thereupon. What is a temporal cross to the eternal joy? No more than a drop of water against the ocean, and a grain of sand against the whole globe.

3. *A Sea.* The prophet *Zachariah* says, *He shall pass through the sea with affliction:* The sea is bad tasting; Affliction is also for flesh and blood. The sea is deep, in some places bottomless, and in some places full of mire: Affliction brings us often in great perils, temptations and grief, so that men must cry out with the *Psalmist, Save me O God, for the waters are come in unto my soul, I sink in the deep mire, where there is no standing.* On the sea blows several and all sorts of wind; in afflictions arises the temptations of Satan, the reproach of men, and their wrong censures, and men's own doubtful thoughts, as *Peter, who began to sink.*

4. *A cup.* The *Psalmist* says, *In the hand of the Lord there is a cup.* This name brings to our remembrance, the forbearance of affliction: A cup is a small vessel, and can be soon emptied; Affliction is not eternal, *but for a moment,* or *a little while. Weeping may endure for a night, but joy comes in the morning. In a little wrath I hid my face from*

you for a moment, but with everlasting kindness I will have mercy on you, says the Lord your Redeemer. Of this name we can remember the certain measure of affliction, in a cup a certain portion goes, whereof everyone gets his part; a child drinks not so much as a man. God gives affliction according to strength, for *he chastened sore, but gives not over unto death*; as, *the fitchess are not threshed with a threshing instrument, neither a cart wheel turned about upon the cummin; but the fitches are beaten out with a staff, and the cummin with a rod:* Likewise *God will not suffer us to be tempted above that we are able to bear.* We can likewise remember the worth: When the Lord of the house stretches out the cup, then must the children drink first, and afterwards the servant: For *the judgment must begin at the house of God.* The beloved Son of God was obliged himself to drink this cup, and has thereby sanctified the same for his brothers and sisters, who must drink after him.

5. *Bitterness and wormwood.* So says the prophet *Jeremiah* in his *Lamentations, He has filled me with bitterness, he has made me drunk with wormwood.* Wormwood is bitter to the palate, affliction is also for flesh and blood: Wormwood purges the bad humors of our bodies; Affliction cleanses the soul from all filthy desires and sin. After the children of *Israel* had been three days in the wilderness, they came to *Marah,* where they found bitter water, and could therefore not drink it; wherefore the Lord showed *Moses* a tree, which when he had cast into the waters, the waters were made sweet. We are not three days old in the world, before we come to the bitter waters of *Marab:* But a true faith is the *Moses,* who casts the Tree of Life, Jesus Christ, into these bitter waters, by which they become sweet.

6. *A Furnace,* so faith the prophet *Isaiah, I have chosen you in the furnace of afflictions.* God has two furnaces, in the one he casts the gold, and in the other the skim. The furnace wherein he casts the skim, is hell, which is called, a *furnace of fire:* The furnace wherein

he casts the gold, is affliction; that as *the fining pot is for silver, and the furnace for gold:* So tries the Lord, men's heart by afflictions, not because he does know them without, but alone to make them public for others.

7. *Chastening.* Of this faith St. *Paul, my son, despise not the chastisement of the Lord, nor saint when you are rebuked of him. For whom the Lord loves he chastens, and scourges every son whom be receives. If you endure chastening, God deals with you as with sons: For what son is he whom the father chastens not? But if you are without chastisement, whereof all are partakers, then are you illegitimate and not sons. Furthermore, we have had fathers of our flesh, which corrected us, and we gave them reverence: Shall we not much rather be in subjection unto the Father of spirits and live? For they verily for a few days chastened us after their own pleasure; but he for our profit, that we might he partakers of his holiness.* In these words lay concealed, two weighty conclusions, why we should patiently receive afflictions. The *first* is, that God has the right to chasten and rebuke his own, since they are not without sin; for where sin is, there is also the punishment for sin. The *second* is, That we should not despair, nor saint away under affliction, since we are thereby assured of the love of God: This is explained with a comparison taken from earthly fathers and their children.

8. *A tempest.* Of this says the prophet *Isaiah, Oh you afflicted, tossed with tempest.* Tempest comes from the Lord, who *raises the stormy winds.* Affliction comes likewise from God. *I form the light, and create darkness, I make peace, and create evil, I the Lord do all these things. Who is he that says, and it comes to pass, when the Lord commands it not? Out of the mouth of the Most High proceeds not evil and good?* God permits some times the Devil, the world, and the corrupted flesh, to afflict his children. Who does not know how Satan afflicted *Job* with the permission of God? *Satan desired to have* Peter, *that he*

might sift him as wheat. The apostle *Paul* speaks of the *fiery darts,* and the *buffets* of Satan. The world is compared by a *sea,* where storm and tempest arise; so do the children of the world occasion much tribulation and affliction to the children of God, *He that was born after the flesh, persecuted him that was born after the Spirit, even so it is now.* The sea is unconstant, first calm then foaming; likewise is the world and her children. The countenance that smiles at us today, will turn and frown tomorrow. Our own corrupted flesh and blood raise likewise many storms against us. The flesh desires against the spirit, and the spirit against the flesh, and *the fleshly lusts war against the soul.* The storm and tempest blows as well on the royal palaces as on cottages; the poor must not alone, but likewise the high and mighty, suffer crosses and affliction: After a great tempest, follow always a great calm; likewise shall there be an end of affliction, if not here, yet hereafter in eternal joy.

When the apostle says in our text, *our affliction,* then makes he thereby difference between the affliction of the godly, and ungodly. The affliction of the faithful proceed from God's love, but that of the unbelievers from his justice and vengeance; and therefore is the affliction of the faithful called, a *chastisement and a trial;* but that of the unbelievers are called, *a plague and punishment.* God mixes his justice and mercy together in the affliction of the faithful. *He retains not his anger forever, because he delights in mercy.* On the ungodly, God sheds out his wrath, for they shall drink the dregs. By the faithful God is present as a loving helper in their afflictions; but by the ungodly, he is as a severe revenger: The faithful are patient in afflictions, saying with the prophet *Micah, I will hear the indignation of the Lord, because I have sinned against him.* The ungodly *murmur, and hearken not unto the voice of the Lord.* The affliction of the faithful is received by them as a fatherly correction, by which God will show them their transgressions; but the ungodly receive the same with obstinacy of heart: wherefore the Lord said of them, *Why should you be striken anymore? you will revolt more and more.* The affliction of the faithful is but for a moment, and shall end in eternal joy; but the affliction of the ungodly and impenitent shall be continually, and end in eternal misery in the furnace of fire.

All the names wherewith affliction is called in the Scripture, can be brought under these four denominations, First, *cross of ransom.* Second, *cross of martyrdom.* Third, *cross of punishment. And* fourth, *cross of trial.*

First, *cross of ransom,* is the painful sufferings of our Lord and Savior Jesus Christ, which he suffered and underwent for the sake of our transgressions, and thereby became a full and satisfactory ransom for the same, and the punishment thereof. None has born this cross but Christ, neither could any other bear the same than he; for therefor was he sent into the world, and took on the form of a servant. In regard to this the prophet *Isaiah* says in his prophecy of Christ, *I have trodden the wine press alone, and of the people there was none with me.*

Second, *cross of martyrdom;* that is, the sufferings of the holy martyrs, which they underwent for the confession of Christ's name. St. *Stephen* is the first on this list, and was afterwards followed by the apostles, and many others both men and women, who were all slain upon the earth for the name of Christ, and the truth of the gospel. It might seem for human thoughts, that the death and sufferings of the martyrs was as painful as that of Christ: But there is as great difference between both, as there is between heaven and earth, light and dark; for the death of Christ was a perfect atonement for the sins of the world, and the martyrs could not satisfy even for the least of their own sins. Christ did feel in his sufferings, the wrath of God, and the terror of hell; the holy martyrs did feel the co-operating power of the Holy Spirit: Christ became in his death a curse for us;

452

the holy martyrs were blessed in their death for Christ's sake: Christ did wrestle with the eternal death; the holy martyrs alone with the temporal.

Third, cross of punishment. When God punishes in his justice either one or another in particular, or else whole countries or kingdoms in general, when they will not repent and be converted; so were the angels who fell, plunged into hell; so was the first world drowned with the sin-flood; so was *Sodom* and *Gomorrah* consumed with brimstone and fire from heaven; so are kingdoms and countries infested with plague, war, tempest, tyranny, famine, and many other calamities, which befalls the ungodly and godly: But all things works good unto them that fear God.

Fourth, cross of trial, when God tries us: Of this says the *Psalmist, You O God have proved us, you have tried us as silver is tried.* This cross or affliction befalls commonly the innocent, not in their person which becomes Christ alone, but in their causes.

Of this cross of trial speaks the apostle in our text, saying, *our light affliction, which is but for a moment.* And describes also affliction by two things. 1st, Of the lightness. 2nd, Of the shortness.

1st, of the lightness. It is an affliction, not a hellish pain, as *dives* suffered. God favors us with many glad hours in the midst of affliction, *I take pleasure,* says the apostle *Paul, in infirmities, in reproaches, in necessities, in persecution, in distresses for Christ's Sake,* God will not let his children bear the crosses alone, but he helps them. The apostles were scourged, and beaten for Christ's name sake, but they rejoiced thereover. St. *Stephen* was stoned, but his soul was rejoiced, and desired to be by Christ, whom *he saw sitting on the right hand of God.*

2nd, of the shortness: It is *but for a moment.* Affliction has its sting, it has likewise wings: Therefore the prophet *Isaiah* says, *sorrow and sighing shall flee away.*

The affliction of God's children, is of little duration in comparison to our time, the time of others, and the time to come.

In comparison to our own time: What is our own time? We reckon the same by years, months, weeks, days and hours, yet the Spirit of the Lord puts such little value thereon, and calls the same *nothing*. It goes with us under affliction, as with a child in school, who thinks the time very long; for they do not consider, that it is for their own benefit, and have therefore always their eyes and ears by the clock, longing for the time, when they shall have their freedom again; and they are the more discontented, since it is a daily work: But when they live and become men, and have the benefit of their learning and school, then they are of opinion, that their school-time was too short. We also are under affliction,

In comparison to the time of others. The time of others is likewise short. We see some suffer one, two or more years: what is that to be compared to the woman with the bloody issue, who was afflicted twelve years, another who was cripple eighteen years, another who laid thirty-eight years on his bed, and him who was cripple more than forty years: And when we also consider our affliction, and compare the same against others, we shall find that *our affliction is* according to the saying of the apostle here in our text, *but for a moment.*

In comparison to the time to come, or properly said, eternity, this hath no end. *A thousand years in the sight of the Lord are but as yesterday.* Sirach says, *As a drop of water into the sea, and a gravelstone in comparison of the sand*; so are a thousand years to the days of eternity. What is a man's age and the afflictions thereof in comparison to the eternal happiness, which God has promised unto the faithful? Who will then complain of this temporal light affliction which is but for a moment, since *eye has not seen, nor ear heard, neither have entered into the heart of men, the things, which God has prepared for them that love him?*

The affliction of God's children is light, in regard to the faithfulness of God, the power of Christ's cross, and the pains of hell.

God is faithful who will not suffer you to be tempted above that you are able, but will with the temptation also make a way to escape, that you may be able to bear it. Therefore as a patient undergoes patiently, all the operations of a surgeon, in expectation of his former health, since he is convinced, that it is done for his best; also is a child of God patient in affliction, knowing that they come from God, who wills him well; and in consideration hereof, is affliction light.

By the power of Christ's cross is the affliction of God's children consecrated and sanctified, so that the same cannot hurt, but profit them, and is to their honor and glory; and when we consider this, then will our affliction become light.

Temporal affliction is in comparison to the pains of hell, as the sting or prick of a needle unto a mortal wound. What is the temporal fire unto the fire of hell? What is the affliction of the body to be compared to the trouble of soul and conscience? Every fiftieth year was a Jubilee year with the *Jews*, when all captives, slaves and debtors, went to their properties, and became free; but there will never come a time for them who are in hell, to be delivered: When we consider this, we shall find, that it is better to suffer here in time, than hereafter in eternity.

When the apostle calls, *affliction light, and for a moment*; he would thereby encourage us to patience in sufferings. We suffer willingly what is light and easy and of a short duration in expectation of a good alteration, or at least an end: Patience is a humble subjection to the will of God, by which we suffer with constancy all what the Lord lays upon us. We can become a martyr without fire and sword, but not without patience: Patience beholds the end of tribulation, and says with *Job, All the days of my appointed time will I wait, till my change comes.* Faith assures us and says, *God will surely come, he will not tarry*; Patience says, I will wait for that time: Faith says, *rest in the Lord, and wait patiently for him:* Whereupon patience answers, *Therefore will the Lord wait, that he may be gracious unto you: Blessed are all they that wait for him.* Faith and patience go hand in hand as two sisters: Faith beholds the eternal glory; Patience waits for the same. This brings me to the second part, namely,

II. What profit we have by affliction.

Our text says, *Our light affliction, which is but for a moment, works for us a far more exceeding and eternal weight of glory.* None must conclude from this, that we can earn or deserve heaven, and the heavenly glory, with our affliction: For although it was possible that a man could suffer all the plagues and afflictions that are in the world, yet he could not deserve thereby any temporal blessings, much less the eternal heavenly glory. But the apostle has regard to the conclusion of God, which is this, that God will not that his children should enter into his heavenly kingdom through any other way, than through crosses and affliction: Men suffers now patiently, lives after the will of God, and cleaves to his promises, (that upon pain shall follow the eternal crown, and upon tears, joy:) So God will perfect his conclusion, that affliction works for the children of God, *a far more exceeding and eternal weight of glory.* This glory is described here by weighty qualifications.

1. By its excellency, since it is called, *exceeding Glory:* Glory is a royal glory, as King. *Solomon* had, or the clearness of the angels; and likewise the godly clearness is called *glory:* Such glory shall God's children receive after this life, when they have conquered all their afflictions and tribulations, according to the promise of our Savior, who faith, *Father, I will that they also whom you have given me, be with*

me where I am, that they may behold my glory, which you have given me: St. John the Divine saw this in a vision, when he *beheld a great multitude, standing before the throne, and before the Lamb, and clothed with white robes, and palms in their hands;* and when he was asked, *who are these which are arrayed in white robes?* Then he answered that he did not know: Whereupon one of the elders said to him, *These are they which came out of great tribulation, and have washed their robes, and made them white in the blood of the Lamb: Therefore are they before the throne of God, and serve him day and night in his temple.* This glory is so great, that the apostle cannot find words to express himself, and therefore calls the same, *A far more exceeding and eternal weight of glory.* The words *far more exceeding,* comprehends a comparison taken of a vender, where one exceeds the other in bidding, until it is raised to a sum: Likewise it is with the heavenly glory, it comes from a mean origin, namely, affliction, but ends in glory everlasting: and it it impossible for human reason, to form any true idea thereof; as we can see by the declaration of the apostle *Paul, That eye has not seen, nor ear heard, neither have entered into the thoughts of men, the things which God has prepared for them that love him.*

2. By eternity. Eternal is long, but long is not eternal, as the old fathers have said. We can imagine some things in our thoughts concerning eternity, but we can never apprehend, much less describe the same: We may call it a bottomless pit, wherein all times and seasons, and even our own thoughts are swallowed up. If we would undertake and could count the drops in the sea, the grains of sand in the globe, and the sun beams in the air, there would once be an end thereof; but of eternity there is no end: It is for the godly, a day without night; but for the ungodly, a night without day. What is now temporal affliction to be compared hereto.

3. By its weight. Weighty is a thing called so, which is heavy in its weight: When the king of *Babylon* had taken *Jerusalem,* he defaced

457

the city, and took away all the vessels out of the temple, and carried them to *Babylon, and the brass of the vessels was without weight*; not because they could not weigh it, but that they would not spend so much time and labor thereon. Would we try to weigh up the temporal affliction against the eternal glory, we would find it impossible; and if such could even be performed, we would find the weight of all temporal afflictions, not to be compared to the weight of the eternal glory; so that we might rightly say thereof, as the prophet *Daniel* said of king *Belshazzar, You are weighed in the balances, and are found wanting:* God who *weighed the mountains in scales, and the hills in a balance*, laid once the sins and transgressions of the whole world in the one scale of his justice, and in the other he laid his beloved Son Jesus Christ, and his meritorious death, and found also the former overweighed by the latter: Christ has also procured the eternal glory to all them who, in a true faith, will embrace him.

But that there should no thoughts be made of any deceit herein, as it often happens in temporal weights and balances, therefore said the apostle in our text, *That we shall look not on the things which are seen, but at the things which are not seen; for the things which are seen are temporal, but the things which are not seen are eternal.* When a marksman would fire and hit a mark, then must he have first a true sight of the mark he is to aim at; so would the apostle say, That in all our afflictions we should aim at, and endeavor to obtain the right mark.

What mark is this? The eternal glory; of which faith the same apostle *Paul*, in another place, *I press towards the mark:* For to obtain this mark has the bountiful God ordained gracious means, and all they who use the same, shall obtain this mark of eternal glory; but they who either abuse, or willfully refuse the same, shall obtain the mark of eternal misery.

The children of the world have their mark, whereat they aim, namely, riches, and worldly glory and honor, so that their cellars and granaries are full, affording all manner of store; and after they have obtained their aim, they account themselves happy: But it goes with them, as with a pur-blind, who cannot see well, except a thing is placed near him, that the same can represent great; the children of this world look always also at the temporal things, and forget thereby the eternal; but the children of God, look not on the temporal things which are seen, but on the eternal which are not seen. Faith has its eyes, wherewith it beholds the invisible and absent things as present, wherefore the apostle *Paul* calls the same, *the substance of things hoped for, and the evidence of things not seen.* *Abraham* saw the days of Christ, not with his bodily eyes, but with the eyes of his faith, as Christ himself testifies of him: *Moses* would not accept the treasures of *Egypt* but by faith had respect unto the recompense of the reward, and therefore *chose rather to suffer afflictions with the children of God, than to enjoy the pleasures of sin for a season, esteeming the reproach of Christ, greater riches than the treasures in* Egypt. On such the children of God meditates always, and in their affliction always looks on this heavenly mark, that they may obtain the same; and are therefore patient, being assured that they shall receive a good end, and be crowned with glory everlasting.

Of this eternal glory, make us all, O God, partakers of grace for the merits of your beloved Son our Savior Jesus Christ. AMEN.

32

Civil Magistrates

T he text, ROMANS 13:1, 2, 3, 4, 5, 6, 7. verses.

Let every soul be subject unto the higher powers. For there is no power but of God: The powers that be, are ordained of God. Whosoever therefore resists the power, resists the ordinance of God: And they that resist, shall receive to themselves damnation. For rulers are not a terror to good works, but to evil: Will you then not be afraid of the power? Do that which is good, and you shall have praise of the same. For be is the minister of God to you for good: But if you do that which is evil, be afraid: For he bears not the sword in vain: For he is the minister of God, an avenger to execute wrath upon him that does evil. wherefore you must needs be subject not only for wrath, but also for conscience sake. For, for this cause pay you tribute also: For they are God's ministers attending continually upon this very thing. Render therefore to all their dues, tribute to whom tribute is due, custom to whom custom, fear to whom fear, honor to whom honor.

INTRODUCTION

IT was not without cause that the Lord chose a man, who was high and stately, to be king over his own people, the children of *Israel*. For we also do read in the first book of *Samuel*, the 10th chapter, 23rd verse, *Saul was higher than any of the people, from the shoulders and upwards*. The Lord shows in this example of the first king chosen by himself, 1. The stateliness, 2. The power, and, 3. The carefulness of this royal condition.

1. The Lord shows us the stateliness of this condition, that they are placed high, and above others; wherefore they are compared in the Scripture by *high trees, high hills*, and *lofty gates*. This stateliness proceeds from, and depends upon God's ordination: *Saul* being at first a person but of a private condition, was not looked upon in regard to his highness or stature, wherein he exceeded all the people; but when he was chosen by the command of God, then was the highness of his person looked upon. wherefore the prophet *Samuel* said to all the people, in the following verse, *See you him, whom the Lord has chosen, that there is none like him among all the people?* As long as *David* went after the sheep, he was not more looked at than another shepherd; but when *the Lord took him from the sheep-cote, from following the sheep, to be a ruler over* Israel, then received he *a great name, like unto the name of the great men, that are in the earth*. It is the Lord, who lays honor and glory upon kings, and takes the same away again when they depart, and are disobedient, as we can see by the examples of *Saul, Nebuchadnezzar*, and others. wherefore *Job* said, *The Lord looses the bond of Kings, and girds their loins with a girdle. He leads princes away spoiled, and overthrows the mighty. He powers contempt upon princes, and weakens the strength of the mighty*.

2. The Lord shows us here, the power of this condition. As soon as *Saul* was chosen and placed king over *Israel*, the Lord ordered and

commanded the prophet *Samuel*, to pronounce and declare unto the people, the right and privileges of the king, consisting therein, *He will take your sons, and appoint them for himself, for his chariots, and to be his horsemen; and some shall run before his chariots. And he will appoint them captains over thousands, and captains over fifties, and will set them to ear his ground, and to reap his harvest, and to make his instruments of war, and instruments of his chariots. And he will take your daughters to be his confectionaries, and to be cooks, and to be bakers: And you shall be his servants.* Hereof we can see the power attending the royal dignity in temporal cases; and concerning their power, in spiritual or ecclesiastical cases we have examples in the proceedings of king *David, Solomon, Jehoshaphat, Hezekiah*, and others more in the Scripture.

3. The Lord shows us the carefulness of this condition. He that is a head higher than others, can overlook them: The magistrates must be careful over the welfare of their country, and subjects, both rich and poor. If there was no magistrates, we could not be secure in our own houses, but it would go as is read of the children of *Israel*, in the book of *Judges; In those days there was no king in* Israel, *but every man did that which was right in his own eyes.* The apostle *Paul* speaks of worldly magistrates in the words of our text, and shows us therein,

FIRST, *Of whom they are.*

SECOND, *What profit we have of them.*

THIRD, *What their due is.*

EXPLANATION of the TEXT

I. The apostle shows us of whom the magistrates are.

Worldly magistracy, is a power and superiority which God has given unto certain persons in the world, that they, among men, should defend his honor, punish the wicked, and reward the good. To such persons are subjects obliged to render tribute, custom, fear, and honor, not only for wrath, but also for conscience sake, that peace and unity may continue in the community, in all godliness and honesty.

The apostle convinces us in the words of my text, that the magistrates *are ordained of God*, when he speaks,

First, of their high and exalted state, saying, *Let every soul be subject unto the higher powers.* Nature has instructed mankind, to put magistrates over themselves; for since man is created to sociable conversation, and cannot live alone, and where there is conversation, there order must be, without which no society could subsist in the world; therefore has man chosen such to be lords and rulers, whom they found to be endowed with wisdom, prudence, and stateliness above others: So that when the common and poor, were oppressed by the richer and more powerful, they have taken their refuge to some such prudent and stately man, who could protect them, and defend them in their rights. This natural order is afterwards placed by God, who is a God of order and decency, in an ampler and better regulation among men, who have a rational sense. Also the magistrates came to the government in the beginning, by either of these two ways, immediate, or mediate.

Immediate, or without means; as when God himself has placed anyone in the magisterial office and power; as we can see by the examples of *Moses, Joshua,* the judges, and afterwards the kings.

Mediate, or with means, either by election, succession, war, or power in subduing of others.

By election. When the highest magistrate ordains other magistrates, as king *Pharaoh* set *Joseph* to be ruler over *Egypt:* Or when the subjects, or their respective representatives, chooses one to be a head and ruler over the kingdom or government; as *Jephtah* was chosen by the elders in *Gilead*, and *David* by the people of *Israel*.

By succession. When one succeeds another in the government, either by heirship, that the son succeeds the father, as the kings of *Judea* from *David* to *Jechoniah*; or by defect of such, that the next heir is chosen, as we can see of *Sealthiel*, who being of the royal blood was chosen after *Jechoniah*, who died childless; or by marriage, as *Adoniah*, who desired to have *Abisag*, in order to raise himself thereby to the royal dignity; or by testament and Will, when the father appoints in his lifetime one of his sons to succeed him after his death, as *David*, who passing by his oldest son, appointed *Solomon*, the youngest son, to be his successor.

By war. It is a natural law, that what one conquers with the sword is his property, and he is the Lord thereof: The children of *Israel* did conquer the land of *Canaan*, and divided therefore the same among them; and many more examples, both in the Scripture, and daily experience, convinces us thereof.

By power in subduing of others. *Nimrod* subdued others with power, and is therefore called, a *mighty hunter before the Lord.* Abimelech *slew his brethren, being three score and ten persons,* in order to come to the government. *Athaliah* did destroy all the seed royal, that she might enjoy the government.

But by and through what means whatsoever, the magistrates come to the government, yet their condition and state is from God, even if they should be tyrants and wicked; which we can prove both by texts and examples in the Holy Scripture.

Of Scripture texts. The apostle says in our text, *There is no power but of God.* The Lord threatens his people by the prophet *Isaiah*, That he *will give children to be their princes, and babes to rule over them*, on account of their disobedience. The eternal wisdom says himself, through the mouth of *Solomon*, of all rulers in general, *By me kings reign, and princes decree justice. By me princes rule, and nobles, even all the judges of the earth.*

Of Scripture examples, both in the Old and New Testament: wherefore the apostle *Peter* admonishes, *Be subject to your masters with all fear, not only to the good and gentle, but also to the froward.*

Secondly, of their power and authority. God has not alone placed the magistrates in a high station, but he has also given them power, or else their highness was of little value and signification: For highness without power, is as a bee without sting, and a shadow without a body. We can prove, that God has endowed the magistrates, both with highness and power.

1. Of the Scripture texts. The Lord himself speaks of the king of *Babylon*, by the prophet *Jeremiah* also, *I have given this land into the hands of my servant* Nebucadnezzar, *the king of* Babylon: And the wise man speaks also to all rulers, *Hear O you kings, and understand, learn you that be judges of the earth; give ear you that rule the people, and glory in the multitude of nations: For power is given you of the Lord, sovereignty from the highest, who shall try your works, and search out your councils.*

2. Of examples. God calls to this dignity, *First*, the patriarchs, as *Noah* and *Abraham*. And *secondly*, the rulers as *Moses, Joshua*, and the other judges. And *thirdly*, the kings, as *Saul, David, Solomon, Hezekiah, Joash*, of whom it was prophesied three hundred and thirty years before his birth; and *Cyrus*, whom God appointed to be a shepherd, and an anointed, two hundred years before he was born.

3. Of the titles. The apostle calls them in our text, *ordinances of God, and servants of God*. The royal *Psalmist* calls them *gods*, not of nature, but in their office and post, since they are the ministers and

465

vicars of God here on earth: In this name gods, is concealed all the virtues that the kings and rulers should be endowed with.

As God is wise, rulers should also be wise, therefore says *Solomon, Where no council is, the people fall*; and again, *Wo to you, O land, when your king is a child.*

God is true and faithful: Rulers should also be true and faithful; whereof is required three things. *First*, that they are willing and ready to hear the complaints of the poor and distressed. *Secondly*, that they search after truth, and believe not every report and story. And. *Thirdly*, after they are truly informed, not to judge partially, neither to have respect to persons, but to judge justly after the laws and constitutions.

God is just and righteous. Rulers should likewise be righteous, for their *throne is established by righteousness.*

God is good and merciful; Rulers must likewise be so; Solomon says therefore: *Mercy and truth preserve the king, and his throne is upheld by mercy.* In regard to this they are called, *gracious lords.*

God hears all without respect: Likewise rulers, *shall bear the small as well as the great.*

God offers himself an example to imitate, saying, you *shall be holy, for I the Lord your God am holy*: Likewise rulers should forego their subjects with good examples.

Rulers or worldly magistrates arc called angels, *As an angel of God, so is the King my Lord*, said the widow of *Tekoah* to king *David.*

They are called, *cherub, You are the anointed cherub*, says the Lord by the prophet *Ezekiel*, of the prince of *Tyrus.*

They are called, *heads and crowns of heads*: That as the head, and the crown of the head, are above all the other limbs, so the rulers are placed in highness above others.

They are called, *gates, and everlasting doors.* That as the gates and doors defends the city and subjects therein, from the assaults of enemies, also the rulers should defend their subjects from the oppression of the wicked.

They are called *signets*. That as a signet ring is much valued, and is worn on the right hand, so are pious rulers much valued in the sight of God.

They are called *hills and mountains*; That as the mountains are above the valleys, so the rulers are lofty and highly exalted above the subjects.

These and all other tides of honor, wherewith rulers are called, convinces us, that they are ordained and instituted by God. When the apostle St. *Peter* calls the kings, *ordinances of men*, he then has regard to the persons, wherein they are of the same nature with others: For it has pleased the almighty God not to place angels, but men to be rulers, for the following three reasons:

First, for God's own sake, and hath therewith showed his goodness and power: His goodness, that he would not rule and govern men by the mighty angels, who are high and mighty princes, but by men themselves, to whom he has given his own name, and calls them *gods*: His power, that he defends them against Satan and all his adherents, and calls them *signets on his right hand.*

Secondly, for the magistrate's sake. God wills that they should consider these three things. 1*st*, God above them: Although they have power upon earth, yet they should know, that there is a Lord over them, who fears no man's person, and to whom they shall be accountable for all their actions, 2nd, their own mortality: That they should not rule forever, as the royal *Psalmist says, you are gods, and all of you are children of the Most High, but you shall die like men, and fall like one of the princes*, 3rd, their subjects under them: Magistrates should consider, that the subjects over whom they govern, are men as well as themselves, and must therefore look upon them as such, and govern them accordingly.

467

Thirdly, for the subjects sake. God will try thereby the obedience of the subjects, if they are willing to obey the magistrates, who are of the same human nature with themselves, although highly exalted in their station.

II. The apostle shows us in our text, what profit we have of the worldly magistrates.

We can best perceive the profit and good, which we have of the magistrates, by the executing of their office, which is two sorts; spiritual, or worldly. Their spiritual office has regard to the first table in the Law of God, and concerns the worship of God, consisting in the following,

First, magistrates must have knowledge in the true worshipping of God; they should love and honor the Word of God, and regulate all their actions according to the same. The Lord himself says thereof by *Moses, It shall be when the king sits upon his throne in his kingdom, that he shall write him a copy of this law in a book. And it shall be with him, and he shall read therein all the days of his life: That he may learn to fear the Lord his God, to keep all the words of this law, and these statutes to do them.* The royal *Psalmist* calls therefore, the *testimonies of God,* his *delight and counsellors.*

Secondly, magistrates should propagate the true Christian religion in their kingdom and countries, and as much as possible oppose and resist all false doctrine and heresies. The Spirit of God calls therefore the kings, *the nursing fathers of the church.*

Thirdly, magistrates should supply the churches with pious and good preachers and teachers, who can righty instruct the people in the true way to ssalvation, and confirm their doctrine with their exemplary life, according to the example of *David, Solomon, Jehoshaphat, Jeboiada, Hezekiah, Joash,* and others.

Fourthly, magistrates should institute schools and colleges, where the foundation of the true religion, and of arts and sciences, can be learned; and they should endeavor to maintain and advance all such schools and colleges, that are erected in their dominions. King *Nebuchadnezzar* erected a royal school in *Babylon*, where he had educated *certain of the children of* Israel, *and of the king's seed, and of the princes, children in whom was no blemish, but well-favored and skillful in all wisdom, and appointed them a daily provision of meat and wine: That they at the end of three years might stand before the king.* *Daniel* who afterwards prophesied of the Messiah, and instructed the kings *Nebuchadnezzar, Belshazzar, Darius*, and *Cyrus*, was also educated and instructed in this school.

Yet notwithstanding, the magistrates must not force nor oblige anyone to religion, for that is contrary to the example and command of our Savior, who commanded his apostles *to teach and baptize the people*, and not to force, much less to destroy them that would not believe. We read in the parable of the Great Supper, that the master of the house ordered his servants, *to compel all to come in:* But we must know that by this compelling is understood the preaching of the law and its threatenings, by which men's conscience is moved, and even compelled to repentance; these are the spiritual weapons, that according to the saying of St. *Paul, cast down imaginations, and every high thing, that exalts itself against the knowledge of God.* The emperor *Maximilian* II said therefore justly, "There is no harder nor greater tyranny, than to govern over men's conscience."

Magistrates of a true Christian religion, should neither tolerate nor allow all sorts of religion, and the public exercise thereof in their countries, except such has been allowed from a long time, and cannot be removed without danger or peril of offence or revolution, then they may be tolerated; as we can see of the example of *David*, who although he hated all strange religions, yet did allow the *Philistines,*

Amonites, Moabites, and other heathen nations, whom he conquered, the free exercise of their devotion and worship.

The temporal office of magistrates has regard to the second table in the law of God, and consists in the following.

1st, Magistrates should make good and wholesome laws for the support of their country, and the maintenance of honesty and justice among the subjects, which laws must be grounded and founded upon the law of nature, the law of God, the nature of the subjects, and the constitutions of the country: The law of nature, shows what is just and reasonable; the law of God shows what is holy, and the nature of the subjects and country, shows what is needful. These are the three diamonds, that must shine forth in all Christian laws, and the subjects are bound to obey such laws not only for wrath, but also for conscience sake, according to our text.

2dly, Magistrates should not alone give and make good laws, but they should also maintain the same: For what signifies a law, that is not kept, and maintained? Not more than a shining sword without edge. Therefore since magistrates cannot be present over their whole kingdom, they should appoint under magistrates and judges, and admonish them to execute justice without exception of persons; as king *Jehoshaphat,* who said to the judges, whom he had set in the country, *Take heed what you do, for you judge not for man, but for the Lord, who is with you in the judgment: wherefore now, let the fear of the Lord be upon you, take heed, and do it, for there is no iniquity with the Lord our-God, nor respect of persons, nor taking of gifts.*

These two articles should and must be with a judge, knowledge and conscience. They are the eyes, whereof the royal preacher speaks, saying, *The wise man's eyes are in his head:* With the one he beholds the law, whereon he should ground and form his judgment; with the other he beholds the cause and evidences that are before him, for to search and find out the truth. Their testimony must be powdered with the salt of conscience, that the same should not become a political fraud. A wise and prudent judge follows the dictates of the law, and will have no regard to persons, nor his own afflictions, for where passion governs, there is reason blind; and it goes then, as in muddy waters, where we cannot see, nor discern anything. If a judge has conscience, then is he also pious: for the admonition of the conscience comes from God, and it is an indisputable truth, that he, who is not afraid of his own conscience, is neither afraid for God: And being pious, he is absolutely just, and will execute his office, without any regard to persons, according to justice.

3rdly, Magistrates should punish all offenders and transgressors of the law, they being destroyers of the common peace; therefore God gave them the sword, that they should not bear it in vain, but to be a revenger to execute wrath upon them that do evil. The Lord said therefore to *Moses, You shall put the evil away from the midst of you; and those which remain, shall hear and fear, and shall henceforth commit no more any such evil among you; and your eye shall not pity him.*

If the subjects are attacked by their enemies, then the magistrates are obliged to protect them against such, in their rights and privileges, so that everyone may live in peace and tranquility under their government. That magistrates may have lawful war, we can conclude by the words in our text, *He bears not the sword in vain; for he is the minister of God, a revenger to execute wrath upon him that does evil.* Since God has delivered the sword to the magistrates, for the defense of their subjects, it then follows by consequence, that lawful wars are permitted. There is four reasons for such wars:

First, needful defense. It is natural to defend myself, when I am insulted; much more is it permitted a king to defend his subjects from the assaults of their enemies, and protect their own dominions; as we can see of king *Saul, Jehoshaphat,* and others; though it is not advisable to oppose an enemy, whom we know and are assured of, to be too mighty and too strong, for then it is best to try articles of agreement, according to the saying of our Savior, *What king going to make war against another king, sits not down first, and consults, whether he be able with ten thousand to meet him that comes against him with twenty thousand? Or else, while the other is yet a great way off he sends an embassy, and desires conditions of peace.*

Second, contempt and injustice. As king *David*, who after he had heard what shame *Hanun* the king of *Ammon*, had done unto his servants, whom he had sent in order to comfort him over the death of his father, warred against *Hanun*, and conquered him.

Third, the breaking of covenants. As when the king of *Moab* rebelled against the king of *Israel*, after the death of *Ahab*, then went *Joram* out against them, and conquered them.

Fourth, retaking of things and possessions, that has been taken away in their own time, or in the time of their predecessors. As *Jehoash the Son of* Jehoahaz *took again out of the hand of* Benhadad, *the son of* Hazael, *the Cities which he had taken out of the Hand of* Jehoahaz *his father by war.*

Unlawful wars, are where there is none of the foregoing reasons, and which could easily and with repute be decided, but are refused: Great lords and princes cannot commit greater crimes, than in beginning of needless and unlawful wars, since they are the only cause and motive of all bloodshed and destructions committed, by which their countries are ruined, and many of their subjects are made both temporal and eternally unhappy, and miserable: So that we may justly compare such princes with a man, who being bereaved of his senses, hacks and destroys his own body and limbs.

472

III. The apostle shows us, what the due of magistrates are.

Since they are the ordinance of God, and are entrusted with such a high office, then we are obliged to obey them, and to render to them their dues; which according to the words of the apostle in our text, consist in the following articles, *to wit*,

First, honor to whom honor. The apostle St. *Peter* says, *Fear God, honor the king.* For whom God exalts above others, them he will have honored above others. To this honor is required,

1*st*, That we are convinced by the word of God, that the powers are ordinances of God; For such conviction is the only foundation whereupon their honor is grounded. St. *Paul* said therefore in our text, *There is no power but of God: The powers that be, are ordained of God, and he is the minister of God.*

2nd, That we address ourselves with due reverence to the magistrates, and with our outward words show and prove our inward thoughts and esteem of this high station; as the widow of *Tekoah.*

3rd, That we likewise honor them with our gestures and actions; when the prophet *Nathan* came in before king *David, He bowed himself before the king with his face to the ground.*

Secondly, subjection and obedience, you *must needs be subject not only for wrath, but also for conscience sake.* Obedience is the cord, where, with all temporal governments are bound and maintained, and when some cord is broke, then must all things fall. This obedience must be exercised towards,

1*st*, All magistrates, either high or low, *Whether it be to the king as supreme, or unto governors, as unto them that are sent by him, not only to the good and gentle, but also to the froward.*

2nd, By all the subjects in the kingdom. The apostle uses in our text, these words, *every soul:* None of what condition, state, or order, is excluded from this obedience.

473

3rd, In all things not being against the honor of God, our own conscience, and our love towards our neighbors: For otherwise we must follow the words of St. *Peter*, and the other apostles, *We ought to obey God rather than man.*

Thirdly, custom to whom custom, and tribute to whom tribute. The subjects are bound and obliged thereto on account of,

1st, The command of God: So says our Savior, *Render unto Cæsar the things which are* Cæsar's. We can best learn and know what belongs to the kings and magistrates, when we consider the constitution of the country and the times, either they are in peace or in war, and according to such must everyone bring forth his quota.

2nd, Reason, *the apostle* Paul *asks, Who goes a warfare any time at his own charge.* The officers and soldiers must be paid; but by whom? Why, the king; therefore it is again reasonable, that the subjects pay their tributes in order to enable the king to discharge the debts contracted for the defense of themselves and their country.

3rd, Examples in the Holy Scripture, *Jehoiakim exacted the silver and gold of the people of the land, of everyone according to his taxation.* And when taxes or tributes are also raised and exacted of everyone according to their taxation, then is there justice in the cause.

Though magistrates must be careful, that they do not impose unlawfully and immoderately upon their subjects: Whereof the Lord speaks also by the prophet *Micah, Hear I pray you, O heads of* Jacob, *and you princes of the house of* Israel: *Is it not for you to know judgment; who hate the good, and love the evil, who pluck off the skin from off them, and they break their bones, and chop them in pieces, as for the pot, and as flesh within the cauldron? Then shall they cry unto the Lord, but he will not hear them, he will even hide his face from them at that time, as they have behaved themselves in their doings.*

4th, Prayers and supplications. We should always pray to God, the King of Kings and Lord of Lords, for our kings and governors, *That the Spirit of the Lord may rest upon them, that the Spirit of Wisdom, and Understanding, the Spirit of Council and Might, the Spirit of Knowledge and of the Fear of the Lord;* may guide them, that they may love peace and execute justice, and not hearken to bad counsellors and advisers, to the glory of God, the welfare of their subjects, and their own salvation.

Grant this, O merciful Father, to all Christian rulers, for your own honor's sake. AMEN.

33

Offense

The text, MATTHEW, 18:6, 7, 8, 9. ver.

Whosoever shall offend one of these little ones, which believe in me, it were better for him, that a millstone were hanged about his neck, and that be were drowned in the depth of the sea: Wo unto the world, because of offence, for it must needs be that offences come; but woe to that man, by whom the offence comes. wherefore if your hand, or your foot offend you, cut them off, and cast them from you: It is better for you to enter into life half or maimed, rather than having two hands or two feet, to be cast into everlasting fire. And if your eye offends you, pluck it out, and cast it from you; it is better for you to enter into life with one eye, rather than having two eyes to be cast into hell fire.

INTRODUCTION

FAULTS and failures accompany everyone, even the holy. As there are spots in the clear shining sun, so are there likewise transgressions in the saints: *Moses* transgressed with doubts, *Aaron* with Idolatry, *David* with adultery and murder, *Peter* with denying his

Master, the angel of the Church in *pergamos* with hypocrisy; for also says the Spirit of the Lord to him, by St. *John* the divine, *Revelation* 2:14 verse. *I have a few things against you, because you have there them that hold the doctrine of* Balaam, *who taught* Balack *to cast a stumbling block before the children of* Israel, *to eat things sacrificed to idols, and to commit fornication: So have you also them that hold the doctrine of the* Nicolaitans, *which thing I hate.*

The Spirit of God makes mention in these words of two false doctrines, that were in great vogue in the church of *Pergamos*, by which the true believers were offended, and whereto the bishop, called here *the angel of the Church*, did consent by his silence, *to wit*, 1. *The doctrine of* Balaam. And, 2. *The doctrine of the* Nicolaitans.

1. *Balaam* was a prophet in *Moab*, who caused great stumbling blocks to be cast before the children of *Israel*, in order to bring, and delude them from the true worshipping of the Lord their God, by whose mighty hand they were brought out of *Egypt*, from the house of bondage, to sacrifice to *Baal-Peor* the idol of the *Moabites*, and to commit fornication with the daughters of *Moab*. wherefore *Balaam* is reckoned among the false prophets, *Which have forsaken the right way, and are gone astray.* The reason of this wicked council of *Balaam*, was, that God being provoked through the disobedience and transgressions of his people the children of *Israel*, might destroy them in the wilderness, and not bring them to the possession of the land of *Canaan*, promised to their forefathers, wherein he gained his aim in part; *for the anger of God was kindled against* Israel, *and killed twenty and four thousand of them in a plague*; though the *Moabites*, with their prophet, were afterwards slain with the sword, by the command of God. By this we can perceive, that the doctrine of *Balaam* consisted in idolatry and fornication, according to the words of St. *John*.

2. The *Nicolaitans* did cast great stumbling blocks of offence, for the

churches in the New Testament, with their false doctrine. They had their origin and name of *Nicolas*, who was one of the seven chosen by the apostles for to take care of the poor in *Jerusalem*: This *Nicolas*, having a beautiful wife, was publicly accused in the presence of the apostles to be jealous of her; whereat he was so offended, that he gave her over to the use of everyone: Of this man the *Nicolaitans* proceeded, and their doctrine consisted chiefly, in these two abominations, *to wit, to eat things sacrificed to idols, and to commit fornication.*

Sacrifices to idols, were the things which the heathens offered to their idols; and whereof they feasted in their idol's temples, and often invited the Christians to such feasts. The Lord abhorred such doings, and eating, of the Christians; wherefore the apostle St. *Paul* says, *The things, which the gentiles sacrifice, they sacrifice to devils, and not to God, and I would not, that you should have fellowship with devils: you cannot drink the cup of the Lord, and the cup of devils: you cannot be partakers of the Lord's Table, and of the table of devils.*

Fornication, or women in common, was practiced among the heathens, and was not reckoned or accounted sin or unlawful; wherewith the apostle St. *Paul* upbraids them in several of his epistles. The *Nicolaitans* did follow the heathens in this abomination, contrary to the commands from the assembly of the apostles and elders in *Jerusalem*, who concluded, and thereupon ordered, *That you abstain from meats offered to idols, and from fornication:* And this abominable doctrine did at last creep in the churches of *Ephesus, Pergamos,* and *Thyatira.*

The Lord was offended at this, and therefore threatened the bishop, that if such abominations were not removed, and they did repent, he *would then come quickly, and fight against them with the sword of his mouth.* For the Lord hates all such things, and punishes severally all them that give offence; as we can be convinced of by the words of our text, where our blessed Savior speaks,

FIRST, *Of offence.*
SECOND, *Of the punishment for offence.*

EXPLANATION of the TEXT

I. Of Offence.

As difficult as it is to walk upon the ice without stumbling or falling, as difficult is it to live in the world without being smitten therewith: For the world is as a coal-pit, wherein everyone that enters in, becomes smitten. There were never so many misfortunes, vermins and insects in *Egypt*, but there are more offences in the world; one offends the other, and the great offend the small. Whereof our Savior speaks in our text, saying, *Whosoever shall offend one of these little ones, which believe in me.* We have to observe here of these words, *First*, what offence is. And, *secondly*, the persons, who give or take offence.

First, what offence is. It is derived in the ground text of limping, when one stumbles against a thing, whereof he becomes lame: and since our whole lifetime, is a continual journey or road; so all what causes us to stumble, or to fall on the way of our salvation into sin, may be rightly called offence.

Offence is therefore nothing else but bad example, that one gives to the other in words, gestures, or actions, by which wickedness is promoted, and the sinner becomes worse and worse. Offence is two ways, either given or taken.

Offence given, is, when one either in actions, or with words, or with omission of God's command, gives bad examples to others, to do the same. Of this offence our Savior speaks here. This offence can be given in the following ways and manner, *to wit*,

With words, when we speak words, corrupting good manners, or in swearing and cursing; which when others hear it, they are willing, and apt to do the same; as daily experience convinces us of.

With actions, when we commit the things which are unlawful, and against the command of God, by which others are deluded to do the same; as the children of *Eli*, who by their evil doings made the Lord's people to transgress.

With omission, when we omit and neglect to do, what God has commanded, by which others are likewise deluded to follow such bad examples; as king *Saul*, who omitted the destroying of the *Amalekites*, according to the command of God, which brought the children of *Israel* to disobedience against the Lord.

Offence taken is, when one speaks, or does a thing that is right in it self, but another hearing or seeing the same, puts a bad construction thereon, and takes cause thereof to slander. The person who spoke the words, or committed the thing, is no cause in such offence, and therefore guiltless; but the person, who through his bad constructions judges wrongfully thereof, is guilty; and we can compare such persons with the spiders, who draw poison of the flowers, wherein no poison is: This is called, *Pharisaical offence*, because the *Pharisees*, were offended at the person, doctrine, and miracles of Christ, since they were evil and wicked themselves; for where there is evil, there proceeds nothing but evil. Our Savior says therefore, *An evil man out of the evil treasure, brings forth evil things.* And in another place, *If thine eye be single, your whole body shall be full of light: But if your eye be evil, your whole body shall be full of darkness. If therefore the light, that is in you, be darkness, bow great is that darkness?* A good man judges always well of the good works and actions of another; but the wicked speaks evil, and is offended without cause.

There is an offence, called, *the Devil's offence*, when the ungodly are offended at the fall of the holy, and takes thereof freedom to sin, and to cloak their wickedness. The fall of saints is mentioned in the holy records, not for us to imitate them, but well to abhor them: And we may rightly call them possessed of Satan, who will rather follow the vices than the virtues of saints; and compare them to the flies, who passing by the sound parts of the body, lights on the wounds. They are as some birds, who, flying by a field of corn, lights on a dunghill or carron.

Second. As there is two sorts of offence, one given, and the other taken; so there is likewise two persons concerned in every offence; one who gives, and the other who takes the offence.

Our Savior speaks in general of the person who gives offence, with these words; *Whosoever offends,* of what state, condition, sex or age whatsoever: For offence is as a plague that spreads about, and we shall find offences in all station in the world.

Preachers and teachers offend their hearers and congregations, with not living according to their doctrine, by which many are offended, and say; *You who teach another, do you not teach yourself? You that make your boast of the law, through breaking the law, don't you dishonor God?*

Rulers and magistrates offend their subjects, when they live irregular, *turn judgment into gall, and the fruits of righteousness into hemlock;* For then it goes as *Solomon* says; *If a ruler hearken to lies, all his servants are wicked.*

Parents offend their children, when they do not agree with one another, but live in difference, and in a wicked course; with swearing, drinking, whoring, gaming, and other bad vices: Likewise, in not bringing up their children in the fear of God, obedience to their parents, and love to their fellow creatures.

Young people offend one another, when they delude and betray one another in debauchery and evil company, by which they are brought astray from the paths of virtue and morality, to all bad vices.

There is a difference in offences, according to the persons who offend: The offence given by a priest is greater than that of a layman, wherefore they were obliged to offer a greater sacrifice in the Old Testament. The offence of an old person is greater than that of a young one. In regard to this *Eleazar*, one of the principal scribes, aged four score years and ten, refused to eat swine's flesh, that the young people should not be deceived, and brought from the true religion, thinking *Eleazar*, an aged man, was gone over to a strange religion.

Our Savior calls here in our text, the persons who take offence, *little ones, which believe in him*; by which we can understand children or little ones, as well by natural as spiritual age: For since the disciples of Christ did dispute, who should be the highest in his kingdom; therefore Christ called a little child unto him, and set him in the midst of them, that they should learn humbleness and simplicity of this little child. Our Savior understands hereby, not alone children of age, but also children of spiritual age; and therefore says; *Whoso shall offend one of these little ones, which believe in me.*

Children in age are offended, when old people speak or do any unsuitable things or words in their presence, thinking that they, being children, will not regard or take notice thereof; although we see daily, that children remember such things long, and afterwards practice the same: For since children have no ripe judgment, for to discern between good and evil, so are they apt to do and follow the steps of old people, and they commonly remember it a long time; for they have nothing to charge their memory with. Children are therefore as a lump of wax, whereon can be printed the shape of a devil as soon as that of an angel. Old people ought therefore to be very careful in their words and actions, especially in the presence of children, who are soon corrupted by the bad examples of their parents, instructors and old people.

Children in mind and heart, are the weak in faith, not thoroughly grounded and founded in the knowledge of God; for faith waxes and grows like a child, who is weak in the beginning, but afterwards becomes a perfect man, with rightly using the gracious means offered; namely, the word of God, and the Holy Sacraments.

St. *Paul* speaks of the Christian liberty, that we should not abuse the same, in offending them that are weak in faith; in idols, offering meat or drink, or in respect of an holy day; or of the new moon, or of the Sabbath-days, which are forbidden or commanded in the law; for there is no difference in meat and drink, except we make conscience thereof; and every day ought to be holy for God: Neither are we bound to the new moons or holy days of the Jews; though it is absolutely necessary that we honor God with keeping one day holy, and entirely, dedicated to holy and pious exercises in the week; which certain day and all other feast days, are regulated according to the liberty granted to Christian churches, and their rulers, which must be done with discretion, since *God is not the author of confusion, but a God of order, and decency, and peace.*

There are some who are offended at others without cause, alone through their own malice and wickedness. We read in St. *Peter* of our blessed Savior, That he should be a *stumbling stone, and a rock of offence:* Not that he should give offence to anyone, but that others through their own wickedness should be offended at him. This was common by the *Pharisees*, who were offended at the person of Christ, saying therefore of him, *Is not this the carpenter's son? Is not his mother called* Mary? They were offended at the place of his nativity, saying, *Search and look, for out of* Galilee *arises no prophet:* They were offended at his doctrine, because he did preach of faith, and not of good works and the law of *Moses:* They were offended at his miracles, saying, *He drives out the devils by* Beelzebub: They were offended at his living, calling him, *A gluttonous man, and a wine-bibber, a friend of publicans and sinners:* They were offended at his mercy and humbleness, because he *eat and drink with publicans and sinners:* They were offended at his poverty, because *he had not where to lay his head:* They were offended at his sufferings, and therefore derided him, *reviling him, and wagging their heads.*

Many are yet offended on Christ, as well without, as within the bosom of the Christian church.

Without the Christian church, the *Jews* and *gentiles* are offended in him; for so St. *Paul* says, *We preach Christ crucified unto the* Jews *a stumbling block, and unto the* Greeks (that is the *gentiles,*) *Foolishness.* The *Jews* did despise him, because his kingdom was not of this world, saying, *We will not have this man to reign over us:* The *Greeks* were offended in him, because his doctrine being above the apprehension of human reason, was not agreeable to their philosophy; and called therefore the apostle *Paul, a babbler, and a setter forth of strange gods, because he preached unto them Jesus and the resurrection.*

Within the Christian church, many are offended, even in these our days, at the person of Christ, since they will not believe the true Godhead and manhood of Christ, through the personal union: Many are offended at his doctrine, judging the same after their human reason, and altering the same according to their weak apprehensions: Many are offended at his kingdom, judging the same by its outward appearance, and despise the same, because the mighty and rich of this world do not belong thereto: Many are offended at the way of Christ's government, because he distributes not his temporal blessings alike; but the best children of God suffer oftentimes most in this world: Many are offended at his cross, not alone because Christ was *despised and rejected of man, and a man of sorrow and grief, in the time of his incarnation*; but also, because he makes the children of God like himself, with cross and affliction: Many are offended at his living, and therefore will not follow his footsteps. They would willingly be partakers of his kingdom, but not of his examples: Many are offended at his mercy, and therefore put off their repentance from one time to another, thinking that his mercy is so great, that he will receive them when they will.

Hereby we can see, that the way of our salvation is full of stumbling blocks; and if we are deceived by them, we will never be saved. A simple faith is the best faith; therefore we should shut the eyes of our reason, and pass by all offences and stumbling-blocks; and in truth, and sincerity, cleave to Jesus Christ, following the light of the gospel, by which we may arrive safe through all the rocks and stumbling-blocks of offences, to the eternal happiness hereafter.

II. Of the punishment for offence.

Our Savior speaks in our text of the punishment for offences, saying; *Wo unto the world, because of offences, for it must needs be, that offences come; but wo to that man by whom the offence comes.* Our Savior shows us in these words; *First,* the necessity, and, *secondly,* the punishment.

First, the necessity. *It must needs be, that offences come:* This necessity proceeds not from God, as if he had absolutely decreed, that there should be offence: No, for God has no delight in ungodliness. Besides, the words of our text convinces us, that God abhors offences, since our Savior calls, *Wo to the man by whom the offence comes:* But these words have regard,

To the malice, envy, and wickedness of Satan; who, *as a roaring lion, walks about, seeking whom be may devour.* He always opposes God and his word, thereby to diminish God's kingdom, and to increase his own. He raises therefore all sorts of offences, and casts stumbling blocks for men in the way of their Christendom; and, *bewitches them, that they shall not obey the truth:* And, *works for them with all power, and signs, and lying wonders;* which God permits; *That they, which are approved, might be made manifest*, according to the saying of St. *Paul*. These words have regard also,

To the wicked and perverse nature of man, which is always inclinable to all wickedness, and is easily deceived: therefrom proceeds all offences, and therefore it must needs be, *that offences come*; for, as we can conclude of the setting of the sun, that the night will follow; so we can conclude the cause of offences by the foregoing reasons; and therefore says our Savior, *It must needs be, that offences come.*

Secondly, the punishment for offence: This is described in our text by two things; 1*st*, Of the certainty; and 2n*dly*, Of the severity.

The certainty of the punishment for offence, is comprehended in this word *wo*, which our Savior, being himself truth, calls out; and we may depend upon it, that it shall never fail: This little word, *wo*, contains great misery, misfortune, unhappiness, and horrible punishment, both here and hereafter. We can be convinced of this, by the examples of them who are punished for offences given to others. The spies that were sent out by *Moses*, died by the plague before the Lord, because they brought evil report upon the land, and thereby offended the people. *Achan* did offend the children of *Israel* with his theft, and was therefore stoned with his whole house, and all that belonged to him. We have also the examples of *Jeroboam, Ahab, Jezebel*, and others.

The severity of the punishment for offence, is described in these words; *It were better for him, that a millstone were hanged about his neck, and that he were drowned in the depth of the sea.* We can see hereof, that our Savior understands by this *wo*, the eternal pain and punishment in hell; for he makes comparison between temporal punishment and eternal pain; and concludes, that it were better to suffer the greatest and severest punishment on earth, than the eternal pain and misery in hell.

It was a great and the severest punishment among the Jews, when one had committed a great crime, that a millstone was hanged about the criminal's neck, and he was drowned in the midst or depth of the sea, as being unworthy to behold the light of the sun, or to breath in the air, or to be in or upon the earth. If this punishment was so severe, then must certainly the punishment which our Savior understands under this word, *wo*, be more severe, and cannot be no other than the torments and pains of hell. The Lord declares them who *make the blind to wander out of their way, cursed*; much more cursed are they then, who cast stumbling blocks and rocks of offences for others, in the way of their salvation.

Since then such a severe judgment and punishment is pronounced against all offences, then a true Christian and child of God, must be careful, and guard himself against them; which may be done with,

1*st*, Mortifying our own members, as our Savior admonishes us in the words of our text, saying; *wherefore, if your hand or your foot offend you, cut them off, and cast them from you; and if thine eye offend thee, pluck it out, and cast it from you.* Our Savior mentions here three of our members, namely, *eye, hand*, and *foot*; not that the other members of our body cannot offend us, but that we by them, can easily form a judgment of the other members. There are some who interpret the three stations in the world, under the similitude of the three before-mentioned members; and understand by the eye, the ministers of the gospel, who must preach and show to others the way of salvation, with their doctrine and life: by the hands, temporal magistrates who must defend the subjects, and not bear the sword in vain: by the feet, everyone in the common wealth, and the whole community, among whom there are manifold offences. I shall bring them under these three heads: senseless things, living things, and man himself.

Senseless things: When man, being blessed with temporal goods and riches, are not concerned for futurity; but, on the contrary, would rather lose God and his glorious kingdom, than to depart from their riches, which thereby becomes an offence to them: Of such may be justly said, that their eyes offend them.

Living things; Your wife is your hand, your foot and your eye, and is therefore called in the Scripture, *a helpmeet for the man:* Many a one are offended thereby, as we can see of *Sampson, Ahab* and others. Your friend is your hand, therefore, when your friend deludes you to wickedness, may be said, your hand has offended you; as we can see by *Absalom, Amon* and others. Our lawful calling is the foot, whereupon our temporal welfare stands: Many a one are so deluded herein, that they forget their own conscience, much more God; as we can see of the men who was invited to the royal feast. It is a common saying, everyone is a thief in his calling: This is a very unbecoming and unsuitable saying, especially for Christians. They ought rather to say, everyone must be an honest man in his calling.

Man himself. *If your hand offends you.* Herein can many offences be given, with over-reaching our neighbors in bargains, and receiving more than the real value of a thing; with taking of unlawful presents, in order to turn the law, or the right of our neighbors; with writing false instruments; with taking of false oaths, and many more ways. *If your foot offends you:* Your servant is this foot, and can offend you with bad advices; and with our feet we walk upon sinful ways. *If your eye offends you:* This member gives the greatest offence; for it is the door wherethrough sin enters into the heart of man; as we can see of *David, Sampson, Achan* and others, in the Scripture, and likewise by daily experience.

Our Savior commands us in the words of our text, That we should *cut off*, and *pluck out* such offending members; that is, as the apostle St. *Paul* explains it; *Mortify your members which are upon earth; fornication, uncleanness, inordinate affection, evil concupiscence, and covetousness.* The same apostle calls it in another place; *To crucify the old man.* So, although it should smart us, when we are disappointed in our evil desires and concupiscence, as much as if a limb, or a member was cut off from our body, yet we should bear it; for, *they that are Christ's have crucified the flesh, with the affections and lusts.* Would it not be better to lose a hand, foot, or any other member, than to endanger the whole body? Is it not better to subdue our wicked affection, and lusts, than in fulfilling the same, to be cast into the eternal torments of hell. We should pluck out the eye of the old *Adam,* in turning them away from all vanity and wickedness; and, *with shutting them from seeing evil:* We should cut off the hands of the old *Adam,* with *shaking our hands from holding unrighteousness:* We should cut off the feet of the old *Adam,* with *walking righteously,* and not in evil and unlawful ways: We should cut out the tongue of the old *Adam,* in *keeping the tongue from evil, and the lips from speaking guile.*

Our Savior commands us, not alone to cut off the offending members, but even to throw them away as hurtful; wherewith he would learn and admonish us to constancy in our good undertakings; for it is not enough, once or twice, or now and then to withstand our evil desires and afflictions, but we should continue and be constant in crucifying and mortifying the old *Adam,* until he is fully conquered and overcome: And this is called,

2ndly, *to deny ourselves:* When Satan, the world, and our own flesh and blood will deceive us, and provoke us to sin, then should we do and act as if we were blind, deaf and senseless, and also oppose their instigations. Our Savior says therefore, *Whosoever will save his life, shall lose it, and, whosoever will lose his life for my sake shall find it.* The temporal life is loving and craved by everyone, and to obtain our will is as pleasing to flesh and blood as life itself; but is it not better to lose all what we value as much as our life in this world, and even life itself, than to be bereaved of the eternal life hereafter?

3rdly, We must abhor and escape all occasions of offence. We live in a sinful world, full of stumbling blocks, and cannot be out of the world; but we ought to live so in the world, that we neither give nor take any offence; as the fish, who although living in the salt water, yet tastes not salty.

4thly, We must have the examples of the holy angels, and the presence of God before us. We must consider, that man is not alone, but God is present over all, and *all things are naked before him*, who knows all our thoughts, words and actions. We ought therefore to be on our guard, and have a due awe and reverence for the presence of our all-seeing and all-knowing God. And, as the holy angels are confirmed in goodness by the continual beholding of God's countenance; there is no doubt, that a child of God, having God always before the eyes of his faith, and following his commands, in sincerity and uprightness of heart, will certainly be free, both from giving and taking offence.

The Lord be merciful unto us, and protect us through the course of our life in this wicked world, where so many offences meet us, that we may appear unpunishable before his tribunal without offence on the grand day of our Lord and Savior Jesus Christ. AMEN.

34

Matrimony

T he text, GENESIS, 2:18, 19, 20, 21, 24, verses.

It is not good that the man should be alone. I will make him a help meet for him. And the Lord God caused a deep sleep to fall upon Adam, *and he slept; and he took one of his ribs, and closed up the flesh instead thereof: And the rib which the Lord God had taken from man, made be a woman, and brought her unto the man. And* Adam *said, This is now bone of my bone, and flesh of my flesh; she shall be called woman, because she was taken out of man. Therefore shall the man leave his father and his mother, and shall cleave unto his wife, and they shall be one flesh.*

INTRODUCTION

OUR church ordinance, concludes the ministration of the matrimonial act with the words of our blessed Savior by the evangelist St. *Matthew*, 19th. 6. verse. *What God has joined together, let no man separate.* These words comprehend three things for our meditation. 1*st*, the worthiness and honor. 2*ndly*, the union. And, 3*rdly*, The inseparable knot of matrimony.

First, the worthiness and honor of matrimony. This can be best perceived, when we consider the institutor thereof, who is no worldly monarch or prince, but the Almighty God, Creator of heaven and earth; who after the creation instituted this holy order, to the glory of his name, and the welfare of man. Hereby can they who live in this holy order be assured, that they live in a condition and state wherein God is well pleased; and they may expect all temporal and eternal blessing, as long as they continue in the fear of God, and are obedient to his will and commands.

This joining must not be understood alone of the matrimonial knot made by the minister, with laying of his hands upon the hands of the man and woman joined together in one another, but also of the persons themselves, whom God has joined together: For since Christ does demonstrate, that a man should not separate himself from his wife for every fault, because God has joined them together; then follows thereby, that God joins them yet together. Herefrom proceeds the common saying, *God has foreseen matrimony.* Matrimony seems to be a lottery, and none can know what partner he or she may have, a *Moses* may get a *Zipporah, David* a *Michal*, and *Abigail* a *Nabal*, yet God has his hand therein. When the same is begun in the fear of God, with prayers, in a pure and sincere love, and in a lawful way; then God orders and governs both parties to mutual consent, and also becomes the saying, *that God has foreseen matrimony*, verified. This can be proved both by Scripture texts and examples.

Of Scripture text: The Lord had appointed *Rebecca* for *Isaac*; in regard to this says *Solomon* in his Proverbs, *A prudent wife is from the Lord.*

Of examples: The patriarch *Abraham*, sent his servant *Eleazar* to bring a wife for his son *Isaac*, who therefore prayed to the Lord for progress and good luck in his errand; and when he knew the maid, and her friends consented, then said they; *The thing proceeds from the Lord.*

Like therefore as God brought *Eve* to *Adam*, and joined them together without means, also brings he married people together yet with means; and it can be said, That God joins them together. Should it happen, as we see daily, that a good man gets a bad wife, or a good woman gets a bad husband, yet is their matrimony from God; for there is no rule without exception; and this happens oftentimes, that the one should learn patience of the other; *For all things work together for good to them that love God.* They who engage themselves without prayers to God, and the advice of their friends, and alone through carnal lust or worldly lucre join themselves together, must blame themselves, if their matrimony is not prosperous and loving; for God permits it as a punishment to themselves, if they do not humble themselves before God, and pray for his assistance and grace: But if they turn to God, and implore his mercy, then he will confirm their matrimony, although began without God.

Second, the union of matrimony. Our Savior calls the same here in these words, *joining together*; wherein is a comparison taken of a couple of oxen yoked together. As long as they go together in quietness, and draw together, the work goes on; but when they begin to disagree, and to draw against one another, then the yoke is broke, and the work is hindered. So it goes likewise among married people; as long as they agree together, and draw as with one accord, then they prosper and have good luck; but when they disagree, then goes the work and all their household backwards. They must be in some measure, as the Milch Kine of *Beth-shemesh*, who went straightway along the highway, and turned not aside to the right hand or to the left; But in another measure, they must not be as the Milch Kine, who went straight-way before the cart, whereupon the ark of the Lord was laid, not knowing the treasure, nor understanding what was laid upon the ark. Married people ought to consider, that they are God's people, and that God has made his covenant with them; therefore should they have God before their eyes, and walk circumspectly according to his command, and be contented with their lot, and cleave together in prosperity and adversity, then shall they obtain everlasting happiness hereafter.

Third, the inseparable knot of matrimony. *Let no man put asunder.* The Jews did in former days, give a writing of divorcement to their wives when they hated them, or had no delight in them; But Christ shows that it was not rightly done; so says he, *From the beginning it was not so*; but *Moses, because of the hardness of your hearts, suffered you to put away your wives.* The reason was, that a man having no delight in his wife, or hating her, might not abuse her with harsh means, since the Jews were a stubborn nation.

But who can separate or divorce married people?

1. The ecclesiastical court may divorce them for certain reasons, whereof fornication is the most principal; and when this is done, we cannot say that they are put asunder by man, but by the laws of God, when his servants the magistrates are to execute justice.

2. Death. Married people shall be put asunder by death; therefore should they, for the little time that they are to live together, agree in love, peace and unity, that they can part on the last day as loving as when they came together on the first day of marriage. Our text speaks of the origin and institution of matrimony; by which we should behold these three heads.

FIRST. *The worthiness and honor,*

SECOND, *The great union, and*

THIRD, *The profit of matrimony.*

EXPLANATION of the TEXT

494

I. The Worthiness and Honor of Matrimony.

We can best perceive the worth and honor of this state, when we consider the following, *to wit*;

1. The majesty and glory of the institutor, who is the Holy God, the Almighty Lord of heaven and earth; who, when he was to create man, went first in council with himself, and likewise now, when he would create a helpmeet for the man, saying; *It is not good that the man should be alone, I wilt make him a helpmeet for him:* And after the Lord had resolved to institute matrimony, then,

First, He created a helpmeet for *Adam. And the Lord God caused a deep sleep to fall upon Adam, and he slept; and he took out one of his ribs, and closed up the flesh instead thereof: And the rib which the Lord God had taken from man, made be a woman.* This sleep was no natural but a supernatural sleep, like the sleep of *Abraham, Siscera,* and the soldiers of king *Saul.* The Lord caused this sleep to fall upon *Adam,* partly, that he should feel no pain in the taking away his rib, and thereby dislike her; partly, that he should not know where she came from before he awoke: For God acts so with his children, and blesses them without their knowledge; and *gives his beloved bread asleep.* She was not created of his lower parts, because man should not undervalue, neither of his head, that she should not take upon her to rule and govern; but of his side, next to the heart, that man should love her as himself, and acknowledge her to be his sole partner and help.

Second, And God brought her unto the man, and married and joined them together. God was not alone Creator of the man and woman, but also Father, to give away the bride, and Priest, to marry the new created couple; which last part was performed with these words; *The man shall leave his father and mother, and shall cleave unto his wife, and they shall be one flesh.* Our Savior convinces and testifies, by St.

Matthew, that these words were spoken by the Lord God himself; with which words the Lord instructs not alone the new created *Adam* and *Eve*, but also, all Christian married people, how they should behave themselves in the matrimonial state; namely, that their mutual love should exceed the love between parents and children, and keep their own families and household separate by themselves, if they are able, in order that the wife should not seemingly be brought under the absolute government and subjection of her husband's parents, which might occasion great offence and discontent.

Third, and the Lord blessed them, not with bare words, as one may bless another, but in effect and reality, generating their seed and procreation of children; which blessing continues yet, and extends to all their posterity.

2. The confirmation of matrimony. Although *Adam* and *Eve* fell from their obedience and love of God, yet the matrimonial state was in its full force, since we see that God, after the Fall, did preach, of the multiplying of their seed, and the *bringing forth of children in sorrow*. Besides, *Adam called his wife's name Eve, because she was the mother of all living*.

3. The renewing this state in the New-Testament. The *Jews*, in the Old Testament, took many wives at one time, and gave a writing of divorcement to them they disliked: But Christ has, in the New Testament, brought the matrimonial state, as it was from the beginning; namely, to two persons, one man and one woman, saying: *They twain shall be one flesh*.

4. The honor showed to this state, by the holy and blessed Trinity. Was it not the greatest honor that the Lord God himself copulated *Adam* and *Eve* together, and blessed them; which he does yet daily by his servants and ministers of the gospel; and blesses married people with children, and prosperity in their lawful calling. Besides, our Savior wrought the first miracle in the temple of his incarnation,

at the marriage in *Cana* of *Galilee*, and compares the Kingdom of Heaven to a marriage, and his church to the virgins that went out to meet the Bridegroom; and the Holy Spirit has dictated the 128th *Psalm*, as a bride song to the honor of the matrimonial state, and the mutual love thereof.

Fifthly, examples in the Holy Scripture, of patriarchs, prophets, high-priests, and apostles, who have lived in this state.

By all this we can conclude and perceive, that the matrimonial state is holy, and well pleasing in the sight of God; and we ought therefore to have a great reverence for his holy order.

II. The Great Union of Matrimony.

They who are inclined and resolved to enter into the matrimonial state, ought to begin the same in the fear of God, after ripe and thorough consulation: For we see that God, who is perfect in holiness and truth, went himself in consultation, before he instituted this state; wherein he convinces us, that we should not run into it thoughtless nor headlong, without the advice of our friends and relations: The bride song is soon sung, but the tune oftentimes lasts a very long while.

But what person then shall man choose in order to clear and pacify his own conscience, that he should not repent afterwards; for we can be careful but once in this cause. *Solomon* asks, *Who can find a virtuous woman?* In these words are two things concealed, 1. A *Difficulty*, 2. A *Carefulness*.

First, the difficulty we can perceive of the question, for it is the way of the Holy Records, to propose all difficulties by questions.

Second, the carefulness is comprehended in this word *find*; which word shows us, that we must first look for it, and be careful in our searching. He therefore that will marry, and live afterwards with content, must look out for a person that is, 1st, His like; and, 2nd, not near related in blood or marriage.

1st. He should look out for his like, since persons alike agree best; whereof the common saying, *that children alike play best together*, proceeds, *Where one eye goes, there goes likewise the other:* That was uneven marriage, when the thistle sends the Cedar of *Lebanon, for his daughter, to be his son's wife.* There must be likeness in the mutual love; for what is marriage without sincere love? Which is the best sauce upon the victuals, the best bed in the house, and the best encourager of their calling. There must be likeness in age, for difference of age causes difference of humor, by which uneasiness is oftentimes occasioned, and mutual love is thereby turned to mutual hatred. There must be likeness of religion, though it is no sin to marry one of a different opinion: For so says the apostle Paul; *If any brother has a wife that believes not, and she be pleased to dwell with him, let him not put her away: And the woman which has a husband that believes not, and if be pleased to dwell with her, let her not leave him.*

2ndly, He shall look out for a person that is not nigh related to him in blood or marriage. Whereof we can read by *Moses* in his book called *Leviticus*, the 18 from the 7th to the 18th verse. 20 the 1, 12, 14, 17, 19, 20, 21. verses, and *Deuteronomy* 27:20, 22, and 23, verses. We must observe here, that where one is forbidden to marry one of them who are related to the same person in the same degree, there is also the other person understood, although not mentioned. As it is forbidden *Levit.* 18:14, and 20, verse. *You shall not approach to your father's brother's wife*, thereby is also meant the mother's brother's wife. Thereof follows by consequence, that no woman may take her sister's husband, since a brother's wife, and a sister's husband are even nigh related to a person.

Married people must be moved to mutual love and unity by the following reasons, *to wit.*

498

1. Of their original likeness. *Adam* said of the new created person whom God brought to him, *This is bone of my bone, and flesh of my flesh.* And shows thereby his joy, and his love.

He shows his joy. He saw before, that all the creatures, which were brought before him had their partners, everyone in its own kind, but found no helpmeet for himself, with whom he could converse, thinking that his lonesome life would be tedious. But now he is rejoiced, seeing and perceiving the goodness of the Lord, who had made and brought to him a helpmeet for him.

He shows his love. Nothing is nearer to a man, than his flesh and bones, so is the wise as nigh to her husband as his own flesh and bones, and she is an image wherein he may behold himself. The apostle *Paul* concludes therefore, *So ought men to love their wives, as their own bodies, be that loves his wife, loves himself.*

2. Of their mutual name. *She shall be called woman*, not that she should rule over the man; But, *because she was taken out of man.* As long as a young woman is unmarried she is called by her father's name, but as soon as she marries, she is called by her husband's name, for she is made partner of the man's goods, fortune, honor and glory. The woman receives her luster from the husband, like the moon its glances from the sun. The learned have very well observed, that the great name of God *Jah*, that is, *Jehovah*, is included both in the man's and woman's name in the Holy Scripture. The man's name is *Ishack*, where the first letter of God's name *Jod* stands in the midst: The woman's name is *Isha*, where the second letter of God's name, *H* stands in the end, and all married people can be assured of the gracious presence of God by them, as long as they live according to his command and will. But when they depart from God, and are disobedient, then God departs again from them, and their name becomes, *Esk, Esk*, that is fire, namely, fire here, and fire hereafter.

3. Of the inseparable knot. *The man shall leave his father and*

his mother, and shall cleave unto his wife, and they shall be one flesh. Children are bound to their parents, and must never leave or neglect them, but married people are bound yet with a greater knot; for the knot between parents and children, sisters and brothers may be separated, but the knot between man and woman lawfully married together can never be separated, except with and through death; and even if this knot is loosened through death, yet can the matrimonial love not be extinguished, but the surviving party will always have a love and regard for the dead party.

Where a loving union is, there is certainly a glorious edifying. The whole world is edified and maintained by the state of matrimony, and the profit thereof extends to all conditions: The same is ordained, and instituted of God.

First, for procreation of children. *Be fruitful and multiply, and replenish the earth.* There are many young wholesome couple married together, that get no children, the reason is by the woman, according to the Scripture, since their wombs are said to be closed up. Procreation is no natural work, but the work of God, as the royal *Psalmist* says, *Lo Children are a heritage of the Lord.* They who are not blessed with children in their marriage must be contented, and patient, considering, that the All-knowing God has causes why they are not blessed therewith; for it is better to have no children, than to have wicked ones, and God has delight in them as well without as with children, as long as they are obedient to the command of God, who can bless them again with other blessings for the want of children.

Secondly, mutual help and assistance. *I will make him a helpmeet for him.* The woman shall be a helpmeet for man.

1. In the bringing forth and educating of children. The woman was created to bring forth children, and was therefore called of *Adam, the mother of all living,* and is obliged to assist the husband, in bringing

up the children in the fear of God, as *Solomon* says.

2. In the household. Therefore is she made of the man's rib, that she should assist him in the care and administration of their mutual house affairs. In regard to this, she is called by the wise man *Sirach, A tower against death to her husband:* And *Solomon* compares her by *the merchant ships that brings food from afar.*

3. In cross and affliction. Married people are subject to many crosses and afflictions. As impossible as it is to go through water without becoming wet, so impossible is it to live in the marriage state and not to meet afflictions. Married people are obliged to help and assist one another herein, and patiently endure under their mutual yoke, comfort one another, and when necessity requires, defend one another.

4. In prayers and religious exercises. Prayers is the best weapon between married people, but when the one prays, and the other curses whom shall God hear? How pleasing is it when one says, *Let us go speedily to pray before the Lord, and to seek the Lord of Hosts.* And the other answers, *I will go also.* Our Savior promises. *If two of you shall agree on earth, as touching anything that they shall ask, it shall be done for them of my Father which is in heaven.*

Thirdly, for a means against evil desires. The apostle St. *Paul* says, For *to avoid fornication let every man have his own wife; and let every woman have her own husband.* There is no need of explaining this, since daily experience convinces us, that since the Fall of *Adam* there are but few who live a modest single life; and if this state of matrimony had not been instituted, the world would be more wicked and corrupt than it is.

Fourthly, for the practice of all Christian virtues. The marriage state is the best school wherein we can learn several virtues, and be instructed in many parts of our Christendom. We can be instructed therein in the following articles, namely,

1. Of God's providence. Many poor people come together, and begin the world together with nothing, yet we see that they maintain themselves, and even prosper and attain to great riches. This is an act of providence. *Jacob* when he entered first in service to *Laban* had Nothing more than the clothes on his back, and a staff in his hand, but the providence of God made him a very rich man, of all temporal and worldly blessings.

2. The government of God. Every house father is careful that his household can be governed regularly, and place therefore his servants everyone to his respective occupation and work, not suffering anyone to be idle, nor neglectful. Also, God rules and governs the whole world, and places everyone to his respective calling, and will not that anyone should stand idle, and be an idle member in the commonwealth.

3. Of the almighty power of God. Married people who are blessed with children, have herein a clear and living argument of the almighty power of God, who can form a child so wonderfully in its mother's womb, and when the time comes, bring it forth to the world from the close prison wherein it was concealed. Must not he be an almighty Lord, who has ordered this so wisely? Has God had his eyes over our substance yet being unperfect, and his visitation hath preserved our spirit, when we were in our mother's womb, and could neither move hand nor foot? Should then the same Lord and God not provide more for us now we are able to ask and pray to him according to the command of his Son our blessed Savior?

4. Of the love of God. Can parents who are of a corrupt and perverse nature love their children so much; how much more is the love of God to his children, whom he has chosen in his beloved Son Jesus Christ before the foundation of the world. For *the Lord is very pitiful, and of tender mercy.* The royal Psalmist says therefore, *Like a Father pities his children, so the Lord pities them that fear him.* And the prophet

Isaiah brings the words of the Lord forth also, *As one whom the mother comforts, so will I comfort you.*

5. Of crosses. When parents chastise their children, it is not through hatred, but for their good: So when the Lord visits married people with crosses and afflictions, then is it not in anger for their harm, but for their good, *For whom the Lord loves, he chastens, and scourges every Son, whom be receives.* And, *though he causes grief, yet will be have compassion according to the multitude of his mercies: For he does not afflict willingly, nor grieve the children of men.*

6. Of prayer. When married people are unlucky, and cannot prosper, but poverty and want comes among them; then is prayers their best refuge: He that did not value prayers and the word of God before, will learn to pray when they are oppressed and want substance.

7. Of patience. When the man is troubled with a bad woman, or the woman with a bad husband, then the grieved party will learn patience, as the example of *Job* convinces us of.

8. Of labor. House-keeping has a great mouth, and may be called a devourer, since it requires bread, victuals and clothing for the family: And if we would support ourselves and our family, then must we labor. Therefore places God labor and bread together, when he said to *Adam, In the sweat of your face shall you eat bread.*

9. Of the mystery of Christ and his church. Man and wife are two in one flesh; the woman is flesh of the man's flesh, and bone of his bone: Christ and his church are one body. Man and wife are bound together with an inseparable knot, which no man can loose: Christ has betrothed his church unto himself forever. Man and wife have everything in common: The faithful have everything in common with Christ, who being the Son of God from eternity, became a man in time, that we being before children of wrath, might become children of God: He took on our infirmities, and made us partakers of his

holiness and righteousness. Man and wife must love one another, and bear patiently with each others faults. Christ loves his church so that he gave himself in death for her, and bears daily over with the faithful. When married people can attain by the grace of God in their marriage state to such thoughts and meditations, and the practice thereof, then are they happy, and all things will be good for them, and they can be assured that the Lord will bless them both here in time, and hereafter in eternity.

The Lord grant this to all Christian married people, for the sake of Jesus Christ, by the assistance of the Holy Spirit: To whom be all honor, might, majesty and dominion, now and forever more. AMEN.

35

Death

T he Text, ECCLESIASTES 12:7 Ver.

Then shall the dust return to the earth as it was; and the Spirit shall return unto God, who gave it.

INTRODUCTION

AS man is not born by a mere accident, according to the opinion of the *Epicurians*, who say, 'We are all born by adventure, and we shall be hereafter as though we had never been;' he also dies not by an accident, but he has his certain time to live, and his certain time to die, which he cannot pass. *Job* speaks thereof in his book, 14:5. *Man's days are determined, the number of his months are with you; you have appointed his bounds that be cannot pass.* Job instructs us in these words, That man has, *first*, his certain time to live in; and, *second*, his certain time to die.

1st. *Job* teaches us, that man has his certain time to live in. As everything in the whole creation has its proper time, so has man likewise, which begins from the moment of his birth, and lasts to the moment of his death. The lives of some are measured with a long, and others again with a short measure, all according to the well-pleasing will of God: wherefore the royal Psalmist says; *Lord, make me to know my end, and the measure of my days, what is it. Behold, you have made my days as a hand-breadth, and my age is nothing before you: Verily, every man at his best state, is altogether vanity.* We may be convinced by many examples, how wonderfully God has freed the lives of many from peril and destruction, because the bounds thereof has been fore-ordained to be longer. *Moses* was cast in his infancy in the river, but was wonderfully saved. *Joseph* was to be destroyed by his brothers, but *Ruben* saved his life, and he was sold afterwards to the *Medianites. Saul* did endeavor to destroy *David,* but could not obtain his will. *Ahab* sent over the whole Kingdom to seek after *Eliam,* in order to destroy him, but could not find him out. We can see hereof, that God has appointed certain bounds unto the life of every man, which he cannot pass. And this brings us to the second part, namely;

2n*d*, that man has his certain time to die; *You have appointed his bounds, that be cannot pass.* The word *appointed,* in the text, signifies determined, or stated, as a judgment that cannot be revoked. The meaning is, that God has determined how many years, months, days, hours, and even moments every man shall live; and when the appointed moments comes, then must he die. *Job* says, That this determined number of man's life is with God, who has recorded all in the book of his omniscience. No man knows the hour or manner of his death; and it is therefore needless to consult the marks of the hands, and the constellation of the planets. *My times are in your hand, O Lord,* says the royal Psalmist. Not alone the time of our death, but also the way how we shall die, is known to God; and even the place of our death is appointed. Though as God does nothing without nature and natural causes, except in miracles; so is there likewise in this case of our appointed time, a condition to be observed, which hath regard to nature, man's life, and several outward accidents.

Concerning nature, although God is not bound to natural causes, as being a free and sovereign Lord, who can do as he will and pleases, yet he lets the natural causes have their progress, and appoints the bounds accordingly. As for example, when man is conceived and formed in his mother's womb, then receives he body and life, consisting of natural heat and moisture, like the lamp of the week and the oil. If this natural heat and moisture be superfluous, and thereby a good temper, then lives man the longer; that is, according to the Scripture, *three score and ten, or four score*; on condition that he fears God, and lives soberly and peaceable. But if there is much of this natural moisture and heat of a weak or irregular temper, then lives man not so long. The all-knowing God sees all this before, and appoints accordingly the time of man's life. Should any defect befall nature through sickness or other accidents, then God has created the medicines by which nature can be helped and supported.

Should anyone fall upon such thoughts; Why has God given a stronger nature to one man than to another? He must know, that *the Potter has power over the clay of the same lump, to make one vessel unto honor, and another unto dishonor.* Why makes a woman one candle to burn a long time, and another to burn but short time? *Woe unto him that strives with his maker. Shall the thing formed say unto him that formed it, Why have you made me thus?* God is the Creator, and we are his creatures, and the work of his hands; and who can prescribe unto him how to appoint the days? He suffered *Methuselah* to live 969 years, *Moses* 120, and *David* 70, according to his godly will and pleasure: So it is yet in his godly power, to extend or shorten our days, according to his godly appointment. His power and will is not forced in the meanwhile, as if he was absolutely bound to something certain: No, for as he has power to distribute his temporal blessing to whom and when he pleases, so he has also power to let our days be long or short; *Time and chance happens to all*, says *Solomon*.

God regulates also the days of men's lives according to their living, so as everyone has acted in his lifetime, either evil or well. If one lives according to the command of God, in sincerity and integrity of heart, and abhors evil, he may expect that *God will fulfill the number of his days*. God has also promised, that if we *honor our father and our mother, our days shall be long in the land*. And although the time of our life should be expired, in regard to our constitution and natural complexion, yet God can prolong the same if he will and pleases, as the example of King *Hezekiah* convinces us of.

The ungodly, who will not obey the word of God, but live up according to the frailty of their corrupt nature, in all sin and wickedness, them God threatens to shorten their lives: For, as *the fear of the Lord prolongs days, so the years of the wicked shall be shortened*. The royal Psalmist says, *bloody and deceitful men shall not live out half their days*. This can be proved by many examples of the holy record.

There are many young persons, who are of a strong and wholesome nature, and could live according to that for many years, but they shorten their own lives with debauchery and excess; and by committing murder, robberies, and other unlawfulness, are executed. Such persons cannot accuse God, and complain that he has appointed the time of this their untimely death: No, but they must consider, that God has permitted them to come to this time and way of death, as a punishment for their sins and wickedness, whereof they themselves are the only cause; and they may depend upon it, that if they had lived otherwise and been obedient, the Lord would have appointed other times and ways for their death, and would have fulfilled the number of their days.

When a pious man dies, whom we think and judge could have

lived, according to the appearance of his constitution or natural complexion, many years longer; then we must conclude, that *he is taken away, left that wickedness should alter his understanding, or deceit beguile his soul*; or, *that his eyes shall not see the evil which the Lord will bring upon the place.*

When we see the wicked live long, and come to a great age, then we must conclude, that God, who wills not the death of a sinner, gives them time to repent and turn from their wickedness, that they may live, and be eternally happy. But if they resist the grace of God, and continue in their wickedness, he is able to keep them to the great Day of Judgment, and then shall their punishment be greater in the torments of hell.

God regulates likewise the days of man's life, according to outward accidents; it often happens, that a man dies suddenly, is shot, drowned, killed by thunder, or any other accident. This is the bounds which God has appointed, though not through an absolute decree, but for certain reasons which are unknown to us. When such accidents happen, then we should first ascribe the same, to the unsearchable will of God, who has his secret though just causes why he permits such accidents; and we should not make any imaginations or search after such causes, but we should rather say, *Righteous you are, O Lord, and upright are your judgments.* Then should we consider, if the person who perished had been pious, and perished in his lawful calling or not; yea, was he pious, and died in his lawful calling; then his appointed time was come, if not according to the appearance of his natural complexion, yet, according to the sacred will of God, and he is happy; for *all things works good unto them that fear God.* A minister and physician may visit sick people in a plague, and a soldier may fight against the enemies of his king and country; and if anything should befall them in such their laudable calling, they may be assured, that God has appointed their time, since they died in their lawful calling. If he was wicked and profligate, and went without reason in the peril, then receives he his just reward, and found the bounds which he looked for himself. In the meantime, we must not judge them, since *every servant stands or falls to his own master.* Besides, it may be, that such a one may repent with the thief in his last moments, and he received in grace; *For God is able to make him stand.*

But one might object here, and say, since God knows it before, is it not then in his power? Why does he not hinder such accidents, which he could if he would? And why does he permit the one to be hanged, the other to be burned, drowned, killed, executed, and so forth? We can answer hereto;

1. That we should give glory to the Lord God in all things, since he is just. He says by the prophet *Isaiah: Say you to the righteous, that it shall be well with him: Woe unto the wicked, it shall be ill with him*; though the Lord can judge better hereof than man.

2. We must consider, that a thing happens not, because God has foreseen the same, but because it happens through its own causes, so has God foreseen the same. God knows and has foreseen the bounds of men's lives, and the ways of their death, therefore he is not the cause or author of the perishing of anyone; *He has rewarded evil unto himself.* Everyone is cause of his own fortune; if not always as an assenting, yet as an assisting cause; if not always as a beginning, yet as a finishing cause. Fortune and misfortune proceeds from the Lord as the first cause, though with this difference, that he wills the one and permits the other; *I form the light and create darkness; I make peace, and create evil; I the Lord do all these things. Who is he that says, and it comes to pass, when the Lord commands it not? Out of the mouth of the Most High, proceeds evil not good.* Good and evil, life and death, prosperity and adversity, comes from the Lord; but it has pleased the Lord to put this condition by: If we do and

observe his commandments, or not. Therefore, he who observes the commandments of God, and fulfills the prescribed condition, he receives the blessings, and prospers; but he who acts on the contrary, he is not blessed, neither prospers. And in regard to this, man is said to be the cause of his fortune or misfortune.

3. Lastly, we should know that God has given unto every man a free-will, to choose either life or death, which we will. Man can shorten his life, but cannot prolong the same, but God alone can prolong the same; as we may see by the example of self-murderers, such as never come from God's absolute will, but their own wicked desires hath entertained such thoughts, by the instigation of the devil: And God has permitted this their wickedness as a just punishment, since they, through their disobedience, departed from the word of God.

This bounds appointed by God, is nothing else but death; for, *it is appointed to men once to die.* Hereof speaks *Solomon* in our text, wherein death is pictured off;

FIRST, *After its origin.*

SECOND, *After its might and power.*

EXPLANATION of the TEXT

I. Death is pictured off in our text, after its origin.

Death is always painted off as a skeleton, with a scythe in his hand, as a mower; by which is showed, that *the days of man are as grass, and as the flower of the field*, which shall be mowed off once by the scythe of death. St. *John* the Divine, describes death, as a rider *upon a pale horse*, not because he is so of himself, but because he makes man so; and may therefore be called *Magor Misabib*; that is, terror round about. He is called in the Scripture, *a destroyer; the firstborn of death; the messenger of death; king of terrors*; and many more names, which would be too tedious to sum up here. Death is no essence nor spirit, much less any corporal thing, having flesh and bones.

St. *Paul* speaks of his *sting*, and St. *John* speaks of his *sword*: but thereby they will show the fierceness and power of death.

The Scripture speaks of three sorts of death, namely, 1st, the spiritual; 2nd, the corporeal, and, 3rd, the eternal death. The first concerns the soul alone; the second the body, and the third, both soul and body.

First, the spiritual death concerns both the faithful and the unbelievers, though in a different way.

The faithful are spiritually dead from sin, the law and the world.

From sin they are dead in two ways, namely: *First*, by regeneration they are justified and freed from sin by Baptism, and are made partakers of the merits of Christ through faith, and *have put on Christ*. Sin cannot accuse nor condemn them longer before the tribunal of God, but has lost its power by the death of Christ, who lived in them, and for whose sake they *are dead to sin, and live unto righteousness*. The apostle St. *Paul* speaks thereof thus, *How shall we that are dead to sin, live any longer therein? Know you not, that so many of us as were baptized into Jesus Christ, were baptized into his death? Therefore we are buried with him by Baptism into death: That like as Christ was raised up from the dead, by the glory of the Father, even so we also should walk in newness of life. Second*, by renewing with the communion of the death and merits of Christ, and the assistance of the Holy Spirit, they crucify and mortify the old *Adam*, with all his desires, that the same shall not break forth in actions. And since the mortification of the old *Adam* cannot be done at once, therefore commands the Spirit of God us, *to mortify the deeds of the body through the Spirit*, as long as we live; and *to crucify the flesh with the affections and lusts:* That is, not alone resist and subdue the old *Adam*, and the evil desires of the corrupt nature, but also acknowledge the same; and repent; which can be done with the practicing of all Christian virtues; and this is called the new spiritual life.

From the law the faithful are dead, not alone the ceremonial law, called by the apostle St. *Paul, the rudiments of the world*, but also the moral Law, because it *condemns not them that are in Christ Jesus*; therefore, says St. *Paul, you are become dead to the law by the body of Christ; that you should be married to another, even to him who is raised from the dead, that we should bring forth fruit unto God. For when we were in the flesh, the motions of sin which were by the law, did work in our members to bring forth fruit unto death. But now we are delivered from the law, that being dead wherein we were held, that we should serve in newness of Spirit, and not in the oldness of the letter.*

From the world the faithful are dead, because the world is dead to them; therefore are they dead from the world: and because they despise the world, therefore are they despised again by the world.

The ungodly are likewise spiritually dead, but in a quite different way, because they live in sin, which is the death of the soul, and have neither Christ, his Spirit, nor a living faith; they are living dead like the profligate Son.

Second, the corporal death is the separation of soul and body, brought into the world by the two first persons *Adam* and *Eve*, through disobedience; and God afterwards, as a just revenger of sin, has appointed, that all shall die. The body rots and returns to earth; but the soul being immortal, goes to heaven or to hell, and shall be united again at the Day of Judgment, with the body, either to reward or to punishment. *Solomon* describes death in our text also, *The dust shall return to earth, as it was, and the Spirit shall return unto God, who gave it:* wherewith he has regard to the creation, and the loss of *Adam*. His creation was from earth; his loss for the sake of sin was to earth: The first was his honor, the second his dishonor. It was indeed, a great honor for man, that God made him immortal, and an image of his own eternity: On the contrary, it was a great, yea, even the greatest dishonor, that man departed, by the instigation of Satan, from the command of his gracious Creator, and fell thereby into death, according to the pronounced sentence of God, *You shall surely die:* We may see hereby, that there are four causes of this corporal death.

The first is Satan, who deludes man to the transgressing of God's command: wherefore our Lord calls him a *murderer.*

The second is sin, which is as a wide gate, wherethrough death enters to all men; wherefore St. *Paul* calls death, *the wages of sin.* That as a warrior sells himself and his life, to be exposed in the war for small wages, so did our first parents sell themselves, and all their posterity to death, for the eating of the forbidden fruit.

The third is man, who, through his disobedience, transgressed the command of God, and became also guilty of the punishment pronounced against them. wherefore St. *Paul* says, *By one man sin entered into the world, and death by Sin; and so death passed upon all men, for that all have sinned.*

The fourth is God, though not as an effecting cause, but as a just Judge, and revenger of sin. For, since man transgressed the command, therefore did God let his pronounced sentence, that they should die, have its full force. Well, says the wise man, *God made not death;* Which is certain; for, *He has no pleasure in the destruction of the living;* but according to his justice, he executed the sentence, and punishes men with death: Therefore, says *Sirach, life and death comes from the Lord;* not to be understood as a Creator, but as a just revenger.

When soul and body are separated by death, then every part goes to its own place. The body, which is called in our text *dust,* returns to the earth; and the soul; called here *the Spirit,* returns to God.

Solomon calls here the body, *dust,* in regard to the matter whereof

God created man's body; by which we may form many meditations. Dust is little valued by man. What is man to be compared to God? *The nations are as a drop of a bucket, and are counted as the small dust of the balance. Behold, he takes up the Isles as a very little thing.* Dust is light, and a little wind can soon blow it away: A little sickness or ailment may soon carry men away; wherefore the Psalmist says, *Our days are soon cut off, and we fly away.* Dust and ashes are always placed together in the Scripture. A burnt tree is ashes and becomes dust; what is meaner than dust? *I am become like dust and ashes,* complains *Job.* Man is cast and tried in the furnace of misery and adversity, and must suffer greatly. Dust and ashes are alike: All men have one entrance into life, and the like going out, as far as concerns the separation of soul and body; there is no difference between the greatest monarch and the meanest beggar. As long as a tree stands and grows, the same is called by its proper or respective name; but when they are burned none can discern the ashes of one tree from another. Go to the bone-house or the church-yard, and see if you can discern the bones and dust of the kings from the subjects, the master's from the servant's, or the rich from the poor's. Dust is an unclean thing; what is man? Worm food, a bag with maggots, an image of misery, and an example of infirmities. Dust and earth is subject to many hardships; it must endure rain, snow, hail, frost, and drought from heaven; it is plowed and sowed by man, and is trodden by man and creatures. *Man is subject to many miseries.* wherefore *Syrach* says: *Great travail is created for every man, and a heavy yoke is upon the sons of* Adam, *from the day that they go out of their mother's womb, till the day that they return to the mother of all things, namely, the earth.* Of dust and ashes man can burn glass, which is an image of eternity, since it never rots. When man dies his body turns to earth, but *the soul,* being immortal, *returned to God, who gave it.* We can prove the immortality of the soul by the following.

1st, Of the Scripture, both the Old and New Testament. The Lord said unto *Moses, I am the God of your father, the God of* Abraham, *the God of* Isaac, *and the God of* Jacob. Was God their God even after their death? Then follows absolutely, that they did live in a certain way, namely, according to their immortal soul; for God is not a God of the dead but of the living. This argument was so great, that the *Sadducees,* who denied the resurrection of the body, and the immortality of the soul, could not refute it. The example of *Enoch* and *Elias,* are plain proofs of the soul's immortality. *Elias* and *David* requested, that the Lord would take their souls into his hands. Our Savior says, that *none can kill the soul.* The souls of *dives* and *Lazarus* lives after their death. The promise made to the thief on the cross, was in regard to his soul; and the apostle St. *Paul* desired to *depart, and be with Christ.*

2nd, Of the image of God. The image of God consists chiefly in the soul; therefore, as God is immortal, also the soul is immortal. The soul lost through the sin-Fall of *Adam*, its wisdom, holiness and righteousness, but retains its immortality, and is like the angels created of God from the beginning, with an immortal nature. If the soul was mortal and died with the body, why should we be concerned for the renewing of God's image, if there was no difference between man and beast? And it would be needless to hear the Word of God, use the sacraments, and to practice any Christian virtues.

3rd, Of the justice of God. The justice of God will, that *it shall be well with the righteous, and ill with the wicked.* We see this not always fulfilled in the world; for it oftentimes goes well with the wicked, and ill with the righteous; therefore there must certainly be another life, where this shall be fulfilled; as we may see of the example of *dives* and *Lazarus.*

4th, Of the conscience. The wicked are not concerned in prosperity and health about their souls, whether the same are immortal or not; but when it comes to adversity or death, that soul and body shall

516

be separated, then they are concerned and would shrine away, and are terrified: The reason is, that their conscience tells them, that their souls are immortal; and shall return to a place, where they shall receive reward for their doings.

But since the soul is immortal, what becomes of the soul after death? *Solomon* says in our text, it *returns to God, who gave it.*

The faithful return to God, as a gracious and merciful Father, and are received into the everlasting habitations, and *are bound up in the bundle of the Lord.*

The ungodly return to God as a just Judge and Revenger, who shall judge them according to the deeds which they have done in the body, and *cast them out into utter darkness, there shall be weeping and gnashing of teeth.* And this is the third death, namely, the eternal.

I come now to the second part, namely, to show

II. The picture of death, after its might and power.

Although the faithful are freed through Christ from the eternal death, yet they are subject, for the sake of sin which dwells in their flesh, to the temporal. And it often happens, that they have a harder death and departure from the world than the ungodly: For death is such a tyrant, and has no regard to persons either good or bad; the one is as welcome to him as the other. He exercises his tyranny in every place and person.

In every place. Death was to be found in no place before the Fall of *Adam*; but now he is to be found everywhere. We have therefore no need to recourse to halter or sword, for he will come of himself. Death is over all; *Though you exalt yourself as the eagle, and though you set your nest among the stars, thence will I bring you down says the Lord.* Death is round about us. The bear stands today before our neighbor's door, and may be brought tomorrow before our own.

Death is in us, and we may say of our bodies with the children of the prophets, Death is in the pot: As many holes and pores in our bodies, as many gates wherethrough death may enter. The pleasantness of a place hinders nor frees anyone from death; neither can walls or fortifications exclude him; but he breaks through them all, and without regard to persons, attacks the king as well as the subject, the master as the servant, the rich as the poor, the young as the old, and the wise as the foolish.

Death may therefore be rightly compared to the ram of the prophet *Daniel, who pushed Westward, and Northward, and Southward, so that no beast could stand before him, neither was there any that could deliver out of his hand, but he did according to his will, and became great.* And by a *deaf viper*, whose teeth lay so deep concealed in his mouth, that none can see the same; but he who is bit by him feels him. Death has too sharp teeth, namely, the law and sin. Man in health and prosperity feel not the same; but when death approaches, then do we feel the sharpness thereof in our conscience. The bite of a viper is incurable. None can take away sin, except Jesus Christ, who has taken away the sting of death; therefore, *He that believes in Christ, though he were dead, yet shall he live. And whosoever lives and believes in Christ, shall never die.* The viper has no regard to persons, neither has death.

Yet there is great difference between the death of the godly and ungodly. The death of the faithful is not a punishment for sin; for *they are reconciled to God by the death of his Son*, and all their sins are pardoned in Christ. But since they bear the remnants of sin in their flesh, so shall they be brought by this corruption into the incorruptible state; therefore their death is called an unbinding from the world, and a departure to the Father: For they die in a true faith in Christ, without whom none comes to the Father. It is called a free-giving from prison, and a gain; for they receive righteousness

518

instead of sin: The heavenly for the earthly, joy for sorrow, and the eternal life for the corporal death: Hereby the faithful are not afraid of death, but are rejoiced at the approach of the same; saying with the apostle *Paul, We are confident and willing, rather to be absent from the body, and to be present with the Lord.* And with *Simeon, Lord, now let you your servant depart in peace.* They behold death as a good messenger, bringing glad tidings, that they shall soon be in the everlasting habitations by God in heaven, who shall wipe off their tears, and make them eternally happy.

The death of the ungodly is a just punishment from the righteous God, who will bare no longer with their wickedness, but calls them to an account, and pronounces the severe judgment upon them, that *they shall drink the dregs*, and *reap according as they have sowed.* Therefore they do behold death as a king of terrors, and are fore afraid: For their consciences tell them, that they shall go from one death unto another, from the corporal to the eternal, which shall have no end. This is the eternal damnation and torments in hell, which is called the eternal death: Although the damned shall seek after death and never find it. Their end shall be destruction, and their honor dishonor.

The Lord mercifully assist us, and grant us a happy and safe departure of this world, with a good conscience, and full sense of a living faith in Jesus Christ, our blessed Lord and Savior, AMEN.

36

Resurrection

T he Text, 1 CORINTHIANS, 15:51–57, inclusive.

Behold, I show you a mystery: We shall not all sleep, but we shall all be changed, in a moment, in the twinkling of an eye, at the last trump: For the trumpet shall found, and the dead shall be raised incorruptible, and we shall be changed. For this corruptible must put on Incorruption, and this mortal must put on immortality. So when this corruptible shall have put on incorruption, and this mortal shall have put on immortality, then shall be brought to pass the saying that is written, death is swallowed up in victory. O death, where is your sting? O grave, where is your victory? The sting of death is sin, and the strength of death is the law. But thanks be to God, which gives us the victory, through our Lord Jesus Christ.

INTRODUCTION

THE Lord kills and makes alive; he brings down to the grave, and brings up. But though he causes grief, yet will he have compassion, according to the multitude of his mercies. The Lord was willing to tell his mournful people in the Babylonian Captivity, understand this: When he carried the prophet *Ezekiel* out, and set him in the midst of the valley, which was full of dry bones, and asked him, *Can these bones live?* And when the prophet, according to the command of God, prophesied upon them, behold a shaking; and the bones came together, bone to his bone; and the sinews and the flesh came up upon them, and the skin covered them above. Again, the prophet prophesied according to the command of God unto the wind, and the breath came into them, and they lived, and stood up upon their feet, an exceeding great army: As we may read in the 37th chapter of the prophecy of *Ezekiel*, from the 1st, to the 11th verse.

This vision of the prophet may be explained, *First*, according to the letter; and, *Second*, according the Spirit.

1st, According to the letter. The Lord explains this vision by the house of *Israel*, saying, *These bones are the whole house of Israel; behold they say, our bones are dried, and our hope is lost; we are cut off for our parts. Behold, I will open your graves, and cause you to come up out of your graves, and bring you into the land of Israel.* The children of Israel were afflicted and cast down on account of their long captivity in *Babylon*, where they were oppressed and condemned by the *Babylonians*; all their joy was vanished, and they thought that they should never come again into their own land. They were sitting by the rivers of *Babylon*, weeping; and the Babylonians did mock them, saying, *Sing us one of the songs of Zion:* This made them as dead men, and their condition was worse than if dead. For, when one is oppressed by his superior, and none will comfort him, then is his condition worse than the condition of the dead. It was with them, as the Psalmist complains of his own miserable condition; *I am as a man free among the dead, like the slain that lie in the grave, whom you remember no more.* But the Lord, who is pitiful and of tender mercy, and will not be angry forever, would comfort them with this vision, and would thereby say as much; can I quicken the dead and dried bones, and gather one bone to another, and bind them together with sinews and veins, and cover them with skin and flesh: Also, I can bring the children of *Israel* again into their own land, and place them in their former prosperity.

It is also the gracious will of God, that we should never despair, nor lose our hope; for God *is able to do exceeding abundantly above all that we ask or think. His hand is not shortened.* And the Spirit of the Lord says by the prophet *Jeremiah, At what instant I shall speak concerning a nation, and concerning a Kingdom, to pluck up and to pull down, and to destroy it. If that nation against whom I have pronounced, turn from their evil, I will repent of the evil that I thought to do unto them. And at what Instant I shall speak concerning a nation, and concerning a Kingdom, to build and to plant it: If it do evil in my sight, that it obey not my voice, then I will repent of their good, wherewith I said I would benefit them.*

2nd, According to the Spirit, the resurrection of the body is concealed in this vision, which can be proved thereby.

First, that the argument which the Lord uses here, to strengthen the hope of the captive and oppressed Israelites, about their coming back to their own country, should have little effect of comfort; if the Lord should prove one uncertainty by another uncertainty: Since they doubted of their freedom and returning back, which they thought could not happen, and the Lord should comfort and assure them thereof with this vision: What comfort would that be, if the one was as certain as the other!

Secondly, there is mention made in the vision, that as soon as the prophet prophesied, and spoke by the command of God, to the dried bones; *There was a noise and a shaking, and the bones came together, bone to his bone.* And when he prophesied unto the wind, there came a breath from the four winds, and breathed upon the slain and they lived. This cannot be understood of the Israelites alone, for many of them were dead in their captivity, the rest were not gathered from the four corners of the earth, but alone from *Babylon*.

Third, all the old church fathers, have explained this vision by the resurrection of the body, and have always confirmed the certainty of the resurrection with this vision: For as the prophet,

1. Saw a heap of dried bones in the midst of the valley, there are also innumerable dead from the beginning of the world. The bones of some are upon the earth, some in the earth, some in the sea, and others are burned to ashes, or rotten to dust; all these shall rise, and every bone shall come to his bone, and the earth and the sea shall give up the dead which are in them.

2. When the prophet spoke the words of the Lord to the bones, they were joined together with sinews and flesh, and covered over with skins. When the dead at the Day of Judgment shall hear the voice of the Son of Man, then shall they rise up again out of their graves, and receive their flesh and skin, which were eaten by the worms, though in a corruptible way.

3. The prophet saw a breath from the four winds, who breathed upon the dead bodies. Christ shall send on the Day of Judgment, his angels with a great sound of a trumpet, and they shall gather together his elect from the four winds, from one end of heaven to the other.

4. The Lord promised to bring the Israelites to their own land again. God has promised us a better land, the land of the living, where we shall remain forever with the Lord.

The apostle St. *Paul* speaks of the mysterious article in the words of our text, by which we will strive to explain these two heads, namely,

FIRST, *The certainty of the resurrection.*

SECOND, *The condition of our quickened bodies.*

EXPLANATION of the TEXT

I. We will explain the certainty of the resurrection.

The apostle *Paul* calls the article of the resurrection in our text, a mystery, saying, *Behold, I show you a mystery.* The apostle shows hereby,

1. The difficulty of the resurrection. What we can't comprehend with our reason, and cannot find cause for in the nature, but is known alone to God, is a mystery. St. *Paul* calls the incarnation of Christ a *mystery.* This article of the resurrection is also a mystery. No man, let him be ever so wise and penetrating, can find out the same with his reason, but must say thereof, the well is deep, and there is nothing to draw with. Who can comprehend with his human reason, that men's bodies drowned in the sea, afterwards consumed by fishes, and them fishes again consumed by men, or burnt to ashes, or destroyed by wild beasts, or rottened, or turned to earth, shall rise up again, and be quickened, everyone with his own respective body, with flesh, bones, sinews, skin, so as they were here before on earth? Many have therefore doubted of the resurrection, and others have absolutely denied the same; as the *Sadducees* in the time of Christ, and the Stoic philosophers in the time of the apostle *Paul.*

2. But the undeniable certainty of the resurrection may be proved, *First,* by the Scripture. St. *Paul* says, *Behold, I show you a mystery.* He had not learned this in the school of the *Pharisees,* but by his apparition in the third heaven; neither did he *receive it of man, but by the revelation of Jesus Christ.* He that will be assured of this article, must be acquainted with the holy record, or he will err as the *Sadducees,* whom Christ upbraided with their ignorance in the Scriptures; saying, you *do err, not knowing the Scriptures.* I will pass by the many Scripture texts concerning this mysterious article; for

he who believes one will believe the others.

Second, of the power of God. The *Sadducees* did deny the resurrection of the body; because they knew not the power of God; which was a great ignorance. God has created all things of nothing, and man's body of the dust of the earth, much easier can he raise the dead, and give to everyone their own bodies again. This power God has shown by the resurrection of several both in the Old and New Testament; of which examples we may be convinced, by the almighty power of God.

Third, of the justice of God. The justice of God requires, that everyone shall receive according to that he has done, whether it be good or bad: Which, since it is not always fulfilled in this world, will certainly be completed hereafter. We are also more sure of the resurrection of our bodies out of our graves than even out of our beds. The bodies of the ungodly have been in this world, *instruments of unrighteousness unto sin*; and their souls have been yoked together with their bodies in sin; therefore requires the justice of God, their bodies and souls should receive due reward and be punished. The bodies of the faithful have been instruments of righteousness; their eyes have wept sorely over their transgressions; their hands have assisted the wants; their hearts have sighed to God for his gracious help and assistance; and their tongues have been the trumpets of God's glory; therefore it is just, that their bodies should be crowned and rejoice. And *though they have lain among the pots, yet shall they be as the wings of a dove covered with silver, and her feathers with yellow gold.*

Fourth, of the resurrection of Christ. Christ is the head, and we are his members. Since the head is risen, then the members must also rise again. He has taken on our flesh and blood, and is therewith placed on the right hand of God. Our bodies are the temples of the Holy Spirit; we are baptized in the death of Christ, and are fed with his body and blood. How should our bodies be lost in the earth, *If*, as St. Paul says, *the Spirit of him that raised up Jesus from the dead dwell in you, he that raised up, Christ from the dead, shall also quicken your mortal bodies by his Spirit that dwells in you.* The ungodly who have no such spiritual union and fellowship with Christ, shall also rise up to the just judgment of God, as St. *Paul* says, *God has appointed a day, in the which he will judge the world in righteousness, by that man whom he has ordained.*

Fifth, of images and types in nature. The grain lies in the earth as if it was dead and should never appear again; but when the time comes, it sprouts up and grows. The birds lie as in a swoon in the winter, but appears again in the summer. The trees withers away in the Fall, seems to be dead in the Winter, but sprouts and buds out again in the Spring. Such visible arguments, has God laid in the nature, that unbelievers, who will not believe the word of God, should be convinced of them in this article of the resurrection.

3rdly, the generality of this resurrection. All shall be changed: *We shall not all sleep, but we shall all be changed in a moment, in the twinkling of an eye, at the last trump; for the trumpet shall sound, and the dead shall be raised incorruptible, and we shall be changed.* When Christ shall appear in his last advent, he will find many alive who shall be changed, and appear to judgment. Some change shall be as death and resurrection at once, in the twinkling of an eye: Their corrupt and mortal bodies shall put on incorruption and immortality. *The dead in Christ shall rise first, then they which are alive shall be caught up together with them in the clouds*, says St. *Paul*. Besides, the words of the Lord, through the mouth of his apostle *Paul*, are general; *Since by man came death, by man came also the resurrection of the dead. For as in* Adam *all die, so in Christ shall all be made alive.*

The righteous shall rise up by the power of Christ's resurrection, since he is their head, Savior, and Propitiator, as he says himself by

St. *John, Whoso eats my flesh, and drinks my blood, has eternal life, and I will raise them up at the last day.*

The wicked, who would not acknowledge Christ to be their head and Lord, shall rise up by the power of the unchangeable decree of God; which is, that God has decreed from eternity, *to take vengeance an them with flaming fire, that know not God, and that obey not the gospel of our Lord Jesus Christ.* And *they that have done evil, shall come forth to the resurrection of damnation.*

Everyone shall rise up again with his own body that he had in this world; Man with man's body, and woman with woman's body; which we can prove,

First, by the answer which our Savior gave to the *Sadducees,* who desired to know whose wife the woman who had seven husbands, should be in the resurrection: *In the resurrection,* says he, *they neither marry, nor are given in marriage.* He does not say there is no woman in the resurrection: No, he hereby shows us, that everyone shall rise again in their own respective sex. If otherwise, Christ had certainly taken this erroneous opinion away.

Second, Christ rose again with the same body that was crucified; whereof the disciples were convinced after his resurrection; for he showed unto them the holes in his hands and Feet: Likewise shall his members rise up again with their own bodies. Therefore, says *Job: Though after my skin worms destroy this body, yet in my flesh shall I set God, whom I shall see for myself, and mine eyes shall behold, and not another.* Therefore, since the same bodies shall rise again, then it is certain, that there will be a difference between the two sexes.

Third, when our Savior describes by *Matthew,* the condition or state of the eternal life, then he speaks of virgins. And St. *John* the divine *saw the dead, small and great, stand before God.*

4thly, The manner how it shall go in the resurrection, is comprehended in these words of our text; *In a moment, in the twinkling of*

an eye, at the last trump: For the trumpet shall sound. It shall not be long, but in *a moment: For as the lightning comes out of the east, and shines even unto the west, so shall also the coming of the Son of Man be. The trumpet shall sound,* which the apostle explains in another place, with *the voice of an archangel.* An archangel shall, as a herald, pronounce the coming of the Lord. For, as an archangel pronounce the first advent of Christ, also shall an archangel pronounce his second advent. And as the trumpets were sounded by the giving of the law on Mount *Sinai,* also shall the trumpet sound by the executing of the law on the Last Day. When the archangel has also pronounced the coming of Christ, *then the Son of Man shall come in his glory, and all the holy angels with him: And he shall send his angels, with a great sound of a trumpet, and they shall gather together his elect from the four winds, from one end of heaven to the other.* Thereupon shall, in a moment, in the twinkling of an eye, the resurrection of the body follow, though not in a confusion; for God is a God of order and decency, and *not an author of confusion.* The dead in Christ shall rise first; that is, all the faithful, who are dead from the beginning until the end of the world, shall come forth out of their graves: Afterwards shall the faithful, who are alive and remain, be changed in a moment; at last the ungodly shall rise and be changed. All which shall be done in a moment, in the twinkling of an eye. In a moment every soul shall come to its respective body. In a moment shall the living be changed, and become immortal. In a moment they shall be caught up together in the clouds, to meet the Lord in the air, and appear to judgment. So that men may ask with astonishment about the souls, *Who are these that fly as a cloud, and as the doves to their windows?*

II. We will now explain the state and condition of the quickened bodies.

But how shall the bodies be in the resurrection? The apostle says in our text, *This corruptible must put on incorruption, and this mortal must put on immortality.* Hereby we may conclude how this change shall be. Before we die we have natural bodies, requiring victuals, drink, rest, &c. But in the resurrection, our bodies shall become changed, and become spiritual and immortal, not wanting victuals, drink, rest, or such like; and yet they shall be true bodies in their essence. This change shall in particular consist in the following, *to wit,*

1. In incorruption. We bear in this world earthen vessels, subject to corruption, and therefore with *Job,* call the grave our *Father,* and the worms our *mother* and *sisters.* Sin is a venomous worm in our bodies; and as rust on the iron, consuming the same: But all such corruption shall be lost in the resurrections, and our bodies shall put on incorruption. *Job* shall not have a body full of sores and boils; *Leo* shall not have weak eyes, neither shall *Barsillai* complain of the weakness of his age; as we may be convinced of by the state of *Lazarus,* when he was in the Bosom of *Abraham.*

2. In immortality. We die daily as long as we are in this world; and there is no need of asking when we shall die. But, when shall we leave off dying? Death is a worm gnawing constantly on the root of the tree of our life; but in the resurrection, this mortal shall put on immortality, and our bodies shall become immortal, and remain to eternity.

The godly and ungodly shall both have these two qualities of incorruption and immortality in common, though with great dif-ference. The incorruption and immortality of the faithful, shall be their greatest salvation, glory and joy: But on the contrary, that of the ungodly shall be their greatest shame, misery, and sorrow. And since the prophet *Daniel* says, *That they shall awake to shame and everlasting contempt*; then it is to be supposed, that they shall awake with the same defected bodies as they had here on earth: *They shall seek death and shall not find it, and shall desire to die, and death shall flee from them.*

The bodies of the faithful shall have according to the words of the apostle *Paul*, in the same chapter of our text words, the following qualifications:

First, clearness and glory. *It is sown in dishonor, it is raised in glory.* When we see a dead person laid in the coffin, then the body is black, and often stinking, so that we cannot forbear the same; but in the resurrection, the children of God shall receive glorious bodies, full of glance and clearness, as the transfigured body of Christ did shine on Mount *Tabor*; And *like apples of gold in pictures of silver*, shall the soul shine in the body after the resurrection.

Second, power and strength. *It is sown in weakness, it is raised in power.* The faithful, who may have had any defect in their bodies in this world, shall receive at the resurrection, complete bodies without any defect: For, as the body of Christ was fully perfect after the resurrection, so shall also the bodies of the faithful be. Therefore says St. *Paul* of the Day of Judgment and resurrection; *Our conversation is in heaven, from where also we look for the Savior, the Lord Jesus Christ; who shall change our vile body, that it may be fashioned like unto his glorious body.*

Third, spiritually. *It is sown a natural body, it is raised a spiritual body.* Our Savior explains this also; *In the resurrection they are as the angels of God in heaven*; not to be understood in essence, as if they should receive the nature of angels, but in gifts and excellency. Angels are wise and penetrating spirits; also the faithful shall be in the resurrection. Angels are glorious creatures; *The righteous shall shine forth as the sun in the Kingdom of their Father.* Angels are strong giants. The faithful shall receive in the resurrection strong bodies. Angels are clean spirits, and are therefore said to be *clothed in pure and white linen.* The faithful shall be in the resurrection, holy and clean without sin; therefore they are said *to have washed their robes, and made them white in the blood of the Lamb.* Angels are quick, and are therefore seen with wings. The faithful shall receive in the resurrection quick bodies: *They shall shine, and run to and fro like sparks among the stubble.* Our bodies are heavy in this world; for when the soul flies up to heaven, it is kept back through and by the heaviness of the body; but in the resurrection, our bodies shall become as light as the souls, and be like birds.

Upon such a change shall follow freedom from death, sin, the law, the devil, and hell.

The righteous and faithful shall become in the resurrection, free

1st, From death. *Death is swallowed up in victory.* The apostle *Paul* has borrowed these words of the prophets *Isaiah* and *Hosea*, and will thereby show and prove the truth of the Scriptures. Death did rule as a mighty tyrant over all men, until the coming of Christ; who by his death, swallowed up death in victory, and *delivered them who through fear of death, were all their lifetime subject to bondage.* Not to be understood, as if they who died before the coming of Christ, were all condemned to the eternal death: For the fathers believed in Christ, and were saved. But because it was then plainly demonstrated, that Christ took away death, and swallowed the same in victory, when he rose from the dead; Death swallowed up Christ like the whale the prophet *Jonah*; but Christ swallowed death up in victory, like *Aaron*'s rod swallowed-up the rods of the *Egyptian* sorcerer's serpent, so that they were seen no more: Death thereby lost the battle, and his claim to the faithful; who, although they are swallowed up by the temporal death, yet will come forth again to the eternal life. If death then be swallowed up in victory, the forerunners of death, namely sin and the law; nor the followers, namely, the devil and hell, cannot prevail.

2nd, From sin. *O death, where is your sting? O grave, where is your victory? The sting of death is sin.* Death consumes and destroys us, even in our lifetime, on account of sin; for when we feel the remorse and check of conscience, then we feel the sting of death, and perceive that we must die: But Christ has taken away the sting from death, by giving full satisfaction for sin through his death and bloody ransom; *There is therefore now no condemnation to them which are in Christ Jesus.* Sin shall be taken away entirely in the resurrection, and the faithful shall not sin any more. But as the holy angels are confirmed in goodness, by the continual beholding of God's countenance, so also shall the righteous be; they shall not alone be free from sinful actions, but also from sinful desires.

3rd, From the law. The law is fulfilled with the holy life of Christ. The children of God must place the law before their eyes in this world; for to learn thereby their own deficiency, and cleave nearer to Jesus Christ, like a child to its mother when the school-master intends to correct it. For the law is our tutor to Christ, and the knowledge of sin comes from the law: But the tables of *Moses* shall be entirely destroyed and broke in the resurrection, and there shall be no occasion for the law, since God himself will be a living and visible law to the faithful.

4th, From Satan and hell. Satan is conquered, and hell is destroyed. Satan cried out before, "victory, victory!" but now the scale is altered, and Jesus Christ calls "victory, victory!" of which victory all the faithful are partakers. We sing of this victory as long as we are here on earth, *In the tabernacles of the righteous:* But in the resurrection we shall rightly learn this victory, when *the God of peace shall bruise Satan under our feet;* then we shall sing and rejoice with all the saints and elect; *Thanks be to God, which gives us the victory through our Lord Jesus Christ.*

We shall then praise and glorify,

First, the truth of God; who has revealed to us in his word, the mystery of the resurrection, and has confirmed the same with so many examples, that we by them should be convinced of the truth of the general resurrection.

Second, the wisdom and power of God. Has human reason looked upon the article of the resurrection to be incredible? Yet, the power and wisdom of God is able to bring it to pass; for nothing is impossible for God. The Lord therefore says of the dried bones by the prophet *Ezekiel, you shall know that I am the Lord.*

Third, the justice of God, who rewards everyone according to his works. Everyone shall receive in the resurrection, as they have deserved. *They that have done good shall come forth unto the resurrection of life; and they that have done evil, unto the resurrection of damnation.* The righteous shall be rejoiced thereof, that God is just, *Who judges the world in righteousness, and minister judgment to the people in uprightness.*

Since we know, and are certainly assured, that there shall be a general resurrection, let us then consider, *What manner of persons we ought to be, namely, in all holy conversation and godliness,* as long as we are here on earth. Is there a resurrection? Then must a happy death go before, that we die from sin, which is called the first resurrection: For he that bewails his sins, prays to God for forgiveness, and is resolved no more to consent to sin, is risen from the death of sin. This is the first resurrection. The Spirit of the Lord says therefore, *Blessed and holy is he that has part in the first resurrection, on such the second. Death has no power.* If there is a resurrection, why do so many live so careless in the world, as if there was no God, who will reward the good and punish the wicked? Many profess, that they believe a resurrection to come, but in works they deny it. If they did believe a resurrection, then would they also believe what is to follow thereon; *to wit, a sharp and severe judgment, where everyone shall receive the thing done in the body, either good or bad.* He who hopes to rise happy, must endeavor to die happy: For in the same condition man dies, in the same he shall rise up. If he dies in a true faith in the grace of God in Jesus Christ, he shall also rise up in faith in the grace of God in Christ Jesus. But he that would die happy, must live a Christian life; for upon a Christian life a happy death follows. After the apostle *Paul* had spoken largely of the resurrection of the body in our text chapter, then he concludes in the 34th verse with these words, *Awake to righteousness, and sin not; for some have not the knowledge of God.* The apostle learns us therewith, that the article of the resurrection of the dead should serve to encourage us to rise from sin, which is the first resurrection, if we will be partakers of the second. Our Savior joins both resurrections together, the first as a fore-runner to the second: The first in repentance, the second in salvation; *Verily, verily I say unto you, the hour is coming, and now is, when the dead shall hear the voice of the Son of God, and they that hear shall live.* Our Savior shows hereby, that they alone, who have heard in this life the voice of the Son of God in the gospel, and by faith are made partakers, of the spiritual life, shall rise to the eternal life in the general resurrection. He who will sprout up in the resurrection to the eternal life, must be grafted here by faith in the tree of life, Jesus Christ. He who will rise with Christ as his head and Lord, must in this life be his true members, and live in him. He who has sought many in this world against the spiritual enemies, and hath conquered by the power of the Holy Spirit, can say comfortably in the hour of death, *I have fought a good fight, I have finished my course, I have kept the faith; henceforth there is laid up for me a crown of righteousness: Thanks be to God, which gives us victory through our Lord Jesus Christ.*

The Lord be gracious unto us, and by the assistance of the Holy Spirit, strengthen our faith and hope of the resurrection, that we may patiently go through the troubles of this world, live a Christian life, and die happy, for the sake of our blessed Lord and Savior, Jesus Christ, AMEN:

37

The Day of Judgment

The Text, 2 CORINTHIANS, 5:10.

We must all appear before the judgment seat of Christ, that everyone may receive the things done in his body, according to that he has done, whether it be good or bad.

INTRODUCTION

SECURITY has cast many more into hell than sin itself; and we man therefore say of sin, and security in sin, the same as the women of *Israel* sung of *Saul* and *David*. Sin has slain thousands, but security ten thousands. Security brought the first world into destruction, and will also cause the destruction of the last world: Our blessed Savior therefore always admonishes, that we should be watchful towards his second coming, and the more, since the hour and day of this his coming is unknown to us; wherefore our Savior himself says by St. *Mark*, Chap. 13:32, 33. *Of that day and that hour knows no man, no not the angels which are in heaven, neither the Son, but the Father. Take you heed, watch and pray, for you know not when the time is.* These

536

words contain two parts; 1*st*, The unexpected coming of Christ to judgment; and, 2*d*, An admonition to a worthy preparation for that day.

First, the unexpected coming of Christ to judgment, is laid before us in these words, *Of that day and that hour knows no man, no not the angels which are in heaven, neither the Son, but the Father.* There has been some who audaciously have dared to peep into this great mystery, and have tried to tell the year and day of the great judgment to come; but they were deceived, and *in professing themselves to be wise, they became fools; they became vain in their imaginations, and their foolish hearts were darkened.* We may conclude that the Day of Judgment is not far off; but *of that day and that hour, knows no man.* For as we may conclude by the symptoms, when a man is deadly sick, his strength decays, and his Spirits seem spent, that he shall die; but the hour or moment thereof is unknown and uncertain. We may also conclude of the foregoing marks according to the revelations in the word of God, that the Day of Judgment is not far off; but *of that day and that hour knows no man, neither the angels which are in heaven, neither the Son, but the Father.* The angels are high enlightened spirits, and behold always the countenance of God in heaven, knowing many mysteries, but this mystery of the great Day of Judgment is hid from them; and they know not the same, neither from natural causes, experience, nor revelations.

But it seems wonderful, that the Son knows not the Day of Judgment. Should the Son, who is not alone, according to his divine nature, the wisdom of the Father, but has also, according to the human nature by the power of the personal union, all the treasures of the godly wisdom and knowledge, know the day and hour of the great Day of Judgment? Yea, certainly he knows the same, for *he and the Father are one,* in essence, power and knowledge: All what the Father has is his; he is in the bosom of the Father and knows all things: Should he then not know the Day of Judgment? He knows the tokens which shall go before this day: Should he not know the day itself? And since the Father has committed all judgment unto him, then he must certainly know the day and hour when this judgment shall be: But we should know that our blessed Savior speaks here in these words of himself as of another man, being now in the state of his humiliation, wherein he knew not all things, not using always the divine attributes. His human nature was well made in the first moment of his conception, by the power of the personal union, a partaker of all the divine attributes, though since he had taken upon him the Infirmities of human nature, by which *He*, like another man, *grew strong in Spirit filled with wisdom*; like another man *marveled*; and like another man *learned obedience.* There were several things which he knew not in this state, whereof the Day of Judgment was one. Besides, our Savior would instruct his disciples, that they should not be concerned about the knowledge of this day: For, since the Son knew not the same, then should they nor none else, have any hindrance thereby in the cause of their salvation; but they should endeavor to prepare themselves for that day, according to,

Second, his admonition to a worthy preparation, saying, *Take you heed, watch and pray, for you know not when the time is.* Our Savior admonished us in these words to three things; *First*, to carefulness; *Second*, to watchfulness; and, *Third*, to prayers.

1st, To carefulness, when we do admonish anyone to carefulness, we always say, *take heed.* We observe this very carefully in all worldly things, much more ought we to observe it in the things which concerns our eternal welfare. We must therefore

Look upwards to God, whose *eyes are upon the ways of man, and sees all his going*, and live therefore in daily repentance, *working out your own salvation, in fear and trembling.* The door of God's grace stands open in this life, but the same will be shut up at the Last Day;

and woe then to the ungodly. We must,

Look downwards: There considering the many souls who lay damned in the eternal torments of hell, on account of sin and wickedness committed in their Lifetime; and therefore take heed that we become not partakers of their crime, and also of the same punishment. We must

Look before us. The way to eternal life is narrow, therefore we must walk circumspectly in the same, like one walking over the sea upon a small plank is always careful of every step he takes. We must,

Look about us, considering the corrupt and deceitful world we live in, and how soon we may be deceived, and brought astray, like they who travel in dangerous places among robbers, and are always on their guard that nothing shall befall them. We must,

Look behind us, not as *Lot's* wife, nor as they who have laid the hands upon the plough, and look behind; but as the wise, who consider rightly what may befall them hereafter. He also who takes heed will strive after,

2nd, Watchfullness. *Watch.* This watchfullness comprehends as follows.

First, the continual remembrance and expectation of the judgment to come. Our Savior uses in regard to this, a comparison, saying, *Let your loins be girded about, and your lights burning, and you yourselves like unto men that wait for their Lord, when he will return from the wedding; that, when he comes and knocks, they may open unto him immediately.*

Second, a worthy preparation. He who sleeps sees no danger, and is therefore not afraid; but he who wakes sees all dangers, and is sore afraid, left he should perish in the peril: wherefore, says *Solomon, A prudent man foresees the evil, and hides himself, but the simple pass on and are punished.*

Third, sobriety and temperance, gluttony and drunkenness will be in great vogue towards the latter end of the world, like as it was in the days before the Flood. The apostle St. *Paul* admonishes therefore, *Let us not sleep as do others, but let us watch and be sober: For they that sleep, sleep in the night, and they that be drunk, are drunk in the night.* Our Savior compares the Last Day to a snare; should we then not live in sobriety and temperance? As a fowler sets his snares out to catch birds, also Satan sets out his snares to catch souls; and they who light and delight in his snares are eternally lost.

Four, diligence in the lawful calling. He who sleeps does nothing. The apostle therefore admonishes, *Watch you in all things, endure afflictions, do the work, and make full proof of your ministry.* But since it is not in our own power to take heed, and watch as carefully as we ought to do, therefore we should implore the mercy and grace of God, with

Thirdly, prayers. *Pray.* Prayers make us watchful, and watchfulness encourages our prayers: They are therefore placed together, *watch and pray.* And that none should think that this admonition concerns him not, therefore our Savior says in the last part of the chapter, *What I say unto you, I say unto all, watch.* Our Savior hereby shows, that, although they should not all live at his coming to judgment, they should not be excluded therefrom, but they should all be judged according as they were found.

The apostle St. *Paul* learns and convinces us in the words of our text, how highly needful it is to be careful and watch for the coming of our Lord Jesus Christ to judgment, either by death, or by the Last Day, saying, *We must all appear before the judgment seat of Christ, that everyone may receive the things done in his body, according to that he has done, whether it be good or bad.* We will, according to these words, treat here of the following parts.

FIRST, *Of the Judgment and the Judge.*

SECOND, *Of the Causes and Objects.*

THIRD, *Of the Process.*

EXPLANATION of the TEXT

I. Part of the Judgment and Judge.

This article of the Day of Judgment, is as incredible and intelligible for human reason, as the article of the general resurrection; wherefore *many scoffers walking after their own lusts, say: Where is the promise of his coming? For since the fathers fell asleep, all things continue as they were from the beginning of the creation.* But that the Day of Judgment will certainly come, we may prove by the following.

1st, Of the Holy Scripture, both Old and New Testament.

In the Old Testament. *Enoch,* the seventh man from *Adam;* did prophesy of this day, saying, *Behold the Lord comes with ten thousands of his saints, to execute judgment upon all. Abraham* willing to move God to compassion over *Sodom,* said, *Shall not the Judge of all the earth do right?* The royal Psalmist speaks also of the Day of Judgment, *The Lord has prepared his throne for judgment, and he shall judge the world in righteousness.* And in another place, *Our God shall come, and shall not keep silence. A fire shall devour before him, and it shall be very tempestuous round about him. He shall call to the heavens from above, and to the earth, that he may judge his people.*

In the New Testament we have many texts by which this article may be proved. It is the promise of our blessed Lord and Savior, in the conclusion of the evangelical writings; *He which testifies these things, says, surely I come quickly, Amen.*

2nd, Of particular judgments. *The angels who sinned, were cast down to hell, and delivered unto chains of darkness.* The first world was destroyed by water; *Sodom* with fire and brimstone from heaven. *Cain* with a curse; *Er* and *Onan* with sudden death; *Core* and his company, with sinking in the earth; The *Egyptians* with ten horrible plagues; and the *Canaanites* with destruction. These and many more examples convince us, that there shall be a day wherein God shall keep judgment.

3rd, Of worldly judgment. God has ordained right and judgment upon earth; and commanded, that they who are to judge, should be careful and judge rightly. Therefore, we may conclude, that there will come a day when everyone shall be called to an account, and receive according as he has done, whether it be good or bad; *Horribly and speedily shall be come upon the ministers of his Kingdom who have not judged aright; for a sharp judgment shall be to them that be in high places.*

4th, Of the sight of the prophet *Daniel*, which is also described: *The thrones were cast down, and the Ancient of Days did set, whose garment was white as snow, and the hair of his head like pure wool. His throne was like the fiery flame, and his wheels as burning fire. A fiery stream issued and came forth from before him: Thousands upon thousands ministered unto him, and ten thousand times ten thousand stood before him. The judgment was set, and the books were opened. I saw in the night visions, and behold the Son of Man came with the clouds of heaven, and came to the Ancient of Days, and they brought him near before him: And there was given him dominion and glory, and a Kingdom, that people, nations and languages should serve him. His dominion is an everlasting dominion, which shall not pass away, and his Kingdom that which shall not be destroyed.* This vision is a type to Christ's ascension and coming to judgment.

Fifth, of the justice of God. They who will not believe the Last Day, make God a blind, wicked, unjust, unmerciful, and false God. Blind, as if he did not see nor care how it goes in the world; neither took notice nor was concerned about men's actions. Wicked, as if he was pleased with the wickedness of the world, since he punishes them not in this world. Unjust, since he rewards not always his faithful servants here in time; for we see many of the wicked often prosper; and on the contrary, many of the pious suffer. Unmerciful, as if he delighted in the evil that befalls the godly, and the good that befalls the ungodly. False, as if he had revealed to us a Day of Judgment, which would not come. Away with such blasphemous thoughts, being alone the Instigations of Satan, in order to bring us to security in sin. On the contrary, we believe and confide in with our hearts, what we confess with our mouths in our Apostles' Creed, That our Lord Jesus Christ shall come to judge the quick and the dead.

Let us now place our eyes and thoughts upon the Judge, who is Jesus Christ. *We must all appear before the judgment seat of Christ.* Jesus Christ, the Son of God and man, shall be our judge in his human nature, that he may be seen by all; for *the Father has given him authority to judgment, because he is the Son of Man.* He shall be our judge according to both natures, for to keep judgment belongs to his royal office; wherefore he is called a *King* by the evangelist *Matthew*, in the description of the judgment, when he shall appear in his godly and majestic glory, and his face shall shine brighter than the sun. If his face shined on Mount *Tabor* as the sun, and his raiment as white as the light, in the state of his humiliation, much brighter will the same shine in the state of exaltation when he will come to judgment. His coming to judgment is therefore called, *The righteousness of his coming. The glorious appearing of the great God. A revelation from heaven with his mighty angels.* He shall come forth *in his glory*, which no angel nor creature has had in common with him. *He shall come in the glory of his Father, the glory as of the only begotten of the Father, which he had with the Father before the world was.* This majestic glory shall appear at the Day of Judgment, both inward and outward.

The majesty and glory of the Judge shall appear inward in wisdom, omniscience, justice, power, and omnipresence. In wisdom: *Solomon* is mightily recommended in the holy records on account of his wisdom; but this Judge is all wisdom himself, *in whom are held all the treasures of wisdom and knowledge*, and *will* therefore *bring to light the hidden things of darkness, and will make manifest the counsels of the heart*. In omniscience: If he knew in the state of his humiliation even the thoughts of men, much more will he know everything at the Last Day: *For all things are naked and opened unto the eyes of him with whom we have to do*. In justice: He shall judge the whole world without exception of persons, and shall *give every man according as his work shall be*. In power: kings, princes, and all the mighty, shall humble themselves before this glorious monarch, and acknowledge his superiority in the power of his glory: Yea all nations shall appear before the judgment seat of Christ, who *shall separate them one from another, as a Shepherd divides his sheep from the goats. And he shall set the sheep on his right hand, but the goats on the left. Then shall the King say unto them on his right hand, come you blessed of my Father, inherit the Kingdom prepared for you from the foundation of the world. Then shall he say also unto them on his left hand, depart from me you cursed, into everlasting fire, prepared for the devil and his angels*. In omnipresence: The brightness of his glorious coming shall be visible to all, so that every eye, on what place whatsoever, shall see him; though with this difference, the faithful shall be rejoiced, but the ungodly shall be fore afraid, and none shall be able to hide themselves, or escape his judgment. For *though they dig into hell, thence shall mine hand take them; though they climb up to heaven, thence will I bring them down: And though they hide themselves from my sight in the bottom of the sea, thence will I command the serpent, and he shall bite them*, says the Lord by the prophet *Amos*.

The majesty and glory of the Judge should appear outwards in the following.

First, in the multitude of angels and heavenly hosts. All the holy angels shall follow him, thousand upon thousands shall minister unto him, and ten thousand times ten thousand shall stand before him, and minister as servants unto him, sitting as Judge upon his glorious throne in the clouds, and their office shall consist in blowing in the trumpets: For *be shall send his angels with a great sound of a trumpet.* Trumpets were used in old time in war to call the assembly and the warriors together: We shall all be called together at the Last Day by the sound of the trumpet, to *appear before the judgment seat of Christ,* who *shall put all his enemies under his feet.* The walls of *Jericho* fell down by the sounding of the trumpet, in the time of *Joshua*, also shall the frame of the whole universe fall down by the sounding of the trumpet at the coming of Christ to judgment: The sounding of the trumpet by the *Jews* in the Jubilee, was not alone a type to the propagation of Christ's gospel over the whole world, but also to the Day of Judgment, *when God shall judge the secrets of men by Jesus Christ according to the gospel.* The office of the angels shall consist also in *gathering together the elect from the four winds, from one end of heaven to the other*, and in *gathering together all things that offend, and them which do iniquity, and cast them into a furnace of fire.* The majesty and glory of the Judge shall appear,

Secondly, In the magnificence and excellency of his judgment seat. Worldly kings and magistrates have their thrones and tribunals. *King Solomon made a great throne of ivory, and overlaid it with the best gold.* Christ shall also have his throne, which shall be partly visible, and partly invisible. The invisible throne of Christ shall be the *right hand of God's majesty* and glory: The visible throne of Christ shall be *the clouds*; these clouds shall shine clear for the godly, but dark for the ungodly, like the pillar of clouds in the time of *Moses*, between the camp of the *Egyptians*, and the camp of *Israel*, it was dark to the *Egyptians*, but light to the children of *Israel.* Christ shall also blot out

545

on the Last Day the transgressions of the faithful as a cloud, but the transgressions of the ungodly shall be as a thick cloud unto them, for that day shall be unto them *a day of wrath; a day of trouble and distress, a day of waste and desolation, a day of darkness and gloominess, a day of clouds and thick darkness.* The majesty and glory shall appear,

Thirdly, of the magnificence of his fellow judges. Worldly magistrates have their fellow judges, who consent with them in the judgment; Christ shall also have his fellow judges, who shall be the apostles and the saints: Christ says himself to the apostles, *you also shall sit upon twelve thrones, judging the twelve tribes of Israel:* That is, that they by their examples and testimony should confirm the Judgment of Christ, to be conformable to the gospel preached by them. The apostle St. *Paul* says of the saints, *Do you not know that the saints shall judge the world?* How? They shall be evidences against them, and hear the pronouncing of the sentence, *Then shall the righteous man stand in great boldness, before the face of such as have afflicted him.* They shall consent in the judgment, and say: *Allelujah, salvation, and glory and honor and power, unto the Lord our God: For true and right are his judgments.* They shall show unto the ungodly their faith and repentance, which they ought to have followed: wherefore Christ says, That the men of *Nineveh* shall rise in judgment with the *Jews,* and condemn them, because they repented at the preaching of *Jonah,* but the *Jews* would not repent by the preaching of Christ himself; they shall also testify of the good actions of the faithful. We must therefore apprehend the words of our Savior in this meaning, when he says by St. *Luke: Make to yourselves friends of the mammon of unrighteousness; that, when you fail, they may receive you into everlasting habitations.*

This coming of Christ to judgment shall be quick and unexpected; therefore is the same compared, by *lightning that lightens out of one part under heaven, and shines unto the other part under Heaven;*

Lightning makes such light that we can see thereby. When Christ comes to judgment, *be will make manifest the counsels of the heart.* Lightning terrifies men and beasts: The unexpected coming of Christ shall be dreadful; for, *then shall all the tribes of the earth mourn.* Lightning breaks forth out of the clouds; Christ shall appear in the clouds at the Day of Judgment: Lightning is of a short duration; the coming of Christ to judgment, the judgment, and the execution thereof shall soon be executed and finished, and the world come to an end. The coming of Christ to judgment is also compared by *a thief:* We must not look in this comparison the person or action of the thief, in regard to the person or action of Christ; No, for there is great difference between a thief, and coming as a thief; but we must behold the time of the coming of a thief, which is always unexpected. The thief comes when he is least expected; The coming of Christ to judgment shall be when he is least expected: The thief steals all he can get, and always the best; the unexpected coming of the Last Day will deprive many from a part in the Kingdom of Heaven. If the good man knew in what watch the thief would come, he would watch, and not suffer his house to be broke open: If we knew the hour of Christ's coming to judgment, we would certainly watch, and be prepared; but, since it is uncertain, therefore is it best that we take heed, watch, and pray. We are careful about worldly things, and can always be watchful about them, how much more ought we to be on our guard, and be careful for the heavenly things, since the eternal welfare of our immortal souls depends thereon. The coming of Christ is likewise compared by a snare; the bird flees about from one limb to another, in the mean while the fowler sets his snares and spreads grains about and under the snare, but the bird coming to feed thereon, is caught in the snare and captivated: They who are overtaken by the Last Day shall not escape; but they who are written among the living shall be saved to eternal happiness. We will now

547

treat of,

II. The Causes and Objects.

The causes which shall be brought forth before this dreadful tribunal, are either concerning the persons, or the cause in themselves. The persons are,

First, the wicked angels. St. *Paul* says therefore, *know you not, that we shall judge angels.* The devils were condemned as soon as they fell, and *were reserved in everlasting chains under darkness unto the judgment of the Great Day*; though they are not so close kept in hell, but they can go about in the world: but at this Day of Judgment they shall be cast out into everlasting fire, prepared for them and their angels. Then *shall the devil be cast into the lake of fire and brimstone, and shall be tormented day and night forever and ever.* And then shall the children of God rejoice over the just judgment of God, that their accuser and tempter is condemned and rewarded for his wickedness.

Secondly, the antichrist, other ways called in the holy records, the beast with the false prophet: Of whom St. *John* the Divine says, *And the beast was taken, and with him the false prophet, that wrought miracles before him, with which be deceived them that had received the mark of the beast, and them that worshiped his image. These both were cast alive into a lake of fire burning with brimstone.*

Thirdly, all men. *We must all appear.* The word all comprehends both the quick and the dead: By the quick must be understood, them who shall be alive at the coming of Christ, and shall be changed in a twinkling of an eye: By the dead must be understood all them who are dead from the beginning of the world unto this Great Day. This word all comprehends both just and unjust, though with this difference, that the sins and transgressions of the faithful shall not be made manifest; since God has promised, That *he has blotted out their*

548

transgressions, and will not remember their sins; but *will cast them into the depth of the sea*; and because Christ is become their propitiations. Besides, we see in the description of the Day of Judgment by St. *Matthew*, that there will be mention made of the good works done by the faithful alone, and not of their transgressions. The faithful will thereby *have Boldness in the Day of Judgment*, and not be afraid.

The causes in themselves, which shall be brought forth, shall be men's belief or unbelief, actions, words, and thoughts.

1*st*, Their belief or unbelief. Christ judges in his word, everyone's faith or unbelief, saying, *He that believes on the Son, has everlasting life; and be that believes not the Son, shall not see life, but the wrath of God abides on him*. But on the Last Day he will make manifest, who has believed or not. And since none can see faith in this world, except as far as we can suppose or conclude of men's actions, therefore shall the judgment be pronounced,

2*ndly*. Over their actions. *Everyone shall receive the things done in his body, according to what he has done, whether it be good or bad*. Then shall the good works which the faithful have done in secret be made manifest, and they will be rewarded according; and the evil which the ungodly have committed in this world shall be made manifest, and they will be punished accordingly, *in outer darkness, where shall be weeping and gnashing of teeth*.

3*rdly*, Their words. *Behold the Lord comes to execute judgment upon all, and to convince all that are ungodly among them, of all their ungodly deeds, and of all their hard speeches, which ungodly sinners have spoken against him*. Our Savior says, *I say unto you, that every idle word, that men shall speak, they shall give account thereof in the Day of Judgment*.

4*thly*, Their thoughts. *Inquisition shall be made into the counsels of the ungodly, and the sound of his words shall come unto the Lord, for the manifestation of his wickedness*. The Lord comes, and *will bring to light the hidden things of darkness, and will make manifest the counsels* *of the hearts. God shall bring every work into judgment, with every secret thing, whether it be good, or whether it be evil.* We are now to treat of,

III. The Process.

It is dreadful to behold a criminal brought to his trial; how the court is opened, the Judge and his fellow judges take their seats; the criminal is brought before the bar and is accused, whereon he becomes ashamed and terrified, and confesses his crime, whereon judgment is pronounced on him, and he is delivered over to the common executioner, who will deprive him of his life: much more horrible will the Last Day be, when the sharpest judgment shall be kept, and justice will be exercised without mercy. The severity of this judgment will consist in the following.

First, in the citation of everyone to appear in their own person. We may send in this world another for us, when we are summoned to appear in court; but at the Last Day everyone shall appear in their person, and hear these words, *Give an account of your stewardship.* God summons us often in his long-suffering in this world; first with the threatening of the law; then with crosses and affliction, and dreadful examples of others: But at the Last Day we shall be summoned but once, by the sound of the last trumpet, in a moment, in the twinkling of an eye, the dead shall come forth, and they which are alive and remain, shall be caught up together in the clouds, to meet the Lord in the air.

Secondly, in the gathering of all before his throne of judgment: Good God! what a multitude will there be; and *Adam* and *Eve* will wonder mightily over the increase of their posterity.

Thirdly, in the separation of this multitude into two heaps. For the angels shall separate the sheep from the goats, the tares from the wheat, and the bad fish from the good fish.

Fourthly, in the trying of the causes by worldly judges, before they pass their judgments, they hear the parties and evidences: The trial at the Last Day shall be before the judgment also, that although the Judge is the all-knowing God, who need no instruction nor evidences, yet since he hath declared to keep this judgment public, *He will make manifest the counsels of the hearts, and bring to light the hidden things of darkness*; and everyone shall, through a particular effect of the godly power, remember their own work, and accordingly be accused or excused by their conscience: Then shall the books be opened, namely,

1. The Book of Life, wherein the names of the faithful are written: For in the Day of Judgment it shall be made manifest unto men and angels, whom God has elected from eternity, *to wit*, them whose names are written in the Book of Life, through a living faith in Christ Jesus; and on the contrary, who were rejected, *to wit*, them whose names are not written in the Book of Life through their unbelief.

2. The book of God's omniscience: From whose all-knowing and all-seeing eyes nothing is hid: This book shall be opened, and the Lord shall make manifest all what has been hid and secret in this world.

3. The book of the Holy Scripture, wherein is to be found *the words of eternal life*. This book shall be opened at the Last Day, *when God shall judge the secrets of men by Jesus Christ, according to the gospel*. The faithful shall be judged according to the gospel, which is a preaching of Christ, in whom, and through whom, they have received remission of their sins, and are declared righteous in the sight of God: The ungodly shall be judged according to the gospel by the law, *because they have not obeyed the gospel of our Lord Jesus Christ*. The law according to which they shall be judged is this, *cursed be he that performs not all the words of this law to do them*. The gentiles who never knew the law of God, shall be judged after the natural

551

law written in their hearts, as St. *Paul* says, *as many as have sinned without the law, shall also perish without the law: And as many as have sinned in the law, shall be judged by the law.*

4. The book of conscience. Conscience is a book wherein our daily actions, words and thoughts are written; this shall also be laid open, and all our secrets shall be brought to light.

5. The book of men's own testimony. The faithful commit their charitable deeds in secret, thereby shunning vain glory; but at the Last Day the Lord will praise them, and they who have received charity and good from them, shall evidence for them.

6. The book of Satan's accusation: It is hid from us here in this world, how Satan accuses us before God day and night, wherefore the ungodly are not afraid of him; but at the Last Day he will publicly accuse us before God, and evidence against us.

7. The book of God's justice: The justice of God is in this world as a closed book, wherein we cannot read, for we see the wicked prosper, and the good ones suffer often times: But at the last this book shall be opened, and *the righteous shall eat the fruit of their doings, and the wicked shall receive the reward of their hands.*

Fifthly, in the pronouncing of the judgment, first to the godly, and then to the ungodly.

1. The judgment of the faithful is grounded upon the gospel. *He that believes on the Son, has everlasting life:* To whom the judge shall say, *Come you blessed of my Father inherit the Kingdom prepared for you from the foundation of the world.*

2. The judgment of the ungodly is grounded upon the law. *He that believes not the Son, shall not see life, but the wrath of God abides on him;* To them the judge shall say: *Depart from me you cursed into everlasting fire prepared for the devil and his angels.*

Hereupon shall follow,

Sixthly, the execution of the judgment. The ungodly shall go into everlasting fire and torment, and the godly into everlasting life and joy: Then shall *everyone receive the things done in his body, according to what he has done, whether it be good or bad.* Then shall everyone reap according to what he has sowed; the ungodly shall then receive the reward of unrighteousness, and the faithful shall receive the reward of everlasting salvation forever and ever.

Though we must not imagine, that since everyone shall receive *according to that he has done,* therefore our actions must be a meritorious cause: No, for the apostle says not, that everyone shall receive for that he has done, but *according to that he has done*; that is, his belief or unbelief, by which he hath done the things: for there is great difference between, to be judged *according* to our actions, and to receive reward for our actions: The Lord Jesus Christ will judge us at the Last Day according to our actions, but will not reward us for our actions. Well, says Christ by St. *John* the Divine, *Behold I come quickly, and my reward is with me, to give to every man according as his work shall be.* Though we must not understand this of the reward for the actions, but of their circumstances, how they are committed either through faith or not; for we cannot deserve anything with our actions, as Christ instructs us in the parable of the laborers in the vineyard.

Since we know, and believe, that *God has appointed a day, in the which he will judge the world in righteousness, by that man whom he hath ordained*; and the coming of this Day is uncertain and unknown to us; Let us then live in daily repentance, take heed, be watchful and pray, that we may be prepared, and this day may be a day of our eternal salvation.

The Lord be merciful unto us, and grant us this, for the sake of our blessed Savior Jesus Christ. AMEN.

38

The End of the World

T he Text 2 PETER, 3:10, 11, 12, 13, 14 ver.

The Day of the Lord will come as a thief in the night, in the which the heavens shall pass away with a great noise; and the elements shall melt with fervent heat. The earth also, and the works that are therein, shall be burnt up. Seeing then that all these things shall be dissolved, what manner of persons ought we to be in all holy conversation and Godliness: Looking for, and basting unto the coming of the Day of God, wherein the heavens being on fire, shall be dissolved, and the elements shall melt with fervent heat? Nevertheless we, according to his promise, look for new heavens and a new earth, wherein dwells righteousness: wherefore, beloved, seeing that you look for such things, be diligent, that you may be found of him in peace, without spot, and blameless.

INTRODUCTION

A person in sufferings, longs and waits for a deliverance: The children of *Israel* did wait for deliverance from the house of bondage in *Egypt*; the prodigal, suffering famine, did long for his father's house: The whole universe expects and longs for the end, when it shall be delivered from the bondage of corruption, as the apostle *Paul* says, in his epistle to the *Romans*, 8. Chap. 19, 20, 21, 22. Verses. *For the earnest expectation of the creature waits for the manifestation of the Sons of God: For the creature was made subject to vanity, not willingly, but by reason of him who has subjected the same in hope; because the creature itself also shall be delivered from the bondage of corruption, into the glorious liberty of the children of God: For we know that the whole creation groans, and travails in vain together until now.* We have three things to consider in these words; 1*st*, The expectation of the creature; 2*nd*, The reason of their expectation; and, 3*rd*, What they expect and wait for.

1*st*, The expectation of the creature, the name "creature," comprehends the whole creation; though there are some excluded. *First*, The holy angels and elect in heaven, who are not subject to vanity, for they are in a higher and more happier state, than that they should groan and wait for a deliverance. *Secondly*, the devils and the damned in hell, who sooner tremble for the Last Day, when they shall come to the eternal shame and torments. *Thirdly*, the ungodly who are not unwillingly, but willingly subject to vanity. So that by this word *creature* must be understood, the dumb and irrational creation, namely, the earth, sea, air and heaven, and all what in them is; which the apostle calls here *creature*, and attributes unto them, human qualities, as to *expect, wait for, hope, groan, and travel in pain.* And the apostle would say as much; O you faithful, who are now in the state of your sufferings in this present time, be comforted;

555

for not alone ye, but even the whole creation expects, groans, and waits for a deliverance; and since the whole creation waits for a deliverance from the bondage of corruption, then must you, who are the children of God, hope more for the deliverance, when it shall be made manifest, that you are the sons of God.

The apostle *Paul* uses here words, to express the expectation of the creature, which signifies, to lift up our head, and wishfully to look about; as we read of *Tobia*'s mother, who went out every day into the way, expecting the return of her son: And of *Sisera*'s mother, *who looked out at a window, and cried through the lattice, why is his chariot so long in coming, why tarry the wheels of his chariots?* Besides, the apostle uses a comparison of a travailing woman, who groans for deliverance: For since the Last Day is called by our Savior, a day of *regeneration*, whereon the earth shall give forth the dead, and the children of the resurrection shall come forth out of their graves, to the resurrection of life; therefore the apostle uses this comparison of the creature's expectation after this Day: And if it was not for the hope, which the creature is subject to, to be delivered from the bondage of corruption, the whole nature would make an Invasion upon mankind; but by reason of him who has subjected the same, it is patient, in hopes to be delivered from the bondage of corruption at the glorious liberty of the children of God. We can thereof conclude,

2. The reason of their expectation, which is the vanity whereto they are subject. We must not understand here, the common vanity, that it shall vanish at the Last Day; but here is to be understood, the vanity of sin, and the variety of punishment for sin.

First, the vanity of sin, whereto the creature created by God to his godly glory, and for the service of men, is employed and abused by sinners, and cannot therefore obtain to the end of their creation; for we cannot find anything created in the whole nature, but the same are employed by mankind to luxury, debauchery, gluttony, covetousness, and many other abominations, which they are not of themselves able to resist.

Secondly, the variety of punishment for sin: The creatures must suffer for the wickedness of mankind, as we can see of the curse laid upon them for the transgression of *Adam*; the golden calf, wherewith the children of *Israel* committed adultery in the wilderness, was burned in the fire, and ground to powder; the beast wherewith a man laid, was to be slain; the water and other creatures did groan over the first world; the heaven and fire did groan over *Sodom* and *Gomorrah*; and the rocks did groan over the cruelty of the *Jews* at the crucifixion of Christ. Such groaning are evidences that,

3. *The creature waits for the manifestation, and the glorious liberty of the sons of God:* The apostle St. *John* explains this manifestation, saying, *Behold, now are we the sons of God, and it does not appear what we shall be; but we know, that when he shall appear, we shall be like him, for we shall see him as he is:* None in this world can certainly know whether another is a child of God or not; for *it often happens unto the just men according to the work of the wicked.* But it shall be made manifest, when the creature shall be delivered from the bondage of corruption, and obtain its freedom; then shall the air not be longer an habitation for the evil spirit, who are now princes in the air; the sea shall no longer be travelled by unjust; the earth shall no longer be plowed and trodden; and all the creatures shall no longer be used nor abused, but they shall be destroyed, and vanish, and be delivered from the bondage of corruption. As a condemned criminal, although desirous to live, must be executed to the honor of God's justice, and for the punishment of his crime; so likewise the creature, who although desirous according to nature, to live, yet for the sake of the sinful vanity of service, whereto it is made subject, the same shall choose rather to vanish, than to continue in that state.

If the dumb and irrational creatures wait, with earnest expectation for the manifestation of the Sons of God, whereof they themselves have no part; much more ought then the children of God to wait for this their glorious manifestation and liberty, which shall be on the Last Day, *when the heavens being on fire shall be dissolved, and the elements shall melt with servant heat?* The apostle St. *Peter* speaks hereof in the words of our text; according to which we will observe here, the following three parts.

FIRST, *Some arguments to prove, that the world shall vanish.*

SECOND, *How the world shall vanish.*

THIRD, *A worthy preparation towards that day.*

EXPLANATION of the TEXT

I. Some arguments to prove that the world shall vanish.

As the world was framed by the Word of God, and had a beginning, so also shall the same be dissolved and have an end, although *many scoffers walking after their own lust, say, where is the promise of his coming? For since the fathers fell asleep, all things continue as they were from the beginning of the creation:* But O you fools, who told you that the world is created? Therefore since you confess that there is a creation and a beginning, must you not also acknowledge a destruction and end; for your own reason convinces you, as also daily experience, that everything you see with your own eyes has a beginning and end. We can prove this,

First, by the name of the Last Day, which is called, *the Day of God;* as a particular day, whereon the Lord will keep judgment. This day shall be an end of days and time, and a beginning to eternity. There are three days called so, with this name, namely; 1. The Day of God's Almightiness, when he created heaven, earth, the sea, and all what in them is, of nothing. 2. The Day of God's Mercy, when our blessed

THE END OF THE WORLD

Lord and Savior suffered, and did thereby satisfy the justice of God, and manifested his mercy to the world. And, 3. The Day of God's Justice, namely, the Last Day, when Christ shall come to judge the quick and the dead. It is not called so, because it shall come on a Sabbath day, commonly called the Lord's Day: No, for none knows the day of his coming to judgment; but it is called so on account of the things which shall be transacted on that day, namely, the coming of Christ to judgment; the resurrection of the dead; the judgment, and the end of the world.

Secondly, by the word of God. The apostle says in our text, *the Day of the Lord will come.* These words are, 1. apostolical words, which are true and undeceivable, for the apostles spoke all by the inspiration; as *Peter* says, *we have not followed cunningly devised fables, when we made known unto you the power and coming of our Lord Jesus Christ, but were eye-witnesses of his majesty. We have also a more sure word of prophecy, whereunto you do well, that you take heed.* Besides, he refers himself to *Paul*, who has written also of the coming of Christ, whereupon the end of the world shall follow. 2. Prophetical words: The prophets have also prophesied of the end of the world; so says the royal Psalmist, *O my God, you have laid the foundation of the world, and the heavens are the work of your hands. They shall perish, but you shall endure.* Isaiah, *Jonas*, and *Haggai*, have all prophesied of the end of the world. And, 3. The Lord's own words; our Savior did often preach in the time of his incarnation of this, as we may see in the holy evangelists, a great many texts proving this article of our faith.

Thirdly, by examples. The apostle *Peter* has in the 6th verse of our text, speaking of the destruction of the first world by the flood, he says also, *that the cities of* Sodom *and* Gomorrah *were turned into ashes, and condemned with an overthrow, for an example unto those that after should live ungodly.*

Fourthly, by the final cause whereto man is created, namely, the eternal life. Since then, man is created to an image of God's eternity, and God knows them, and the number of them that shall be saved, for their names are written in heaven, and he knows his own; then is it certain, that then, when this number is completed, the world shall perish and have an end.

Fifthly, by the tokens, and forewarnings, which shall go before the end of the world; whereof our blessed Savior and his apostles have spoken in several places. Our Savior says, *there shall be signs in the sun, and in the moon, and in the stars:* That is, as he says in another place, *the sun shall be darkened, and the moon shall not give her light, and the stars shall fall from heaven, and the powers of the heavens shall be shaken.* The eclipses in the sun and moon have all their natural causes, yet they are tokens of the Last Day, as sickness is a presage of death, although death follows not always upon it. *There shall be signs upon the earth, distress of nations*; that is, you *shall hear of wars and rumors of war. For nation shall rise against nation, and kingdom against kingdom, and there shall be famines and pestilences, and earthquakes in divers places,* and *the sea and the waves shall be roaring.* Some of these tokens are fulfilled, and others are not: And, since our Savior says, *as it was in the days of Noah, so shall it be also in the days of the Son of Man. They did eat, they drank, they married wives, and were given in marriage. Even thus shall it be in the day, when the Son of Man is revealed.* Also, there shall be great security towards the latter end of the world, *when the ungodly shall say, Peace and quietness, and safety, then sudden destruction comes upon them, as travail upon a woman with child.* The apostle *Paul* gives us a picture or draught of this day, in his epistle to *Timothy,* saying, *In the last days perilous times will come. For men shall be lovers of their own selves, covetous, boasters, proud, blasphemous, disobedient to parents, unthankful, unholy, without natural affections, truce-breakers, false accusers, unconstant, fierce, despisers of those that are good; traitors, heady, high-minded, lovers of pleasure more then lovers of God, having a form of godliness, but denying the power thereof.* He who will observe the world, and the transactions therein, will find, that all the foregoing are fulfilled. Where do we find now, even among, Christians, true piety without hypocrisy, willingness to serve others without self love? Contentment without covetousness? Truth without blasphemy? Obedience of children and servants without murmuring? Friendship without falsehood? Love without envy? Chastity without lasciviousness, and so forth. And although such crimes have been in vogue in the world, ever since the beginning, as we can be convinced of by the words of the Lord, saying, *all flesh has corrupted his way upon the earth*; yet they shall be more in vogue towards the end of the world, for *the devil will have then great wrath, because he knows, that he has but a short time.* All such tokens admonish us, that the Last Day and the end of the world is,

1. Nigh-by. For all the tokens and forewarnings in heaven, earth, and the sea, call to us as with one voice, the end of the world is nigh-by. Beloved, behold, if the world was even so much corrupted, as it is now in our days. The whole world is involved in sin and abomination, and buried entirely in security; we hear of wars and rumors of wars, bloodshed, unrighteousness, falsehood, fraud, deceit, blasphemy, and all other vices and abominations. Although God is long-suffering, and looks on, as if he did not observe the wickedness of men, neither punishes at once their transgressions, wherefore men's heart becomes more and more evil, yet he will come at last, and the world becomes by this worse; so that our Savior says, *when the Son of Man comes, shall he find faith on earth?* This Last Day is,

2. Put off. But not made to naught nor annihilated. The apostle says, *the Lord's Day will come.* The Lord prolongs well his promise, but he takes it not away, *he is long-suffering toward us, not willing that any should perish, but that all should come to repentance.* This

prolonging on account of, *first*, God's eternity, for *one day is with the Lord as a thousand years, and a thousand years as one day*. We men who live in this time, where everything goes so gradually and slow according to the course of the sun, time, and season after another, day after day, and year after year, thinks that God has forgotten his promise, because he tarried so long: but the High and lofty One, that inhabits the eternity, whose years and days cannot be measured according to time, and by whom there is no mutation nor alteration, think not the time too long. *Secondly*, God's long-suffering is so great, that he forbears with men, and *will have all men to be saved, and to come unto the knowledge, of the truth*. If we do not repent, and are converted, he will, *thirdly*, with severity punish and condemn the unconverted sinners; so that the ungodly shall have no excuse, that they are suddenly overtaken with the judgment. Which shall come,

3. Sudden *as a thief in the night*. As little as the good-man knows the time, when the thief comes, as little do we know when the end of the world will be. We can see hereby the greatness of God's grace, that we should be always prepared to meet the Lord with joy. If men knew the time of the end of the world, they would become more wicked, and too secure in their wickedness, thinking it is time enough to repent and be converted, when the end is drawing nigh. Many, yea the greatest part, are secure now as it is, that we know nor the end of time: But if this time was known, yea a less part would live in the fear of God, and others would thereby become yet worse than they are already. And if anyone should think, the Day of Judgment will not fall in my time; he must know, that there is a Last Day of life, which none can escape, but this day of our death is certain, and will come *as a thief in the night*, and we shall be judged according as we are found at the moment of our death; for as the tree falls, it shall remain. We will now observe,

II. How the world shall vanish.

The apostle St. *Peter* shows us in the words of our text, how the world shall vanish, saying, *the heavens shall pass away with a great noise, and the element shall melt with fervent heat. The earth also, and the works that are therein, shall be burnt up.* The apostle describes in these words,

First, what shall perish, namely, the heavens, the elements, the earth and the works therein.

The heavens shall pass away with a great noise, both the firmament, which *God stretched out as a curtain, and spreads out as a tent,* and wherein, the sun, moon, stars, and the planets were placed, as also the sky, wherein the birds do fly. The heavens suffered not in the destruction of the first world by the flood, but in the destruction at the Last Day, *the host of heaven shall be dissolved, and the heavens shall be rolled together as a scroll, and all their host shall fall down as the leaf falls off.*

The elements shall melt with fervent heat. That is, fire, air, water and earth, which are the first created original things, whereof all other natural things are composed.

The earth and the works that are therein shall be burnt up. That is, all things created under heaven, the earth and the sea, with all what in and on them is.

The apostle describes in these words,

Secondly, the manner thereof, namely with a great noise, and with fire.

With a great noise. When a great building falls, there is always a great noise. When this great frame of the universe shall fall and pass away, there shall be a great noise, everything shall then vanish away, not alone according to its form, so that they shall be burnt and scattered and receive a better form; No, but they shall vanish as a

563

smoke, according to their essence and being, and shall be no more; the earth and the heaven shall flee away, and there shall be found no place for them any more.

With fire. The first world was destroyed with water, and this shall be destroyed with fire: what fire this shall be, is alone known to God: Our Savior speaking of the end of the world, shows to us the example of *Sodom*, when it rained fire and brimstone from heaven. The old ones have observed, that there are two colors red and blue in the rainbow, and have explained thereby the two destructions of the world, the first with water, and the second with fire; water and fire are two contrary elements, water against heat, and fire against cold. The first world was overheated in lasciviousness, and was destroyed in water; the second world shall *be cold in love*, and shall perish with fire. The element of fire shall then take the upper hand over all the other elements, not in a natural, but in a supernatural way; for the Last Day shall be full of miracles, namely, the sudden coming of Christ with the angels and archangels, who shall sound in the trumpet, the resurrection of the dead, the changing of the quick, the appearing of all before the judgment seat, and the destruction of the whole universe with fire and fervent heat, with a great noise.

The Lord shall show in this great work, his power, justice, and honor.

His power. That he will in a moment destroy heaven and earth, and the works that are therein: So that although the heavens are seemingly *as strong as a molten looking glass*, yet they are for God as a smoke. wherefore the prophet *Isaiah* says, *the heavens shall vanish away like smoke.*

His justice: That he will punish heaven and earth with utter destruction for the sins, which they themselves have not committed, but are employed and used to by others; the heavens shall pass away, because it has been a cover for the ungodly angels and men; and the earth shall be burnt up, because it has been the habitation of the wicked; and the elements shall melt with fervent heat, because they have been abused by evil doers; like unto one who has committed a crime against the majesty, is not alone punished in his own person, but also in his whole family, and even in his habitation, which is demolished, and an infamous monument is erected instead thereof to his shame. And truly the whole world, and all what was in it, would have been destroyed through the justice and vengeance of God, over the Fall and disobedience of *Adam*, if the Son of God, the Lord Jesus Christ, had not interceded, that the same might stand and remain for man's sake, that the Christian church might have a place on earth, until the number, of the elect were completed. Therefore are *all things that are in heaven, and that are in earth, visible and invisible, said to be created by him*, and *that he upholds all things by the power of his word.*

His honor. He shall not act then with the elect and faithful any more by means, as in this world, where they are called to the communion of saints by the word and the Holy Sacraments; but without means, for *he shall be all in all.*

Thirdly, the apostle shows us, what there shall remain in the end of the world, namely, the good and bad angels: The godly and ungodly shall all remain; the good angels with the elect shall enter into the Kingdom of Heaven, and praise God there eternally; but the bad angels with the ungodly shall be cast out into eternal torment, to *be punished with everlasting destruction, from the presence of the Lord, and from the glory of his power.*

Fourthly, the apostle shows us, what there shall be again, saying, *we look for new heavens and a new earth, wherein dwells righteousness.*

New heavens. The old heaven shall then be passed away according to its essence, and not altered according to its form or shape, as some wrongfully conceive. For, as the heavens was created of nothing, also shall the same pass away and come to nothing. As the new *Jerusalem* will differ much in essence from the old, also will the heavens, namely, the new, differ much from the old. We must not understand by that new heaven and earth, a created or bodily heaven and earth, nor any worldly kingdom; but we should know, that it is a comparison, in order to make it more intelligible for our weak apprehensions; and should therefore understand thereby, heaven and the eternal life.

A new earth. The word new, in both places, signifies, that it shall be glorious and excellent, exceeding the old in all manner of ways: Our Savior called the wine which he was to drink in his Father's Kingdom, *a new wine.* This new earth will have a quite different shape from the earth which we inhabit, and is corporal; the same shall be spiritual; for the Paradise which our Savior assured the malefactor of on the cross, could not be any temporal or earthly place. St. *John* the divine gives us a description thereof, saying, *I saw a new heaven, and a new earth, for the first heaven and the first earth, were passed away, and there was no more sea. And I John saw the holy city, new Jerusalem, coming down from God out of heaven, prepared as a bride adorned for her husband.*

The apostle says, that we look for the new heavens and new earth, *according to his promise.* Faith is looked for, and grounded upon the promises of God; and we may depend upon it, that all what the Lord has promised in his word, shall certainly come to pass, although it may seem wonderful and incredible for our human reason. God has promised, that he will make a new heaven and a new earth, saying, by the prophet *Isaiah, Behold, I create new heavens, and a new earth, and the former shall not he remembered, nor come into mind,* which we should understand aforesaid: This we must believe, although we cannot apprehend it with our reason.

The apostle further says, That *righteousness dwells* in this new heaven and new earth: Over the gate stands these words; *This gate of the Lord, into which the righteous shall enter.* All in the new heavens are holy and righteous spirits: There were many crimes and transgressions committed in the old world, but *there shall in no wise enter into the new Jerusalem anything that defiles, neither whatsoever works abomination or makes a lie, but they which are written in the Lamb's Book of Life.* All the inhabitants shall be righteous and holy, having received here the remission of their sins, and being made partakers of the righteousness of Christ, through a living faith; and having practiced holy and charitable actions, they shall become there perfectly righteous, and the root of sin and evil shall be taken away from them; so that they shall not want *to wash their hearts from wickedness,* for, *they have washed before their robes, and made them white in the blood of the Lamb. The church of Christ shall then be glorious, not having spot, or wrinkle, or any such thing; but it shall be holy and without blemish, being arrayed in fine linen, clean and white, which is the righteousness of saints.*

III. A worthy preparation towards that day.

We should worthily prepare ourselves against that day; and if we should not live to that day, we should then prepare for the day of our death, which shall be our last day: We should prepare ourselves with holy conversation and godliness, with a hearty looking for, and with purity of heart.

With holy conversation and godliness: The apostle St. *Paul* explains this also, *That denying ungodliness and worldly lusts, we should live soberly, righteously, and godly in this present world.* Soberly towards ourselves, righteous towards our neighbors, and godly towards God: Soberly in words and gestures, righteous in actions, and godly in heart. Our lives in this world shall be a daily repentance. Now, while it is the day of alvation, it is time; but it will be too late hereafter, when time and the world shall have an end, and eternity shall begin; and we should always consider, that all the days which God grants unto our lives in this world, is alone for that one day, that we should be worthily prepared.

With a heartily looking for. The apostle says, *we look for a new heavens and a new earth*; and if so, then do we certainly believe the coming of that Day; For expectation is an effect of faith, therefore the faithful are said to *look for the Savior the Lord Jesus Christ*, and to *look for the glorious appearing of the great God, and our Savior Jesus Christ.* Did we certainly believe the coming of that Day, we would endeavor to prepare ourselves for the same with holiness and godliness, that it might become a Day of our Salvation, and not a day of destruction and damnation. A bride looks with great desire for the coming of the bridegroom: A soul that is a true bride of Christ looks with great longing the coming of the cridegroom, the Lord Jesus Christ; for *the spirit and the bride say, Come*; that is, a soul wherein a true Spirit dwells, being a bride of Christ, faith, with a hearty looking for, *Amen, even so come Lord Jesus.* Consider the course of the world, and you shall find, how carefully the children thereof are concerned for their temporal gain and profit. If one has assurance of an heirship, how wishfully looks he for the same? The wicked intending mischief, wait always an opportunity. *The eye of the adulterer waits for twilight.* The wicked *lay wait for their own blood, they lurk privily for their own life.* Should we not much more look for our salvation, and that the more, as we are *hastening unto the coming of the Day of God.* We consider not that the end of the world is drawing on closer and closer, and that time slips away towards eternity, it goes therewith as with a ship, they who are on board perceive not the course of the ship, which comes daily closer unto the desired port.

With purity of heart. *Be diligent, that you may be found of him in peace without spot, and blameless.* The heart *is purified by faith*, by attributing unto us, and embracing by a living faith his holiness and righteousness; although the remnants of sin and imperfection dwells in us, yet we should withstand sin and the evil lusts, which war against the soul, being clothed in the garment of the holiness and righteousness of Christ, and serve him faithfully all the days of our life; then *he who is the God of all grace, and has called us to his eternal glory in Christ Jesus, will make us perfect, establish, and settle us* in all what is good, for the obtaining of this eternal glory of grace for Christ's sake.

The very God of peace sanctify us wholly, and grant that our whole spirit, and soul and body may be preserved blameless, unto the coming of our Lord Jesus Christ. AMEN.

39

Hell

T he Text, ISAIAH, 30:33 ver.
    For Tophet *is ordained of old: Yea, for the King it is prepared,*
    he has made it deep and large: The pile thereof is fire and much
wood; the breath of the Lord, like a stream of brimstone, does kindle it.

INTRODUCTION

IT is a common saying, *As you have made your bed, so you must lie on it:* Would we lie easy, and rest well, we should make our beds accordingly. Would we rest hereafter in the bosom of *Abraham,* then should we make our beds in this world, of the under-bed of repentance, the bolster of faith, and the cover of good works, and a Christian life, which should be our daily work. *Dives* did not consider this: he was concerned in this world alone, for the satisfying and gratifying his carnal lusts and appetites, not regarding what would become of his soul hereafter; as we may read in St. *Luke* 16:23. that after he was dead and buried, *He lift up his eyes in hell, being in torments.* We should understand this of his soul, since there is mention made a little before, of his body, that *he died and was buried*; by which this conclusion follows, that his soul did live after death, and was in a certain place. This place is described here, 1st, by its name; 2nd, by its condition.

First, by its name: The same is called here, hell. It is a horrible name, wherein is contained all the pains and torments that can be.—A miserable change! *Dives* never thought of this, while he was here on earth, therefore says the evangelist, *He list up his eyes, being in hell, in torments:* He was clothed here in purple and fine linen, there he was clothed with the purple flame he fared here, sumptuously every day; there he had not a drop of water to cool his tongue: He lay here at nights upon an easy bed, there he was in torments; where *the worm was spread under him, and the worms did cover him.* He depended in his lifetime on his riches, fared sumptuously every day, was uncharitable towards the poor, and was an atheist, not believing *Moses* and the prophets.

We may prove by the following arguments, that there is a hell.

1st, By the Holy Scripture. Both the Old and New Testament are full of texts wherewith this may be proved, which would be too tedious to sum up here.

2nd, By the examples of the damned in hell; as the wicked angels, and ungodly men; as *Corah, Dathon, Abiram*, and his company; *Saul*, the King of *Babylon, Capernaum, Dives, Judas*, and many others.

3rd, By the justice of God; it is just by God, that everyone should receive according to what he has done; which, although it happens not always in this world, shall be fulfilled on the Last Day.

4th, By the curse of the law. We should not imagine, that the curse wherewith the Lord threatens the transgressors of his law, is in vain, and will be of no effect: No, for the power of these words shall be made manifest on the Last Day, when the great judge shall say to the ungodly, *Depart from me you cursed, into everlasting fire, prepared for the devil and his angels.*

5*th*, By the testimony of our own conscience. A bad conscience is a spark of hell fire, which we may fee both by the godly and ungodly: Of the godly, the royal Psalmist complains, in a comparison, of his *broken bones:* Of the ungodly, *Judas* the traitor is an example above all, and said therefore, *I have sinned, in that I have betrayed the innocent blood.*

6*th*, By the example of the possessed of evil spirits. We read in the writings of the gospel, of many possessed of the evil spirits, who were miserably tormented. We may conclude hereby, that there are devils, and as there are devils, there must also be an abode for them, which is hell.

7*th*, By the descension of Christ into hell. If we believe that Christ descended into hell, then there must certainly be a hell. He first tasted the terrors of hell in his soul, when he sweated drops of blood; but descended afterwards into hell, not for to be pained, but to convince the evil spirits of his victory.

Second, hell is described here by its condition: This is comprehended by this word, *torment*. There is nothing else but torments, and even eternal torments, in hell. Hell therefore bears such terrible names, namely a pit, a bottomless pit, the smoke of a pit, a stream of pitch, the second death, the eternal death, the eternal damnation, the eternal destruction, prison, pit wherein there is no water; eternal fire, fiery furnace, the lowermost parts of the earth, a worm, immortal worm, eternal pain, a pit burning with brimstone and fire, eternal shame and misery, the wrath to come, and utter darkness.

The words of our text give us further occasion to speak of this place; and we shall accordingly speak thereof under these two heads.

FIRST, *What hell is.*

SECOND, *How it is in hell.*

EXPLANATION of the TEXT

I. We will speak of what hell is.

Should men often go into hell with their thoughts, they would not go so easy therein with soul and body, to their eternal damnation. It hurts none to be afraid of hell; but to live all in security, without dread or fear of this place of eternal torments. The prophet speaks also of this place in the text; *Tophet is ordained of old.* In which words two things are ordained for our meditation, namely, *First*, that hell is a place; and, *second*, an ordained place.

1*st*, That hell is a place, and in a certain place, we may conclude by the words of the prophet, who described the same by its depth, breadth, and largeness, which agrees with the place where *dives* was tormented, that was separated by a great gulf from the abode of the elect. We can also describe hell, that it is a horrible place of torments; that God of his justice, has prepared from eternity for the devils and the ungodly, where they shall be cast out from the presence of God, and be eternally tormented. The prophet calls this place *Tophet*, which was a certain place without the city of *Jerusalem*, otherwise called the valley of *Ben Henriom*, after a man named *Henriom*, in whose lot this valley was. The children of *Israel* did sacrifice their children alive in this valley, according to the custom of the heathens unto *Moloch*, the idol of the *Ammonites.* This *Moloch* was a great image made of copper, as a king, with extended arms, wherein the children were laid; the image was hollow within, wherein a fire was made until the image was quite hot, and the children miserably burned to death. The priest in the meantime, deceiving the people, gave forth, that the children were not apprehensive of any pain; and the better to conceal their fraud, they beat upon drums, and made a great noise, for to prevent the parents from hearing the laments

ARTICLES OF FAITH

of their sacrificed children. This place or valley was therefore called *Tophet*, which signifies a drum. Our Savior applies this in the New Testament to hell, which is the place where the damned shall be tormented eternally with fire and brimstone: And since the prophet speaks of this place, as of an abode, having its breadth, depth and largeness; we may thereby conclude, the hell is a certain place: For, if the faithful are in a certain place, then must the damned also be in a certain place; they cannot be all over, neither can they be in no place; they must be therefore in some certain place. The Scripture mentions not where hell is, neither is it manifested to any: Therefore said the Lord to *Job, Have the gates, of death been opened unto you? Or have you seen the doors of the shadow of death?* It cannot be in the lower parts of the earth, as some imagine, because the same is described by a descending into the lower parts of the earth; and because *Corah, Datban* and *Abiram*, and their company, were swallowed up in the earth, and went down alive into the pit: No, should hell be in the earth, what would become of the same, when the heavens, the earth, and all the works that are therein, shall vanish? The earth that swallowed up that murmuring company, was not the place whereto, but wherethrough they all went: Thus their being swallowed up by the earth, and going down alive into the pit, shows the horrible pains wherewith their souls and bodies were tormented on account of their murmurings, and the earth was here used as a means to bring them therein. Hell is a place beside the world, in utter darkness. We should not be so much concerned about where hell is, but endeavor to escape this cursed place of eternal torments.

2nd, That hell is an ordained place: The prophet says, *Tophet is ordained of old.* Who has then ordained hell? We may well think, that the devil has not made the same, but there are three causes why hell is ordained; 1st, The wickedness of Satan; 2nd, The ungodliness of mankind; And, 3rd, The justice of God. The devils laid the first wood

574

to the eternal hellish Fire; The unbelief of men laid the second, but the justice of God did kindle it.

First, the wickedness of Satan. Satan did not ordain hell, but was the cause of the same being ordained; for, since, he and his company *kept not their first estate*, and remained steadfast in their original truth, *but left their own habitation*, and gave themselves up to lie and murder, therefore *they were cast down to hell, and reserved in everlasting chains under darkness, unto the judgment of the Great Day.* And since the devil goes round in the world, and instigates men to evil, so is hell also ordained.

Second, for the ungodliness of men: According to the eternal decree of God; *He that believes not, shall be damned. Every tree which does not bring forth good fruit, is thrown down, and cast into the fire.*

Third, the justice of God, who, as a just revenger of sin, hath ordained hell for the devils and unbelievers; not through an absolute decree, as if they were created alone for to be damned, and eternally tormented; no, God created none bad among the angels, neither wills he the death and damnation of a sinner: But, because he, the all-knowing God, saw before from eternity, that some of the angels would fall; and that man, being deceived by Satan, should also transgress, therefore he ordained hell, wherein the devils and the ungodly should be tormented.

God had ordained hell before the devils fell; wherefore the prophet says here, *Tophet is ordained of old*; that is, from eternity; yet he was not the cause that they fell, and that the prophet says, *Yea, for the King it is prepared*; by which *Senacherib*, the king of *Assyria*, is understood, who was a great tyrant, and plagued the people of God sorely: Under this name should be understood, all ungodly and wicked men, great and small, high and low, kings and subjects. We should think well otherwise, that the common and mean people alone came in hell. It is certain, that Satan has no regard to persons or their stations;

and we may suppose, that he, being a proud and haughty spirit, is overjoyed when he can gain the souls of high and mighty, yet he refuses none. Hell is prepared for all the transgressors of the law of God, as idolaters, blasphemers, condemners of God's word, heretics, hypocrites, false teachers, unrighteous, rebellers, murderers, fornicators, adulterers, effeminate abusers of themselves with mankind, thieves, covetous, drunkards, revilers, extortioners, and all other evildoers and unbelievers. Above all, hell is prepared for them, who remain impenitent and without faith, until their lives end. For, as all sickness is mortal in itself, and he that condemns the remedy die effectually; So also the eternal death is in common the wages of sin; yet alone they who condemn the heavenly means offered in the gospel, are effectually condemned.

II. We will now behold how it is in hell.

Let us open the door of hell, with the key of God's word, and behold how it is therein, that it may terrify the ungodly, who often wrongfully imagine that hell is not so hot and terrible, as it is described: By the word *hell*, must be understood all the torments, wherefore hell and torments are placed together. Take all the torments and tortures, that can be invented in this world, yet the torments of hell exceeds them all; for the same is,

First, a miserable torment. The prophet called the same in our text, *Tophet*, that is *deep, large*, and *broad*. It is called in other places, a deep dark prison, a deep pit, wherein is no water, a dark pit, outer darkness, a great gulf burning with fire and brimstone. The condition of the damned shall be in eternal darkness, where they shall never see light. Their greatest pain shall be, that they shall be eternally cast out from the glorious presence of God and his beloved Son Jesus Christ. God has turned his gracious countenance from them, so that they shall never behold him more, and that to their eternal shame and misery; and since they are cast out from the presence of God, then they are also excluded from the company of the holy angels, from the heavenly paradise and *Jerusalem*, and from the company of saints and elect, who praise God always. They are excluded from all comfort, hope, and commiseration. The torment of hell is miserable,

1st, On account of its dreadfulness. *The breath of the Lord like a stream of brimstone, does kindle it.* The Royal Psalmist says, *upon the wicked the Lord shall rain snares, fire, brimstone, and a horrible tempest: This shall be their portion of the cup.* As none can number the days of eternity; so neither can the torments of hell be numbered. *They shall be bound hand and foot, and cast into outer darkness, there shall be weeping and gnashing of teeth.* The torments of hell are miserable,

2nd, On account of its multiplicity. *They shall be tormented night and day forever and ever.* Their conscience shall accuse them continually, and death shall feed on them; they shall be tormented in their soul through the remembrance of their sins and transgressions, and in their bodies by fire and the worm, for *their worm shall not die, neither shall their fire be quenched.* They shall be tormented always from above, by the *burning anger of God, which burns unto the lowest hell*, from beneath of the eternal hell's fire, which shall burn, and not consumed: *Burning coals shall fall upon them, and they shall be cast into the fire, into deep pits, that they rise not up again,* from round about of the evil spirits and tormentors; yea, they shall be tormented in all their senses; their sight with dreadful specters of the damned; their hearing of their own weeping and gnashing of teeth; their smell of the stinking stream of brimstone; their taste with hunger and thirst; and their feeling with this horrible eternal fire. This torment is miserable,

3rd, On account of its continuation. St. *John* the divine says, *They shall be tormented night and day forever and ever.* When one is sick, he has often times intermission; but the torments of hell shall continue, and be always alike; their tormenters shall not be tired, neither their tormenters cease; *They shall seek death, and shall not find it, and shall desire to die, and death shall flee from them.* This torment is miserable,

4th, On account of eternity. *The smoke of hell shall go up forever,* and the fire shall burn forever and ever. The shame and contempt of the damned shall be everlasting; their torment eternal; their death an eternal death; their condemnation an eternal condemnation; and their prison an everlasting prison, wherefrom they shall never and never escape, nor be released. This torment is miserable,

5th, On account of its being dissatisfactory. After the damned have suffered thousand and thousand of years, it is not satisfaction at all; so that if they could weep as many tears as there are drops in the sea, yet it will not procure the remission of one sin unto them; for the door of God's grace is then shut, and will never be opened again.

Secondly, it is a command, though unequal torment. Princes here on earth have their dominion and kingdom, but in hell the princes shall be nothing. The prophet *Ezekiel* numbers up a great many princes and kings that are condemned, as the kings of *Tyre, Assyrian, Egypt, Etam, Mesech, Tubal, Edom,* and the princes from the North: Whereof we can see, that Satan has no regard to persons of what state, condition or age whatsoever, but he goes round as a roaring lion, seeking whom he may devour. We must conclude that they who have committed the greatest sins here in this world, shall receive the greater torments hereafter. That there shall be a difference in the torments we can prove,

1st, By Christ's words. *It shall be more tolerable for the Land of* Sodom *and* Gomorrah *in the Day of Judgment, than for that city* that condemns and rejects the word of God, and the doctrine of the gospel. *Woe unto you* Chorazin, *woe unto you* Bethsaida; *for if the mighty works which were done in you, had been done in* Tyre *and* Sidon, *they would have repented long ago in sackcloth and ashes. But I say unto you, it shall be more tolerable for* Tyre *and* Sidon *at the Day of Judgment, than for you. And you* Capernaum, *who are exalted unto heaven, shall be brought down unto hell: for it the mighty works, which have been done in thee, had been done in* Sodom, *it would have remained until this day. But I say unto you, that it shall be more tolerable for the land of* Sodom *in the Day of Judgment, than for you.* The Jews of the Old Testament, shall be tormented more than the gentiles; the Christians more than the heathens and Muslims. For, *that servant which knew his lord's will, and prepared not himself, neither did according to his will, shall be beaten with many stripes, but he that knew not, and did commit things worthy of stripes, shall be beaten with few stripes: For unto whomsoever much is given, of him shall much be required.* Though the least torment in hell shall be greater than all the tortures on earth.

2nd, We can prove it of the inequality of sin and transgressions, which are not all alike great and heinous; therefore shall the torments in hell not be alike neither. The sin of *Judas* the traitor was greater than of *Caiphas*, and that of *Caiphas* than of *Pilate*, which we can conclude of Christ's saying to *Pilate, he that delivered me unto you hath the greater sin.* The sin of *Judas* and *Caiphas* was greater than that of *Pilate* in several degrees and respects. *First*, because they delivered Christ unto *Pilate. Secondly, Judas* and *Caiphas* knew of the prophets, that Jesus was the Christ, but *Pilate* was a heathen. *Thirdly, Judas* and *Caiphas* delivered Christ out of covetousness and spite, but *Pilate* condemned him through fear of a tumult and the emperor. We can conclude thereby, that *Judas* shall receive greater punishment than *Pilate.* This is the meaning of the apostle, when he says, *that* Judas *went to his own place.* That is, the place of torment in hell, which he had prepared for himself by his transgression. This we can conclude by the following. *First*, of the person whom he betrayed. *Secondly*, of the remorse in his conscience, which drove him to the halter. The torment in hell is all alike for the damned, yet they shall not all be tormented alike, but one shall be tormented more than another.

3rd, We can prove it of the condition of the eternal life. If there be a difference in the honor and glory of the elect in heaven, to be understood in regard to the degree, but not in the glory itself, then shall there also be a difference in the torment of the damned in hell; for as are there is many rooms in heaven for the elect, so also are there many rooms in hell for the damned.

Thirdly, it is eternal and without end. No torture in this world is so great and tormenting, but the same will have an end; but the torments of hell is without end, *the worm shall not die, neither shall the fire be quenched,* for the same is eternal; and that in regard to the following.

1st, In regard to *the breath of the Lord, which is like a stream of brimstone, and does kindle it.* There is no satisfaction, no ransom, no remission of sins, nor redemption from hell: For this inscription stands over the gate of hell, *Verily, you shall by no means come out thence, till you have paid the uttermost farthing.*

2nd, In regard to the bodies of the condemned. An iron remains iron even in the midst of a great furnace, so also shall the bodies of the damned, after the general resurrection, remain burning eternally in hell; for the Lord Almighty will take vengeance of them in the Day of Judgment, in putting fire and worms in their flesh, and they shall feel them, and weep forever and ever.

3rd, In regard to the fire and wood. The prophet says in our text, *the pile thereof is fire and much wood.* The fire we have here on earth, is not to be compared to the fire in hell. Our earthly fire is kindled of the breath of man, but the fire of hell is kindled by the breath of the Lord, *which is as a stream of brimstone.* Our earthly fire can be quenched, but hell's fire is never quenched; our earthly fire must be supplied, but the hell fire has much wood from the anger and wrath of God; our earthly fire consumes everything, but the hell fire burns forever, and the bodies and souls of the damned are not consumed; our earthly fire gives glances, and is shining, but the hell fire is dark and black. The prophet says in another place, that *their worm shall not die:* we can conclude thereby, that there shall be worms in this fire: These worms shall be gnawing, biting, and burning, for each of them has four stings, namely; *First,* the deprivation of past good. *Secondly,* the remembrance of past transgressions. *Thirdly,* the suffering of the present torment. And, *fourthly,* the long tail of eternity. *Dives* was very much gnawed of this worm, when *Abraham* said unto him: *Remember that you in your lifetime received your good things, and likewise* Lazarus *evil things; but now is he comforted, and you are tormented.* If we consider those words rightly, we shall find all those four before mentioned stings in them.

Since then the torments of hell is eternal, and so horrible that the same cannot be described, are then the condemned not dealt unjustly by, that they are punished with eternal torments for temporal crimes and transgressions? No certainly, God rewards them not unjustly. A criminal is not punished alone according to the greatness of his crime, also according to the greatness of the person, against whom the crime is committed: He who sins against a king, commits a greater crime then he, who sinned against a private person. Now God is infinite Lord of Lords, and King of Kings; therefore must they, who sin against him, be punished with infinite torments. God is the eternal good; Then it is just, that they, who depart from him, should be rewarded with eternal evil. The ungodly sin in the eternity of their life here on earth, and if they were to live forever, they would also sin forever; therefore are they punished in God's eternity: In the same condition a man dies, in the same he remains in eternity. The ungodly dying in their sins, remains so, and shall never be redeemed therefrom.

Let us think often upon hell with our thoughts in this world, that we shall not come there hereafter with soul and body: When we see a criminal executed, we enquire always the cause of his suffering, thinking the Lord may preserve us from such shameful death; we should much more be careful and shun sin, by which so many are become eternal criminals in hell. Was there but two or three to be damned, we should then be afraid that we might be even one of them; much more must we now, while we know, that the road that leads to destruction is broad, and many thousands walk on the same: For as in the destruction of the first world, there were but eight saved, in the destroying of *Sodom* and *Gomorrah* but four; and of six hundred thousand but two came in the land *Canaan*; so shall but few be saved in comparison to the great multitude that shall be damned. Our Savior Jesus Christ admonishes us, *Strive to enter in at the straight gate, for many will seek to enter in, and shall not be able.*

The Lord be gracious unto us, and open our eyes, that we may see and find the way, that leads to the eternal life, and thereby escape the broad road that leads to the eternal destruction. Hear us good Lord for Christ our Savior's sake. AMEN.

40

Heaven

T he Text, MATTHEW, 13:43, ver.
Then shall the righteous shine forth as the sun in the Kingdom of their Father.

INTRODUCTION

WHAT shall be done unto the man, whom the King delights to honor? We may also ask: What shall be done unto the man, whom the heavenly King delights to honor? We should call them *sons of God.* This is the greatest honor, that can befall them in this world; whereupon shall follow the everlasting honor in heaven: But that we should not think, that the honor of God's children in this world consists only in a bare title, whereupon nothing shall follow; therefore says the apostle St. *John,* 1st epistle 3:2. *Behold now are we the sons of God, and it does not yet appear, what we shall be, but we know, that when he shall appear, we shall be like him; for we shall see him as he is.* The apostle describes in these words, 1. The honor of the sons of God in this world. And, 2. Their honor after this life.

1. The honor of the sons of God in this world, that they are *sons of God*. Adam and *Eve* were the two first children of God, but they became through their disobedience soon fatherless; since them, no sons of God are more born, for they are all children of wrath by nature; God needs no more children, for he has his firstborn Son, whom he has generated of his own essence from eternity, sitting upon the throne by him; but we need a Father. We were therefore, having by nature no child's right, chosen and adopted of mere grace; and this adoption is made in the holy child Jesus, whom God sent in time unto the world, that we through and by him might receive the adoption of sons, We can best perceive this honor by the following.

First, of the precious worth, where this adoption is purchased. For, if a thing must be prized of its cost, then certainly this purchase is of the greatest value: It is not obtained with a great sum, as the *Roman* freedom in old days; neither with the foreskins of *Philistines*, as *David* gave for *Saul*'s daughter; neither with any corruptible things as silver and gold, *but with the precious blood of Christ*, the only begotten of the Father from eternity.

Secondly, of the majesty of him, after whom we are called, namely God. David *said unto* Saul'*s servants*, who offered unto him *Micah* the king's daughter: *Seems it unto you a light to be a king's son in law*. We read of *Moses*, that *when he was come to years, he refused to be called the son of* Pharaoh'*s daughter*. What comparison is there between God and *Saul*, between the King of Heaven, and *Pharaoh*'s daughter? Was it not a light thing to be a king's son in law? neither a light honor to be called *Pharaoh*'s daughter's son? Much more honor is it, to be called *sons of God*. It is a great honor to be God's servants, a greater honor to be God's friends, but the greatest honor is to be *sons of God*. Thereof follows, that being *children of God, we are heirs of God, and joint heirs with Christ*.

Thirdly, of the privileges and freedom, which God's children have before and above others. The Lord gives unto his children many freedoms, because they are become through grace well-pleasing in his sight. Of all these freedoms we will mention here but these three following.

1st, A child of God is made free from sin and damnation. The apostle St. *Paul* says thereof, *There is no condemnation to them which are in Christ Jesus.*

2ndly, A child of God received a new name; he was before a slave, now a son; a sinner, now a saint. The Spirit of the Lord says thereof by St. *John* the divine, *to him that overcomes, will I give a white stone, and in the stone a new name written.* The white stone signifies the remissions of sins; for a white stone was given in old days to a person that was pardoned, and a black stone to the condemned.

3rdly, A child of God is heir to all the promises of God. The apostle *Paul* calls them therefore, *The children of promise.*

This is hid from the world. *It does not yet appear, what we shall be.* Many of the children of God live herein this world in the greatest poverty, sickness, and adversity, so that men would not think that they were children of God. *Lazarus* laid before *Dives*'s gate full of sores and boils, and *Dives* did not imagine, that he was a child of God, but when he was in *Abraham*'s Bosom, it did appear he was a child of God. *Then we shall be like him, for we shall see him as he is.*

2, The honor of God's children after this life, consisting in the following,

First, they shall be like him. Not in eternal godhead, neither in the majesty of the personal union, neither in the excellency of the redemption, neither in the exaltation to God's right hand, nor in the honor of adoration, for all these becomes unto Christ alone, who is God forever and ever; but like him in glory, everyone according to his measure; for as one star differs from another star in glory, also the elect shall exceed one another in glory.

Secondly, see him like as he is. We see God here through a glass darkly, but we shall see him hereafter face to face: None in this life can imagine, nor comprehend, much less speak out, what glory this shall be; in the mean while we must wait therefore with desire, and prepare ourselves thereto with holiness, and live here in the gracious kingdom as children of God, that it may appear hereafter in the glorious Kingdom, what we should be; where *the righteous shall shine forth as the sun in the Kingdom of their Father.* We will of those words consider the eternal life, or heaven, as,

FIRST, *A Kingdom.*

SECOND, *A Kingdom of Light.*

THIRD, *A Kingdom of Righteousness and Holiness.*

EXPLANATION of the TEXT

I. We will consider heaven as a kingdom.

As every man can be divided in the internal and external; so also there are two lives, the natural and the spiritual in everyone: The natural life is supported by natural things, and the spiritual by spiritual. The natural life begins at our birth, and ends at our death, but the spiritual life begins here in the gracious Kingdom, and continues eternally in the glorious Kingdom, where the souls of the righteous united with their respective bodies at the Last Day, shall be eternally rejoiced with unspeakable glory and honor. When the Spirit of God would describe the eternal life in the holy record, he in regard to our weak understanding uses expressions full of joy and glory, that we may conclude thereof, what glory and honor we have to expect, and calls the same, *The third heaven. The habitation of God's holiness. The place of God's habitation. The holy city. The city of the living God. A city whose builder and maker is God: The heavenly* Jerusalem. *A building of*

God, and house not made with hands, eternal in the heavens. A weeding paradise. Abraham's Bosom. It is called in our text, a *kingdom*; not the kingdom of God's power, which extends over the whole creation; neither the kingdom of God's grace, which is administered in the Christian church, by the Spirit and the word of God; but the glorious Kingdom of God in heaven, called in other Scripture places, *The Kingdom of God. The Kingdom of Christ. The Kingdom of Heaven. A glorious kingdom. An eternal kingdom. A kingdom, which cannot be moved.*

Heaven is called a kingdom on account of the following,

First, on account of its greatness. The heavens, which we see with our eyes, is greater than the earth; for the whole globe is but a step in comparison to the great extent of the firmament, much greater must then the invisible heaven be. St. *John* the divine saw an angel, who had a golden reed to measure the new city, measured the same with reed *twelve thousand furlongs.* The Spirit of the Lord uses here a certain number for an uncertain, showing thereby the greatness of his Kingdom: There are many kingdoms on earth. Every kingdom is divided into many countries, every country has its cities, every city has its burgers, every burger has his house, and every house its own family: But the Kingdom of Heaven is one kingdom, one heaven, and one house. Well says our Savior, *in my Father's house are many mansions:* Not to be understood, that it is divided in many rooms, but for the following.

1*st,* For the great room that there is. They who are willing to take in strangers to lodging, say always, as *Rebekah* said to *Abraham's* servant, There is room enough that you can lodge in; but they, who are unwilling to lodge a stranger, makes always excuse of having no room to lodge in: Our Savior says therefore, *in my Father's house are many mansions*; showing thereby his Father's willingness to receive the faithful in the Heavenly Kingdom.

2nd, For the many inhabitants, that are there. The angels, patriarchs, prophets, apostles, martyrs, confessors, faithful, and elect,
who, although a small number, in comparison to the devils and
the damned in hell, make up a great multitude, which no man can
number; as St. *John* the divine says.

3rd, For the differing honor and glory. All subjects in an earthly
kingdom are not alike in degree, honor and condition; also shall
there be degrees of glory in the Kingdom of Heaven. The apostle
Paul says thereof, *there is one glory of the sun, and another glory of the
moon, and another glory of the stars, for one star differs from another
star in glory; so also is the resurrection of the dead:* Though everyone
shall have an unspeakable joy.

Secondly, heaven is called a *kingdom,* on account of its ruling power
and highness. There is but one king in every earthly kingdom. All the
elect are made in heaven, kings and triumphing conquerors: They
have warred here against sin, the devils, the world, death, hell and
their flesh; but they shall there hang up their armors in token of
victory, and reign with Christ a thousand years.

Thirdly, it is called a *kingdom* on account of the privileges and
freedoms. Every kingdom has its own privileges, and every condition
and degree in a kingdom has their particular privilege: But the elect
shall have in heaven alike privilege; they shall be free from sin and
all causes of sin.

Fourthly, it is called a *kingdom* on account of its justice. There is
often little justice exercised in earthly kingdoms. For *in the land of
uprightness, the wicked will deal unjustly;* and *devours the man that is
more righteous than he:* But heaven is a kingdom where righteousness
dwells.

Fifthly, it is called a *kingdom* on account of the peace that is there.
Peace is the most precious pearl in a king's crown: But where can we
find the same constant here on earth? Kings and princes conclude

always eternal peace together, but their eternity is as inconstant as themselves: In heaven there is eternal peace, the Prince of Peace dwells there, and the saints shall come there to the eternal peace.

Sixthly, it is called a *kingdom* on account of the superfluity of all good there. No kingdom on earth is so rich, but there are some defect: But in heaven the elect shall have plenty of all things; they shall know all things; they shall drink of the fountain of wisdom; they shall behold the eternal light of truth and wisdom; they shall be delighted with the harmonious melody of the angels; they shall behold God face to face; they shall dwell in the eternal habitations made without hands; and they shall be clothed with white garments and robes of righteousness. Oh Lord God, wherefrom shall we take words, of comparisons to express the glory of this Heavenly Kingdom? Was *Solomon* in all his glory not arrayed like the lilies of the field? How can this mortal glory be arrayed like the heavenly lilies of the beautiful gardens of God's Paradise?

Seventhly, it is called a *kingdom* on account of its constancy. Earthly kingdoms can be conquered and destroyed by the enemies; but the Kingdom of Heaven is an everlasting kingdom: No enemies can war against the same, nor age and time consume the same, but it shall last as long as the king, that is, eternally without end: We are here on earth, sojourners; but shall be there, inhabitants to eternity.

But who has formed or made this heavenly kingdom? Earthly kingdoms have their beginning and origin from men. *Nimrod* founded the *Babylonish, Cyrus* the *Persian, Alexander* the *Grecian*, and *Julius Cæsar* the *Roman* kingdoms: But the holy blessed Trinity, Father, Son, and Holy Spirit, has prepared the Kingdom of Heaven.

The Father, in that he has made us able to the inheritance of the saints in heaven, and has heaven for the faithful from eternity; and hath promised the eternal salvation through grace to the faithful, and fulfills his promises for Christ's sake.

The Son, in that he as high priest has fulfilled the law of God through his obedience, and thereby procured our salvation; as the prophet has declared unto us in his Heavenly Father's will; and as the king defends his church, and assures unto us, in his word and sacraments, the eternal life.

The Holy Spirit, in making us free from the law of sin and death, wherefore he is called, *the Spirit of life in Christ Jesus.*

The means which God uses to help us to the eternal life, are the following.

1st, On God's side, his word and sacraments, the ministers who preach the gospel, and administer the sacraments; and the holy angels, who carry the souls of the faithful into the Bosom of *Abraham*, and shall at the Last Day gather together the elect from the four corners of heaven.

2ndly, On our side, faith. wherefore the apostle *Peter* calls *the salvation of souls*, the end of faith.

II. We will consider heaven as a kingdom of light.

The righteous shall shine forth as the sun. What is brighter in this world, than the beams of the sun, for it sends forth bright beams, and dims the eye. Although these words of our Savior in our text, are proof enough of the glory and clearness which the elect shall enjoy in the Kingdom of Heaven, yet we will prove the same by the following.

First, by Scripture texts. *Barack* and *Deborah*'s song also, *Let them that love the Lord, be as the sun, when he goes forth in his might.* The prophet *Daniel* says, *they that be wise, shall shine as the brightness of the firmament, and they that turn many to righteousness, as the stars forever and ever.* The Apostle *Paul* confirms, *that Christ shall change our vile bodies, that they may be fashioned like unto his glorious body.*

Secondly, as the brightness of the angels. *In the resurrection the elect are as the angels in heaven.* The angels are called *flaming fire,* and have always made their appearance here on earth in shining forms. The prophet *Daniel* saw an angel *clothed in linen, whose loins were girded with fine gold; his body was like the beryl, and his face as the appearance of lightning, and his eyes as lamps of fire, and his arms and his feet like in color to polished brass.* The angel that descended from heaven, and rolled the stone from the door of the Sepulcher; *his countenance was like lightning, and his raiment white as snow.* Also shall the elect be in the Kingdom of Heaven, and are therefore *clothed with white robes.*

Thirdly, of the shining face of *Moses.* The face of *Moses* became clear and shining, by being forty days and forty nights by the Lord on Mount *Sinai.* How much more shining shall the elect become, when they shall be eternally by God in his glorious Kingdom, and see him face to face as he is?

Fourthly, by the transfiguration of Christ on Mount *Tabor;* when *his raiment became shining, exceeding white as snow.* We can partly conclude of this, what glances and clearness the elect shall enjoy hereafter.

Fifthly, by natural images. We find in nature many clear shining bodies, as diamond glass, and other precious stones. Why has God created them? They are certainly created for the use and diversion of mankind; but the Lord will also admonish us by them of the clearness which our bodies shall have in heaven. We might otherwise repent that God had given such a clear body to these lifeless creatures, thinking, why has the Lord created the sun, pearls, diamonds and such like, with such a transparent body; and us, who are created after his own image, and are his handy works, with such coarse and dark bodies? Is man the Lord of the world, the sun the servant of the world, the pearl and precious stones, the ornaments of men. Why hath the Lord given clearer bodies unto the servants than unto the Lord? In the Kingdom of Heaven the righteous shall shine forth as the sun. *This kingdom has no need of the sun, neither of the moon to shine in it, for the glory of God did lighten it, and the lamb is the light thereof.* An heavenly clearness shall go forth from the essential uncreated light, which shall enlighten all the elect, wherein they shall walk, and be enlightened by the light of God's countenance forever and ever.

This clearness shall consist in the perfect restitution of God's image; in the happy beholding of God's countenance, and in eternal praise.

In the perfect restitution of God's image. *Adam* lost through his transgression the image of God, and the Lord did renew the same by his gracious promise concerning the seed of the woman, which *Adam* was to embrace through faith. The Lord renews his image daily in us by his Spirit and word, when we do not resist the same through obstinacy; which image never becomes in this world entirely free from the spots of sin, but that the remnants of sin hangs in us: But in eternal life, the image of God shall be perfectly restored both in soul and body.

The souls shall shine forth of the knowledge of God's mysteries, *they shall be taught of the Lord,* and shall know the Lord as he is. We know God here in part, and the veil of *Moses* is over our eyes, as upon the heart of the *Jews:* But the veil shall be taken away hereafter, and we shall see him face to face. We shall then perfectly understand the following mysteries.

1st, The mystery of the Holy Trinity. How one can be three, and three one, is wonderful and unintelligible for human reason, and we can therefore form only some dark thoughts thereof: It is a bottomless pit, which our understanding cannot fathom; but in the eternal life we shall see God perfectly as he is.

2ndly, The mystery of the holy incarnation of Christ, who took on the human nature in his personal union. This is a mystery, that the angels desire to see into. The Lord said of *Adam, "Man is become like one of us"*; but we may say, "God is become like one of us": The Incarnation of Christ is a golden chain of miracles, unintelligible for human reason; for the Creator is become a creature; the Father of eternity is become a birth in time; he whom the heaven of heavens cannot contain, laid concealed in a womb; he who upholds all things, is held up on human arms; he who maintained all things, is maintained by woman's breast; a virgin has brought forth a child; Christ is born of a woman, his own Creature; the mother was younger than the child; the child was greater than the mother; the Spirit from eternity is become flesh in time; he has two natures, and is but one person: Behold, what multitude of miracles is concealed in this mystery; but in the eternal life, this shall not be longer hid from us, for we shall receive perfect knowledge thereof, and we shall see him as he is.

Our bodies shall shine forth as the sun; for they shall be,

1. Clear, shining and transparent. What would not the learned give, that they might see in this world, a transparent human body, in order thereby to see and be instructed in the wonderful connection and being of this little world: In the eternal life, the righteous shall receive glorified bodies, like unto the glorified body of Christ, and shall shine forth as the Sun in all eternity.

2. Spiritual. They shall be equal unto the angels, and shall not need eating, drinking, sleep, nor any carnal exercises.

3. Immortal. This mortality shall be swallowed up by the eternal life. The elect shall never die: In heaven there is neither sickness nor death; for as the soul is immortal, also the body shall become immortal: When sin, the cause of death, is removed, then must, also death the effect of sin, depart.

4. Beautiful. The bodies of the righteous shall be like unto the angels, yea like unto the glorified body of Christ: They who have had

any defect in their bodies in this world, shall receive glorified bodies without defect. That our blessed Savior, had after his resurrection, the holes in his side, hand and feet, was not through any natural infirmities, but alone to confirm the disciples in the belief of his resurrection. The disciples were wounded in their belief through his death, but he healed this wound, by convincing them of his resurrection by these holes in his side, hand and feet.

5. Invisible. Their bodies shall be glorified bodies, so that carnal eyes shall not be able to see them, as Christ's body was invisible after the resurrection to the disciples on the road to *Emmaus*.

6. Free from natural infirmities, as, hunger, thirst, cold, heat, labor, crosses, sorrow, and such like. *They shall hunger no more, neither thirst any more, neither shall the sun light on them, nor any heat: For the Lamb, which is in the midst of the throne, shall seed them, and shall lead them unto living fountains of waters: And God shall wipe away all tears from their eyes. And there shall be no more death, neither sorrow, nor crying, neither shall there be any more pain; for the former things are passed away.* And how shall any pain or trouble befall the elect, since they shall have,

The continual happy beholding of God's countenance. *They shall see his face, and his name shall be in their foreheads.* This beholding of God's countenance shall be,

1*st*, Clear. We see God's back parts here in this world; but we shall see him hereafter face to face, as he is. This shall be the greatest joy of the elect in heaven: For since God is the highest good; the greatest salvation; the greatest joy; the essential light, life and salvation; also shall the beholding of God's countenance be their greatest joy, light, life, and salvation.

2*nd*, Glorious. If Christ was glorious in his Transfiguration on Mount *Tabor*, in the time and state of his Humiliation; how much more glorious will he be at his Exaltation on God's right Hand.

594

3rd, Joyful. The apostle St. *Peter* says thereof, *you shall make me full of joy with your countenance.* It will be very joyful to see, after a severe winter of crosses and afflictions in this world, the Son of Righteousness come forth in his glory: *The elect shall be abundantly satisfied with the fatness of his house, and be shall make them drink of the river of his pleasure.* The prophet *Isaiah* says, *the ransomed of the Lord shall return, and come to* Zion *with songs, and everlasting joy upon their heads.*

4th, Pleasing. There is nothing in the universe, that can please us; but the beholding of the Holy Trinity shall please the elect. The royal Psalmist says, *I will behold your face in righteousness; I shall be satisfied, when I awake with your likeness.* Solomon says, *the eye is not satisfied with seeing.* But in heaven the eye shall be satisfied with beholding God, who can alone satisfy the eye and heart.

5th Not tedious. We grow weary and tired with beholding the things of this world; but the elect shall never be tired with beholding the countenance of God in the Kingdom of Heaven; the more they behold God, the more they are drawn into a holy desire and joy. And of such shall proceed,

Eternal praise. The elect shall have fullness of joy, and shall stand before the throne, and the Lamb, clothed with white robes, having palms in their hands, and saying, *Amen, blessing, and glory, and wisdom, and thanksgiving, and honor, and power, and might be unto our God forever and ever, Amen.*

III. We will consider heaven as a kingdom of righteousness and holiness.

Since then our blessed Lord and Savior assures us, *That the righteous shall shine forth in the Kingdom of their Father as the sun:* Then we ought, being desirous to enter into this Heavenly Kingdom, to strive after righteousness, as long as we are in this world, for none that does iniquity, shall enter into the heavenly *Jerusalem.* No man is righteous by nature: wherefore *Job* says, *What is man, that he should be clean, and he which is born of a woman, that he should be righteous?* Neither can anyone obtain the eternal life by an imagined righteousness; as the *Pharisees* did conceit; who *being ignorant of God's righteousness, and going about to establish their own righteousness, have not submitted themselves unto the righteousness of God.* We must seek the true righteousness in the Lord Jesus Christ, *Whom God has set forth to be a propitiation, through faith in his blood, to declare his righteousness for the remission of sins, that are past through the forbearance of God.*

The Lord has ordained for the obtaining of this righteousness, certain means which are on God's side, the word, and the sacraments; and on our side, faith.

By baptism, the first sacrament, we are regenerated to a new life in Christ Jesus. We become of children of wrath, children of God; the old sinful garment is taken away, and we are clothed again with a new garment of salvation, the righteousness of Christ; and we are assured of the spiritual and eternal life. We become also new men in the baptism, receiving the renewing of God's image, by the operation of the Holy Spirit; But, since the remnants of sin cleaves always by the regenerated, as long as they live in this world, therefore God uses the second means, namely, the word, by which we are sanctified unto daily renewing; for the Spirit of God kindles by the word a new light in our understanding, and new desires in our heart, to subdue the old

Adam, with all its lusts and appetites, and to walk in newness of life, according to the command of God. And since the old *Adam* is tough like a viper, and lives always again, therefore has God ordained and instituted the second sacrament, the Lord's Supper, by which the new life is strengthened in us, and the fruits of righteousness waxed, that as Christ died for our sins, we should also mortify sin in us, and as he rose for our righteousness, we should also live in righteousness for. God and man. For God, that we live according to his word and command, let the Spirit of God govern us, walk as children of light, and serve him in righteousness and holiness all the days of our life: For man, that we behave our selves justly towards all, hurting none with free will, considering, *That the unrighteous shall not inherit the Kingdom of God.* This is,

Faith. Which shall embrace the righteousness of Christ, and shine forth in an unpunishable and just conversation towards men: He who will obtain the crown of righteousness, and he who will enter into the life-everlasting must walk in uprightness. For *in the way of righteousness is life, and in the pathway thereof, there is no death.*

O merciful Lord God, Heavenly Father, who has created us to the eternal life, in your beloved Son Jesus Christ, and upholds the spiritual life in us by your words and Holy Sacraments, assist us with your Holy Spirit, and graciously strengthen us, that we may live so in this world, that we may hereafter obtain the eternal life in your heavenly Kingdom, which shall continue forever without END.

Made in the USA
Las Vegas, NV
19 April 2022

47688546R00334